THE
CONFIDANTE

THE
CONFIDANTE

The Untold Story of the Woman
Who Helped Win World War II
and Shape Modern America

—◆—

CHRISTOPHER C. GORHAM

To Susan's Friends & Family, I hope you find Anna's story inspiring!

CITADEL PRESS
Kensington Publishing Corp.
www.kensingtonbooks.com

CITADEL PRESS BOOKS are published by

Kensington Publishing Corp.
119 West 40th Street
New York, NY 10018

All Kensington titles, imprints, and distributed lines are available at special quantity discounts for bulk purchases for sales promotions, premiums, fund-raising, educational, or institutional use. Special book excerpts or customized printings can also be created to fit specific needs. For details, write or phone the office of the Kensington sales manager: Kensington Publishing Corp., 119 West 40th Street, New York, NY 10018, attn: Sales Department; phone 1-800-221-2647.

CITADEL PRESS and the Citadel logo are Reg. U.S. Pat. & TM Off.

ISBN: 978-0-8065-4200-3

First Citadel hardcover printing: March 2023

10 9 8 7 6 5 4 3 2 1

Printed in the United States of America

Library of Congress Control Number: 2022947432

ISBN: 978-0-8065-4201-0 (e-book)

For Elizabeth

*I'm not a crusader or a reformer, but there are a lot of things happening
you just cannot sit by watching idly.
I decided to do something about it.*

—ANNA ROSENBERG

—

Anna, you have quite a book to write someday.

—EDWARD R. MURROW

Contents

Prologue: The Eagle's Nest   1

1. Roman Candle   7

2. The Tammany Instinct   17

3. The Busiest Woman in New York   24

4. This Man Roosevelt   33

5. Action in Albany   44

6. A New Deal   51

7. Hyde Park   65

8. The Inner Circle   74

9. Sign It, Mr. President!   93

10. Mrs. Fix-It   107

11. War Is an "All-Out" Business   119

12. The Buffalo Plan   131

13. Ask No Questions   142

14. Wartime Mission   156

15. When Johnny Comes Home   169

16. Casualties of War   177

17. Homecoming   190

18. General Marshall Calls   208

19. Enemies Within   223

20. A Woman Is Running the Army!   237

21. Every Ridge a Heartbreak   256

22. Drafting Eisenhower   269

23. Happy Birthday, Mr. President   284

24. A True Friend across All These Years   293

Epilogue: The Last New Dealer   306

Acknowledgments   315

Notes   318

Selected Bibliography   353

Index   359

THE
CONFIDANTE

THE EAGLE'S NEST

KEHLSTEIN MOUNTAIN, BERCHTESGADEN, BAVARIA, GERMANY,
SATURDAY, MAY 19, 1945

Anna Marie Rosenberg stood in the Great Room of the Eagle's Nest, Adolf Hitler's redoubt in the Bavarian Alps. She gazed into the valley below, with its deep blue glacial lakes bordered by wildflowers. The jagged peaks on the other side punctured the horizon as shafts of brilliant late-spring sunshine angled through the giant octagonal room. Here, she thought with a chill, the Führer had sat in the armchair by the fire, his German Shepherd at his feet, while high-ranking Nazis and their courtesans clinked glasses of looted champagne, their faces flushed as they delighted in transforming Europe into a slaughterhouse.

How could such a beautiful spot have housed such depravity? She thought of her family: Hungarian Jews forced to flee Budapest more than thirty years before due to the caprice of the Austro-Hungarian Emperor. Anna's father, Albert Lederer, responded to his exile by becoming a fiercely patriotic American, a posture he encouraged his daughter to adopt as well. "My father was vehement in his belief that everyone born outside the United States owed a special obligation to this country," Anna explained later. "His influence on me was so great . . . he drilled into me that I must serve the United States, and that attitude of great love, you couldn't help but assimilate." While Anna and her family struggled to find their footing in New York, back in the Old World the Emperor's nephew was assassinated, plunging Europe into the world's first industrial, modern war. A generation later, dispatched to battle-torn Europe by President Franklin Roosevelt in the fall of 1944 to serve as

1

his personal emissary, Anna found the land of her childhood caught up again in the dragnet of war.

On this second mission Anna was in the heart of the imploding Nazi state. Though she had heard terrible stories of roundups, ghettos, and camps, Anna was unprepared for the tragic scenes she witnessed at the Nordhausen concentration camp just days after its liberation by American troops in April 1945. Wearing a borrowed Women's Army Corps uniform, Anna climbed down from her jeep into a nightmarish world of suffering and anguish. Among pyres of corpses the survivors shuffled in a daze, their striped prison uniforms in rags. Medics, chaplains, and soldiers raced about saving the living, comforting the dying, and digging long trenches for the dead. "I saw the survivors, ragged and ageless," Anna recalled; "few could stand up." One woman, shocked at the sight of an Allied woman in the camp, slowly approached her. After a moment's hesitation, Anna groped for items at the bottom of her purse and the man's briefcase she always carried. She tenderly put them into the woman's hands caked with dirt. Anna was ashamed at the insufficiency of her gesture. *How could she give lipsticks and note pencils to a starving woman?* But seeing the face of the woman as she closed her hands over the small tokens gave Anna hope. "To this woman, it was everything. It was the first thing she had owned in years. Everything had been taken from her. Even her name had been blotted out by the Nazi stamp 'Juden.'"

Gazing at the edelweiss in the valley below, Anna thought of the young men who would never get to go home. Or who, like her son, Thomas, a lieutenant in the U.S. Army, would return carrying the trauma of what they had seen. In a field hospital in Saint-Lô, a wounded American brought in a French child, "her body torn and shattered by a wood mine" left by the retreating Germans. "He cried, he cursed, he prayed," Anna said. The soldier promised: "I'll pay them back for this."

She thought of the generals she now considered friends: Supreme Allied Commander Dwight D. Eisenhower, Omar Bradley, and George S. Patton. What toll had been taken on them as they saw the terrible price exacted by Hitler's divisions from the beaches of Normandy, across the Rhine River into the very heart of the Third Reich?

But most of all, as she stood there watching dust particles suspended in the sunlight, she thought of the man who had sent her here:

President Franklin Delano Roosevelt. She remembered the last time they were together, sharing a lunch in the small sun parlor of the White House on a pleasant spring Saturday in March, just a few weeks before he died. Before leaving the White House that day for what would be his very last time, the President directed her to make this second mission to learn from the soldiers themselves what they hoped for when they returned home.

Anna took one last look at the magnificent Bavarian Alps as the shadows lengthened across the valley; she turned and walked into the library that abutted the Great Room. On one end was a huge stone fireplace, and at the other sat a mahogany desk. She picked up the folded copy of *Stars and Stripes* that sat on the desktop. An article caught her eye. An American private would be giving a piano recital at the Mozarteum concert hall in nearby Salzburg.

Classical music was one of the few indulgences she allowed herself. Moving through most days like a hummingbird, she prized the moments she found to slip into a hall or conservatory, just another anonymous listener, as the orchestra went through its afternoon rehearsal. She ached to go to the private's performance but knew she could not. There was too much work to be done.

She looked up from the newspaper at the tall bookcase behind the desk. A title caught her attention: *10 Jahre Hitler, 10 Jahre Roosevelt* (10 years of Hitler, 10 years of Roosevelt). She stood to her full 5'3" and with the substantial heels of her WAC boots was able to reach it. Flipping it open, she saw images of Depression-era Americans. A man in a dirty undershirt ladled soup amid the pitiful detritus of a makeshift homeless camp. Idle, unemployed men squatted on a bench, their caps pulled low over their eyes. There were photographs of President Roosevelt shaking the hand of a Black man and with Jewish American leaders. Anna flipped through the pages and saw a photograph of her friend and mentor Bernard Baruch; the German text beneath decried America as the home of mongrels and gangsters. Juxtaposed against these images were columns of neatly uniformed youths marching in a mountain valley, a swastika flag held high. Dozens of strong, tall Aryan women in matching outfits performed calisthenics. Hitler, surrounded by his generals, was fixated on a military map.

Ten years. A decade before, Anna would have been in New York or Washington or on a train between the two. It was peacetime then, but the Great Depression hung over America like a heavy curtain. Now here she was, at the end of a world war. The immigrant girl who was inspired to a lifetime of patriotic duty, the woman who became a vital wartime adviser to the American President, standing in the crown jewel of Hitler's evil empire.

Just then, she heard her aide speaking French in the corridor with a few officers of the French Second Armored Division. The men were still gloating over the French and American flags atop the Eagle's Nest, a great symbolic prize they had dreamed of since D-Day. Lieutenant Commander Fischer stuck his head into the library.

"Mrs. Rosenberg?"

Anna slipped the book into her briefcase and tucked on her khaki cap at the angle she liked. It was time to go. There was work to do.

———◆———

That a civilian woman came to be President Roosevelt's personal envoy to wartime Europe is but one episode of a lifetime spent at the pivot points of history. She was a pioneer in the new art of labor mediation, and by her mid-twenties Anna Rosenberg was known as "the busiest woman in New York." Her success brought her to the attention of Franklin and Eleanor Roosevelt at the moment he was running for Governor of New York. Anna's combination of skill and social ease was valued by FDR as he won the presidency, and by her thirties she was the nation's only woman in charge of implementing massive New Deal programs. When World War II erupted, she pushed President Roosevelt to make defense jobs available to Black Americans. By 1944 Anna's labor mobilization plan had become the nationwide model.

The *Chicago Tribune* called Anna perhaps the closest person to FDR during the war years, with the exception of Harry Hopkins. "Outside of the President's personal Secretary," echoed General Walter Bedell Smith, "FDR relied more upon Mrs. Rosenberg than any other single individual."[1] Roosevelt trusted her with a remarkable array of tasks while enjoying her company. Prior to her first wartime mission for Roosevelt, Anna was instrumental in securing the vital secrecy of atomic power. She later guided the direction of the G.I. Bill of Rights, transforming the lives of millions of Americans. For her efforts during World War II, Anna Rosenberg was the first person, man or woman, to be awarded the Presidential Medal of Freedom, the nation's highest civilian award. She "meant business in winning World War II," Secretary of War Robert P. Patterson told *Independent Woman*.

Her long connection to FDR, the greatest American of his time, was followed by a second act. "She knew how to make connections with very powerful people and leverage those connections," explains her grandson, Thomas P. J. Rosenberg. Anna had the uncanny ability to find her way into the inner circles of power, and the discretion to stay there. After FDR's death, Anna remained a key Washington policy maker in the administrations that followed. As the top woman in government during the Truman years, *Life* magazine called her "far and away the most important woman in the American government, and perhaps the most important official female in the world."

It was a pinnacle she may never have reached. In 1950 a cabal of extremists led by Senator Joe McCarthy accused Rosenberg of being a Communist. Anna knew she wore the bull's-eye: "I was Jewish, an immigrant, pro-labor, and a woman. What could have been worse?" Worse was the unfortunate coincidence that she shared a surname with atomic spies Ethel and Julius Rosenberg. After their arrest, unrelated Rosenbergs around the country were dismissed from government positions, shunned by their friends, and their children were ostracized at school. "I remember a lot of hysteria," reported the daughter of Milton Rosenberg, a civilian Air Force analyst summarily dismissed without pay. "My parents lived under a halo of shame."* While Anna was not ashamed of her name, the Rosenberg affair provided another reason for her to, as she said, "fade out of the picture."[2]

---

* Completely unrelated to Anna Rosenberg, the married couple Ethel and Julius Rosenberg were arrested and tried for passing atomic secrets to the Soviet Union and executed in 1953. By a second unfortunate coincidence, Anna's first husband was also named Julius Rosenberg (she called him "Mike"). For other unrelated Rosenbergs, see The Free Library s.v. "The Other Rosenbergs: They Had the Wrong Name at the Wrong Place at the Wrong Time: An Investigation into Discrimination against Jews Who Worked for the U.S. Army Corps at Fort Monmouth, NJ, in the Wake of Julius Rosenberg's Arrest," by Nadine Epstein, *Moment*, March 1, 2011.

As I was writing this book, the most common remark from friends, colleagues, and readers was, "Wow, what a woman!" followed up by, "How is it that I haven't heard of her?" This book seeks to illuminate *what* it was about Anna Rosenberg that led Presidents Roosevelt, Truman, Eisenhower, and Johnson to seek her counsel and service, while solving the puzzle *why* have so few heard of this once-national figure. Who is this woman of uncommon ability who played a seminal role during World War II and in shaping and implementing many of twentieth-century America's most significant public policies? "She was a famous person in her day," explained a contemporary of Anna's. So why have historians been "remarkably silent" about her?

This book seeks to break the silence.

CHAPTER ONE

ROMAN CANDLE

As dawn broke over New York City on Friday morning, April 6, 1917, newsboys hawked the city's papers from street corners up and down Manhattan. Shouts of, "America's at War!" competed with the rumble of the subway, the screeches of the el trains above, the clattering of wagon wheels, and hoots of automobile horns. The throngs hustling to work couldn't miss the huge headlines that screamed from the city's many newspapers. "NATION'S GIGANTIC RESOURCES MOBILIZED," read the *New York Times*. "WAR WITH GERMANY," cried the *New York Tribune*. "WILSON PROCLAIMS WAR," echoed the *Evening World*.

Just hours before first light, at 3:12 in the morning, the U.S. Congress voted to declare war on Imperial Germany. The debate in the House of Representatives lasted sixteen and one-half hours, included over one hundred speeches, and left some lawmakers sobbing. In the end there were 373 yeas to 50 nays. It was official. The United States of America was in the Great War.

In mobilizing the nation for the First World War, President Woodrow Wilson had an enormous task ahead of him. From the time of the Roman legions, a nation at war needs four things in great abundance: soldiers, food, weapons, and money. Wilson would need to raise by far the largest army in the nation's history. The army of the Spanish-American War in 1898 was the size of the New York City police force. That would not do in a world war, where a single day of battle could cause sixty thousand casualties, as the British Army discovered to its horror along the river Somme in 1916. Families would have to do without meat and wheat and grow their own vegetables, so as to provide for the huge army that would be crossing the Atlantic to fight in the trenches of France. The nation's industries would need to produce the rifles, machine guns, and helmets needed to fight, and all of this would cost the national treasury unprecedented sums. In an instant, America's prewar stillness was shaken; the country was "boiling with preparedness agitation."

And time was short. The war was in its fourth year, and America's allies, primarily France and Britain, desperately needed fresh troops to defend Paris against Kaiser Wilhelm's powerful German Army.

For New York City, the years before the war were a time of transition between old traditions and the modern world. Automobiles coursed along the city's grand avenues, but horse-drawn carriages still carted vegetables in the neighborhoods. Masted sailing ships in the harbor were docked gunnel to gunnel with steamships. New York was a cosmopolitan city, home to families like the Morgans, whose fortunes were among the largest in human history; it was also the landing spot of millions of immigrants who lived, studied, worked, and prayed in crowded neighborhoods such as Little Italy or the Jewish Lower East Side. Echoing down the streets of New York were voices in Italian, Russian, Yiddish, and the Irish brogue.

Political unrest was also part of the street scene. Workers were fighting for the right to organize, and young women were agitating for the right to vote. In December 1909, a strike of thirty thousand garment workers, mostly young Jewish women, dragged on for four weeks. "When all America is eating and drinking and having a good time," reported the *New York Times*, "hungry girls . . . wait on recognition of their union."[1] When a strike of textile workers in Lawrence, Massachusetts, dragged on into the cold winter months, the children of the strikers were picked up at Grand Central Terminal and "adopted" by New York families for the duration of the strike.[2] In 1912 the city's waiters and hotel staff went on strike. The men were "badly fed, badly quartered," and "shamefully underpaid." To fight for a living wage, a safer workplace, and a less-than-sixty-hour workweek, the strikers faced not only hunger but arrests, beatings, and exposure while picketing.[3]

Women, too, were waging a battle on the streets of New York: for the right to vote. Suffrage marches and parades were common in the years before World War I. One such march was witnessed by a half-million spectators. Another led a reporter from the *New York Times* to marvel:

"It was a line, miles long . . . of women deeply concerned in the cause they are fighting for [and] girls in their teens overflowing with enthusiastic exuberance."[4]

It was in this world that a young Anna Marie Lederer first made her mark.

———•••———

Anna's remarkable journey began in the Austro-Hungarian Empire on the eve of the twentieth century. She was born in Budapest on July 19, 1899, the second daughter of Albert and Sarolta Lederer. Albert Lederer owned a furniture factory, and Sarolta was an author and illustrator of children's books. The family lived a comfortable middle-class life in Budapest. In the summertime, Anna and her older sister, Klara, looked forward to picnics in one of the city's many parks, where the family would watch suntanned countrywomen set up their flower stands. After a lunch of summer sausage and rye bread, they often strolled to the café, where the girls were treated to a piece of plum cake. Fortified, they would hike up Gellért Hill with its panoramic views of Budapest. As the sun set behind the Buda hills, the girls were mesmerized by the floodlit castle and the blue-green patina of its Baroque copper dome. Gazing down at the lacy Gothic spires of Parliament and the Chain Bridge spanning the shimmering Danube, young Anna could not imagine living anywhere else.

Albert Lederer provided furniture by appointment to His Majesty Franz Josef I. From his seat at Schönbrunn Palace in Vienna, Franz Josef was Emperor of Austria and King of Hungary. The House of Hapsburg had ruled a vast and diverse area of Central Europe since before the time of Columbus, its dominion stretching from the beaches of the Adriatic Sea to the steppes of Ukraine. Muslim peasants in rural Bosnia celebrated the Emperor's birthday, as did Bohemian businessmen and Budapest café-goers.[5] The ancient capitals of Budapest, Krakow, Prague, and Sarajevo all answered to Vienna, where sat Franz Josef and his fourteen-hundred-room Rococo palace, which for three centuries had evolved along with royal taste.

Having secured an exclusive contract to provide extensive furnishings to Schloss Schönbrunn, Albert Lederer invested nearly everything he had scouring the salons of Europe and procuring the fine Louis XV pieces then in favor among the aristocracy. Once the cash-poor landed gentry sold him their bombé chests and bergère chairs, their fauteuils and fruitwood canapés, Albert returned to his workshop and reupholstered the pieces. To the toile, silk, and velvet coverings he added the custom detail for which he was known: passementerie.

When it came to running the braids, cords, fringes, piping, and tassels along the seams of the furniture and cushions, Albert was no mere craftsman; he was an artist. Once his work was installed in the royal palace, his clientele and his wealth were sure to multiply. His investment in time and money was risky, but if he could please the Emperor he would become a rich man. But the Emperor arbitrarily canceled the large contract after the furniture was delivered. Never paid for his work and never given an explanation for the cancellation, Albert Lederer was ruined.

Disgusted that the whim of a monarch could destroy his life's work, he scraped up the last of his savings, determined to leave the Old World behind. Having exported many shipments of fine Eastern European textiles to buyers in New York, Albert was aware of that city's thriving garment industry. In May 1910, Anna and Klara tearfully bid adieu to their papa as he boarded the train to Genoa, from where he would sail to America.

Once in New York, Albert found himself among the thousands of Eastern European Jews working in the city's needle trades. After twenty months of toiling as an employee, unsure whether to stay or return, Albert found his footing. In February 1912, Albert partnered with a furrier supplier named Henry Davis, and Davis & Lederer opened its workshop at 142 W. 23rd Street. For the first time, he felt secure in his new country. In August 1912, Sarolta and the two girls left Budapest, toting their worldly belongings in a pair of steamer trunks. At the port of Hamburg, they boarded a two-funneled ocean liner, the *Kaiserin Auguste Victoria*, bound for New York. The anticipation of seeing her father again was tempered by Anna's realization that this journey would take her away from her grandparents, her friends, and the house with the green shutters where she had been born.

During the crossing, a topic of conversation among the passengers was the recent sinking of the RMS *Titanic* and the poor souls who breathed their last in the freezing North Atlantic. Anna may have felt fortunate to be in a second-class cabin, rather than in steerage, the locus of so many of the *Titanic*'s victims. With a second-class berth, Anna was free to spend time in the ship's stately spaces. Anna passed afternoons with her mother and sister in the ship's airy conservatory, decorated in pale green and pink, a huge palm tree under a domed skylight. She drew flowers in her souvenir Hamburg-American Line writing pad, and listened as a young German crew member proudly told her that the ship had been the largest in the world until the launch of a British liner, the *Lusitania*. When the crew and her family weren't around, Anna would sneak to the top of the ornate staircase to the men's smoking room to gaze at the large oil paintings of port scenes from the era of sail.

If Anna worried on the ocean crossing, she need not have. The voyage was uneventful, and after nine days at sea Anna caught her first view of the Statue of Liberty and her beckoning torch.

Albert and his family tearfully reunited at Ellis Island, where Anna's mother Sarolta's name was Anglicized to Charlotte (she was still Mater to the girls). The Klara who left Hamburg became Clare in New York, but Anna steadfastly refused to become Anne. In the arrival documents, the Lederers' "race" was noted as "Hebrew." From Ellis Island, a ferry took them to the pier in Manhattan, where throngs of people were shouting and waving American flags. They descended the gangplank to a waiting truck, with "Davis & Lederer" in gilded letters on its side. The girls and Charlotte climbed aboard, Albert hoisted the trunks onto the flatbed, and they chugged north on Broadway. The Lederers' new life in America had begun.

For the first few years, they lived in a small apartment in the Bronx and struggled to assimilate along with the other Central and Eastern European immigrants who inhabited New York's northernmost borough. Anna struggled with English—especially spelling—and when her parents enrolled her in school they fibbed about her age, claiming she had been born in 1901 rather than 1899. That made her two years younger, to give her two years more of public schooling.*

---

* The historical sources do not agree on Anna's birthdate or her naturalization date. Her birthdate is incorrectly cited as July 19, 1901, or, less commonly July 19, 1902, and some sources place the birth month as June. For the sake of consistency and to avoid confusion with sources that placed her birthdate as July 19, 1901, I will use the 1899 date.

Though she was older than her classmates, the extra life experience did not at first translate into street smarts. When their Budapest-born nanny escorted the girls to their first day of school, a group of neighborhood boys mocked them for their accents and their traditional Hungarian dress. Afterwards, Albert persuaded Charlotte to dress the girls in store-bought clothes rather than the homemade aprons embroidered with decorative designs of roses, hearts, and birds.

Public School 31 was a handsome new building, but to get there and back Anna had to pass through a tangle of trains, trolleys, and construction. She missed her old school, the girls' gymnasium, located in a fashionable district of Budapest and surrounded by gardens. Her new modest circumstances and unsettled future might have brought to her mind lines from "The Roses of Saadi," a little poem found in many French primers:

All the roses took wing
The wind carried the flowers to the sea
they followed the water, never to return.

Anna especially missed her grandmother Marie, for whom she was named. Nagymama Marie had given her a parcel of cookies at the Budapest Keleti train station when they departed. Anna couldn't bear to eat the cookies, so they sat in her dresser drawer along with a box of letters and other memorabilia from the old country. While she was normally a meteorite of energy and curiosity, Anna's nostalgia for home dulled her spirit. She longed to be sixteen, so she would be "very grown up [and] do almost anything," and she dreamed of becoming a "scientific gardener," but imagining a life of freedom among her beloved flowers did not shake her out of the doldrums.[6]

In late June 1914 a reverberation from the Old World shook the Lederers in their new home. Emperor Franz Josef's nephew, the heir to the Austro-Hungarian Empire, was assassinated in Sarajevo, the capital of Bosnia. The murder set off a series of events that drew the empires of Europe closer to war, but in the United States the crisis was largely ignored. President Wilson delivered a Fourth of July speech. A week later, he attended a baseball game, seeing the Washington Nationals lose to the Detroit Tigers. While it was business as usual in America, the powder keg in Europe exploded. On July 28, 1914, Austria-Hungary declared war on Serbia, which it blamed for inciting the assassination, and by August 6 the empires of France, Great Britain, and Russia were at war with those of Germany and Austria-Hungary. The Great War had begun.

Unlike Anna, Albert had taken quickly to his new country despite a lack of fluency in English. His business ruined by an absolute monarch and his family forced to emigrate, Papa Lederer was a "fiercely patriotic immigrant" who happily performed jury duty and was delighted by the idea of voting. He instilled in young Anna the value of freedom and of making her voice heard. "We went to see the Statue of Liberty so often," she remembered, "I thought it would start calling me by my first name."[7] Her father's message was reinforced when Anna joined the local Girl Scouts of America troop. "I often think back to those pleasant days and the many things I learned through scouting," she recalled. "The respect and love for one's country that a young person acquires as a scout stays with him all through his life. One learns how to compete honorably and how to get along with others."[8] "I remember how proud I was as a child in this land of opportunity."[9]

By 1915 the Lederers had returned to the middle class. After Clare moved out following her marriage, Anna and her parents lived in an apartment on Manhattan's West Side. Davis & Lederer was now manufacturing and importing furniture trimming, buttons, and furriers' supplies, and Charlotte was working for respected American publishers. Spending Sunday afternoons in Riverside Park along the Hudson River was a comforting reminder of their old lives.

That year Albert and Charlotte enrolled Anna in the Wadleigh High School for Girls at Seventh Avenue and 114th Street, a public school a few blocks above the northern boundary of Central Park. There she immediately displayed her patriotism. Anna founded the "Coming Voters League" dedicated to women's suffrage, and despite admonitions that they were at Wadleigh to be groomed as gentlewomen and ladies and not agitators, Anna's group came to include over one thousand high school girls. Her principal noted that she was "efficient . . . public spirited, popular and aggressive without being disagreeable." One schoolmate called Anna "an ignited Roman candle darting into space."

His home established, his girls in school, and his business thriving, Albert Lederer was ready to become an American citizen. One month before the United States declared war on Germany, in March of 1917, he petitioned for naturalization. "I absolutely and entirely renounce all allegiance and fidelity to any foreign prince," read his Oath of Allegiance, "particularly the Emperor of Austria and Hungary."[10] Albert's business partner, Henry Davis, supported his petition with a sworn affidavit that Albert was "of good moral character, attached to the principles of the Constitution of the United States, and is in every way qualified to be admitted a citizen of the United States." On June 7, 1917, Albert Lederer became an American citizen, and because girls and women were naturalized through the father or husband at that time, so did Anna.

In the fall of 1917, Anna and the other young suffragists joined twenty thousand demonstrators in a Votes for Women march. The *New York Times* reported "women of all ages, from the nearly feeble to the vigorously youthful" marched south along Fifth Avenue from 59th Street to Washington Square.[11] Black women marched alongside Finnish immigrants in brightly colored traditional dress; factory girls wearing aprons flanked college women in their caps and gowns. Many wore the purple, white, and gold sash. Unwilling to be anonymous among this rank and file, Anna volunteered to carry an American flag at the head of her column. After an hour of marching, the flagstaff being "thrice her size and half her weight," Anna began to waver.[12]

At that moment, Papa Lederer, who had stepped out of his workshop on 23rd Street to join the thousands of onlookers that packed both sides of the street, spotted his daughter from the curb. He rushed into the avenue, relieved her of the flag, and ordered her to go home at once. That night, Anna went to bed exhausted, slightly humiliated, and very proud. Like her father, she had become an "enthusiastic patriot."

Her enthusiasm carried over to the war effort. Anna volunteered at an embarkation hospital for soldiers. Leaving school early, she took the long subway ride south to 18th Street, where the hospital was set up.[13] There she learned first aid and how to make and fold dressings. Her duties also included cheering up the men in the recreation room. One wounded soldier asked her to stand by him while his arm was amputated. Twenty years later, the man still corresponded with Anna from his home in Oklahoma. As part of the Hero Club, Anna and the girls also wrote letters to lonesome and homesick soldiers of the American Expeditionary Force.

Anna also did her part to help finance the war effort by selling Liberty Bonds. In a single week she sold nearly $10,000 worth from a booth at 145th Street and Broadway ($200,000 in today's dollars). By 1917 Anna Marie Lederer was committed to serving her adopted nation.

On October 12, 1917, seven months after America's declaration of war, Anna appeared in the *New York Times* for the first time. But it wasn't suffrage that landed her in the papers; it was the war's impact on teenagers. In the name of military preparedness, the New York Board of Education had mandated a lengthened school day for the city's high school boys to accommodate compulsory military training after school. The mandate meant that the school day wouldn't end until 5:30 PM.

Taking a cue from a popular labor tactic against management, boys from three high schools, many of whom worked or played sports after school, immediately went on strike. The students threatened further walkouts if the school day wasn't returned to normal. The Wadleigh girls joined the boys in solidarity. A total of ten thousand New York City high school students were now threatening to stay away from school. A contingent of student strikers this large needed a leader.

Anna, who had been voted to the student council at Wadleigh, was their choice. Addressing hundreds of student strikers in the overflowing Wadleigh auditorium, she told them she agreed with the objectives but not the tactics. Her first public statement of her long public life is also the first time we hear her voice. She told the striking students:

> We will stick with you to the end but for God's sake don't queer things by striking. I have circulated petitions which now have fifteen thousand names and will be presented to the Board of Education. If our petitions are unavailing, we will bring the matter to the Mayor; if he refuses to listen, why—our parents are voters and they have one last resort, the polls!

Despite her advice, three more schools joined the strike, and the New York City high school strike, now seventeen thousand strong, was making news in Buffalo and Glens Falls and across the state. A meeting was called before the Aldermanic Committee for Public Welfare.

Waving away a cloud of cigar smoke, Anna rose to speak. With "preciseness and fluency" she made the case for returning to the normal school day. The student paper of DeWitt Clinton High School went on to report that "Miss Anna Lederer, the principal speaker" for the student delegation, "brought down the house" with her "enthusiastic eloquence." Anna's advocacy impressed the aldermen, as well as a reporter for the *New York Globe*, who asked bystanders, "Who is that girl with the forceful personality?"

"That is Anna Lederer," one responded.

"She is the power behind the students in the school," another Wadleigh girl added.

In the end, the school day was shortened. Anna had settled her first strike. Moreover, she was making a name for herself in her adopted city and beyond. During the impasse, her efforts were reported as far away as Reno, Nevada, and Spokane, Washington. But Anna did not need news reports to grasp the important lesson she learned from the episode. "That was the first time," she recalled, "that I realized the power of polls and the power of politics."[14]

Anna had found her voice.

CHAPTER TWO

THE TAMMANY INSTINCT

The girls of Wadleigh High School would always remember where they were when they heard the boys overseas were coming home. As the school day clanged to life on the morning of Monday, November 11, 1918, the news that Germany had signed the armistice at midnight ricocheted along the corridors of the handsome French Renaissance–style building, its stained-glass windows filtering the autumn light into reds, greens, and yellows. The war was over.

As the calendar turned to 1919 and the first demobilized troops returned, Anna was in her senior year, and looking forward to graduating in May. She never got the chance. The administration discovered that Anna was over eighteen and she was asked to leave the school.

In October 1919, Anna, twenty years old and living with her parents, married Julius Rosenberg, an infantryman whom she had met through the Hero Club letter-writing campaign. Mater protested that this was no way to meet a husband, but Anna had fallen for the young soldier. In a photo taken upon his return, Julius gazes from under a crown of bushy light brown hair, wearing the tunic and trousers of the Fifty-First Pioneer Infantry Division, his hands jammed in his pockets, and with the merest hint of a smile. The petite Anna, in a crisp checked gingham dress with a bow in front, tilts her head coquettishly, her right arm wrapped over his shoulder and her left on her hip.

Julius, who went by the more "American"-sounding Mike, was the youngest son of Austro-Hungarian immigrants who had been in the United States for much longer than the Lederers. Mike was a quiet boy who didn't talk much and who didn't like school. After being drafted into the Army, Mike was shipped to France in September 1918, in time to see action in the last stage of the Great War. Like millions of other veterans, he returned home with invisible psychic wounds, inflicted by the trauma of trench warfare.

But he had survived, he had a new wife, and together they would build a life. The newlyweds rented an apartment on the Upper West Side, at 342 W. 71st Street, a seven-story building, and began to plan for the future. Upon returning from their honeymoon, Mike got a job as a rug salesman and Anna persuaded the administration at Wadleigh to allow her to complete the requirements for her diploma. While there, she reconnected with her suffragist club. The young women had a lot to talk about: the Nineteenth Amendment had passed the Senate but had not yet been ratified. One evening, the girls went to hear Margaret Fay, one of the first women leaders of New York City's Tammany Hall political machine. Fay's speech ignited Anna to leave Wadleigh again, this time to fight for women's suffrage. America had won the war, but American women still had a battle to wage to gain the right to vote.

———◆◆◆———

James Joseph Hagan was a veteran Irish politician, who carried with him the toughness he forged growing up in the Lower East Side tenements. A Tammany Hall man, where favors and patronage were traded for votes, Hagan was vociferously opposed to equal suffrage. Anna heard how Hagan liked to tell people he had broken every knuckle in his right hand. "See that hand?!" he'd yell. "That's how I became district leader!" But for all his bare-knuckled bluster, Hagan had lost a series of elections to Republicans. Maybe he wasn't as strong as people said.

Anna and the girls of her suffrage group squared their shoulders and walked into a meeting at Hagan's smoke-filled clubhouse, the Amsterdam Democratic Club, at 131 W. 64th Street, and took seats in the back, careful to avoid the spittoons that sat on the floor. Old Jim Hagan was in the front of the room, railing against a woman's right to vote. When Hagan took a mocking tone, Anna could take no more. She rose to respond.

"Mr. Chairman, you are wrong. Women will—"

"Sit down!" ordered Hagan.

"Mr. Chairman," she shot back, "if that's your idea of a political argument, no wonder you can't carry the district!"

There was a ripple across the room, as attendees soaked in what they had just heard. Hagan had controlled the Democratic vote in his district for forty years, and Republicans beat him in thirty-two of those years. This young woman, not even twenty-one years old, had just jabbed the Tammany Tiger where it hurt him most. Everyone could see that.

Hagan sought out Anna at the end of the meeting. He wasn't angry with her. On the contrary, he was intrigued. Who was this young woman of "noisy acumen" who had had the courage to talk back to the boss like that?[1] The old Tammany salt came away impressed by the young suffragist. She confounded his prejudices with her logic and common sense. She appealed to him with her combination of practicality and idealism.[2] Within weeks, the tough old Irishman had taken the young Jewish woman as his protégée. Jim Hagan would teach Anna Rosenberg the practical politics of New York City.

If Hagan was Anna's political father, Belle Moskowitz was her mother. A quarter century older than Anna, and from a family of German Jewish immigrants, Belle Lindner Moskowitz provided a model for the younger woman. Moskowitz was a publicist, lobbyist, networker, and fundraiser. More importantly, she was a close adviser to New York Governor Al Smith. In an era in which women never achieved proximity to political power unless related by blood or marriage to political figures, Moskowitz was a force in New York politics, writing speeches, preparing legislation, and acting as Smith's gatekeeper.[3] Unlike the bellicose Jim Hagan, who walked around the neighborhood like he owned it, Belle Moskowitz kept a lower profile but exercised greater power.

Like many people from the Austro-Hungarian Empire, Anna spoke both German and Hungarian. Whether it was this fact, or Anna's pluck, or a combination, Mrs. Moskowitz hired the younger woman. Anna reserved hotel ballrooms and contracted orchestras for the luncheons, dinners, and banquets for Jewish philanthropies. These charities flourished in the years after World War I as a way for wealthier families to help those arriving in America from Poland and Russia, driven by war, famine, and violence. The opportunity to work with Mrs. Moskowitz came with a warning that would've been clear in any language: "If you don't make good on this one, don't come back to me for another one."[4]

Working for Belle Moskowitz, Anna saw the power behind the throne. Moskowitz displayed a "selfless, nonthreatening loyalty" to Governor

Smith. "She never grabbed credit for herself," explained Frances Perkins, who would later be the first woman to be a presidential cabinet member, "she gave it to the Governor." When people remarked that Smith was her protégé, she corrected them: *he is my mentor.* "Women in politics," Moskowitz counseled, "can achieve more behind the scenes than in office."[5]

As much as Anna wanted to enter the political arena herself, her career would have to wait. On July 16, 1920, Anna gave birth to a baby boy, Thomas John.* The summer of 1920 brought with it another new responsibility: the vote. In the run-up to what would be the first voting experience for women in most states, the League of Women Voters had staged mock elections, taught citizenship classes, and practiced with pretend ballot boxes.[6] For Anna Rosenberg and other New York Democratic women casting ballots in their first presidential election, 1920 would be especially memorable. A tall, handsome New Yorker with the most famous name in politics was on the ticket: Franklin Delano Roosevelt, thirty-eight and married to the niece of former President Theodore Roosevelt. The younger Roosevelt supported a woman's right to vote, and his bold willingness to ignore precedent as a lawmaker had caught the attention of President Woodrow Wilson. After eight years serving in Wilson's Navy Department, Roosevelt knew his way around Albany and Washington and had already logged a fine record of public service.[7] Moreover, he had accrued foreign policy experience after being dispatched to the battlefields of World War I as Wilson's emissary. His star on the rise, the Democratic Party made Franklin Roosevelt the candidate for Vice President, running with James Cox. It seemed destined that Franklin Roosevelt would one day follow cousin Teddy to the Presidency.

The election of 1920, against Republican Congressman Warren

---

* It was a busy summer for the Lederers. Just weeks before Anna gave birth to her son, Anna's sister, Clare, was involved in an embarrassing episode that made statewide news. Clare's husband of five years, Victor, was found in a hotel room with the wife of his business partner, John Livingston; when detectives broke in, Victor was in his pajamas and Mrs. Livingston was wearing only a curtain. Clare sued Victor for divorce and named Mrs. Livingston in the complaint. In *his* complaint, the cuckolded Mr. Livingston sued his wife and named his business partner. The *New York Tribune* printed a headline with alliterative glee: "Business Partners Figure in Double Divorce Decree," June 13, 1920.

Harding and his V.P. candidate, Calvin Coolidge, was a referendum on the rapid pace of change in the United States following World War I. Arts, fashion, habits, and attitudes all had changed. The response was an unsettling tribalism. Henry Ford's *The International Jew* provided a textbook for anti-Semites. In Tulsa, Oklahoma, the Black Wall Street was destroyed and its residents massacred. In Frankfort, Illinois, Italian Catholics had been burned out of their homes by an angry white mob. Most troubling of all was the fact that the reanimated Ku Klux Klan was no longer limited to southern states. Targeting Blacks, Jews, and Catholics, the Klan was on its way to 4 million members, many of them middle-class northerners.[8] Large segments of the country, it seemed, longed for a return to the slower pace of life, the world in which women, immigrants, and Blacks knew their place.

On the evening of Tuesday, November 2, 1920, the Amsterdam Democratic Club was decorated with red, white, and blue bunting and, for the first time, radios were set up in the hall to broadcast the incoming election results. The euphoria of voting for the first time was tempered by losing: Warren Harding overwhelmingly defeated the Cox-Roosevelt ticket. The American public had spoken: it wanted, to use Harding's inventive phrase, a "return to normalcy."

The national race might not have gone her way, but for Anna there were local campaigns to win. In 1922, at the culmination of her three-year tutelage with Old Jim Hagan, Anna got her chance to prove herself when he put her in charge of his son Walter's campaign to be city alderman.[9] It was a long shot: the seat had been traditionally Republican.

Maybe it was because of her self-consciousness about her poor spelling and barely legible handwriting, but Anna was ahead of her time in her profligate use of the telephone. "She was always on the telephone, cooing, flattering, threatening, joking. Virtually every voter in the district who had a telephone heard the sound of her voice."[10] Anna had the uncanny ability to make and receive dozens and dozens of daily phone calls, often skipping any type of greeting to get right down to business and always ending them with her trademark, "goodbye, *dollink*."[11] It was a new kind of retail politics, and it worked. But the telephone was just one of Anna's innovations that "[Jim Hagan] had never heard of": his pupil went house to house, knocking on doors and "merchandising" young Walter Hagan as if he were a new Premier Duplex electric vacuum cleaner. Then, relying on her wealthier contacts, Anna convinced several society ladies to endorse "the handsome young Irishman" on "their own elegant stationery."[12] Anna's blitz worked: to "everyone's surprise," Hagan's son won in a landslide. Even Pop Hagan was "amazed at his son's election."[13]

Anna was one of the first women in American history to manage political campaigns.[14] Following Hagan's win, she managed campaigns for the New York State Assembly, the New York State Senate, and Theodore Peyser's run for U.S. Congress. Her political work brought in much-needed income, but Anna did not consider this her career. She was a young mother, busily caring for Thomas and learning to cook chicken paprika and other homey Hungarian fare. Anna saw herself as "primarily a housewife who dabbled in politics."[15]

Her modesty notwithstanding, Anna was prepared for success. She had learned ward heeling from the veteran Irishman, and how to be the unseen hand shaping the policies of political candidates. To these skills, Anna added her own irrepressible charm and relentless work ethic. And her timing was perfect. Anna was a member of the generation of women who benefited at the end of the long struggle for suffrage while also being in the vanguard of the modern woman. Anna wore the cloche hat of the flappers, smoked the occasional cigarette, went out dancing, and possessed "a vocabulary that would make a longshoreman blush."[16] Once, when leaving a memorial service full of long-winded speeches, Anna vented, "God damn all politicians!" Not everyone was thrilled with Anna's modern, liberated ways. When a truck driver recognized Anna on the sidewalk one day and yelled out, "Hey, Anna!" Mother Lederer, on a shopping excursion with her youngest daughter, was none too pleased. Anna, of course, waved back.

Unlike the matrons of the Progressive Era, Anna was free to be forthright, candid, and a woman. A profile in *Independent Woman* magazine later recalled what made Anna so potent:

> [Barely out of her teens and] Neck Deep in New York City politics she learned the tricks and wiles of bringing quarreling factions together . . . she knew when to be feminine and cajoling, when to use her soft voice and luminous eyes

to flatten opposition, when to pound the table and scream, [and] when to use fatigue as a weapon to bring spent factions together. She also learned that there is no substitute for hard work, none for facts, none for patience.[17]

———— ••• ————

Anna may have regretted that she lacked a high school diploma, but she had completed an internship with a Tammany Tiger and attended class with the dean of American political women. She had seen the inner workings of the great metropolis, the gears of the crooked meshing with those of the reformers, and the power generated by pragmatic couplings. Geometry, Chemistry, and English Composition had been replaced by a host of practical skills. Anna raised charitable contributions from society ladies with her "silky uptown talk" and used her "Tenth Avenue argot" to appeal to downtown teamsters.[18] Managing campaigns, she was a speechwriter, a field organizer, a spokesperson, a media buyer, an event planner, and a shaper of policy. "What have I done?" she told a reporter for the *New York Times*. "Almost everything."[19] "I am a graduate of the 'learning by doing' school. I had to *do* things when I should've been learning." The broad experience paid off: she had become a "savvy political advisor, public strategist, and astute intermediary of competing local groups"—skills she honed in the "laboratory of urban liberalism."[20] Hers was a master's program in practical politics, her campus was New York City, and Anna Marie Rosenberg had graduated with highest honors.

CHAPTER THREE

THE BUSIEST WOMAN
IN NEW YORK

Under a cloche hat haloed with silk ribbon and wearing a pleated skirt and patterned sweater, Anna Rosenberg exited the subway station at 72nd Street and Broadway. In the heels that added an inch to her 5'3" frame, she walked briskly along 71st Street admiring the stately apartments on West End Avenue. Stepping into the foyer of her more modest apartment building, she greeted the doorman, picked up the bottles from the small milk room, scooped up the letter that sat in her mailbox, and took the elevator to her apartment. Putting the milk and her handbag on the kitchen counter with a sigh, she opened the letter on stationery that read: "Mrs. Dr. Henry Moskowitz," expecting a request for her assistance on some or other matter. Instead, she found a large check enclosed. "If your time is worth nothing to you," Belle Moskowitz had written, "it's worth nothing to others. Keep the money."[1]

The payment was from the concert Anna organized that was attended by thirty-five hundred women and resulted in a large sum for the charity. When the letter of thanks soon arrived at the Rosenbergs' apartment, along with the sizable check, Anna returned the draft, believing the task had been voluntary. Now, pinching the check on each end and holding it up, she examined it as if looking for answers. With Mike's ulcers, and with the expense of little Thomas, they needed the money. The letter was a green light, a boost of confidence: Anna would open her own business.

Fueled by her ever-expanding connections and by her sixteen-hour days, Anna M. Rosenberg, Public Relations & Labor Relations soon gained its first clients. A bus company hired her, then a milk producer. Drivers for these companies had unionized, and the owners sought her advice in dealing with them. Her "fast, frequent, and furious telephone conversations" gained yet more clients.[2] Soon she was receiving retainers from jewelry makers, clothing manufacturers, food service concerns, hotels, trucking firms, and textile dyers.

These companies and the unions they employed were often headquartered downtown, in lower Manhattan, or in nearby Brooklyn. At first, after hiring a nanny to look after Thomas, Anna commuted downtown, sometimes stopping at her father's workshop on 23rd Street with a lunch of stuffed cabbage leaves or a plate of plum cookies. But she soon had her first office. Through her work with the Jewish charity the Joint Distribution Committee, Anna knew Assemblyman Irwin Steingut, a power broker in Brooklyn's Democratic Party. He had space at 32 Court Street, Brooklyn, in a twenty-two-story building known as the borough's first skyscraper.[3]

Busy as she was, she still made time for politics. As it had four years before, in the summer of 1924 the Amsterdam Democratic Club hosted a listening party during the Democratic National Convention, held that year at Madison Square Garden. Like her fellow New York Democrats, Anna listened to the club's radio hoping hometown hero Governor Al Smith would be the nominee for President to defeat Calvin Coolidge, who as Vice President had taken over following Harding's untimely death in office.* If Smith won the general election that fall, there was the intoxicating possibility that Mrs. Moskowitz's ideas would affect the daily lives of all Americans.

As the convention began and the radios in the Amsterdam Democratic Club crackled to life, Democrats were in a "cocksure mood." Harding was gone, but surely voters would remember his scandals, such as the Teapot Dome affair, in which oil reserves in Wyoming set aside for the Navy were leased to a Harding cabinet member. But over several days "fierce factional quarreling" over Prohibition broke out between the "wets," led by Al Smith, and the "drys."[4] Governor Smith was also the target of anti-Catholic smears stirred up by the resurgent Ku Klux Klan.

With the Democratic Party mired in infighting, there was one indisputable bright spot. It was at Madison Square Garden that Franklin D.

---

* Harding disregarded the White House physician and insisted that he be treated by a friend from Ohio. This doctor misdiagnosed Harding, who died. Harding never was a good judge of talent.

Roosevelt made his return to the national spotlight after fighting back from the debilitating polio he contracted in the summer of 1921. As Roosevelt rose to give the keynote address on behalf of Governor Smith, the radio announcers painted a dramatic picture. Supported by crutches and assisted by his son James, Roosevelt made his way to the podium with painful slowness. Once there, he was "a commanding figure of a man despite his crutches."[5] After his rousing speech in which he hailed Smith as the "Happy Warrior of the political battlefield," the delegates responded with an ovation that went on for three minutes.

But the dream of Al Smith—and Belle Moskowitz—was not to be. Corporate lawyer John W. Davis "emerged with the worthless nomination."[6] That November, Republican Calvin Coolidge easily defeated Davis. After losing a second consecutive election to Republicans, the only solace for those hoping for an energetic and progressive national government was the reminder of the Roosevelt magic.

<hr/>

Looking out from her office at the Brooklyn Bridge, the young businesswoman took in the full measure of the complex task that lay ahead. Politics would have to make room for the practicalities of earning a living. How should she counsel companies to adapt to the mounting challenges posed by union organization? What advice should she give on how to navigate the growing media scrutiny? In the seven years between 1916 and 1922 the United States recorded its highest levels of strike activity ever. By the mid-1920s, this turbulence was fresh in the minds of management and workers. Some factory and mill owners responded with harsh, union-busting tactics, mobilizing violent strikebreakers, or insisting workers sign "yellow-dog" contracts that made joining a union a fireable offense.

Other owners traded profits for labor peace by offering workers "pensions, holidays, sporting and musical clubs, Americanization classes, safety committees, in-plant concerts, sermons, dances, and exhibits of consumer goods that could be bought on installment."[7] Whether they used the stick of harshness or the carrot of corporate beneficence, the private companies that hired Anna "were suspicious, if not hostile, toward unionism and its presence in the American workplace."[8]

To Anna Rosenberg, there was a third course: mediation. Rather than picking the side of the businesses that paid her, knowing that she would lose the trust of the unions they employed, Anna's novel approach was to solve conflicts through internal discussion geared toward promoting accommodation.[9] If they were willing to try this approach, Anna advised the businessmen, they would be able to retain managerial authority in the face of union challenges—power the owners were keen to keep.

The unions were comforted by Anna's background of social and political activism, her "refusal to adopt an adversarial position against labor," and encouraged by her efforts to liberalize policies and practices of the workplace.[10] "She knows what the workin' stiff is up against," said one union man. "We don't have to spell out our side of an argument for her. When she tells us a thing we know it's true." Rosenberg is "on the level," said another. "She's always kept her word with us."[11] A labor reporter spoke of "her ability to make you feel she is *your* advocate, and that she cares for *you*."[12] The rank and file's appreciation for Anna was matched by their leaders. Throughout the 1920s, she cultivated strong relationships with men such as David Dubinsky of the International Ladies' Garment Workers' Union and Sidney Hillman of the Amalgamated Clothing Workers of America.

Her equitable treatment of labor and her efforts to liberalize labor relations did not cost her corporate clients.[13] On the contrary, coming to a mutually beneficial agreement was much more cost-effective than walkouts. One businessman learned his lesson the hard way: "Half an hour of her time would have been worth $10,000 to me."[14] Anna had a sense of moral fairness that was appealing to both labor and management. *Fortune* magazine called it "intuition."[15] According to scholar Elizabeth A. Collins, "Her emphasis on fairness (or the appearance of fairness) to labor won her the respect of labor leaders."[16] Adept at "soft-soaping labor and management into agreements," Anna "managed to earn the trust of the unions at the same time she was earning large fees from their employers."[17] "It is strange," Anna told the *New York Times*:

> how many active business men keep their noses so close
> to the grindstone that they are not able to see the changes
> that are taking place in the world around them. Even today
> there are many firms trying to conduct their affairs in the
> same manner they did fifty years ago. They do not realize

that the world has progressed and that human relations are different and workers are no longer slaves.[18]

In conference rooms with the owners on one side, the union men on the other, and Anna at the head of the table, she worked her magic. Perching on a telephone book or a dictionary and resting her elbows on the table, Anna was polished and in control in her skirt and jacket, a large brooch on her lapel, and her brown hair neatly done and crowned by an elaborate hat. When the men were seated, she stopped writing, folded her hands, and calmly looked up. Her pleasant face was animated by her large eyes, expressive brows, and the merest hint of a smile at the corner of her mouth. As she spoke, her eyes made contact with all those in the room. Hers was not an officious tone, but a measured one delivered with a slight tilt of her face, which signaled sincerity. If the parties needed a push, Anna leaned forward on her elbows and added volume to her voice. If the parties were stubborn or recalcitrant, Anna expanded her vocabulary and candor.

Adelaide Kerr of the Associated Press was amazed when she first saw her in action:

> [Ms. Rosenberg has] never read a single book on labor relations. Her technique is a mixture of intelligence, energy, sympathy, toughness, diplomacy, common sense—and a hard, fast smack when she thinks a smack is needed. In one second she can switch from soft-voiced cajolery to the language of a stevedore. Some call it shrewd showmanship. Others say it stems from a genuine liking for people, and understanding of their problems in a capacity to go straight to the core of a question.

When a drug manufacturer turned to her for advice, Anna advised an educational campaign that would show its workers how important their work was to human health. "One of the main keys of her labor relations policy," explained Adelaide Kerr, "is her strong belief that people who have been given a sense of responsibility, service, and pride in their work will do a better, faster job. She advises her clients to use every possible means to make their employees understand the social significance of the product they manufacture and work they do."[19] As Anna herself described it: "I'm trying to instill new ideas into old businesses."[20]

Her methods worked. Settling a strike or striking a deal, Anna would command, "Pipe down, boys, and listen to me."[21] Whether union or management, she would tell them not what they wanted to hear, but what they needed to hear. "Do you want to settle this or don't you? You have two choices. You can take a strike, and if you want to take it, it's none of my goddamn business, or do you want to settle this thing? If you want to settle it, here's what I suggest to you."[22] Then boom, boom, boom. The deal done, she would clap her hands together, bracelets jangling, and congratulate the parties, "Wunnerful job, gentlemen!" Denying Anna Rosenberg was like denying a "buzz saw."[23]

In the first decade as a consultant her client list grew to include financier John Hay Whitney; I. Miller, the shoe magnate; the investment house Lazard Frères; and Nelson Rockefeller, the grandson of the founder of Standard Oil. Her annual reports from the 1920s show her mediation practice earned over $20,000 a year, about $300,000 in 2022 dollars.

Deep-pocketed titans of finance and captains of industry were not her only clients. In 1926 the all-Jewish soccer team SC Hakoah Vienna retained Anna to arrange a tour of the United States to play matches for charity. The tour was a smash. At Ebbets Field, home of the Brooklyn Dodgers, soccer outdrew baseball for the first time. The team's elegant style was a draw in Boston, Chicago, Philadelphia, Providence, and everywhere they played. Awed by his opponents' skillful teamwork, one defeated goalkeeper complained Hakoah "had the ball for 87 [out of the 90] minutes."[24] Besides being a huge draw, the tour was "a moral success," in the words of one reporter. "Only by promoting the spirit of brotherhood and sportsmanship among the nations of the world," wrote the *Jewish Daily Bulletin*, can "international peace . . . be effectively developed."

Life had settled into a contented rhythm for Anna Rosenberg. The young businesswoman's office routine began with her a daily phone call to Mater, a call to Ms. Elsie, her live-in help, and a check-in with Thomas on his schoolwork.[25] When they could, Anna and her sister, Clare, met their mother for lunch. Under a café umbrella, the three women caught up, reminisced, and when there was a particularly juicy bit of gossip they lapsed into Hungarian.

Sunday was family day for the Rosenbergs. They would dote on little Thomas, take a walk to Riverside Park, and enjoy a glass of wine afterwards. Anna might indulge in a cigarette as she shuffled through the kitchen drawer looking for one of her grandmother's handwritten recipes. "I'm a good cook, and can get up the best Hungarian dishes you've tasted," she boasted.[26] If Clare and her husband joined them for dinner, Anna would serve a multicourse meal on her best set of china; at the center of the table, as always, sat a vase of freshly cut flowers.

It was during this time that Anna was perfecting her dualistic public persona. "Blustery, hearty, and businesslike on the one hand, and visibly feminine on the other."[27] With her bobbed hair and large brown eyes, journalists routinely recorded that she looked "younger and prettier than her photographs." Perhaps it was the girlhood incident where she was mocked at school for her traditional Hungarian dress, but Anna was dressed and coiffed immaculately. To the office she wore a uniform of "smart suits, seasoned with a pretty blouse," and she adorned her wrists "with gold bracelets and some accent like a gold flower clip with a diamond heart." Her hats, "a froth of pastel plumes, are conversation pieces." The overall impression was that of a pretty, chic young professional, a "petite, dark-eyed sparrow of a woman," whose presence carried a caffeinated charm.[28]

Just before Christmas 1926, Papa Lederer died. His remarkable journey had taken him from the periphery of a nineteenth-century Imperial Court to the heart of New York City during the very moment it was becoming the world's financial hub. Albert instilled in his youngest daughter a gratitude toward the nation that gave the Lederer family a second chance. "My father," Anna explained, "was vehement in his belief that everyone born outside of America has a special obligation to this country. Father's influence upon me was so great it constantly keeps before me my own obligation to the United States. I seldom say no when asked to participate in public affairs."[29]

Shortly after her father's death, Jim Hagan's long-running district leadership was put to the challenge, and, as busy as she was, Anna couldn't say no to a return to the political game. Nathan Straus, Jr., a "financial prince" of the Macy's department store kingdom, put up a candidate against Old Jim. It was a "real fight" even by the bare-knuckled standards of 1920s New York City. "He is not fit for even the smallest position of public trust," railed Straus.

Old Jim Hagan called on Anna to run his campaign. She used the phones to emphasize his opponent's inexperience and trumpet Hagan's Tammany favors. In the end, Straus' man was defeated and Hagan retained leadership of the district. Though on the losing side, Nathan Straus was so impressed with Anna that he vowed to work with her in the future. Straus was just the latest addition to Anna's list of connections that was growing to include politicians, businessmen, union bosses, and scions of industry.

———— ••• ————

As the 1920s wound down, it was clear that much had changed in New York and across the nation. Radio and newsreels competed with newspapers. Horse-drawn carts had given way to cars and trucks. The "el" had been torn down; New Yorkers now went underground to commute via the gleaming new subway trains. New York was transforming into a city of superlatives. The Port of New York was the world's busiest seaport. The Woolworth Building in lower Manhattan was the world's tallest building. Harlem, a hundred blocks north, was home to some of the era's greatest literature, music, and arts.

New York City's kaleidoscopically electrified Times Square may have portended a bright future, but all was not well. Women voters were demanding that attention be paid to their priorities, such as ending child labor and capping the hours of the workweek. Consumers had indulged their hunger for goods like the Kodak Brownie camera, electric refrigerators, and RCA radios, but much of this purchasing had been made through installment buying, dependent on future income. Middle-class families had joined the wealthy in buying up stocks in the nation's fast-growing companies, but it seemed impossible that the stock market could keep going up indefinitely. The fast pace of change had caused a latent malaise. Some wondered when the bubble would burst.

Anna Rosenberg's life had changed, too. She was a wife and mother, pursuing the dual tracks of politics and business. Her political efforts fed into her business, and her business connections fed into her politics—the result was a list of contacts so enviable the *New Yorker* described her as "a kind of switchboard."[30] With an ever-expanding network that included politicians like Fiorello La Guardia, the future Mayor; and business leaders like Nelson Rockefeller, by the end of the decade Anna Rosenberg was dubbed "the busiest woman in New York."

If managing campaigns for Tammany small fry and engaging in local politics had been the sum of her activities, Anna might have simply enjoyed a long and prosperous career in labor and public relations. But it was through her political activity that she came to meet another ascending politician, one who would change her life, the lives of millions of Americans, and indeed the fate of the nation: Franklin Delano Roosevelt.

CHAPTER FOUR

THIS MAN ROOSEVELT

Most people who are nominated for the Governorship have to run, but obviously I am not in condition to run, and therefore I am counting on my friends all over the state to make it possible for me to walk in.

—Franklin D. Roosevelt,
a 2-to-1 long shot in the race for New York Governor[1]

Anna nervously looked again at the business card to make sure she had the address correct: "Mr. and Mrs. Franklin Delano Roosevelt, 47-49 East 65th Street, New York, New York." Anna exited the cab and looked up at the massive arched doorway of the Roosevelts' limestone and redbrick twin town house.

Days earlier, Anna had attended a tea for the Women's Division of the New York Democratic Party hosted by Eleanor Roosevelt. When Mrs. Roosevelt, who was always looking to promote women in politics, learned that Anna was in labor relations and that they had a common friend in Belle Moskowitz, she invited Anna to meet her husband, who was about to run for Governor of New York.

The butler led Anna into the parlor, where Eleanor Roosevelt greeted her before leaving to teach her class at the Todhunter School. While Anna waited for Mr. Roosevelt, she thought of the rousing convention speeches she'd heard on the crackly radio. Just then that sonorous tenor voice filled the room with a hearty hello. Franklin Roosevelt extended a hand from what looked like a homemade wheelchair, a narrow wooden dining chair with double-rimmed wheels and a bracket that held an ashtray. He was a large man with a handsome, finely chiseled face. His dark hair had a hint of silver. He wore a white dress shirt and bow tie. His strong upper body contrasted with his withered legs, over which were draped dark trousers.

Like many people meeting Franklin Roosevelt for the first time, Anna shared the notion conveyed by the press that Roosevelt was mildly handicapped, that he was able to stand, albeit with some difficulty. But he remained seated.[2] His temperament and magnetism, though, were exactly what she expected. On his upturned face was a pair of gold-rimmed pince-nez glasses like those worn by Theodore Roosevelt. Like his kinsman, Franklin smiled easily and laughed often, and the overall impression was one of vitality. In Roosevelt's right hand was a Camel cigarette at the end of an ebony holder.

When Anna left the Roosevelt home that morning, it was with instructions to go to the Biltmore Hotel the following day and ask for Louis.

—◆—

Anna stepped from the elevator on the fourth floor of the Biltmore on Madison Avenue and walked toward the pungent cloud of cigarette smoke drifting from an office suite. Amid the clacking of typewriters, she saw a wizened figure in the epicenter of the cloud. The hunched man looked up, revealing a pockmarked face bookended by large ears and topped with combed-over strands of greasy hair. He continued typing while at the same time croaking into a telephone receiver cradled between his slight shoulder and skinny neck. As he talked, typed, and smoked, a series of assistants handed him documents to sign and newspaper clippings to review. *This must be Louis.*

Louis McHenry Howe (pronounced Louie) was in charge of Franklin Delano Roosevelt's political fate, and had been since covering the state legislature beat in Albany in 1910, when he saw the potential of the young politician. Like others before her, Anna could scarcely imagine a more unlikely partnership than that between Franklin and "Louie," the "grim little bulldog."[3] Roosevelt was handsome and gregarious, while the older Howe was "the oddest little duck" with a "brusque irritable manner" who "made no effort to be friendly."[4] Wearing the starched white collar that was fashionable at the turn of the century and rumpled trousers covered in fallen cigarette ash, Howe stood in contrast to the elegant patrician. Despite their differences, Franklin and Louie were fiercely loyal to each other. Louis Howe's "only ambition was to be the 'manager' of the man whom he genuinely thought to be the greatest human being history had ever produced."[5]

As for the candidate, he owed Howe a tremendous debt. More than Franklin's wife, Eleanor, and his mother, Sara Delano Roosevelt, Howe had been instrumental in keeping Roosevelt's political career alive after Franklin contracted polio. Whether rehabilitating in Georgia or on his houseboat with his personal secretary and companion, Missy LeHand, Roosevelt was absent from New York for long periods. During these absences, Howe maintained lines of communication between Roosevelt and the powers in the New York Democratic Party.

Howe was treated as family, living in the Roosevelts' town house during the week, but he spent most of his time at the Biltmore headquarters. Howe issued publicity, gathered campaign intelligence, and was the foreman of a "vast letter writing factory, with people specifically trained to forge the candidate's 'personal' signature to form letters issued by the hundreds."[6]

Half Howe's sixty years and with a build like a rugby player was Sam Rosenman. Capable of "prolonged bouts of concentrated labor," the bookish lawyer was more at home working quietly than throwing elbows in the scrum of politics. Sam was on FDR's team to travel with the candidate and to transform his dictations, insertions, revisions, and instructions into winning speeches. Sammy the Rose, as FDR called him, was just a few years older than Anna, but over the many years she worked with him he seemed ageless, "neither youthful when young nor elderly when old."[7]

As if to make up for the soft-spoken Sam Rosenman was Jim Farley, a big, bald-headed Irishman whose "insatiably gregarious" personality made him seem younger than his forty years. Farley hailed from rural Rockland County, New York, and it was his job to work the moribund upstate counties.

The other Irish Catholic on the team was Edward J. Flynn, the Democratic leader of the Bronx and, like Anna, a Tammany protégé. Flynn was close in age to Jim Farley but seemed older, with a head of prematurely silver hair. Flynn and Farley shared Irish roots, but not much more. Unlike the backslapping Farley, the tall and handsome Flynn was "aloof, solitary." Flynn could go into depressive moods but was also capable of conversational ease with "sophisticated people."[8] The lodge and the fraternity were not for him. Flynn, slated to be FDR's Secretary of

State of New York in the unlikely event they could win an election in a Republican year, would whip up the urban vote.

The last recruit to the campaign cabinet was Anna Rosenberg, who possessed "the experience, brains, and liberal values" that Roosevelt sought in his aides. Anna would hone the candidate's message to labor unions while keeping him palatable to factory owners and industrialists, a vital task in a campaign in which labor relations was one of the key planks in the platform. Roosevelt had Frances Perkins as a labor adviser, but no one in New York knew what the union worker wanted and what the owner was willing to grant better than the young labor mediation expert. By bringing her on board, Roosevelt was not merely acceding to his wife's wishes; he was making a politically wise move. The businesswoman's "mixture of political savvy and considerable knowledge of labor issues [was] invaluable," according to scholar John Thomas McGuire. "Contacts to labor leaders such as William Green of the American Federation of Labor and David Dubinsky" were bonuses Anna brought to her "first important work with Roosevelt."[9] Echoing this sentiment, business historian Jacqueline McGlade describes the "considerable clout that Rosenberg had amassed with the New York business community" in the 1920s.[10] Her contacts and reputation set her up for "successful pre-presidential advising."[11]

But that morning at the Biltmore, Anna was like any other professional woman trying to navigate her first day on the job. Her older male colleagues were nice enough, but there was no question who was running things. "Remember this," Louis Howe told the assembled quartet. "You're nothing. Your face means nothing. Your name means nothing. I don't want to catch you or anybody else trying to crowd into a photograph. All you have to worry about, night and day, day and night, is this man Roosevelt."* Howe took a long drag from his ever-present Sweet Caporal cigarette and dispatched Team Roosevelt to work their various constituencies.

---

* Elliott Roosevelt and James Brough, *A Rendezvous with Destiny: The Roosevelts of the White House* (New York: G.P. Putnam's Sons, 1975), 21–22. Elliott Roosevelt recalls Howe giving this "pep talk" to campaign staff in the presidential race in the fall of 1932, but given Howe's single-minded devotion to FDR and knowledge that the New York Governor's race was a stepping-stone to the presidency, such advice in the fall of 1928 seems entirely in character.

The election was in less than three weeks.

—◆—

That this man Roosevelt was a candidate for Governor of the nation's most populous state in 1928 was a minor miracle, capping a decade that started with unlimited political promise, and brought unimaginable personal agony. The year after his unsuccessful run for Vice President, Roosevelt went for a swim in the cold waters near his vacation home on Campobello Island, hoping to ease a stiff back. Over the next few days Roosevelt felt his legs become increasingly weak. When Roosevelt climbed into bed on the evening of August 10, it was the last time he would ever stand unassisted again.

Roosevelt was thirty-nine.

In time, Roosevelt overcame the psychological wound of his disease, and tried to heal himself physically. He took water immersion treatments in Warm Springs, Georgia, where he built a modest cottage and created a haven for children stricken with polio, who affectionately called him Rosie. Swimming in warm water activated his body, but whether it was in the Peach State, on his houseboat, or in New York, Roosevelt was often confined to bed. To activate his mind, Roosevelt renewed his interest in his boyhood hobby of stamp collecting. Besides passing the time, by examining postage stamps from around the world—Japan, Clipperton Island, Mexico, Galápagos—he was soaking in geography, history, and culture.

During his long absences from the Empire State, Roosevelt's political past was in danger of being forgotten and his future cast in doubt. But Louis Howe kept him connected to Democratic politics in New York and stoked his political ambition. Roosevelt's performance at the 1924 convention reminded followers of his magnetism, but he was not yet ready to return to politics. In the meantime, Howe encouraged Eleanor to become more involved in New York's Democratic Party, where she could serve as FDR's eyes and ears—a role Anna Rosenberg would also come to play.

In the fall of 1928, as New Yorkers celebrated another World Series victory by the Yankees and a stock market that saw its heaviest trading ever in a single month (nearly 10 million shares), FDR was persuaded to leave his rehabilitation and return to the political arena. Roosevelt's opponent in the New York Governor's race was Albert Ottinger, the New York State attorney general and the first Jewish gubernatorial candidate in the state's history. The fear in the Roosevelt camp was that Ottinger would appeal to New York City's large Jewish population, so to offer voters an alternative, Roosevelt chose Herbert Lehman, another Belle Moskowitz protégé, as his lieutenant governor. The *New York World* endorsed the Democratic ticket, adding: "Leading Democrats hope the vote of the Jewish citizen of Greater New York" will go to Roosevelt-Lehman.[12]

In the "religiously sensitive campaign" against Ottinger, Franklin Roosevelt relied on a number of Jewish advisers.[13] In addition to Rosenman and Rosenberg, FDR was advised on farm issues by his Hyde Park neighbor Henry Morgenthau (whom Franklin and Louie called Henry the Morgue); on criminal justice by Judge Joseph Proskauer, and FDR rekindled his friendship with Felix Frankfurter, the only Jewish tenured professor at Harvard Law School. These aides would help the candidate "navigate the treacherous waters of New York politics and guide state policy."

Appealing to New York's Jewish voters was just one of the many challenges the candidate faced in the fall of 1928, when President Herbert Hoover was popular, the stock market was strong, and it was looking like a replay of the 1920 Republican landslide. A decisive victory for Hoover would mean Democratic losses at the state and local levels—and maybe even the end of Roosevelt's political career, once and for all.

Once in the race, however, Franklin Roosevelt was committed to winning. To carry the state, Roosevelt would have to appeal to all of New York: upstate rural voters and urban liberals alike. He would have to appeal to farmers and factory workers, to Protestants, Jews, and Catholics. He would need labor unions and fat cat donors, "wets," who were against Prohibition, and "drys." To harmonize these various elements of New York politics, he relied on Louis Howe and his team.

On October 17, 1928, Roosevelt launched a sprint of a campaign. With high energy and political charisma, the candidate barnstormed by automobile, train, and barge. Visiting every corner of the Empire State and delivering as many as fourteen speeches a day, FDR turned the race into a contest of ideas one reporter described as "reactionary-ism versus progressivism." Albert Ottinger represented a Republican Party "barren of imagination," charged Roosevelt. In contrast, his was a movement of ideas.

To win rural upstate Protestants, Roosevelt championed the public development and ownership of hydroelectric power. For farmers ruined by postwar lack of demand, Roosevelt promised state aid to get them back on their feet. Although Eleanor and Franklin had agreed that she should remain at national headquarters working on the presidential campaign of Al Smith, Eleanor made "a very complete campaign throughout the state" to promote her husband.[14] Along with Caroline O' Day and Nancy Cook, Eleanor carpooled upstate to meet with Jim Farley and connect with women progressives in the critical upstate counties and to change the minds of rural women who saw the Democratic Party as "a collection of Catholics . . . immigrants [and] urban workers of the lowest class."[15]

In that first week on the campaign trail, besides illustrating what an energetic government could accomplish, Roosevelt made the case against the racial and ethnic bigotry that had spread during the decade. Appalled at KKK activity in his beloved upstate, allied with Roman Catholic Al Smith, and with Herbert Lehman sometimes at his side, Roosevelt made combating bigotry a part of his stump speech.

In small cities like Binghamton and rural towns like Hornell and Wellsville, Roosevelt spoke out against the Klan: "I have noticed this un-Americanism, this type of assault on the principles on which our country was founded, exists most greatly where there is least education." This intolerance was not to be found in the cities, but in the "out-of-the-way farms and small towns."[16] The candidate thought his strong stance was "not only good morals but also good politics," but he misjudged his rural audiences.[17] Back at headquarters, Louis Howe was receiving "several violent comebacks on this."[18] FDR's moralizing came off as criticizing the very voters he needed if he had any chance of winning.

Roosevelt and Sammy the Rose arrived in Buffalo the night of the nineteenth to a desperate wire from Howe commanding a return to a bread-and-butter issue on which there was a consensus among New

Yorkers. FDR chose labor, an issue on which he did not own as much expertise as, say, rural electrification or upstate dams. Fortunately, Roosevelt had two labor specialists on his team. Forty-eight-year-old Frances Perkins' understanding of the labor landscape dated to the Progressive Era, a time when change was driven by idealism and by a mistrust of the largeness of American industry. A generation younger was Anna Rosenberg, who had also been nourished at the well of New York City social justice. Instead of seeing business leaders as potential enemies, her success in labor mediation led her to see them as partners in a new liberalizing movement that was shaping up to be a more pragmatic descendant than its doctrinaire parent. By positioning herself in the middle, she could act as a switchboard. The "entrepreneurial consultant" Anna Rosenberg proved to be a "vital link" in "facilitating dealings between business groups and the state in formulating industrial policies."[19]

In addition to her labor expertise and connections, Anna brought practicality to a candidate rusty from his political absence, and who could, at times, be taken with his own idealism. In her way, Anna played a role in FDR's evolution to a more practical politician. In the tough world of machine politics, Anna had earned a reputation as an "outstanding manager of local political campaigns."[20] As a woman "at a time when public power and business position was largely a realm held by men," her success is all the more striking.[21] "When I want something done," Anna explained, "I call up a friend. He says all right, and the next day the job is done. Later, I find the proper procedure was to go through eighteen offices, make seven carbons, wait three weeks, and spend several dollars in the process."[22]

Though he had carved out a name for himself as a fighter against Tammany Hall corruption as a young state senator, as Roosevelt evolved as a politician he allowed himself to soak up valuable lessons from Tammany insiders such as Anna and Herbert Lehman. Historian Arthur Schlesinger, Jr., describes Roosevelt's learning curve: "[A]s a practical politician, Roosevelt was learning a good deal— about patronage, about party organization, about working with congressmen, about living with bosses." Author Terry Golway states that "this shrewd, ambitious man learned valuable lessons about politics as he observed the wiles and ways of the down-to-earth, pragmatic, and likeable Tammany figures."[23] As Anna later explained, Governor Roosevelt "would have been the first to admit . . . that the social benefit programs" used as tools to reduce the gross inequality in New York "influenced his thinking."[24] Idealism could live in harmony with pragmatism, but sometimes it had to give way, a lesson that Roosevelt clearly internalized when he snapped at Sam Rosenman, "You have to get the votes first—then you can do good things!"[25]

Roosevelt's chance to pivot to a unifying campaign topic was October 20 in Buffalo, where he was to deliver a speech to the blue-collar audience. The night before, FDR handed Sam Rosenman the thick labor file with contributions from Perkins and Rosenberg, containing both theoretical ideas and practical implementation. On his way to a fundraiser, Roosevelt wheeled out of the room winking to his speechwriter and saying, "Don't stay up all night."[26]

Rolling out his labor plank the next night, Roosevelt hammered his opponent, who "had the nerve to talk about what the Republican Party has done for labor." Working New Yorkers would only get "half-way measure[s]" and "smoke screens" from Republicans, Roosevelt railed. "Somewhere . . . in a desk of the Republican leaders of New York State," mocked Roosevelt, "is a large envelope, soiled, worn, bearing a date that goes back twenty-five or thirty years." This envelope, he continued, has "Promises to labor. . . . But nowhere is a single page bearing the title 'Promises kept.'"[27]

Labor proved to be a winner.

In the last two weeks of the campaign, audiences from Buffalo to the Bronx cheered as Roosevelt described how the Democrats would add to those measures. If elected, he would favor an eight-hour day, and a forty-eight-hour week for woman and children in factories; he would promote a minimum wage for women in industry; and he would expand the Workmen's Compensation Act to give the "greatest protection to injured workers and their [dependents]." Anna was instrumental in the tactical decision to fight for women first. There would be "much less opposition," she explained, because there was "a sympathy for women in industry." Moreover, "women were not unionized much, and there was nobody to fight their battles."[28] The strategy succeeded. Heralding that "labor has a true friend in Franklin D. Roosevelt," at a campaign event at the Commodore Hotel on October 30, 1928, labor leaders representing nearly 1 million workers pledged their support to the candidate from Hyde Park.

Franklin Roosevelt's whirlwind campaign ended on Monday, November 5, in Poughkeepsie, where he was greeted by a parade of twenty thousand supporters. Over the course of nineteen days, he had crisscrossed the cities, towns, and villages of the Empire State, traveling over thirteen hundred miles and delivering nearly fifty speeches. Standing on his braced legs, from the back of his convertible touring car Roosevelt greeted voters from the five boroughs to the countryside flaming with autumn's colors. With Sam Rosenman at his side and Louis Howe directing operations from midtown Manhattan, Roosevelt made the case that their progressive platform would improve the lives of the state's farmers, workers, women, and children. Team Roosevelt had done all it could.

Would it be enough?

As the evening of the election wore on, bad news trickled into headquarters at the Biltmore. By ten o'clock, the presidential race was decided. Republican Herbert Hoover had beaten Democratic candidate New York Governor Al Smith, and a Republican landslide was unfolding not just in New York, but across the nation. At midnight, with Albert Ottinger's lead upstate holding, the first editions of the Wednesday morning papers announced the Republican had won. Roosevelt took the news "with his usual good nature," but Louis Howe was "brokenhearted."[29] After saying their goodbyes to the team, Eleanor and Franklin went home to get some sleep before making the concession speech.

Although she, too, must have been disheartened, the candidate's intrepid mother, Sara Delano Roosevelt, remained at the Biltmore, kept company by the rest of team Roosevelt. At two o'clock in the morning, Ed Flynn noticed an unusual delay in the upstate vote tallies and immediately issued a statement to the press that "fraud [was] being committed" and that a "staff of 100 lawyers" would be on their way upstate at first light.[30] Within minutes, the vote tallies returned to normal speed. Frances Perkins noticed Roosevelt gaining on Ottinger. "Forty votes here, one hundred votes there, and seventy-five votes somewhere else. They mounted up," she recalled.[31] At 4:00 AM Roosevelt took a slim lead and held it. Just before dawn, Sara Roosevelt hopped in a taxi to the 65th Street town house to awaken the new Governor of the Empire State.

On November 12, Louis Howe telegrammed Roosevelt, who had taken a post-election rehabilitation in Warm Springs, to report that six hundred letters had poured into headquarters since the election, of which "four hundred were out-of-state [and referred] to national matters." Howe's longtime dream for this man Roosevelt was very much alive, but even he could not have foreseen the ways in which this election would shape the nation's destiny.

CHAPTER FIVE

ACTION IN ALBANY

[The Jazz Age] leaped to a spectacular death
in October, 1929.

—F. Scott Fitzgerald, "Echoes of the Jazz Age," 1931

Governor Roosevelt spent the first months of his two-year term at the towered and turreted Executive Mansion in Albany wrangling over the budget with the legislature, signing and vetoing bills, and filling vacancies. His days began early, with breakfast in bed, an old sweater thrown over his pajamas to keep his shoulders warm, and continued to late in the evening, when, after hosting dinners and state affairs, Roosevelt would draft speeches, including radio addresses he delivered from his study.[1] On Columbus Day weekend Governor Roosevelt spoke at the Saratoga Battlefield, where British general "Gentleman" Johnny Burgoyne had lost his army in a decisive battle in the fall of 1777. The clouds thickening over the ancient battlefield that Sunday afternoon portended the storm about to burst.

On Tuesday, October 22, 1929, the front page of the *New York Times* reported a stock sell-off and that "amid scenes of wild confusion and drastically lower prices, the stock market continued to pay the piper for its long dance of advancing inflated prices." After a brief rebound the next day, stocks plummeted Thursday—Black Thursday—and again on Friday. The weekend failed to calm the market, and the sell-off continued on Monday. On Tuesday, dawn broke over Manhattan at 6:24. Two and a half hours later, the shouts of, "Sell! Sell!" were so cacophonous that the opening bell of the New York Stock Exchange could not be heard. By that afternoon 16 million shares had been sold and $14 billion had evaporated forever. Forty percent of the wealth of the United States had been wiped out, never to return.

The Great Depression had begun.

The effects in New York were immediate and terrible. When the New York–based Bank of United States collapsed in December 1930, 450,000 depositors discovered they were ruined—banks had been allowed to speculate in stocks with their deposits. Eight thousand desperate people formed a queue in front of one branch in Brooklyn. Out-of-work bond salesmen worked as shoeshine boys, five cents a shine. Erstwhile executives peddled cheap neckties and roasted chestnuts. Managers and office staff stood outside in long lines for a long-shot chance at a day of manual labor and a nickel sandwich. When office rents dried up, the newly constructed Empire State Building stopped running the elevators from the forty-second to the sixty-seventh floors; Depression-weary New Yorkers called it the Empty State Building.*

The men who'd lost their jobs and their will joined the human flotsam that washed up in the city's parks, sheltering themselves in shacks of tar paper, carboard, and tin. Central Park's "Hooverville" was filled with homeless men covered in old topcoats or newspapers, "Hoover blankets." One desperate couple, a carpenter and a maid, sheltered in a cave in Central Park. In 1931, 238 persons were admitted to New York hospitals due to malnutrition; a quarter of them died.

———◆◆◆———

The languishing "Empty State Building" might've frightened off most real estate developers, but not the family of John D. Rockefeller. Their ambitious project to construct a towering Art Deco skyscraper at the heart of a larger urban complex during the Great Depression was a stroke of good fortune for Anna Rosenberg. When Nelson Rockefeller retained her to handle relations between the unions and management during the construction of Rockefeller Center, he called Anna the "most influential personality in the labor situation in New York."

With clients like Macy's and the Rockefellers, Anna and her family moved to a new apartment at 78th Street and Broadway. The ten-story building was newer and taller and had a two-tone Tudor façade of soft white and half-timbered beams. Inside, cream-colored beams, dark-stained moldings, and leaded glass gave the apartment the feel of

---

* One of the remaining tenants was Belle Moskowitz, who ran her public-relations firm from a small office in the Empire State Building.

an especially spacious and well-lit English cottage, but the views of the downtown skyscrapers, the Hudson River, and the New Jersey smokestacks were unmistakably New York. Sales of luxury goods were down, but Mike's job as a rug merchant was safe. Tommy was enrolled in the private Horace Mann School, and Anna was self-sufficient at a time when unseen forces were wreaking havoc on jobs, careers, and livelihoods. "By that time I had seen a number of people forced to retire when they were at the height of their energy and power," she remembered. "I didn't want that ever to happen to me. I wanted to be in business for myself."[2]

If the ambitious "city within a city" were to be realized, it would take every ounce of Anna's considerable skills. The House of Standard Oil did not become one of the richest concerns in human history by bargaining with unions. Its aged king, John D. Rockefeller, was resolutely anti-union, refused to pay overtime, and relied on armies of company workers.

Anna's mediation soon infused trust and transparency into the relations between the construction tradesmen and the family; she pointed out areas of common agreement and urged better communication. It worked: Anna "[served] as Nelson's Sherpa on the treacherous slopes of organized labor."[3] When the union that represented janitors, elevator operators, and "scrubwomen" found itself shut out of the project, Anna lobbied state officials. The Building Maintenance Craftsmen union was certified almost immediately, without the usual public hearings. "Overnight, the company [teams] were dissolved," and the new union went to work. Anna's efforts solidified what was to be a lifelong mentorship to the young Rockefeller, as well as her reputation as an "über-lobbyist" with a "direct pipeline" to power.[4]

Literally cementing the Rockefeller legacy in midtown Manhattan, the grand project combined urban idealism and architectural magnificence. The plaza included unprecedented public space, including gardens and the famous ice-skating rink. Towering above the complex was 30 Rockefeller Plaza, its spire 850 feet above the bronze statue of Prometheus, who in Greek mythology stole fire to give to humankind—including the foundry workers in Queens who cast the work. In December 1931, the union men pooled their money to buy the first Rockefeller Center Christmas tree, a grand balsam fir adorned with homemade garlands.

This small act of optimism in New York City took place at a moment of national inaction. Like Calvin Coolidge, President Herbert Hoover was a prisoner of his own economic orthodoxy. A believer in the rugged individual, he was unwilling to use the national government to mitigate the misery. When the storm broke in 1929, by contrast, Governor Roosevelt promptly saw that localities would be overwhelmed as they tried to combat the Depression. What was needed was action by the state. The use of government to help struggling citizens upset many of Franklin Roosevelt's old Harvard classmates, who were doctors, lawyers, and captains of industry. "It was too bad," one classmate told reporters, "that Franklin hadn't taken more economics and government courses at Harvard."

"I took economics courses in college for four years," FDR shot back, "and everything I was taught was wrong."[5]

While Governor Roosevelt formulated the response to the Depression from Albany, Anna remained in contact with the Roosevelts mainly through Eleanor. Together with the First Lady of the Empire State, Anna was a "patroness" for the fundraisers put on by the Democratic Junior League. Much like the charity work she'd done for Belle Moskowitz, in which wealthier New Yorkers aided poorer ones, Anna arranged ladies' luncheons, kids' carnivals in Democratic clubhouses, and bus trips to the coastal village of Lindenhurst on Long Island. These events financed summers for impoverished city kids at Camp Gerard on the banks of the Hudson River and funded Christmastime dinners for those without.[6]

In these first years working together, Anna and Mrs. Roosevelt maintained a respectful but businesslike *Mrs. Roosevelt/Mrs. Rosenberg* status. Though Anna found the progressive women of Eleanor's coterie to be "extremely kind" and that they "tried to involve me in their activities," a close personal bond failed to materialize.[7] Molly Dewson was a graduate of Wellesley College, Nancy Cook and Marion Dickerman had met at university, and Caroline O'Day was from a socially prominent family and married to an oil executive. The gulf of ethnicity, education, and differences in age and temperament proved to be too wide.

But neither was Anna Rosenberg a working-class Jewish feminist. She existed in between worlds—she identified as Jewish but was nonobservant; she was an immigrant and ardent patriot, married but self-reliant. She was unlettered but capable of executive leadership, and her social justice bona fides coexisted with her financial success. While some women who were accepted into male networks of power "saw themselves as exceptional [and] failed to question women's second-class status in American society," Anna advocated for greater equality.[8] An early profile on her in the *New Yorker* was tellingly titled "Middlewoman." It was her positioning herself in the middle that allowed her to navigate relationships with both Eleanor and Franklin Roosevelt without stepping on their marital landmines. If the couple didn't compete for their circles, they certainly collected them apart from each other. Eleanor had the Women's Division and her friends at Val-Kill Cottage and the Todhunter School, and Franklin had his inner circle. "He didn't want you to be very friendly with her," Anna explained. "I don't want you to go on that trip with Eleanor and Caroline O' Day," he commanded, "you just work with me."[9] Anna heeded his directive. "I'm not dumb, dollink."[10] Very few individuals could walk the tightrope that connected Eleanor and Franklin as Anna Rosenberg did.

While the women's charity events bandaged some of the wounds of poverty, the Governor was formulating a comprehensive and revolutionary cure. Roosevelt believed states were laboratories of democracy and the Great Depression was "an opportunity to advance a program of his own."[11] The Roosevelt program was massive government action never before advanced on such a scale:

> Minimum wages and maximum hours, old age insurance, unemployment relief through public works . . . unemployment insurance, regulation of public utilities, stricter regulations of banks and on the use of other people's money . . . farm relief, public development of water power, cheaper electricity . . . greater use of state funds for education [and the disabled], repeal of prohibition laws, reforms in the administration of justice, [and] reforestation and proper land use.[12]

Would it all work?

Beginning in 1930, it was clear that the answer was "yes." That year, the Governor pushed through a bill establishing old-age insurance; his hydroelectric plants gave "back to the people the waterpower which is theirs." He promised strong banking regulation to "those meanest of criminals who squander the funds of . . . small depositors in reckless speculation for private gain."[13] Most importantly, Franklin Roosevelt became "the first governor in the United States to stress openly and emphatically that unemployment was a major and growing problem."[14] When Republicans pushed back, Roosevelt skillfully used radio addresses to press his case in a homey, familiar style that in time would be known to all Americans. As the Depression deepened elsewhere, Governor Roosevelt's bold programs "provided an economic lifeline by which thousands of stricken families have climbed back to self-support."[15]

With every policy success, Franklin Roosevelt increased his national stature. Elected twice by New York voters, Roosevelt went from being a "Governor as Presidential Candidate" in his first term to a "Presidential Candidate as Governor" in his second.[16] "The work in Albany," Eleanor Roosevelt wrote in her memoir, *This I Remember*, was "invaluable for the work that was to come." Delighted by Franklin's success, Louis Howe publicized Roosevelt's accomplishments and strategized Roosevelt's run for the presidency of the United States. As his agenda continued to give hope and encouragement to New Yorkers while providing a blueprint for combating the Depression, Roosevelt came to be seen as the strongest Democratic opponent against Herbert Hoover, whose chances for reelection withered with every dollar lost to the Depression.

During the 1932 presidential campaign, Hoover was no match for Roosevelt's strengths. FDR had "carved out [an] enviable career in public service and politics . . . he had been a successful State Governor, perhaps the best single qualification for a Presidential candidate . . . and he possessed pleasing and attractive personal qualities . . . he was an eloquent and persuasive speaker." In contrast, the man FDR nicknamed Herbie the Hoov suffered from an overt lack of charm and empathy. His shortcomings as a leader were magnified the summer before the election, when the U.S. stock market bottomed out, having lost 90 percent of its value from September 3, 1929.

That hopeless season had one bright spot when Franklin Roosevelt

flew to Chicago to accept the nomination of the Democratic Party—
never before had a nominee accepted in person, let alone by flying. As
the klieg lights added to the heat of that July evening, the winning
candidate vowed, "I pledge you, I pledge myself, to a New Deal for the
American people."

<hr />

In New York City that November the lights of a different kind were shin-
ing. The glass and steel of the Chrysler Building and Empire State Building reflected a metropolis stubbornly progressing even during a calamity
of historical scale. New Yorkers had helped Franklin D. Roosevelt win
in a landslide, and now the president-elect vowed the government would
have a new relationship to its citizens. Scaled up the Roosevelt program
would help "the forgotten man at the bottom of the economic pyra-
mid."[17] He had buoyed New Yorkers as their Governor; when he was
President, Franklin Roosevelt's optimism would give hope to citizens
nationwide. As Americans headed into their fourth winter of the Great
Depression, they did so with newly strengthened morale.

In December Anna took Thomas to Rockefeller Center; its giant
Christmas tree adorned with electric lights and thousands of shiny
ornaments was a symbol of joy in a midtown dotted with boarded-up
storefronts and passed by figures who could only dream of the pretty
items in the display windows. As Anna's gaze went from the Prometheus, that symbol of human striving, toward the star atop the balsam fir, to the skyscraper's spire, she squeezed her son's hand thinking
of what was possible. Franklin Delano Roosevelt was to be the thirty-
second President of the United States, his New Deal might beckon,
and better days lay ahead.

CHAPTER SIX

A NEW DEAL

They were Americans, and it was the country's responsibility.
—Anna Rosenberg

It was a typically busy weekday morning at the Rosenbergs' apartment, Tommy finishing the last of his breakfast, Ms. Elsie packing his book bag and dropping a small stack of subway tokens in its zippered pouch. Mike set down his coffee, straightened his tie in the mirror, and headed for the elevator down the hall. Unlike her teenage son, soon holding a strap on the 1 train north, and her husband, behind a newspaper on the Broadway Express south, Anna's commute was anything but typical. Each morning, the limousine of New York City Mayor Fiorello La Guardia stopped in front of the stately Tudor building at 210 W. 78th Street and Anna and the Mayor drove to work together, La Guardia exiting at City Hall and Anna, just a few minutes south, at 45 Broadway.

They had known each other for years, but it wasn't until 1933 that the two rising stars in the New York City political firmament combined forces. While the "origins of their relationship [are] unclear," it is hardly surprising that Fiorello La Guardia and Anna Rosenberg found each other.[1] Fiorello—"Little Flower" in Italian—was, like Anna, an early recipient of Tammany outreach to immigrants. Both of them benefited politically from proximity to Old Jim Hagan—she as his defender and he as his accuser of corruption.[2] La Guardia was a New York City alderman at the same time Anna was managing her first political campaigns. Both were allied with the policies of Franklin D. Roosevelt, Rosenberg as a committed New Dealer and La Guardia as a reform-minded Republican. Even their backgrounds bear a similarity: La Guardia's mother was a Jewish native of Trieste, which, like Budapest, was part of the Austro-Hungarian Empire; his sister, Gemma, married a Hungarian Jew and settled there. Like nearly all people who came from the Austro-Hungarian Empire, both Anna and La Guardia spoke German. In temperament, they were both colorful personalities; in politics, they were more pragmatic than partisan; and in appearance, they could have been siblings. Standing only five feet tall and with his hair boyishly parted in the middle, Mayor La Guardia, like Anna, looked younger than his years.

After he was elected "the People's Mayor" in 1933, Fiorello La Guardia and Anna Rosenberg formed a potent political partnership. Serving as one of the Mayor's "closest advisors on labor and public relations matters" confirmed that Anna was "the city's leading arbitrator of labor problems and disputes." This, in turn, attracted more clients and contacts, which further boosted Rosenberg's "status as a public power-broker and accomplished industrial mediator."[3] For the Mayor, who aspired to national politics, Anna's relationships to powerful business and labor leaders made her a valuable asset, as did her proximity to Franklin and Eleanor Roosevelt.

The stakes were astronomically high for President Roosevelt in the opening moves of the New Deal, and nowhere more so than the Empire State. "Burdened with special pressures not felt by other states," New York was the home state and policy laboratory of the new President. Programs pioneered in New York were scaled up nationwide: the Works Progress Administration and the Civilian Conservation Corps put people to work, while the Tennessee Valley Authority provided electricity to the Southeast. When it came to the industrial pillar of the New Deal, the National Recovery Administration, FDR had an especially "vested interest" that New York succeed. The President needed New York, the largest economy in the country and the home to its largest metropolis, to "serve as a model" to other states and cities.[4]

The National Recovery Administration was meant to do for industrial workers what the New Deal was doing for farmers: controlling supply and thereby raising wages. In the farm sector, the federal government paid farmers to not plant and to cull livestock. This brought supply in line with demand, and farmers' incomes rose. Trying to get industries to comply with regulations on hours, wages, and fair competition proved a much more complicated task. Agricultural commodities—oranges, hogs, wheat, and the like—are a manageable number. Moreover, U.S. businesses were cutthroat competitors, not guilds working together. Not only would businesses have to adopt cooperation, but labor unions would have to make concessions.

The innate difficulty of drafting workable industrial codes and garnering compliance from both business and labor was made more difficult by "indecision and inertia" from Washington. The national director of the National Recovery Administration, General Hugh Johnson, named Nathan Straus, Jr., as head of the agency in New York. Straus, in turn, called on Anna Rosenberg to implement the new program. A "savvy political advisor, public strategist, and astute intermediary of competing groups," Anna would have the chance to run a New Deal agency as "chief administrative officer at the NRA."[5] Immediately, Anna got to work hiring personnel and establishing field offices in Albany, Buffalo, and New York City. She staffed boards from industry and labor and worked to put Straus in contact with large business associations and labor groups.

Despite these efforts, Nathan Straus was unable to deal with General Johnson; the two men engaged in "volatile, ego-centric clashes" that hobbled New York's industrial recovery. Finally, the "frequent, highly publicized" fights between the national agency and its New York office became untenable. Straus resigned, and General Johnson was forced out. While the other New Deal seedlings were taking root nationwide, the NRA was beset with confusion and a lack of leadership. By the summer of 1934, the agency was foundering badly.

A rudderless National Recovery Act was a black eye for the President. The White House began casting about for someone who could provide stable leadership in public while privately inspiring the rank and file, someone who could secure labor cooperation and business compliance and who was a well-known figure, to act as the face of this vital agency. It soon became clear that the person they were looking for was already there.

One year after Franklin D. Roosevelt stood under a blustery, overcast sky in Washington, D.C., swore to uphold the Constitution, and buffeted Depression-weary Americans by telling them "the only thing we have to fear is fear itself," the New Deal had indeed beckoned Anna Rosenberg. At age thirty-five, Anna Rosenberg became the only woman regional director in the entire NRA administration. Her promotion was met with widespread praise. The *New York Evening Journal* commended her "efficient manner," the *Brooklyn Daily Eagle* enumerated the many congratulatory telegrams she received from labor leaders, including William Green of the powerful AFL, and her connections to "several business houses" were highlighted by the *New York Times*.[6] Wearing a plaid taffeta blouse and a dark skirt, Anna smiled for press photographers.[7] "Her appointment," said Nathan Straus, "proved that demonstrated ability and devotion to duty are being recognized in promotion in the NRA." General Hugh Johnson called her "the ablest woman in American public life," and Anna Rosenberg became a new entry in *Who's Who of American Jews*, taking her place among composer Ernest Bloch, actor George Arliss, and boxer Max Baer.[8] "Anna is a very energetic woman who has an intelligent grasp of the situation," Mayor La Guardia told reporters. "She will make a great success."[9]

———————— •••• ————————

After a friendly argument about the relative merits of the cuisine in the La Guardia kitchen versus that in the Rosenberg kitchen, the Mayor exited at City Hall. A few minutes later the limousine pulled along the curb in front of 45 Broadway, near Morris Street, at the southernmost tip of Manhattan, and the driver opened the door for Mrs. Rosenberg. The site had a rich history. After his vessel *Tiger* was burned in November 1613, Dutch sea captain Adrian Block built four huts on the site—the "first habitation of White Men on the Island of Manhattan," read the historical marker. Three centuries later, Block's huts had been replaced by a massive ten-story stone building owned by the government of Imperial Germany. The tenant was giant German shipping company the Hamburg-American Line, and the Kaiser himself was one of its largest shareholders. In World War I the building was seized by the U.S. government. During the early New Deal years, the building was the New York headquarters of the National Recovery Administration.

The theory behind the NRA was that as businesses competed for customers, they cut prices and wages in a never-ending struggle to get the cost of production to its lowest point so as to maximize profit. The issuance and enforcement of hundreds and hundreds of legalistic fair-practice codes and a ban on unfair trade would, so went the theory, stimulate business recovery. Behind the Blue Eagle was a numbing number of industry codes and the sprawling effort to enforce them. Responsible for drafting the codes and policing them in the nation's most populous state, the one with the largest economy and home to the most corporations, was Regional Director Anna M. Rosenberg.

The Imperial German two-headed eagle was now the Blue Eagle, the symbol taped to the window of every participating factory and retailer and known to every American housewife who proudly did her family's shopping at compliant shops. The building still housed the furnishings and decorative flourishes of its former tenant, and, to Anna, it reminded her of the German ship of the line that carried her to America. As if to exorcise the room's imperious spirits, Anna cheerfully and democratically greeted everyone from the elevator man to department heads by first name.[10] Opening the glass door with the gold-stenciled "Regional Director," Anna Rosenberg was about to add to the site's ancient and worldly history.

When the New York Times sent S. J. Woolf to pay a visit to the "woman who sits in judgment," the journalist found "a slip of a woman . . . her hair carefully dressed, her clothes chic." Woolf was struck by Anna's temperament. "She radiates a spirit of friendliness throughout the organization," he wrote. "Her straightforwardness inspires confidence, her informality cuts red tape." Her efficiency extended even to the layout of her office. In one corner of the mahogany-paneled room sat an unused rolltop desk; instead, Anna pushed a flat desk against the long conference table at a right angle. To the single telephone line in the room, she added two telephones atop her desk.

There was a philosophical ballast to Director Rosenberg's hummingbird activity. Showing Woolf around the spacious office, Anna pulled a file from a carton on the floor; inside were letters "written in shaky hands by frightened workers telling of abuses in factories." "Last winter," Anna explained,

> we were called upon to deal with a number of cases of underpayment under some of the codes. We managed to

persuade many of the employers to settle claims just before Christmas. Some $50,000 was paid out. I for one was curious to discover what was done with the extra money. Some paid doctor bills, others bought clothes of which they were sorely in need, and one woman, who had never been able to give her children any presents, went out and bought gifts for all of them.

"There is something more than money in the world," Anna went on, getting to the heart of what the New Deal meant to her. "This Depression has brought in its wake an entire realignment. For years labor had had no chance, now a new scheme has been worked out under which . . . labor and capital have been put on an equal footing. [The] effect is evident upon the workers. Men and women who once regarded themselves as a little more than slaves have a new outlook upon life. They have lost that cowed attitude. They come into our offices with a new sense of freedom. Right through the ranks there is a new spirit."[11]

When it ran at the end of March 1935, the *New York Times* feature included a finely rendered sketch of Anna Marie Rosenberg in profile made by Woolf himself. At the end of the interview, he asked the "inevitable question"—what was it like to be a woman in such a high public position?

"I want to be regarded as a public official," Anna explained. "The fact that I am a woman plays no part. I like theatres, art exhibitions, and concerts. Unfortunately, I have been deprived of these."

But the worst part, she told the reporter, is that "I have to order my hats and clothes over the phone, and that's bad for a woman, even if she is Regional Director of the NRA."[12]

If Anna Rosenberg was among the advisers who helped President Roosevelt tack toward pragmatism, his idealism remained a beacon for her and other New Deal public officials. Reflecting on her first federal post for FDR, Anna explained:

> I was in government because I was so fascinated by what he was doing. . . . You never heard Franklin Roosevelt say this is a state or a local responsibility to care for the sick, for dependent children, for the aged . . . *they were Americans,*

and it was the country's responsibility. . . . I think his real
legacy is one of caring. Caring for the old, for the sick, for
the young, for the unemployed . . . with Social Security
legislation, the Works Progress Administration, and the
Civilian Conservation Corps.[13]

And, of course, the National Recovery Administration. Anna's
unique combination of skills brought stability to the critical agency.
Possessed of a "rare set of credentials as an executive able to strike
a . . . balance [among] business, government, and labor," Anna leaned
into the job she "seemed born to do."[14] Bridging the traditional differences between business and labor, and with the imprimatur of the federal government, Director Rosenberg worked to engineer the industrial
recovery of the nation's largest economy.

Her job wasn't easy. She was in charge of the drafting of the state's
NRA codes despite never opening a law book. Once the codes were
written by the team of lawyers, Anna sent investigators across the
Empire State to enforce compliance. The NRA foot soldiers faced business executives not only enraged by having to comply with the NRA's
codes but resentful of having to abide by a woman administrator—a
woman sitting in judgment.

These dual challenges came together one evening at the NRA headquarters, when Anna presided over a "highly charged" meeting of cigar
manufacturers and the jobbers who rolled them. As she listened quietly
to an hour's worth of "impassioned speeches" without a single comment,
one attendee wondered "how she had come to hold such a position."
But when she rose and began speaking, "she really came to life." To
one owner's "scathing rhetorical attacks" she answered "in a way that
he had no reply to make." She disarmed another by cooing, "[N]ow let's
hear your pretty little speech." Simultaneously tamping down emotions
and making astute recommendations, Anna's "cool, tough manner" and
recital of facts ended the mudslinging and led to an agreement. Director
Rosenberg, who "moved like a goddess and looked like an angel," had
"awed" the parties "into smiling submission."[15]

The sense of optimism that Anna described to the *Times* as a
"realignment" and "a new scheme" for workers was not to last. On
May 27, 1935, the U.S. Supreme Court rendered three unanimous

anti–New Deal decisions, the last of which, *Schechter Poultry Corp. v. United States*, destroyed the parent act of the NRA—the industrial centerpiece of the whole New Deal.

Within hours of the court's decision, the $15-per-week minimum wage was reduced to $9. One million New Yorkers relied on the NRA for survival, and Mayor La Guardia railed against the Supreme Court's narrow definition of interstate commerce. "When the farmers in Iowa and Kansas can't get enough for their farm products, workmen in New York can't get a job!" he shouted at reporters.[16] An irate President Roosevelt complained, "We have been relegated to the horse-and-buggy definition of interstate commerce." At Anna's headquarters, complaints immediately poured in: a motion picture company cheated a troupe of chorus girls; a printer cut wages; textile factories ran full shifts on Saturdays; and ushers, doormen, grocery clerks, and dressmakers saw their hours increased from forty-eight hours per week to fifty-four, sixty-five, and even 70.[17] Price-cutting wars broke out all over the city, further depressing wages and requiring ever more working hours. By Friday, the number of complaints by telegraph, telephone, and walk-ins amounted to an "avalanche."[18] After Anna handled nearly one hundred thousand cases during her year-long tenure at the NRA and earned the nickname Frances Perkins No. 2, there was little she or Mayor La Guardia could do under the banner of the powerless Blue Eagle.[19] Speaking to the press at the end of May, Anna Rosenberg announced she no longer had the authority to enforce the codes and suspended action on thousands of pending cases.

FDR responded to the *Schechter Poultry* case by hatching his "court-packing" scheme, allowing a new (and pro-Roosevelt) Supreme Court justice to be appointed for every current sitting justice over the age of seventy. The plan was ill-fated from the start. To the Roosevelts' friend Marion Dickerman, it went against "a very well-founded tradition and smacked a little too much of a smart method of meeting a problem."[20] To Anna, it was the worst decision of his long presidency and it was the response of a man used to getting what he wanted. "I think it was just symbolic, of sometimes wanting his will done, packing of Supreme Court."[21]

One of Roosevelt's point men on the court-packing plan was Thomas Corcoran, a brash young lawyer from Harvard Law School.[22] For a time, many considered "Tommy the Cork" the second most powerful man in

Washington, even elbowing out Harry Hopkins, who jealously taunted his rival: "Remember, Tommy, anything you spend an entire day doing I can undo in ten minutes after supper."[23] When a beanpole-thin young politician from Texas first met FDR in 1937, the President handed Lyndon B. Johnson a slip of paper. "Here's a telephone number," he said. "When you get to Washington, ask for Tom."[24]

But it was Anna Rosenberg who helped ensure that Lyndon Johnson made it to Washington. When the candidate made an emergency appeal on the eve of his 1937 special congressional election, Anna sent a $500 contribution. Johnson won and at twenty-eight years old commenced his extraordinary career in Washington. As she recognized him as "a dynamo, a real liberal," Anna and the young Texas lawmaker were allies from the beginning.[25] They had come to the New Deal from different paths, she as an immigrant girl raised in the city and he from Texas hill country, but they shared a faith in government's power to transform the lives of the neediest citizens. Anna appreciated that Johnson "fought very hard for President Roosevelt's social legislation," and found him "eager, terribly hard-working, [and] determined to get things done." The tall Texan's liberalism was revealed early, when Johnson fought on behalf of Black farmers in his district shut out of government loans—"the first man in Congress from the South ever to go to bat for the [Black] farmer."[26] His blend of empathy and ability was again illustrated in 1938, when he rescued a young Jewish Austrian orchestra conductor from Nazi persecution, and maybe death. On tour in the United States and nearing the end of his visa, Erich Leinsdorf found himself without a country to return to when Nazi Germany swallowed Austria in the Anschluss. He was put in touch with Lyndon Johnson, who worked Sundays, pulled strings, and bypassed rules to obtain a permanent visa. It was the beginning of a lifelong friendship.[27]

While Congressman Johnson figured out how to get things done on Capitol Hill and Harry Hopkins and Tom Corcoran engaged in palace politics, Anna Rosenberg was doing her part to implement the New Deal in New York. In January 1936, Anna Rosenberg met one-on-one with President Roosevelt for the first time at the White House.[28] In time, Anna would come to easily recognize the items that filled the President's second-floor study: the wooden ship models, the nautical prints, the collection of Democratic donkeys, and the large portrait of FDR's mother over the fireplace mantel, but at this initial meeting there was no time for sight-seeing. Wearing a neatly tailored skirt and jacket and a bevy of bracelets on her wrists, she made sure to wear her trademark stylish hat—a touch she knew the President would appreciate. "A woman can never afford to let down," she explained, "she cannot be late to meetings, [or] appear tired while working, [and] she must always look her best."[29] Roosevelt was particularly fond of her collection of elaborate hats—he always noticed them and often commented on them.

While we do not have the minutes of her meeting with the President, Anna was back in Washington a few months later for the announcement that she was to be named regional director of a new national program that would transform the lives of American families: Social Security.

The old-age pension idea had been kicking around for decades, but a grassroots movement ignited the nation and led to the 1935 Social Security Act. Elderly activist Francis Townsend, a doctor by training, lost his job as a public health official in Long Beach, California, when the Depression hit. Desperate as he was, facing old age without a source of income, there were those worse off. According to his memoir, *New Horizons*, one morning early in the Depression he looked out his window and saw two old women, dressed in ragged clothing, picking through his garbage cans for scraps of food. The Townsend Plan, a national old-age pension program, was born. Within two years over thirty-four hundred Townsend Plan Clubs were exerting pressure on Congress to pass a monthly stipend for Americans beyond their working years. Faced with the groundswell of support, Roosevelt told his Secretary of Labor, Frances Perkins, "We have to have it [Social Security]. Congress can't stand the pressure of the Townsend Plan unless we have a real old-age insurance system."[30]

Dr. Townsend wasn't the only critic of President Franklin Roosevelt. Despite his energetic first term, the Great Depression persisted, and FDR found himself beset by criticisms from conservatives who bristled at his expansion of executive power and by progressives who feared the New Deal was not doing enough for ordinary Americans. For the first time in two decades, Roosevelt did not have Louis Howe's candor and instincts. In April 1936, Howe's frail health deteriorated to the point where he could barely breathe. Confined to one of Franklin's wheelchairs when not under an oxygen tent, Howe whispered to the Roosevelts he would be on his feet again, in his suite at the Biltmore, running FDR's reelection, but it was not to be. When the end came at last, on April 18, Roosevelt felt that "for him it must be a blessed release."[31]

Faced with critics from the left, like Louisiana Governor Huey Long, and a recalcitrant Supreme Court, and without Howe's guidance, FDR doubled down. His 1936 presidential campaign called for more jobs from the massive Works Progress Administration, a stronger federal role in labor relations, the expansion of Social Security—all paid for by increased taxes on the wealthy. In late June, this more muscular New Deal was touted at the Democratic National Convention, held in Philadelphia. Anna Rosenberg, with experience in all three planks, attended as a delegate from the state of New York.

The next month, the Supreme Court paved the way for the expanded New Deal. Departing from his own decision in a prior case that a state minimum wage was unconstitutional, Justice Owen Roberts' reversal in the *Parrish* case swung the court 5–4 in Roosevelt's favor. The jurisprudential about-face made FDR's court-packing plan unnecessary. Anna told reporters the court's approval of state minimum wage laws was "gratifying."[32] A quick wit called Roberts' change of heart "the switch in time that saved nine." Though expanding the court had been unnecessary after all, the boldness of the plan snapped several old friendships, some going back to FDR's Harvard days. One of the relationships that was irretrievably frayed was with Vice President John Nance Garner. "Cactus Jack," whose political career was backed by "reactionary press lord" William Randolph Hearst, disagreed with the President on the scope of executive power, bristled at the massive relief spending, and was anti-union.[33] To FDR's second-eldest son, Elliott, the Vice President "was a good Republican."[34] Garner would in time become an enemy of the New Deal, but for the moment Franklin Delano Roosevelt was in command of a national recovery advancing on all fronts and Anna Rosenberg was a commissioned officer in his New Deal army.

In 1938 Anna was profiled in the *New Yorker*. When the prestigious magazine's Richard O. Boyer paid a visit to the Social Security regional offices at 11 W. 42nd Street, he, too, noticed her "brown bobbed hair, and attractive, pert face" and that when she exited the elevator she shouted a "Good morning!" to her office force. He also took note of the three telephone lines atop the desk of this "animated lady"—and he immediately saw why.

"Mrs. Rosenberg," called Anna's secretary, "it's Aubrey Williams." Bypassing a "hello" to the New Dealer from the South, Anna jumped right in: "Why, *hell* no, Aubrey, I haven't cared *one damn* what they thought about my supporting La Guardia."

Anna took a softer tone with the wife of labor leader Sidney Hillman, who was on line two. Then it was back to mediator mode, when Anna's secretary handed her the third phone. "Well, now, listen. Chosinsky is a nice fellow and wouldn't approve of that. . . . I'll arrange a nice lunch and you two [will] get together. . . . Goodbye, dollink."

Boyer sat there, amazed at her pace, writing his copy: "The secretary enters again to announce that the department executives are ready for their conference. After that is a meeting with a committee from the American Arbitration Association. Also, the Mayor wants to see her before five. One of the telephones rings."[35]

There was an intimate human contact in administering the Social Security Act. A middle-aged woman confided to Anna that she feared signing up for Social Security would reveal her real age to her husband. "If she wanted her husband to think she was a little younger when they married," Anna reasoned, "why should anyone expose her now?"[36] A factory worker, "gray about the temples," worried that the owners would find out he lopped off a few years. A "young blond stenographer" fretted that news of her marriage would get back to her boss and cost her her job. To these and the many other anxious New Yorkers signing up for their old-age pension accounts, Anna had the same response: "Give your true age and circumstance, and Uncle Sam and I will keep your secret."[37]

Despite managing a staff of several hundred working out of thirty-two field offices, Anna found time to calm distressed individuals. Among the 1,050 walk-ins in one week in 1936 was an impoverished elderly couple, worried that they would have to split up after nearly fifty years of marriage; they insisted they speak to "Miss Government Lady." Ushered into the regional director's office, the old woman broke down sobbing. A few phone calls later, Anna had arranged for enough public assistance to keep the couple in their apartment. Mrs. Rosenberg, one reporter noted, has a "quick heart" for "human problems." "I was participating in the evolution of dynamic legislation," she recollected. "There is nothing static about the Social Security Act, because there is nothing static about human progress."[38] Anna went on:

> When I go to our office in Baltimore where almost 48,000,000 cards are kept—as far as the eye can see— *I'm thrilled!*
>
> Each card represents a contract of a worker with the government. On the one hand, the government recognizes that it owes something to each person who has contributed to its growth and prosperity. On the other hand, every worker is helping build this nation and is investing in it.[39]

What the New Deal may have lacked in coherence it made up for in persistence. Roosevelt's boldly charted course rocked congressmen, cabinet members, and Supreme Court justices. His fireside chats sought to explain the new relationship, but it was left to the New Deal administrators to take it to the street level. Industrial workers continued to struggle with depressed wages and long hours, and, as vividly described in the novel John Steinbeck was readying for publication, *The Grapes of Wrath*, sharecroppers were left to survive amid unthinkable hardships. Worse still, Black Americans were left out of much of the New Deal benefits.

But the experiments worked. WPA jobs building roads, bridges, airports, and playgrounds were a lifeline for nearly one in five Americans. Two million citizens were taught to read by WPA teachers, and interviews were conducted with formerly enslaved people to preserve what might have otherwise been erased. "I'm proud of our United States, and every time I hear the 'Star-Spangled Banner' I feel a lump in my throat," remembered one worker. "There ain't no other nation in the world that would have the sense to think of the W.P.A."

Farmers' incomes rose 55 percent by 1937, and in 1938 workers celebrated the forty-hour workweek and the first federal minimum wage. Stability was brought to banking and securities, and hydroelectricity illuminated poor regions. Three million young men were spared the worst of the crisis by working for the Civilian Conservation Corps and sending money back home to help support their families. "The CCC," one recalled, "gave me the job experience that I've built on the rest of my life."

No New Deal program revealed the changed relationship between Americans and their government more than the Social Security Act. In Anna Rosenberg's words, the law gave Americans "a new sense of participation and partnership and the feeling that the government was assuming a new role in helping the individual establish some measure of protection against the hazards of daily life."[40] Just as union members were more invested when they were treated as partners by management, so, too, did ordinary Americans take pride in this new cooperative venture. "Workingmen come up to me after meetings," explained Anna, "and proudly pull out their Social Security account cards and show them to me."[41] Anna was proud, too. "The things that make life for [ordinary] people of a country more than bearable," she wrote, "are the things that make a nation great."[42]

After the rollout and initial implementation of the Social Security Act, and after Regional Director Rosenberg and her staff had enrolled 6 million New Yorkers in the new program, it was clear that New York had come through for FDR as a model for other states. But because the complexity and novelty of the law lagged in some regions, the twelve regional directors met in Washington to hear Don Nelson of Sears, Roebuck & Co. speak on simplifying the ins and outs of the law so it could be understood by academics and illiterates alike. The First Lady paid the directors a visit, and in a following session President Roosevelt surprised the group by appearing unannounced. Noticing Anna's elaborate feathered hat, the President quipped, "Anna, I think that's a very elegant hat, but I can't tell which is front and which is back, so I don't know whether you are coming or going."

"Exactly, Mr. President," she said with a smile. "It's a New Deal hat."

CHAPTER SEVEN

HYDE PARK

Solidarity forever
Solidarity forever
Solidarity forever
For the Union makes us strong.

—Ralph Chaplin, "Solidarity Forever"

Just after Christmas 1936, autoworkers at General Motors' massive factory in Flint, Michigan, went on strike in a bid to galvanize the United Auto Workers union into a force capable of negotiating on even terms with the industrial behemoth. It was no ordinary strike: at 7:00 AM on December 30, the men at Fisher Body Plant No. 2 put down their tools, turned off their machines, and simply sat down, occupying the second floor of the factory and making it impossible for GM to send in replacement workers. At 10:00 PM, just after the night-shift lunch break, workers at the larger Fisher Body Plant No. 1 followed suit. The massive factory that employed seventy-three hundred workers who produced fourteen hundred Buick and Chevrolet bodies every day went silent.[1]

The Great GM Sit-Down Strike was novel in its tactics, but labor strife was commonplace in the 1930s. Longshoremen paralyzed ports along the West Coast, Teamsters engaged in bloody fighting with police in Minneapolis, and in Chicago the Republic Steel strike turned deadly.

In the bitterly cold days that followed the sit-down, the strikers' wives sent food, newspapers, and clean clothing. Inside the factory, men smoked, played cards on the floor, and got what sleep they could on bench-style car seats. Meanwhile, company leaders were simmering, as was the aristocratic Du Pont dynasty, which owned 10 million shares of GM stock. Calls to remove the sit-downers by force echoed in conservative circles, as company guards and Flint police stood by, ready to pounce. The tension ratcheted up as orders were given to train machine guns on the factory.

On Monday, January 11, when the temperature dropped to 16 degrees, GM had its moment. Shortly after noon, the company turned off heat to the plant. A group of armed men removed the ladder and destroyed the wives' public announcement equipment. Trapped inside without food or any way to communicate, the strikers waited to see what the owners would do next. On cue, a group of police squad cars screeched to a halt in front of the factory. "For God's sake," someone shouted, "it's a tear gas squad!" Brandishing tear gas guns and wearing gas masks, the policemen opened fire.

The battle with police and the stalemate that followed further enraged GM'S powerful owners, who now called on Michigan Governor Frank Murphy to send in the National Guard. Governors had done the bidding of property owners for decades, and further violence in Flint seemed certain. Even Vice President John Nance "Cactus Jack" Garner called for troops to evict the strikers. But President Roosevelt signaled a pro-worker approach, calling on GM to recognize the nascent United Auto Workers union and hoping for an end to the strike without further bloodshed. Anna Rosenberg publicly reinforced the President's message: "Nobody is going to get hurt. This is because the labor men know that there is today a man in Washington who has their interest at heart and who has shown that he will see to it that the interest of the workingman will be protected, who sees to it that they do not have to fight with violence because they can get what they want through more peaceful ways."[2] On February 11, 1937, GM signed its first ever contract with the United Auto Workers, which by the end of that year had a half-million members. "The greatest industrial crisis in history," summarized Governor Murphy, "was settled in an atmosphere of justice and reason, without the suppression of a liberty or the loss of a single life."[3]

To prove that labor peace was achievable in the aftermath of the Sit-Down Strike, President Roosevelt commissioned a group of advisers to go to Great Britain and Sweden and report back on the progressive labor legislation and stability of those two nations. Secretary of Labor Frances Perkins was charged with naming the members of the commission. William H. Davis, a patent lawyer, was chosen to head the group, which included Gerard Swope, the president of General Electric, and five other men, all of whom brought their wives along, with the exception of Charles Hook, a steel mill owner, who at fifty-seven retained a slender physique and boyish features. The President's Commission on Industrial Relations was set to sail for Europe in late June 1938.

New York Senator Robert F. Wagner shared with both Franklin and Eleanor Roosevelt the conviction that a woman should also be in the study group, and that Anna Rosenberg was the best person. Simultaneously holding progressive labor views and the respect of large industrialists made her a perfect choice. As Secretary Perkins was making final preparations for the trip, Senator Wagner called her to suggest she add Rosenberg to the study group.

"She did splendid work in the NRA in New York. I think she'd be very valuable."

"She doesn't know anything about [labor] matters," Perkins snapped back.

The commissioners had already boarded the ship without Anna when FDR called his Secretary of Labor directly on the ship-to-shore line to inform her he'd appointed Rosenberg. Perkins also objected to the addition of Marion Dickerman, the vice principal of the Todhunter School in New York and a close friend of Eleanor Roosevelt, who lived part of the year in Val-Kill Cottage at Hyde Park. Ms. Dickerman would represent education, and Anna would represent the White House. The nine-member commission, including the two women, set sail for Europe on June 18, 1938.

While in London, the group toured factories and met with their British counterparts in a suite of rooms on the first floor of the U.S. Embassy, where they discussed methods for raising wages, lowering hours, and preventing the loss of "man-hours" to strikes. After tea service at four o'clock, the group continued until six. At the end of the day, the married couples returned to whichever hotel they were staying at in London. Whether they were installed at the Berkeley, the Connaught, or the Grosvenor, they left the three unattached members: Ms. Dickerman, Anna, and Charlie Hook, to fend for themselves.

Anna chose the newly built Dorchester hotel, opposite leafy Hyde Park. There an unlikely friendship formed among Ms. Dickerman,

Charlie Hook, and Anna. Anna had met Marion a decade earlier, when she was introduced to Eleanor's women friends during FDR's run for Governor. Marion Dickerman was often seen as older than her years, but Anna seems to have rekindled what one insider described as her "resiliency of youth"—a trait that Anna certainly shared.[4] Ignored by the married couples, the trio had also been dismissed by their boss— Frances Perkins. Marion, "probably born an old maid," had "been a school teacher . . . [who'd] bought some old private girls' school in New York . . . hardly one of the great educators of America." Charlie Hook "led a Presbyterian life somewhere in the center of Ohio." As for Anna, the youngest and most outgoing of the three, she was merely an opportunistic lightweight not to be given a second thought.[5]

Whether any of the three knew what Perkins thought of them at that time is unclear, but there was virtually no interaction with the Secretary of Labor while in Europe. "I was busy with a lot of other things," Perkins explained, "and I undertook to keep myself out of the social life of the commission."[6] While Frances Perkins was busying herself with "a lot of other things," Anna was leading her troop on weekend sight-seeing jaunts to Buckingham Palace and the less regal home in nearby Grosvenor Square where John Adams lived from 1785 to 1788 as the first U.S. Minister to the Court of St. James's. Back at "the Dorch," the bookish Marion was keen to catch a glimpse of poet Cecil Day-Lewis or novelist Somerset Maugham, habitués of the hotel. In the evening, the cabaret might feature Danny Kaye or the Jack Johnson orchestra.

Being in Europe was liberating for Anna, whose demanding jobs in New York and Washington kept her tethered to a telephone by day and working on a stack of papers each night. European travel "is a wonderful thing," she later told journalist Edward R. Murrow, "because it is five hours away from the telephone. . . . By the time people want to call you they find out there's a five-hour difference and during that time they solve their problems."[7]

Free from having to be "Seven-Job Anna" that London summer, after workdays at the Embassy, Anna took Marion and Charlie out dancing. "I never thought I'd live to see the day," gossiped one of the married ladies, "when I saw Charlie Hook dancing around . . . having such a good time."[8] On another occasion Charlie rounded up an English gentleman to be Marion's date and the foursome went to dinner and dancing. "I doubt when she was sixteen and eighteen she had anybody take her out to dances," remarked the wife of Commissioner Robert Watt. On the weekends and during lunchtime, Anna treated Ms. Dickerman to shopping excursions on Bond Street that ended at high tea at the luxury department store, Harrods. Before the final celebratory dinner hosted by the British Board of Labour, Anna took Marion to one of London's finest dressmakers.

"You've never had any fun. Come on, buy yourself a good dress. We'll go get you a fine dress."[9]

Anna then took her to a hairdresser where Marion had her hair curled, waved, and jazzed up. "She looked like a different person," said Mrs. Watt. "I'd never seen Marion look the way she did the night of the dinner . . . she never had such a handsome dress before."[10]

The toasts and dancing with their British colleagues contrasted with a subsequent incident that Marion described as "an ugly, anxious moment." After tours and meetings with their Swedish counterparts, the commissioners ferried from Göteborg, Sweden, to Hamburg, Germany, and boarded a train bound for France, where they would embark for the return home. As the train rumbled across Adolf Hitler's Germany, the red, white, and black swastika fluttering amid the wisps of steam at every station, it pained Anna to think of the life she would have had had she remained in Central Europe. Just that spring, Hungary had adopted anti-Jewish laws modeled on the Nazis' Nuremberg Laws. Jews were second-class citizens, forbidden to intermarry, barred from prestigious professions and from civil service.

A train attendant entered the commissioners' cabins: Nazi officials were boarding at the next stop to examine their passports.

The whistle sounded and the train came to a halt. Anna, Marion, and the other Americans dug out their travel documents from their luggage. There was a knock at the door. Two men stood in the doorway—one in a dark suit, holding his fedora under his arm, and a uniformed soldier in a field-gray tunic cinched by a wide black belt. The first man in perfect English asked to see the passports, and, one by one, the group handed over the burgundy passport booklets bearing the words "E Pluribus Unum." Everything seemed to be in order until

Gerard Swope, who was Jewish, was unable to find his passport. As Mr. Swope dug deeper, neckties and his shaving kit dropping to the floor, the first man grilled Swope about the purpose of his travels. The soldier blocked the doorway. If he did not present his passport by the end of the brief station stop, Swope would be taken from the train to the local bureau. Seconds before the whistle blew, Mr. Swope found it. "In the nick of time," according to Marion, but the chairman of GE, one of the world's largest companies, was "absolutely harassed, undone." The aftermath of the experience left Swope with a "cold fury" toward his fellow Americans who harbored sympathetic views of Hitler and his Nazis.* The uniforms might have been more modern, but Anna recognized in the incident the age-old anti-Semitism that lay just below the surface of Central Europe. Less than three months after the Americans left Germany, on the night that came to be called Kristallnacht, Jewish shops, homes, schools, and synagogues were smashed and plundered, and ninety-one people were murdered. The anti-Jewish laws had hardened into open state-condoned violence.

After six weeks in Europe, in mid-August the group boarded the ocean liner *Washington* bound for New York. During the five-day crossing, the commission members handwrote the draft labor report for President Roosevelt. As the ship made its way into New York, Anna found herself on the deck once again catching sight of the Statue of Liberty, nearly a quarter century after the reunion with her father. Before disembarking, Marion approached Anna: "Come on up to Hyde Park to my house with me. Spend the weekend. We'd be delighted to have you."

———— •••• ————

The English Crown in 1697 granted land along the Hudson River to nine prominent New York merchants. One of the nine, William Creed, built a house above the shore of the Hudson, which was later

---

* Marion Dickerman, *Invincible Summer*, 149–50, 128–29. Joseph P. Kennedy was one such American. This was not the first time that Kennedy was a divisive figure among New Dealers. When he was named the first chairman of the new Securities and Exchange Commission, there was an outcry—the Boston-based Kennedy had been one of the nation's most notorious stock price manipulators. To these critics, FDR privately replied, "Set a thief to catch a thief."

remodeled in the Italianate style. In 1866 the grand home with its tower overlooking the river valley was purchased by James Roosevelt, Franklin's father. By 1938 the estate known as Springwood sat on three hundred acres of parkland that included apple orchards, a horse track, marshland, and an ice pond—all connected by a series of paths carpeted by needles from the towering pines that made a canopy overhead. The Hyde Park estate was bordered to the west by the shore of the river and to the east by a rustic cottage made of fieldstone. Known as Val-Kill, the cottage was the seasonal home of the Roosevelts' close friends Marion and her partner, Nancy Cook.

On Sunday, August 21, 1938, following the church service at Hyde Park, Marion and Anna paid a visit to the "Big House," as Marion wanted to present President Roosevelt with a souvenir of Swedish glass. The two women were greeted by a smiling President Roosevelt in the wood-paneled library. Sitting in one of his homemade wheelchairs, its ashtray "[receiving] the tapping of his ever-present cigarette in a long holder," FDR was in his element, cocooned among his beloved collections.[11] Anna, wearing a summer dress suitable for an August Sunday in the country, stood in the President's wood-paneled library, amid the naval paintings, taxidermy birds, model ships, stamps, and thousands of books.[12]

Relaxed in the home where he was born, surrounded by the things he loved, the President was in fine spirits. His schedule was free until four o'clock, when the Roosevelt entourage was off to nearby Pawling, New York, where the softball team called Nine Old Men was taking on a team of journalists and correspondents. As Eleanor heard all about London from Marion, Anna "regaled [the President] with stories of the adventure, the details he was eager to hear."[13] FDR roared with laughter imagining Charlie Hook on the hotel dance floor, and lit up hearing Anna's little jokes about "stuffy old Mrs. Swope and pickle-eyed Mrs. Davis." Roosevelt appreciated the touches of the life he remembered, the carefree gaiety of dancing parties and double dates, people having a good time. The train episode could wait for another time. . . .

Franklin Roosevelt's informality extended to how he conducted his professional responsibilities as President. He didn't need armies of experts and reams of reports in order to make important decisions shaping the destiny of the country. "When Roosevelt appointed a commission," Anna explained, "he would say, 'Come tell me about it before the Commission formally comes to present it.'"[14] Eschewing formality was both efficient and a way to get the unvarnished truth. FDR was able to take advice and add to that his own keen political instinct, and out of that alchemy came the Roosevelt magic: thinking that was both quick and comprehensive, idealistic and pragmatic, addressing immediate problems while looking over the horizon.

As his stamp collection proved, Roosevelt was always eager to learn how other nations solved problems. After their gossip session, Roosevelt wanted to know what they learned on the study trip, and Anna gave him the highlights of the report. The British government, Anna explained, had come to see strong unions in a favorable light, as they were better able to keep agreements. Union membership and collective bargaining were generally respected by employers and the nation could boast of an industrial peace that was elusive in many U.S. factories.

After a few hours of chatting, the entire Hyde Park extended family piled into their cars and were off to Clover Brook Farm to take in the ball game, enjoy a barbecue supper, and listen to the old-timey music of The Lumberjacks. It was good to be home, thought Anna, especially after the long stay in Europe. It was true what her father often told her: being outside the United States makes you appreciate it so much more. "Every time I come back and see that flag waving," she explained, "it does something to me."[15] Home also meant getting back to work. By midday tomorrow, the nostalgic strains of the fiddle drifting through the river valley would be replaced by automobile horns, heels on pavement, and the shouting voices of a city beginning a new workweek.

"That's a bully report!" Roosevelt told his Secretary of Labor as he commenced his workweek at the White House. How had he seen the report, Frances Perkins asked, when it was still in draft form?

"Anna Rosenberg told me all about it."

The President planned to use the commission's findings for his upcoming Labor Day address. "See that the p.r. on this is handled perfectly well," he ordered his Secretary of Labor.

As the President wheeled away from Perkins, he mused, "Isn't she wonderful?"[16]

As Roosevelt readied his Labor Day remarks, the reverberations of the worker unrest in Flint, Michigan, and elsewhere shook Washington. From the office of the Vice President to the House of Representatives, a plan was hatched to weaken the New Deal from within. With the support of Vice President Garner, witch-hunting young Congressman Martin Dies, Jr., formed the House Un-American Activities Committee (HUAC). Described as having a "face the color of boiled ham," Congressman Dies weaponized his committee to take aim at those he considered enemies of America: leftists, labor leaders, and immigrants—all easily smeared as "communists."

"I saw 100,000 Communists parade in New York," claimed the beefy young Texas Congressman, referring to the pro-worker march. "I did not see an American in the crowd, they openly insulted and derided everything we hold sacred. If I had my way we'd deport every one of them and cancel the citizenship of those who have been naturalized."[17]

The members of the Dies Committee and HUAC would use disunion and division to make names for themselves. To rise through the ranks, careers would be destroyed, regardless of the truth. One of the Dies Committee's first targets was the outspoken young woman who was quickly becoming recognized as FDR's top labor troubleshooter: Anna Rosenberg.

CHAPTER EIGHT

THE INNER CIRCLE

*The inner circle [is] where the really important
decisions in . . . politics are made!*

—Eleanor Roosevelt[1]

Donning one of her less elaborate hats due to the drizzly rain, Anna stepped out onto 78th Street, where Mayor La Guardia's driver was holding the rear door open for her. He took her briefcase from her, as Anna, retaining her purse, slid into the back seat of the limousine. It was Friday, the first day of September, but the normally glorious late summer weather had not appeared, which annoyed the Mayor, as the dreary weather was dampening attendance at the 1939 World's Fair, then in full swing in Queens. Anna would be going in the opposite direction the next day, north up the Hudson River for an event at the Yonkers Social Security field office. Their chitchat ended at City Hall, where the Mayor departed, and the driver headed to 45 Broadway.

Waving an unlit cigarette between her index and middle fingers, Anna began the morning dictating remarks for the Yonkers event to her secretary: "Passed in 1935 to take effect in 1936, the first year when taxes were collected and benefits paid out was 1937. Two years later, nearly six million New Yorkers have been enrolled." Then an aide set up an easel in the old directors' room and Anna perused the new promotional posters that described the recently expanded benefits: "Under the amended plan, Wives of Annuitants will get Monthly Benefits when they reach 65."

As another poster was placed on the easel, her secretary announced Mrs. Lederer on line one. It was Mater, and she was crying. "Have you seen the news?" she asked in English before switching to her faster Hungarian: *Hitler uralkodni akar Európában!*" then back to English: "What fools at Munich! The phone lines to Europe have all been cut!"

Just then Anna's assistant walked in, caught Anna's eye, and placed the *New York Times* on her desk, the headline facing her: "GERMAN ARMY ATTACKS POLAND; CITIES BOMBED." Anna paced in a small circle, trailing the phone cord with her left hand. "What about our family in Budapest?" her mother asked. "Will there be another world war?" *Oh dear. Thomas.* Thomas had turned nineteen that summer. Anna waved the visitors from her office.

In Washington, President Roosevelt had been alerted at 2:50 AM by special telephone in the White House. One and a half million German soldiers, more than two thousand airplanes, and more than twenty-five hundred tanks had crashed over the Polish frontier. "God help us all," said the President, when told by his ambassador to France that German armor was already deep into Polish territory. "It's come at last."[2]

On Sunday, after Hitler ignored demands that he quit Poland, Great Britain and France declared war on Germany. Over the crackle and whine of their radios, Americans listened to war correspondent Edward R. Murrow reporting from a bunker across the Atlantic Ocean. "This is London," he intoned, where soldiers rolled coils of barbed wire to protect the Houses of Parliament and "the air-raid warning sirens screamed through the quiet calm of this Sabbath morning."[3] Later that day, President Roosevelt addressed the nation: "This nation will remain a neutral nation, but I cannot ask that every American remain neutral in thought as well. Even a neutral has a right to take account of facts. Even a neutral cannot be asked to close his mind or his conscience." As *Time* magazine pointed out, the line about conscience was "the most striking sentence in the broadcast" because of the contrast with President Woodrow Wilson's 1914 edict that Americans remain "impartial in thought as well as action" in the early years of World War I. Only days into the war, Roosevelt clearly favored the British side and seemed to be asking his citizens to follow his lead.

In the first months of the war in Europe a national debate arose between those in the America First movement, where anti-democratic factions took refuge under the umbrella of "isolationism," and those who saw the dangers of Nazism as an existential threat to democracy. The America Firsters were a handsomely financed coalition of Roosevelt haters and anti–New Dealers: "old mid-western isolationists, anti-Semites . . . Fascist sympathizers, and idealist Christians."[4] They had a hero in Charles A. Lindbergh, the pioneering solo transatlantic flyer, and a powerful establishment voice in bitter ex-President Herbert Hoover.

Events in Europe that fall and winter bolstered the isolationists. On September 17, Russia attacked Poland from the east, its free hand guaranteed by a nonaggression pact with Hitler. In October the Soviet Union invaded its Baltic neighbor, Finland. But Great Britain was protected by the English Channel, and France by the Maginot Line. For the time being Hitler was stalled. What the press was now calling the phony war concerned the President. In December he wrote one of the founders of the Committee to Defend America: "What worries me, especially, is that public opinion over here is patting itself on the back every morning and thanking God for the Atlantic Ocean (and the Pacific Ocean). We greatly underestimate the serious implications to our own future."[5] By early 1940, the vastness of the oceans seemed to offer less comfort. In March, Imperial Japan demanded recognition for Manchukuo, the puppet state in China it conquered with appalling brutality. Days later, Germany invaded Denmark and Norway. The false sense of security was falling away.

On May 10, 1940, German paratroops floated down to occupy roads and airfields in Belgium and the Netherlands, armored divisions crashed toward the northern and eastern borders of France, and the sirens of Stuka dive-bombers wailed overhead. Alerted that the Battle of France had begun, Franklin Roosevelt resolved to run for an unprecedented third term that fall. That evening Roosevelt dined with Harry Hopkins, still recovering from a near-fatal gastrointestinal illness, and installed him in the White House as his right-hand man. Hopkins lived in the Lincoln Suite at the White House for the next thirty months.

On May 28, Belgium fell. Days later German tanks sighted the French Atlantic coast, trapping the British Army on the beaches; only a miraculous evacuation from Dunkirk by an armada of civilian boats saved the British soldiers. On June 10, Italy's Benito Mussolini sent his troops across the border into southern France. "The hand that held the dagger," FDR said in a speech that evening, "has plunged it into the back of his neighbor."[6] The French government fled Paris for Bordeaux, and on June 14 German columns goose-stepped under the Arc de Triomphe. A week later, it was over: the huge French Army was knocked out of the war, leaving Britain to stand alone. FDR's ambassador to London, Joseph Kennedy, counseled against loaning Great Britain weapons and to "steer clear of a sinking ship," but Prime Minister Churchill countered this defeatism with his exhortation to the House of Commons:

> We shall go on to the end. We shall fight in France. We shall fight on the seas and oceans, we shall fight on the beaches, in the fields, in the streets, in the hills. We shall never surrender.[7]

The alarming reversals for the democracies in the war in Europe coincided with the departures of FDR's innermost advisers. Harry Hopkins together with Louis Howe, Missy LeHand, and Thomas Corcoran had formed the innermost circle of power from the earliest days of the Roosevelt presidency—Howe and LeHand went back even further. Howe was now gone, and both Tommy and Missy were on their way out.

Four years after Louis Howe's death, Thomas Corcoran was let go. Perhaps because he had been made the knight-errant on the doomed court-packing plan or somehow gotten too close to family secrets as the "fixer" who steered the Roosevelt sons Elliott and James out of trouble, Tommy the Cork had run his course as a Roosevelt favorite.[8] When Corcoran told FDR he had decided to marry Margaret "Peggy" Dowd, a woman from a modest family, Roosevelt objected.

"You can do better," chided Roosevelt, before telling him to marry a woman with money so that he could eventually run for office.[9] Defying Roosevelt, Corcoran married Peggy, then asked FDR to receive them. On the appointed day, the newlyweds arrived at the White House and were made to wait two hours. Finally, Harry Hopkins emerged from the Oval Office to say that the President was too busy to see them. The humiliated Corcoran never worked for FDR again.

The fall of the Kingdom of Norway to the Nazis also had repercussions for the Roosevelt cohort: Missy LeHand's long tenure as personal secretary, companion, and gatekeeper was coming to a tragic end. In August 1940, King Haakon and his daughter-in-law, Crown Princess Märtha, who was the First Lady of Norway after the death of Queen

Maud, fled Oslo for exile in Sweden. President Roosevelt sent a destroyer across the Atlantic to fetch Princess Märtha, whom he had met in 1939 when she and her husband, then Crown Prince Olav, toured the United States. In September she and her three children were installed in the White House, and the young, elegant royal became a presidential favorite. As President Roosevelt entertained the Crown Princess, Missy grew jealous. A reporter described how Märtha met the presidential car "in high-heeled slippers and black silk hose. She would race to the car, leap in and off it would go."[10] Twenty years younger than the President, Märtha "behaved like an 18-year-old flirt," saying little, "just [giggling] and looking adoringly" at Roosevelt. The President, of course, loved it, but such behavior tormented LeHand.[11] Adding to Missy's misery was the fact that when FDR brought his former flame, Lucy Mercer, to the White House, it was Missy who had to log her in using an alias to protect their secret dalliance. It became too much to bear. "Missy is very ill again," Eleanor Roosevelt wrote her daughter, Anna. "She's been taking opiates & had a heart attack & then her mind went as it does."

Occupying the place closest to Franklin Roosevelt after Louis Howe's death was the slender, chain-smoking Harry Hopkins, a "mixture of idealism and back-alley ruthlessness." While he was a true believer in the New Deal and a "first-class adjutant" to FDR, one figure, no matter how good the fit, was not enough.[12] Roosevelt's was a presidency in which "personal and political influence intertwined," according to scholar Frank Costigliola, one that "pivoted on personality."

> Roosevelt needed a family circle: emotionally committed, multitasking devotees, who kept him company, helped him relax, discouraged hare-brained schemes, overcame his procrastination by knowing how and when to push, translated his notions into pragmatic policy, and helped maneuver that policy through Congress and the bureaucracy.[13]

At this moment of world crises compounded by personal loss, the President invited Anna Rosenberg to take her seat at the Roosevelt round table. She was provided with an office in the East Wing of the White House and began meeting with the President one-on-one. "How is your day, Mr. President?" she would say in her slight accent, walking into his office with a jar of caviar or chicken paprikash prepared by her mother that the two would eat in secret "like naughty children."[14] Just as he looked forward to Hopkins walking down the stairs, drink in hand, before dinner, Roosevelt looked forward to Anna's visits; if she couldn't make it, the President would lightheartedly threaten her: "If you're not willing to come down, you'll have to do chores for me."[15] Between the invasion of France and Christmas 1940, Anna met with Roosevelt every two weeks. In October, Rosenberg asked Major General Edwin "Pa" Watson, Roosevelt's secretary, if the President minded if she "skipped a week in Washington."

The few who enjoyed this rarefied access, figures such as Bernard Baruch, rankled the senior officials who were made to jockey for private time in the company of FDR (often unsuccessfully). During the war, wrote a Chicago reporter, "Mrs. Rosenberg was regarded in Washington as possiblay the closest person to President Roosevelt with the exception of Harry Hopkins."[16] President Roosevelt "relied a great deal upon Anna in making many of his decisions," confirmed General Walter Bedell Smith. "Outside of the President's personal Secretary, [FDR] relied more upon Mrs. Rosenberg than any other single individual."[17] The official White House calendars and off-book accounts corroborate these assertions. In the words of Roosevelt biographer Joseph Lelyveld, "Anna Rosenberg found her way onto [FDR's] appointments calendar more easily than most cabinet members."[18]

Like the few others welcomed into this small and special family, Anna was devoted to FDR. When Roosevelt sent her a photograph signed "from her old friend" after a White House visit, Anna gushed in her thank-you letter, written in a girlish cursive:

> My dear Chief,
>
> Please forgive me if this note is a little incoherent. I am so thrilled by the memory of my visit with you last Saturday—and by your sweetness in sending me your autographed picture that there is a lump in my throat and my eyes are wet . . . you have made me very happy.[19]

Anna fit the Rooseveltian pattern in that she, like others in the sanctum, was an actual or virtual "bachelor." Anna Rosenberg was very much her own woman. She was married, but Mike played no role at all in her public life and remained in New York when Anna was in Washington or traveling at the behest of the President. Like Missy LeHand, and later Crown Princess Märtha, and even Harry Hopkins, Anna came across as unattached, so much so that White House schedulers noted her as "Miss Rosenberg" well into FDR's second term.[20] This availability fed into Roosevelt's need for undivided loyalty from those closest to him. Years earlier, as the sun set on his own political fortunes, Al Smith had asked FDR to employ the skills of Belle Moskowitz, and each time he had refused. Although he respected her greatly, "he thought it impossible for anyone to transfer loyalty after working so long and so closely with someone else."[21] In Anna, he had someone with a range of skills that matched Moskowitz's, free of any question of divided loyalty. Her devotion to Franklin Roosevelt never wavered. As she recalled in a televised interview decades later, "There were times that he made decisions that took your breath away and you had the feeling, 'God, this is a great human being. A great human being, not only a great president.'"[22]

Seven-Job Anna was a media nickname, but it was literally true. Officially, Rosenberg remained as the regional director of the Social Security Board in New York, where she continued to tackle a variety of assignments for Mayor La Guardia. In Washington for part of each week, she was the President's unofficial labor adviser, even as she was pivoting to problem solver in areas of civil defense and civil rights. But "no listing of positions," according to scholar Anna Kasten Nelson, "could do justice to Anna Rosenberg's influence" at this moment in her career.[23] Her extraordinary ability was combined with a winning personal charm, a trait she shared with Hopkins. The President's right-hand man "was an extremely charming person," observed journalist John Gunther, "and Roosevelt, a charmer himself, liked charming people." Gunther, who knew Hopkins well, goes on:

> He was an admirable, patient listener. FDR could talk to him as if nobody was in the room . . . he could laugh and banter and give a humorous touch no matter how serious the situation. [H]is mind was stubborn and penetrating to an advanced degree. Also he knew everything; he was a bottomless well of news and gossip. He brought Roosevelt

gaiety and scuttlebutt. Then too FDR liked him because he
did things [emphasis in original].

Gunther's description could easily apply to Anna Rosenberg. She had
an uncommon ease in the presence of Franklin Roosevelt and shared his
appreciation for the lighter moments. "Somehow or other you didn't feel
you were dealing with the president," she recalled, "you felt like this was
a person you were working with. I thought of nothing to walking in to
tell him something. . . . Sometimes you see something funny, 'well, I'm
going to tell him about this.'"[24]

Whether at Hyde Park, Warm Springs, or the White House, Franklin Roosevelt enjoyed one or two cocktails before dinner. Gin was the
spirit of choice, and mostly in the service of dry martinis, but as with
food, FDR was not picky. He shook up cocktails with ginger ale, grape-
fruit juice, or whatever was on hand. The resulting concoction, the "little sippy," lubricated the predinner chat with whoever was in his company. During cocktail hour, FDR discussed all manner of topics with
the "utmost frankness" and regaled his guests with many "a good anec-
dote . . . worth endless retelling."[25] A "natural raconteur," FDR possessed
an "immense store of personally lived experience." Whether the audience
was one or many, Roosevelt was in his element repeating jokes, reciting
his woes with Congress, and telling stories. In Anna's case, the site of the
stories was most often the Oval Study on the second floor of the White
House, and the lead-up was always the same. His ivory cigarette holder
between his teeth, "the cigarette at an angle so steep that when he tossed
his head back . . . he risked shaking ash into his eyes," FDR would fix his
gaze on his listener like a teacher waiting for a class to quiet down. Then
he would begin: "Well, as I was saying . . ."[26]

"I sometimes had dinner with him alone in his study," Anna related
to ABC's Diane Sawyer in 1982. "He would sit at his desk before they
brought in dinner and fix drinks. And he knew I had a very small capacity for drinks. And he would really fix a [strong cocktail]! When he wasn't
looking, I poured it into the rubber plant. I didn't think anybody noticed
it, but one day Mrs. Roosevelt said to me 'Anna, you ruin so many rubber plants.'"[27] Adjacent to the study was the President's bedroom, where
he kept a notepad. The doodles and naughty jokes he scribbled on the
pad were a source of great amusement between Anna and the President.

"After a tiring day, to blow off steam," Anna explained, he would write little notes on the chits. In the morning, "Pa" Watson would have the chits delivered in a sealed envelope to Anna at the Shoreham Hotel.

Anna was an indulgent listener to Roosevelt's yarns, but she could also spin her own lively tales. After her visit to Hyde Park in the summer of 1938, Roosevelt came to value her wit, her charm. "What a smart girl," Roosevelt told his secretary Marvin McIntyre and General Watson. One time, Anna told FDR, she had gathered intelligence for a labor dispute in New York City by putting on an old raincoat and sitting in waterfront beer parlors and cafés where the longshoremen came in. Roosevelt was delighted: "What that woman didn't learn!" he laughed to Labor Secretary Perkins.[28] In Anna's company, the president could relax. Anna could say things to the President that virtually no one else could. "You could raise hell," she told journalist John Gunther, "never feel any restriction about saying anything. You forgot he was President."[29] Anna once scolded Roosevelt for always taking the side of his mother, Sara, rather than his wife, Eleanor. Sara, who never remarried after FDR's polio diagnosis 1921 at age thirty-nine, loomed large in the Roosevelt marriage.

"You don't know what I owe her," the President protested. "She was a beautiful young widow. She never remarried because of me."

"Well, did anyone even ask her?" Anna shot back.

After a lengthy pause, FDR threw his head back and roared with laughter.

Anna had the ability to identify a problem with an efficiency that led to straightforward solutions. This, too, was shared by Hopkins, whom British Prime Minister Winston Churchill called "Lord Root of the Matter." Churchill might have called Anna "Lady Heart of the Problem." One of Anna's assistants observed that "in meetings and discussions, she cuts immediately to the core of a question."[30] A labor reporter noted that "she takes abstracts and breaks them down, like wedges of a pie."[31] When Connecticut Senator William Benton first met Anna in 1940, he was told, "Here is one of the half dozen most influential people in the United States." This surprised Benton, who thought he "knew the country pretty well." But he came to conclude that Anna Rosenberg "is the most extraordinary human being that I have ever known." Why? Because she

> had the uncanny talent for going to the real heart of the problem. [She] knew what people wanted . . . and what was actually in their minds regardless of what they said. [She] knew where the dangers and risks lay [and] how to use incentives and rewards. [Her] genius for candor [was] keyed to a keen and unwavering sense of reality.[32]

Anna Rosenberg was charming, loyal, socially graceful, candid in the face of power, and had an uncanny ability to solve problems—all of which FDR appreciated. Roosevelt wanted "assistance without strain, diversion without effort," and Anna gave that to him.[33] But she wasn't just a companion there to entertain the weary President or to provide a frank sounding board. She was a tactical adviser, acting as Roosevelt's mobile aide-de-camp, walking from the White House to Capitol Hill to act as the liaison between Congress and the President. "Talk to the Budget about this," "Get up an Executive Order on this," and "Go up and talk to the men on the Hill" were common Roosevelt commands.[34]

There was something else about Anna that Roosevelt appreciated. In his handwritten notes of an interview in Paris in 1951, John Gunther wrote down Anna's recollections of being with FDR: "[H]e courted and wooed . . . he liked a challenge . . . he loved to flirt in his last years, [he had a] great interest in women. *Watch yourself!* [He can] charm birds off trees."[35] In a 1969 interview with journalist and historian Joseph P. Lash, Anna confessed FDR "was a man who loved women, good-looking women, a flirt."[36] She begged Lash to keep the comment confidential, but Lash jotted in his notes that "FDR was always trying to get her to come down to D.C." A decade after the Lash interview, Anna was asked by Diane Sawyer, "Why did FDR like you?"

> I was useful to him. He liked women, maybe it was more fun for him. I wouldn't say he asked me [the] things he asked me to do because I was a woman. He felt "she could do it. Let's take a chance; let's see how she can do it" . . . I had a good familiar relation where I could fight with him,

I could argue with him, so maybe being a woman made that easier.

Anna's rise in the Roosevelt court led to rumors, gossip, and jealousy, particularly from Frances Perkins. That this younger, stylish, but unlettered woman was invited into FDR's inner circle rankled the Secretary of Labor, whose long and successful professional association with Roosevelt had never evolved to a warm, easy friendship. Regarding Anna, Perkins claimed to have heard "nasty, dirty things [said] about her and the President."[37] Rather than bond in a sisterhood of the reform-minded, Perkins judged Anna to have overstepped her bounds.

Although Anna was sometimes called in the press "Frances Perkins No. 2" or even the "de facto Secretary of Labor," the overlapping expertise of the two women was their only similarity.* Nearly twenty years older than Anna (and almost two years older than FDR), Perkins was the product of the women's network that included Eleanor Roosevelt and other members of the Women's Division of the Democratic Party. According to *Ladies of Courage*, by Eleanor and her friend Lorena A. Hickok, the leader of the Democratic women, Molly Dewson, "pushed open the door. She practically made a career out of promoting Frances Perkins."[38] There was no such champion for Anna Rosenberg. She had mentors—Belle Moskowitz and Jim Hagan—but the doors she opened, she opened by herself. The women's network "may have seemed to her impractical, and the women themselves academic," but neither was Anna the product of a male network.[39] Instead, she was "a woman who penetrated [the] 'old boy network' through her ability, friendship with men of influence, and force of personality."[40] To Eleanor, Anna Rosenberg was a "leading figure in a new generation of women reformers."[41] Mrs. Roosevelt respected her, "trained as she was in the tough, realistic school of the district club," as a woman who rose up the ranks by herself. "That, to Anna, is how the great game of politics is played. You're on your own, it's rough, but, if you've got what it takes, you succeed."[42]

Frances Perkins was from an old Maine family that traced its lineage to the War of Independence. She held an Ivy League degree and

---

* In his April 27, 1942, "Washington Merry-Go-Round" syndicated column, Drew Pearson called Anna Rosenberg the "de facto Secretary of Labor."

spoke with an upper-crust accent: "theater" was "thee-a-tah"; "tomato" was "tomahhto."[43] To the small group of women who knew her well, she was the "most reserved of New Englanders," a women of "puritan austerities."[44] A *Collier's* profile of her titled "The Woman Nobody Knows" revealed that despite Washington gossip that "Mrs. Roosevelt's influence is about all that keeps Miss Perkins in her job," the two women "are not particularly good friends."[45] While she was "[d]aring in politics and economics, she was conservative in morality."[46] As if to prove this last point, "she adopted a wardrobe of plain, matronly clothing."[47] To protect herself from "self-indulgence," she practiced "a thousand little acts of self-discipline," including, later in her life, visits to a convent.[48]

The youngest daughter of Albert and Sarolta Lederer spoke with a trace of Hungarian and whisper of the Bronx, where she had attended high school. Neither a puritan nor a libertine, Anna Rosenberg was a realist. Her workdays were too long and too charged for her to indulge in anything more than mail-order shopping for another fashionable outfit or a stolen puff of a cigarette. Her 1938 *New Yorker* profile, "Middle-woman," touted her enviable network of business and political contacts and her centrality among them. A labor reporter admired that she was "a great lady with the common touch."[49] Anna never minimized her femininity; she knew that she was a "normally attractive female, [and dressed] smartly to emphasize this."[50] A relative of Anna's once observed that "there wasn't a religious bone in her body"—a claim perhaps supported by the fact that, when the moment called for it, Anna could "'god-damn' and 'what-the-hell' all over the place."[51]

Whether by using their type of tough talk or by emphasizing her womanliness, Anna's appealing dexterity of personality could disarm male skeptics. "Her secret in getting along," wrote one commentator, "lies in looking soft, coy, charmingly feminine."[52] *Fortune* magazine explained how she used "her coyness and femininity to her advantage," but she also relied on "humor and diplomacy," and she was not above using "direct or strong language" when challenged. Frances Perkins did not possess Anna's social graces. When organized labor learned of her appointment to the cabinet, they were, in the words of Robert Moses, "grim and unimpressed." The Secretary of Labor was an "incorrigible chatterbox," known for droning on pedantically in her cultured Boston Brahmin accent.[53] Perhaps for this reason, she remained in the group of advisers perpetually eager for a one-on-one with the President, only to be disappointed when such meetings didn't materialize with any consistency.

In the capital, the Secretary of Labor was known "not always fondly as 'Ma' Perkins."[54] White House staffer William D. Hassett referred to her as "the Perk" in his memoir, along with Wordsworth's lines "A maid whom there was none to praise / And very few to love."[55] Perkins' rectitude resulted in poor public relations. "It is too bad," lamented Eleanor Roosevelt, "that she could not have been more relaxed in her contacts with the newspaper people."[56] As a result of her refusal to "live in a goldfish bowl," to pay the price of public officialdom, "newspaper reporters, both men and women, were indifferent to her, if not outright hostile."[57] Perkins was paralyzed by a "sheer terror" of public relations, while Rosenberg was gifted with "an extraordinary public relations sense."[58] Anna was unafraid to deal with the press. "You can be wise," Anna told author Margaret L. Coit, "but if you only talk to yourself, it's no good."[59] If the press was indifferent to Frances Perkins, they were fascinated by Anna Rosenberg.*

Frances Perkins also found it impossible to be indifferent about Anna Rosenberg. While she omitted Rosenberg in her 1946 me-and-FDR memoir, *The Roosevelt I Knew*, Perkins had rather a lot to say about the younger woman in a series of interviews she gave after leaving government service.

"She's not a dumbbell," Perkins admitted when asked about her relationship with Anna. She is "quick as a cat . . . a bold person who had no hesitance about pressing herself into various things," who tries to "worm in."[60] Rather than staying in New York, "she wanted to come down here [to Washington] and mess in things." Once there, Rosenberg "imposed her presence on the public," and "[threw] her weight around." To the chagrin of Perkins, Anna "established herself as a friend of the President's [*sic*] who was to be admitted when she asked to be."[61] Worse still, the President enjoyed her company. "She's an entertaining person,"

---

* Toward the end of her tenure as Secretary of Labor, *Collier's* ran a piece on Frances Perkins titled "The Woman Nobody Knows" (Jerry Kluttz and Herbert Asberry, "The Woman Nobody Knows," *Collier's*, August 5, 1944). Kirstin Downey's *The Woman behind the New Deal* did much to bring Perkins' accomplishments to a wider audience.

granted Perkins; she could tell him "bedside stories . . . about things he enjoyed."[62] To the sober Secretary of Labor, the relationship between Anna and Roosevelt could only be comprehended as "an acquaintance-ship" based on "humor, enjoyment, and so forth."

Commenting on her "extreme dressiness," Perkins sourly observed that Anna had "a new hat on every week . . . made at some or other place where they cost forty-five or fifty dollars apiece or more." It bothered Perkins when Anna stayed at the deluxe Dorchester in London on the 1938 trip, and it bothered Perkins that Anna had a suite at the Shoreham. "I used to see Mrs. Rosenberg blowing in in the morning at a time when you couldn't get a room in Washington to save your life." As for what motivated the young presidential adviser, Perkins had a take on that, too: "She's not an adventuress, really. She's a very strange mixture of things. I would say she wanted money." Regarding Anna's mediation career, Perkins said, "You charge through the nose for that kind of work. . . . The fees are just preposterous. . . . So I think what drove her on was money, and perhaps some longing for power."

Perkins continues:

> What her real ambition is, I don't know, because I never wanted to become well-enough acquainted with her to find out. However, she had that extraordinary quality which those who don't like her say is Hungarian. She's a Hungarian Jew and people will say, "That's just like the Hungarians. They're pushers."[*]

President Roosevelt was aware of Perkins' coolness toward Anna, but there were more important issues than palace politics in May and June 1940.

———◆◆◆———

* Frances Perkins Oral History, 386–456. Perkins told *Collier's* in 1944 that she had not met Anna until 1938 on the fact-finding mission to Britain and Sweden. This seems odd, given that Perkins and Rosenberg had sometimes-overlapping roles for Roosevelt going back a decade, to his governorship in New York. In fact, when Anna arrived in London in 1938 she greeted Perkins with, "So nice to see you again, Frances." See Jerry Kluttz and Herbert Asbury, "The Woman Nobody Knows," *Collier's*, August 5, 1944.

As panzer divisions scythed through France in May and June 1940, Roosevelt urgently turned to his privy counselors Harry Hopkins and Anna Rosenberg. With Hopkins' help, FDR established the National Defense Advisory Commission, the first wartime agency to address what was now becoming clear: American factories would need to convert to war production and there must be sufficient workers to staff the machines. In due course, Anna would play a vital role in keeping the Arsenal of Democracy firing, but the immediate task was to save Great Britain.

Any eventual U.S. involvement in the European war would be unthinkable if Britain were not to survive. The Miracle of Dunkirk had saved the British Army, but there was no such miracle for their weapons, which were forfeited or destroyed in occupied France. When the British desperately cabled for 375,000 artillery shells, the U.S. Army rejected the plea, saying they didn't have any to spare. "I turned the thing over to Harry," said a frustrated President Roosevelt. "He found 100,000 shells at Fort Bragg left there since 1919, and another 150,000 in Manila. Then he got five manufacturers to produce 10,000 more apiece."[63]

Roosevelt wasn't done. Working "seventeen hours a day," the Commander in Chief scrounged up what arms he could to keep Churchill's Britain in the fight. A half-million rifles from the Great War were soon on their way to Britain, along with eighty thousand machine guns and nearly a thousand 75mm cannon. But there was a political cost as U.S. taxpayers were subsidizing the island's defense. To gift the Brits millions of dollars in government money would give plenty of ammunition to the America First crowd. To head off those who would criticize the outright gift of arms, FDR linked the defense of the European democracies with U.S. national security. "We defend and we build a way of life, not for America alone, but for all mankind."[64] Keeping U.S. allies sufficiently supplied to counter the Nazi offensive in the months before the American entry into the war continued to draw attacks from FDR's critics. With the election later that year, it was vital for FDR to win his argument to the American people.

Franklin Roosevelt had been president of his college newspaper, the *Harvard Crimson*, and his greatest champion, Louis Howe, was a journalist. FDR knew the important role journalism could play in politics as a means to gauge public opinion. Until 1940, he relied on aggregated newspaper clippings, information scouts (such as Eleanor), and information reports to take the temperature of the electorate. These unscientific measures led to poor information. In 1936, for instance, a leading publication predicted a presidential victory for Republican Alf Landon by a 2-to-1 margin. Roosevelt crushed Landon, winning every state save Maine and Vermont. When, in 1940, many of these same prognosticators were confident of a victory in the fall for the Republican presidential candidate, Wendell Willkie, FDR became fed up with the erroneous intelligence.

There was another reason to shift to more scientific public opinion polling. As the violence escalated in Europe, Roosevelt became more interested in ascertaining public sentiment. What did Americans think of the President's armaments lifeline to Great Britain, and more critically, could the nation be galvanized for war? And who could test FDR's "one major issue," as the leading pollster, George Gallup, a Republican, was untrustworthy to the chief executive?

For answers to these questions, President Roosevelt turned to Anna Rosenberg, who suggested retaining a contact of hers, Hadley Cantril of Princeton's American Institute of Public Opinion. In short order, Cantril polled the question "Which of these two things do you think is more important for the United States to try to do, keep out of the war ourselves or help England win, even at the risk of getting into the war?"[65] Anna set up meetings at the White House with Cantril and the President, and when the polling expert had his initial polling numbers he sent them to Anna. Beginning in May 1940, respondents were given a binary choice: "Keep Out" or "Help Defeat Germany." In the initial poll, the "Keep Outs" won; fewer than one-third of Americans were willing to help defeat Germany. Armed with this knowledge, the President went to work.

On May 16, in a message to Congress, FDR made the case that the Atlantic and Pacific Oceans did not insulate the United States in the face of "the brutal force of modern offensive war," in which "motorized armies" were capable of rapid thrusts hundreds of miles into enemy territories. The steam-powered warships of the past, he argued, capable of perhaps 20 knots per hour, had been replaced by increased naval and air power; fighters and bombers could attack at 300 miles per hour.[66]

Next, he took his case to the American people through the magic of the Roosevelt fireside chat. "Tonight we sit down together, you and I," he began on Sunday night, May 26, "to consider the grave problems we confront."[67] Careful to not panic listeners, FDR calmly but forcefully stressed the need for a strong defense, preparedness for war, and the fragilities of the European democracies. Throughout the summer and into fall, Roosevelt made a series of similar speeches to lawmakers and directly to the American people. "His fireside chats," Anna later recalled, "I'll never forget, you got into a cab the morning after [a chat] and the taxi driver would say to me 'Franklin Roosevelt said to me.' It was this belief that he talked to everybody."[68]

With Cantril's numbers, charts, tables, and reports, President Roosevelt was moving the needle. On the issue of whether U.S. ships should ferry weapons to the British, a July poll indicated that 54 percent of Americans were against it, but that number dropped to 47 percent the next month. As the year progressed, the results confirmed this growing receptivity toward lending war matériel to the British. In November the incumbent Roosevelt cruised to victory over Wendell Willkie with 449 electoral votes (Gallup had predicted 283 for Roosevelt) and became the first third-term president in American history. In a decision that no doubt cheered many New Dealers, "Cactus Jack" Garner was replaced as Vice President by Henry Wallace, the popular but idiosyncratic Secretary of Agriculture. The good news continued in December 1940, when Hadley Cantril sent Anna a table showing that an amazing change of public opinion had taken place. On the question of "Keep Out" or "Help Defeat Germany," a majority of those polled now wanted the nation to join the battle against Hitler.

That was all Roosevelt needed to hear.

President Roosevelt wanted to aid Britain with the toll of war, but the British treasury was depleted. Communicating the solution in terms everyday Americans would understand, Roosevelt explained his idea during a press conference on December 17: "Suppose my neighbor's home catches fire, and I have a length of garden hose . . . if he can take my hose and connect it up with his hydrant, I might help him put out his fire." The fire out, the neighbor returns the garden hose; no money changes hands. "What I am trying to do," explained FDR by way of a solution, "is eliminate the dollar sign." In a fireside chat delivered four days after Christmas, FDR continued to "line up opinion for what he proposed to do," urging Americans, "We must be the arsenal of Democracy."[69] Prime Minister Churchill's house was indeed on fire, and if Roosevelt's messaging took effect, the destroyers and other weapons so valuable to the British as to be "measured in rubies" would be on their way to save the island kingdom.

Twelve days later, President Franklin Roosevelt used his State of the Union address to articulate America's guiding principles should war come. Recognizing the uncertainty, instability—and even danger—that lay ahead in the new year of 1941, President Roosevelt presented four freedoms supported by Americans, liberties they might find themselves fighting for on foreign battlefields. "We look forward," he told Congress in the first State of the Union delivered by a third-term President:

> . . . to a world founded upon four essential human freedoms. The first is freedom of speech and expression—everywhere in the world. The second is freedom of every person to worship God in his own way—everywhere in the world. The third is freedom from want—which, translated into world terms, means . . . a healthy peacetime life for its inhabitants—everywhere in the world. The fourth is freedom from fear—which, translated into world terms, means a worldwide reduction in armaments [so that] no nation will be in a position to commit an act of physical aggression against any neighbor—anywhere in the world.

The Four Freedoms speech was idealistic; it was Wilsonian in that it recalled the idea of making the world "safe for democracy," but it also gave Americans a reason to be in the fight. If the Axis leaders sought empires and grandeur, the United States would fight for the establishment and preservation of essential human dignity. In this fight, Roosevelt would not be alone. "Our strength," the President said in conclusion, "is in our unity of purpose."

In the meantime, Anna continued to work with Cantril to sift through public opinion data that would help shape the policy direction of the Roosevelt third term. Appreciating the historical moment, the pollster sent Anna a quote from Abraham Lincoln, given just after his inauguration in 1860: "What I want is to get done what the people desire to have done, and the question for me is how to find that out exactly."[70] Determining the will of the people was not as difficult for the thirty-second president as it had been for the sixteenth. While Roosevelt's idea for Lend-Lease seemed to come out of nowhere and was even called a "flash of almost clairvoyant knowledge and understanding" by Labor Secretary Perkins, the idea was in fact guided by months of carefully considered statistical work carried on behind the scenes and discussed over meals and meetings in the sanctum of the second-floor study of the White House.

It had not been easy, but with the pioneering work of Anna Rosenberg and Hadley Cantril, President Roosevelt was finally able to announce the action that matched the rhetoric of the Four Freedoms. An Act to Promote the Defense of the United States, known as the Lend-Lease Act, was passed by Congress just before four o'clock on Tuesday, March 11, 1941. With the Lend-Lease Act the United States took its first step toward war, when President Roosevelt duly put his signature to H.R. 1776.

Far from being a materialistic gadfly who flitted between New York and Washington and who had the means and connections to do so, by 1940 and with the United States preparing for war, Anna Rosenberg was in the inner circle of the most famous American of his time, where, as Eleanor Roosevelt well knew, "the really important decisions are made."

CHAPTER NINE

SIGN IT, MR. PRESIDENT!

Nothing counts but pressure, more pressure,
and still more pressure.

—Asa Philip Randolph

Poem for a man / Who plays the checkered game /
Of king jump king—

—Langston Hughes, "Poem for a Man"

Aubrey Williams was summoned into President Roosevelt's office. Tall and slender, square-jawed, and with a head of dark hair, the fifty-year-old Williams was a white southerner whose liberal values had earned him the friendship of Eleanor Roosevelt and the trust of the Black community. As the head of the National Youth Administration, Williams trained white and Black youths for skilled jobs in the U.S. defense industries, which were feverishly building ships, tanks, and airplanes under government contracts. "When I got into the President's office," Williams recollected, "I saw that he was tired and irritable. I said nothing waiting for him to speak—he rubbed his eyes, and leaned over toward me.

"'Aubrey, I want you to go to New York . . . the missus is up there and you can get in touch with her. Get the missus and Fiorello and Anna, and get this stopped.'"[1]

* * *

Franklin Roosevelt had shepherded the nation through the Great Depression and was now preparing it for world war. He was no stranger to personal or political crises, but even FDR staggered under the burden of events in the first half of 1941. That spring, British and American intelligence, alarmed by German arms massing in the east, had warned

Stalin of the threat of a Nazi invasion—warnings the Russian dictator ignored. Hitler's brilliant successes in 1940 portended doom for an
ill-prepared Soviet Union. But to equip the Communist giant would be
politically costly: the America Firsters would make sure of that. If the
political path were cleared, would precious Lend-Lease equipment be
nonetheless wasted on the Russians? If the Soviet Union was knocked
out of the war, would the United States allow Britain to stand alone
against Hitler? In the event of U.S. entry into the war, could the American Navy defend the Pacific against Japanese aggression and the Atlantic
from the U-boats and battleships of the Kriegsmarine?

Focusing on these questions of national security was made even more
difficult by a personal drama playing out at the White House. Missy
LeHand, Roosevelt's work-and-play companion, his gatekeeper, and his
de facto Chief of Staff, was in rapidly declining health. On June 4, a
party at the White House came to a sudden end when Missy let out a
scream and collapsed. The stroke left her partially paralyzed and barely
able to speak. To care for her, she was installed in an unused third-floor
room opposite the sewing room. On the few occasions he visited Missy
there, the normally loquacious FDR couldn't find the words.

Days later, a new crisis on the home front demanded the attention of
the weary President.

On July 1, one hundred thousand Black Americans were going to the
Lincoln Memorial in Washington, D.C., to demonstrate for the opportunity to work in the nation's mushrooming defense industries, which
had excluded them. With the war in Europe expanding, the U.S. government was placing contract after contract to build the tools of war. The
factories and shipyards offered good-paying jobs to tens of thousands of
workers, but only whites. The Office of Production Management did little to discourage companies like Standard Steel, which stated: "We have
not had a Negro working in 25 years and we do not plan to start now," or
Vultee Air, which echoed: "It is not the policy of this company to employ
other than of the Caucasian race."[2]

When Blacks were hired, it was for menial, low-paying work.
"Negroes will be considered only as janitors," North American Avia-
tion flatly stated.[3] "What happens," asked Walter White of the NAACP,
"when a Negro who has had excellent training at one of NYC's technical

or trade schools applies for one of the thousands of new jobs opening up? . . . Wanted—Colored: Porters, Cleaners, Janitors."[4] The Black press was incensed. The *Pittsburgh Courier* reported, "Negroes who are experienced machinists are being refused employment, while white men and boys with no experience in this type of work are being hired and trained later."[5] "Our war is not to defend democracy," wrote a Black journalist, "but to get a democracy we never had."

In early 1941, Aubrey Williams' New Deal agency sent one hundred male graduates to an aircraft factory near Buffalo, New York. Ninety-nine of them were hired; the top graduate of the class, a young Black man, was sent back.[6] What was the point of training Black youth for defense jobs, Williams wondered bitterly, if owners and labor unions refused to hire them?

But no one was more driven to end the discrimination than Asa Philip Randolph. Courtly and intense, with the "diction of a Shakespearean actor" and an "eagle stare," the fifty-two-year-old labor leader was by the early 1940s "the one pole around which divergent elements in the Black community could unite."[7] Randolph grew up in poverty in Jim Crow–era Florida before making his way to New York, where he took a job as a railroad porter. Taking classes at City College, Randolph was inflamed by the collective power of socialism. He rose through the ranks of labor organization, and, by the 1920s he had become the president of the powerful union the Brotherhood of Sleeping Car Porters.[8] For the next four decades Randolph launched from his union base a series of campaigns against racial injustice. As the threat of war neared, Randolph used his position to advocate for the twin goals of ending discrimination in employment and integrating the armed forces.

Tired of watching Black Americans excluded from the booming defense industries, Randolph barnstormed by train to Chicago, to the Mississippi Delta, to Harlem, and past the Virginia fields where his forbears had been enslaved, everywhere calling on his legion of supporters. Such economic discrimination was "wholly untenable and indefensible," he declared. "Decorous middle-class pressure" would no longer be applied; something stronger was needed. On May 1, Randolph formally called for a March on Washington to be held on the first of July. "You possess power, great power," he told his followers; "harness and hitch it up for action on the broadest scale."

Word that the march was gathering momentum was not welcome at the White House. Several times that spring, the Black leaders sought an audience with the President, only to be brushed off each time. "The pressures of matters of great importance," General Watson responded condescendingly, "is such that it does not seem probable that he will be able to comply with your request for a personal conference."[9]

Born of frustration, the March on Washington movement cemented Randolph as the nation's most prominent civil rights leader in the decades before Martin Luther King, Jr. "No one had ever tried anything like this before in black America," according to Black scholar Lerone Bennett, Jr., and "no one knew for sure whether 1,000 or 300,000 would march. But the threat was there, and the threat was real."[10]

To many, including Congressman Martin Dies, A. Philip Randolph was the most "dangerous Negro in America," a leader with socialist leanings who was "dancing on the edge of sedition."[11] Roosevelt did not share this view, but he feared the planned march. Washington was so segregated that Aubrey Williams couldn't have a cup of coffee in public with his Black counterparts. The capital remained "a Southern town, with a Deep South mentality."[12] According to historian David M. Kennedy, "[t]he prospects of one hundred thousand Negroes" marching in Washington, D.C., "did not present a comforting vision."[13]

Roosevelt was in a tricky position. Needing to maintain working relationships with the southern congressmen who chaired committees, Roosevelt was loath to challenge the segregationist policies.[14] But the president also needed to hear out Black Americans, who comprised an increasingly important part of his Democratic coalition.[15] According to Aubrey Williams, while FDR saw the need for an order against discrimination, he feared that the issue might slow war production at a time when it needed to accelerate.[16]

Perhaps something could be done in the future related to civil rights, but for now, the March on Washington must be called off.

———— •‥• ————

On Friday, June 13, Aubrey Williams took the express train to New York, FDR's order ringing in his head—*Aubrey, get the Missus and Fiorello and*

Anna, and get this stopped. After meeting Eleanor Roosevelt for breakfast, the two of them joined Mayor La Guardia and Anna Rosenberg at City Hall. The quartet were "the biggest white liberal guns of the administration. . . . If they couldn't talk Randolph and his ally Walter White out of the march, nobody could."[17] Despite Eleanor Roosevelt's conviction that Anna Rosenberg "could stop fights before they started," it quickly became clear that the City Hall meeting was not going to resolve the issue.[18] FDR's emissaries found the Black leaders steadfast: they would not call off the march unless Roosevelt immediately issued an executive order prohibiting discrimination, and they wanted to discuss the order with him face-to-face.

The next day, Anna called the President's secretary, "Pa" Watson, and sent Roosevelt a memorandum urging him to arrange a meeting with La Guardia and Black leaders at the White House. Within four days of Rosenberg's memorandum, and with the march only two weeks away, the meeting was set up for the middle of the following week. Meanwhile, Aubrey Williams, who had failed in his mission to "get it stopped," urged Randolph to halt preparations for the march "pending the conference."[19] The civil rights leader refused.

On Wednesday, June 18, just after lunch, Anna Rosenberg met one-on-one with the President. He considered her the best labor-relations troubleshooter in his administration. "H.L.H.," began a note from the President to Harry Hopkins, "any change in labor tell Anna and she will straighten it out. FDR."[20] According to one New Dealer, Anna was "the President's unofficial liaison officer with labor leaders," and to journalist John Gunther, the "courageous, incisive" Rosenberg was FDR's "most valued advisor on labor during the war."[21] "Get Anna," the President ordered his assistant James F. Byrnes, "to clear all orders affecting labor."

His confidence in her expanding, FDR had taken to calling her his "Mrs. Fix-It," but this problem relied on her primary expertise: mediating a labor dispute. According to Roosevelt biographer Joseph Lash, Anna "briefed [the President] on what the Negro leaders wanted," and that if he wanted to prevent the march he would need to do more than set policy; he would need to issue a mandate.[22]

At two o'clock, the others were shown in: A. Philip Randolph and Walter White, Secretary of War Henry L. Stimson, Secretary of the

Navy Frank Knox, and William S. Knudsen and Sidney Hillman, who represented the very agency that had ignored inequality in hiring.* Aubrey Williams attended, but Eleanor did not, as she was at the Roosevelt property at Campobello.

As he so often did, Roosevelt, seated behind his large desk, initiated the meeting by playing the raconteur. But after a few political anecdotes, Randolph grew impatient, and fixed him with the eagle stare: "Mr. President, time is running out. You are busy, I know, but what we want to talk with you about is the problem of jobs for Negroes in defense industries."†

Momentarily stung by the fact that his storytelling did not have the expected effect, and noticing Randolph's polished delivery, President Roosevelt then tried a new tack. "Phil," Roosevelt started anew, "which class were you in at Harvard?"

"I never went to Harvard, Mr. President," came the cool reply.

"I was sure you did. Anyway, you and I share a kinship in our great interest in human and social justice." While he was in favor of an order against discrimination, the President explained that raising the issue at this moment would slow war production just as it needed to quicken.

"Phil, what do you think?"

Randolph rose to speak. "We came here today to ask you to say to the white workers and to management that we are American citizens and should be treated as equals.

"We ask no special privileges; all we ask is that we be given equal opportunity with all other Americans for employment in those industries who are doing work for the Government."[23]

"Why," replied the President, "I surely want them to work, too. I'll call up the heads of various defense plants and see to it that Negroes are given the same opportunity to work as any other citizen in the country."[24]

---

* In some accounts, Robert P. Patterson, the Undersecretary of War, is noted as attending rather than Secretary Stimson. FDR's calendar notes Stimson was there, so perhaps Patterson was a last-minute replacement.

† Doris Kearns Goodwin, *No Ordinary Time: Franklin & Eleanor Roosevelt: The Home Front in World War II*. Note that the precise wording of the exchange differs slightly among the accounts based on A. Philip Randolph and Aubrey Williams (as retold by Jervis Anderson, Lerone Bennett, Roger Daniels, Doris Kearns Goodwin, David Kennedy, and Ted Morgan).

That wasn't good enough for Randolph. "We want you to do more than that," he said, "We want you to issue an Executive Order making it mandatory that Negroes be permitted to work in these plants."[25]

Roosevelt demurred. "You know I can't do that," he explained, envisioning the wrath of southern congressmen. He requested that Randolph call off the march. "Questions like this can't be settled with a sledgehammer."

"Call it off and we'll talk again," the President parried.[26]

"I'm sorry, Mr. President, the march cannot be called off," replied Randolph.

After pausing for a minute, FDR asked, "How many people are you planning to bring?"

"One hundred thousand," replied the labor leader.

Incredulous, Roosevelt turned to Walter White of the NAACP and looked him in the eye. "Walter, how many people will really march?"

"One hundred thousand, Mr. President."

The President was rattled.

"Somebody might get killed."

It was not his policy, he added, to make decisions like this "with a gun at his head."

"Well, Mr. President," Randolph countered, "something must be done and done at once."

"Something *will be* done," FDR countered, again hoping to defuse the situation by promising future action, "but there must be no public pressure on the White House."

"Mr. President," boomed Randolph, "*something must be done now!*"[27]

The President was desperate. The buses were hired; the trains were chartered. In thirteen days, the streets of Washington would again erupt in the kind of deadly racial violence last seen in Washington in 1919, when an angry white mob attacked Blacks, including returning veterans still in uniform. As the nation prepared to fight fascism abroad, it would suffer the embarrassment of having its own caste system publicized before the world.

As the clock struck three, the sour mood of the meeting let up when Mayor La Guardia chimed in. "It is clear that Mr. Randolph is not going to call off the march, so I suggest we all begin to seek a formula."[28]

At that point, Anna was sent by the President to the Cabinet Room, along with the Black leaders, to "draft the kind of order they thought he should issue."[29] Her account is corroborated by Aubrey Williams, who joined the others in the Cabinet Room. Neither Knudsen, the "annoyed" Sidney Hillman, nor the military men were invited. They were, Anna reported, "reluctant . . . to do anything about discrimination."[30] Time was running short, and if a compromise was to be forged, it would be by and among Walter White and A. Philip Randolph representing the Black workers, and La Guardia, Williams, and Rosenberg—"the biggest white liberal guns of his administration."[31]

As Anna knew, any compromise must confer dignity to Randolph and his supporters while minimizing the political cost to the President. Having mediated disputes with southern factory owners and seen their biases up close, Rosenberg knew that white businesses and southern lawmakers would ignore the president's order unless it included a watchdog provision. Even with an enforcement mechanism, Roosevelt was sure to lose some congressional support. The Black leaders, too, stood to lose some support, as they had postponed their call for desegregated armed forces. Both sides had made concessions, but could both sides claim a victory?

They finished the first draft by the following day, Thursday, June 19, but the parties continued to haggle over terms for the next week, with Randolph communicating directly with La Guardia and Anna Rosenberg. The White House meeting had initiated the conversation, but it had failed to break the stalemate. The march was on, the threat was real, and the executive order remained unsigned. Then, on the night of June 21–22, two additional crises converged. The President was sleeping when news arrived in the middle of the night that Nazi Germany had broken its nonaggression pact and invaded the Soviet Union. Operation Barbarossa was the largest land invasion in human history. The numbers staggered American and Allied observers: 150 German divisions, 3.5 million men, attacking a nation that spread across eleven time zones. That same night, one floor above the President, a smaller tragedy was unfolding. Two weeks after the small stroke at the party, forty-four-year-old Missy LeHand suffered a major stroke. She was taken to hospital, never to return to the White

House. Overnight, America's chances at staying out of the war dimmed as FDR's closest companion for two decades disappeared.

The beleaguered FDR had more bad news to process on Monday, June 23, when A. Philip Randolph "tightened the screws" by inviting Eleanor Roosevelt to speak at the march. It was a risky move. The First Lady was an outspoken champion of civil rights, and she would have trouble refusing the invitation. If she accepted, it would reflect badly on her husband. How could the leader who inspired the world's democracies with his Four Freedoms speech only months earlier stand by and watch as millions of his own citizens were systematically discriminated against? How could he stand so public a break with Eleanor? Randolph had played a sharp card, and Anna Rosenberg knew that things were coming to a head.

That afternoon, Anna gathered her things from her office in the East Wing and departed the White House.[32] A few hours of shopping would calm her nerves. Eleanor Roosevelt suggested the shopping excursion and told Anna to wear her "newest and prettiest hat" when she returned to see the President.[33] As Anna stepped outside, she was hit by the day's heat and humidity. She waited for the car that would take her to the boutiques in the chic Georgetown neighborhood. Passing Farragut Park and turning northwest at Washington Circle, Anna took out her compact, reapplied her lipstick, and made her plan: she would window-shop at the florist, say hello at her favorite salon, and then indulge herself with a new hat at the millinery boutique on Wisconsin Avenue that carried the Sally Victor brand, her favorite.

All the while, folded neatly in her purse was the draft executive order Anna Rosenberg hoped would break the impasse.

That afternoon Rosenberg returned to the White House carrying a hatbox and armed with resolve. She marched straight into the President's office, skipping her customary greeting, "How's your day going, Mr. President?" and walked over to his desk. She pulled the papers from her purse, spread them across Roosevelt's desk, and thrust a pen in his hand.

She took a breath. Franklin Roosevelt would be the first President since the Civil War to use his power against racial injustice, or he would be diminished by a spasm of violence that would sap American unity just at the moment it was needed most.

"Sign it, Mr. President; sign it!"

———◆◆◆———

Executive Order 8802 was issued on Wednesday, June 25, 1941, stating, in part:

> By virtue of the authority vested in me by the Constitu-
> tion . . . and as a prerequisite to the successful conduct
> of our national defense production effort . . . I do hereby
> declare that it is the duty of employers and of labor organi-
> zations . . . to provide for the full and equitable participation
> of all workers in defense industries, without discrimination
> because of race, creed, color, or national origin.[34]

The executive order also created the Fair Employment Practices Committee, a five-member body with the power to investigate grievances,
monitor compliance, and strip contracts from discriminatory defense
companies. Milton Webster, one of Randolph's key aides, was named to
the committee by the President at the suggestion of Anna Rosenberg.[35]

Black organizations, leaders, and the Black press rejoiced from coast
to coast. The *New York Amsterdam News* described it as "epochal" and
compared Lincoln's proclamation to end physical slavery with Roosevelt's order "to end, or at least curb, economic slavery."[36] The *Chicago
Defender* celebrated that "faith in democracy" for Black Americans
"was renewed throughout the nation." Prominent Black attorney and
politician Earl B. Dickerson hailed the law's mandate that the right
to work was now a civil right owed to all Americans.[37] The figure who
united the Black community as "never before in the history of the
nation," Asa Philip Randolph, led the chorus of those who saw it as
the "Second Emancipation Proclamation," and carried out his end of
the bargain. "The President has just drafted the Executive Order," he
telegraphed Eleanor Roosevelt. "I therefore consider that the proposed
Negro March on Washington is unnecessary at this time."[38]

According to David M. Kennedy, the order "represented a spectacular
victory for Randolph and defined a crucial pivot in the history of African
Americans."[39] Although it said "nothing whatever about segregation in

the armed forces—an important part of the origins of the March . . . it represented one of historical breakthroughs of the black struggle."[40]

But while Roosevelt scholars generally agree with the contemporary assessment of the law, they have never given Anna Rosenberg her due for being among the principal authors of the history-making executive order. Of all the participants, only she and Fiorello La Guardia were present for each meeting over the ten days in New York and Washington. For all his many talents, the Little Flower was not a professional mediator, but his friend and adviser Anna "knew more about labor relations and human relations than any man in the country."[41] For nearly two decades, Anna Rosenberg had made a lucrative career out of bringing antagonistic parties to mutually satisfactory agreements without resorting to trials or strikes. This was essentially a labor-relations issue, albeit an extraordinary one. Labor leader A. Philip Randolph represented not just a powerful union, but millions of Black Americans, and Franklin D. Roosevelt was the chief executive, not of a large corporation, but of the United States of America. No one was better equipped to bring the sides together than Anna Rosenberg.

Part of her method in midwifing solutions was earning the trust of both sides. In the absence of Eleanor Roosevelt, Anna and Aubrey Williams were seen as the closet allies of the Black community. Joseph Rauh, a government lawyer called in to reduce the agreement to formal legalese, and who is sometimes credited with the negotiations and drafting, complained, "Who the hell is this guy Randolph, and what does he have over the President?" A fighter for social equality since the suffrage era, Anna Rosenberg respected A. Philip Randolph and the position he had taken. What Randolph was fighting for was nothing less than the first federal prohibition against job discrimination based on race in American history. Since the end of Reconstruction in the late 1870s, politicians from the southern bloc of states had prevented the federal government from taking action in any way helpful to the cause of Black Americans. Poll taxes designed to prevent voting were allowed to stand; not even anti-lynching laws could pass through Congress. What was *perhaps* possible was an order from the President, whose wife, Eleanor, was sympathetic to the cause. If the March on Washington movement could get Franklin Roosevelt to put an end to workplace discrimination, it would be the first national action on civil rights since the administration of Rutherford B. Hayes; it might even lay the foundation for a postwar push for civil rights.

In every detailed account in both primary and secondary sources, Anna was among the small group directed to start the negotiations with Randolph and White in the Cabinet Room on June 18. Of that group, she was the only one with mediation experience and, notably, the only woman. She herself admitted that being a woman was part of the secret of her success. "I have no axe to grind, and I am a woman," she explained to journalist S. J. Woolf. "Men will talk more freely to a woman than to another man, and when men talk freely nine times out of ten misunderstandings vanish."[42] When they talk to a woman, rather than "a male competitor," Anna observed, "it's easier for men to back down from a strong stand."[43]

Anna was content to let others take the credit, to do things quietly. Once the trouble was settled, she remarked, "then I fade out of the picture."[44] Her penchant for talking through problems rather than engaging in a written back-and-forth is another reason her role largely escaped historians' notice. Anna was less interested in the rhetoric of national unity than in doing something concrete to forge it. Executive Order 8802 bears the hallmarks of Anna Rosenberg's work: it's a concise five hundred words, it was done quickly and out of the public eye, and there was something in it for both sides. Just a few months later, it would become clear just how important it was to broker national unity rather than surrender to internal dissension. For A. Philip Randolph, while he may have been bluffing regarding numbers of marchers, it didn't matter: the threat was real. Historian Lerone Bennett, Jr., calls Randolph's maneuver "one of the most brilliant power plays ever executed by a Negro leader, if not the most brilliant."[45] For the Black community, the order was the first step in a long-overdue economic emancipation, but not the last step. Anna counseled her union clients to consolidate their gains. She had fought for a minimum wage for New York women knowing it would lead to a minimum wage for all. Likewise, A. Philip Randolph's hard-fought victory set the stage for the future: it led to the establishment of civil rights organizations like the Congress of Racial Equality and, of course, a postwar March on Washington.*

Even the watchdog provision, the Fair Employment Practices Committee, bears the mark of the woman the *New York Times* called "a top-notch investigator, trouble-shooter, and peacemaker for high government officials."[46] The FEPC was itself mainly an investigative apparatus, similar to those that conducted inspections and monitored compliance for Director Rosenberg at her two New Deal agencies in New York. As with the White House meeting, even the personnel on the committee were influenced by Anna Rosenberg: she recommended David Sarnoff (a client of hers) and labor leader William Green. While it was imperfect in that it lacked muscular enforcement power, Walter White stated that "more progress was made by the FEPC towards employment on the basis of ability in the face of racial and religious discrimination than any other in American history."[47] Historian Roger Daniels shares this sentiment when he writes, "In the long sweep of American history, the FEPC order [was] the modest beginning of the first federal action against race discrimination since Reconstruction."[48]

Even more important is Roosevelt's insistence that Anna Rosenberg be at the meeting in New York, where the March on Washington movement emanated, in his office at noon on June 18 to personally brief him, at the subsequent conference at the White House, and in the anteroom afterwards to commence the drafting. The President clearly expected her to bring her considerable skills to bear, and she delivered. At the end of the crisis, it was, after all, Anna Rosenberg, buoyed by Eleanor Roosevelt, and crowned by the new hat bought just for the occasion, who pulled the order from her purse and urged the President to sign without delay.† "Just as the United States was committing itself to a war for freedom and

---

* On the eve of A. Philip Randolph's seventieth birthday, Langston Hughes sent Martin Luther King, Jr., a poem to read at the celebration: "Poem for a man / Who plays the checkered game / Of king jump king— / And jumps a President: / That order 8802 / For me and you."

† Joseph Lash relates that Eleanor Roosevelt urged Anna to shop for a new hat to screw up the courage to deliver the order to the President. Aubrey Williams saw the exchange between Anna and FDR in which she said, "Sign it, Mr. President; sign it!" See Anna Rosenberg, oral history interview with Joseph Lash, 1969.

democracy," writes historian Anna Kasten Nelson, Anna's "unseen hand influenced" the agreement that avoided a damaging display of disunity.[49]

———— •◦• ————

On Tuesday, July 1, 1941, the day of the scheduled March on Washington, there were no buses, no special trains, and no procession down Pennsylvania Avenue. But on that quiet summer night, along the banks of the Potomac River, A. Philip Randolph and a handful of supporters met under the gaze of the illuminated Lincoln Memorial and celebrated their victory.

CHAPTER TEN

MRS. FIX-IT

*The crown of many titles does not rest too heavily upon
her dark brown hair, and in her walks with kings
she has never lost the common touch.*

—*St. Louis Post-Dispatch*, 1942[1]

The second half of 1941 offered no respite for either Franklin Roosevelt or Anna Rosenberg. That fall, the President assigned his top troubleshooter a politically sensitive task that involved redirecting both Fiorello La Guardia and the First Lady. Under pressure from Mayor La Guardia to give him a war assignment, as it would bolster his chances at a 1944 presidential run, Roosevelt reluctantly made him the director of the Office of Civilian Defense, an agency for home front security measures such as urban blackouts and emergency evacuation. The agency was beset by problems from the beginning. It had "no official structure," little funding, and was conceived in "great hurry." Anna called it a "mess organizationally."[2]

Compounding matters was that Roosevelt's naming Mayor La Guardia to head the agency worried many White House advisers. Cabinet member Harold Ickes felt "La Guardia would not work with the team but would run all over the field with the ball." This sentiment was echoed by powerful financier and presidential adviser Bernard Baruch, who knew something of war, having been the czar of America's wartime industry in 1917 and 1918.[3] "He is a poor executive and won't work with anyone," predicted the elder statesman. It wasn't long before "La Guardia was in the president's hair."[4] As some had anticipated, the ebullient Mayor strained Roosevelt's patience with budgetary mismanagement and his mishandling a subordinate's resignation.[5] Once she was dispatched by the White House, it was the job of Anna Rosenberg "to stick close to the mayor and, above all, keep him away from the president."[6]

Anna harbored no illusions about the Mayor, his leadership style, or his ambitions. Anna described La Guardia to an interviewer as a "fiery little man, you know, who only understood things being done the way *he* did them."[7] In one telling episode from March 1940, just as FDR started summoning her to Washington more frequently, Mayor La Guardia called on Anna to settle a transit strike that paralyzed the city. The strike was over the pending municipal takeover of the subway and bus lines, which had been run by private companies. Faced with a gridlocked metropolis, La Guardia installed Anna in City Hall with the transit owners and the city negotiators.

Negotiations dragged on all day and into the evening, and by eight o'clock all parties were eager to get out of the chilly conference room to go get dinner. Anna led the party to the exit, where she encountered a policeman. "I'm sorry, Mrs. Rosenberg, you people can't get out."

"What do you mean we can't get out? Why, we have got to eat."

"The Mayor said you eat when you settle the strike."[8]

Back to the drafty room they went. The negotiations took all night, but by eight o'clock in the morning Anna had brokered a deal. The strike was ended.

While she could laugh about this years later, the Little Flower's imperiousness was one of the reasons Roosevelt thought him unfit to take on a war-related position of great authority. Instead, the civilian defense post was a third-place prize to keep him content.

Making matters even worse at the civilian defense agency was the fact that its assistant director was Eleanor Roosevelt, who was not so much an executive or administrator as a "guiding spirit" and "inspiration" for the multitudes of women expected to take part in civilian defense.[9] Eleanor's role, too, was by design, as Anna later explained. President Roosevelt, she said, "was glad to channel [Eleanor's] energies into one area so that she would leave him alone in other areas."[10] Roosevelt's plan backfired when his wife clashed with the flamboyant La Guardia. They were as different in temperament as in appearance. The First Lady "was very tall, very New Englandy," while the Mayor "was short . . . and wore a big black hat."[11] The odd couple in charge of the Office of Civilian Defense clashed over everything, from whether La Guardia could be Mayor of New York *and* lead the civil defense agency, to details like the women's uniforms. "After you have seen the costumes and the insignia," said the Little Flower, having commissioned New York's finest fashion houses, "do please let me have the benefit of your criticism." Naturally, Eleanor chose an apron of blue-gray cotton that cost less than three dollars.[12]

The blame wasn't all La Guardia's. The First Lady contributed to her own public political embarrassment by hiring her friends at OCD, one of them at the then-astronomical salary of $4,600 to lead a dance troupe to build children's morale.[13] Republican newspapers snapped at Mrs. Roosevelt's heels and congressional opponents soon voted to transfer the agency's $100 million budget out of civilian hands and into the War Department. Republicans, the President griped to Anna, were targeting Eleanor to get to him.[14] Something had to be done.

Caught between the two, and with a reluctant nation poised to officially enter World War II, President Roosevelt asked Rosenberg to intervene. As Anna vividly remembered, the president gave her a direct order: "I can't take Eleanor and La Guardia. Each one comes with a story; each one is right; each one comes to me: I cannot cope with it and I want you to try and keep them away from me and reconcile their differences."[15]

Eleanor Roosevelt and Anna Rosenberg had known each other for thirteen years. They were allies in the campaigns of FDR, believers in the goal of social equality for all Americans, and the two women had been instrumental in getting Executive Order 8802 signed. If not a warm friendship, theirs was a relationship of mutual respect. Outwardly, Anna was always deferential to the elder First Lady, but this episode revealed the complexity of their evolving relationship.

"I didn't like her so much when [FDR] was alive," Anna confessed; "I thought she didn't take care of him sufficiently."

"I would be very annoyed sometimes when I would stay for dinner. And he would be so tired and so worn out during the war, after a very busy day, and [Eleanor] would say, 'Now, Franklin, there's a boy—' and some insignificant incident. . . . It wasn't insignificant to her because it was about a human being. But it wasn't the kind of thing to bother him about when he was worn out."[16] The First Lady's efforts to influence policy extended to "the Eleanor basket"—which sat under Roosevelt's night table collecting "memoranda, communications, and reports for the president to read—a sort of private post office between husband and wife."[17]

Eleanor persuaded Franklin to take a more active stance on civil rights and many other issues that she thought needed addressing—desires not always welcomed by her husband.

Soon the portfolio of tasks Anna Rosenberg was doing for the President expanded to include running interference between the first couple. "I remember him saying, 'We're not going to do that now. Tell Eleanor to keep away.'"[18] The President, Anna later recalled, "knew that [Eleanor] felt frustrated because many of the liberal programs had to be put aside."[19] It was his wife's moral certitude, according to Anna, that was at the base of his annoyance. Eleanor "bothered him because she had integrity. It is very hard to live with someone who is almost a saint. He had his tricks and evasions."[20]

The First Lady's dogged interest at the atomic level of the New Deal was a feature of her personality that Anna knew firsthand. No person was too insignificant for Eleanor Roosevelt to plead their case with a "terrier's tenacity."[21] Cabinet secretaries would recognize "Mrs. R's handwriting," Anna remembered, "and say, 'Oh my God, here's another one.'"[22] Anna was herself the recipient of several such letters. While in charge of New Deal agencies in New York, Mrs. Roosevelt wrote to her dozens of times to seek positions for out-of-work acquaintances. "Dear Mrs. Rosenberg," begins each letter, "can you find a job for Brooklyn man Frank Brodsky?" Or "Miss Elspeth Connichie, a rest room attendant at the Girls' Service League?" "Could you come to the apartment Friday at 4:30 to speak with a Mr. Leigh, who has a story which I think if widely told would do infinite harm to the whole cause of labor?" As for Mrs. Crystal Byrd Fauset, a Black campaign aide, she "would have to have a salary"; Mrs. Eliot Pratt "is much too capable to be allowed to remain idle"; and Mr. Karl Hesley "is capable of doing a good job."[23]

Anna being Anna, she diligently followed up on every such case and responded promptly and with the utmost respect to Mrs. Roosevelt. Because they both spent part of each week in New York, Eleanor would invite Anna to her apartment, and in the absence of Mr. Roosevelt they genuinely enjoyed each other's company. "It was grand seeing you and the boys," concludes one letter from Anna. "It was wonderful to see you the other day," ends another. "The yellow roses are lovely," the First Lady wrote in return; "many thanks for your sweet thought of me."[24]

But when Anna spent time with the Boss and the Missus together at the White House or Hyde Park, their fault lines appeared, and Anna usually blamed Eleanor.

"He loved food. He never went out to eat, imagine never in a restaurant, never in anybody's home. I would think, 'At least do things in the White House that he would enjoy.' Her food was abominable. She had no taste for food, she had no interest in food." The Roosevelts' second son, Elliott, shared this observation: "Mother's prowess as a cook was limited to scrambled eggs." While his mother "cared nothing about fine food," his father "would have been an epicure if he had been given the opportunity."[25]

For someone like Anna, who collected fine china and who served extravagant multicourse meals to her family on Sundays, Eleanor's utter indifference to the pleasures of dining and the austerity she forced on her husband irritated Anna's motherly instincts.

Seeing the Roosevelt marriage up close, Anna could sense the tension. "The strain between them when I knew them was annoyance. . . . [There was a] definite strain about the children." One day when Anna was at Hyde Park with the President and First Lady, the private school of the couple's youngest son, John, telephoned to report he'd crashed another car.

"Eleanor said not to buy him another car," but Franklin said that was up to his mother, Sara. "You have to let Ma-MA do what she wants."

"Ma-MA was the ruler," Anna explained.

Sure enough, John "drove up to Hyde Park and Sara bought him a brand-new car."

Eleanor "turned white."[26]

"I was so hurt and angry for her," Anna told Eleanor's biographer. "She looked so utterly defeated."[27]

One can only imagine what Anna, whose own son, Thomas, was then an undergraduate at the University of Wisconsin and preparing for Army officer candidate school, thought of this episode.

While she was sorting out the mess at the top of the civilian defense agency in the summer of 1941, itself a "very difficult . . . extracurricular activity," President Roosevelt added another case to the Rosenberg docket.[28] Anna would head the newly created Office of Defense, Health and Welfare. Assisted by David Rockefeller, Nelson's younger brother, Anna was given emergency powers to ensure adequate transportation, housing, schooling, health facilities, and public safety for the "swollen towns" and expanded military bases in New York, Pennsylvania, New Jersey, and Delaware. Once a month, Anna and her staff met with military, municipal, and industry leaders in the ballroom of the Hotel Astor in Times Square. Perched on the stage were Anna and her staff. On the long table sat two telephones, a black one and a red one. The red one, she said, was a direct line to the White House.

The monthly meetings started with a recap of the last meeting's priorities. "David, where's our list? Okay. Now, Admiral, last month you promised you would soon have more housing in your Navy Yard, yes?"

"Well, Mrs. Rosenberg, you see . . ."

"Not yet, Admiral? Am I seeing the housing?"

"Well, no, Mrs. Rosenberg. There's a problem. We can't get enough lumber."

Anna grabbed the red phone. "Anna Rosenberg here. Is he there? Good . . . fine . . . listen . . . Admiral Smith says . . . thanks . . . see you soon . . . goodbye, dollink."

It took just a minute. According to David Rockefeller's assistant: "In the several meetings I attended, I was unable to ascertain whether the red phone was actually connected to any terminal, let alone one at the White House. Nevertheless, the missing lumber, the elusive plumbing, or the scarce medical supplies somehow soon appeared where needed."[29]

In early September 1941, Sara Delano Roosevelt's lifetime of devotion to her son, a closeness that negatively affected his marriage, came to an end, when she died at Hyde Park. In his season of disappointment, FDR had been accused of being coldhearted to the ailing Missy LeHand, but when he returned to his ancestral home to deal with the probate of the estate, Roosevelt wept upon finding that his mother had saved the cradle that rocked him as a baby and the tiny robe he wore to his christening fifty-nine years earlier.[30]

Back in Washington, an annoyance popped up from an unlikely source. The House of Representatives proposed investigating waste and inefficiency in the booming defense industries. Fearing that it would be used as a political cudgel, Roosevelt and his wartime assistant James Byrnes maneuvered the investigation into the hands of Senator Harry S. Truman of Missouri, who they trusted would be more pragmatist and less grandstander. Over the next three years, the Truman Committee saved taxpayers billions of dollars as its chairman raised his national stature. One defense project was kept secret from Truman: the Manhattan Project. President Roosevelt hid from Truman the fact that he was "surreptitiously channeling millions into the search for the atom bomb."[31]

On Wednesday, November 26, 1941, the President publicly turned his attention to lighter matters. On that day, he signed a bill fixing the Thanksgiving holiday on the fourth Thursday in November and joked with reporters that he would be eating three feasts. That bit of news was drowned out that same day in U.S. newspapers by a series of somber reports from the war fronts. In the broad Russian theater of war, the Germans had captured a series of towns in the Moscow defensive belt as well as a key highway leading to the Soviet capital.[32] In the Libyan desert, Italian and German forces had locked the British into a bloody stalemate. FDR had hoped to celebrate the holiday in Warm Springs, but he remained in Washington to confer with Secretary of State Cordell Hull, Secretary of War Henry Stimson, and Army Chief of Staff George C. Marshall regarding the maintenance of peace with Japanese envoys then in Washington. The President was not optimistic. Two days earlier he admitted to British Prime Minister Winston Churchill: "I am not very hopeful and we must all be prepared for real trouble, possibly soon."[33]

As the U.S. high command sat at the conference table just after noon in an effort to maintain the state of peace that had existed in the United States for two decades, the next day was dawning one-third of the way across the globe. Beneath the light of the rising sun, a Japanese Imperial Navy armada was out to sea. Six aircraft carriers, 414 planes, and the finest combined air and naval forces in the world were steaming west toward a launch site roughly 230 nautical miles from the Hawaiian island of Oahu, all the while maintaining strict radio silence.

———•••———

At 9:30 in the evening of December 6, President Roosevelt was shown a multipart cable from Tokyo to Japan's diplomats in Washington that had been decoded by Naval Intelligence. It was clear from the decoded message that the Japanese were poised to attack. "This means war," said the President. A Japanese attack was imminent, but where?[34]

Sunday, December 7, 1941 was a windy, raw day in the nation's capital, and President Roosevelt was wearing a threadbare sweater to ward off the chill. He had just finished lunch with Harry Hopkins in his oval study, among his maritime lithographs, wooden ship models, and under the gaze of the portrait of his departed mother, when he learned that a Japanese surprise attack had decimated the U.S. fleet while still at anchor in Oahu.

That night, as Americans gathered around their radios taking in the dreadful news and realizing that life for their generation would never be the same, President Roosevelt worked on his message to a Joint Session of Congress to be delivered the following morning. His scheduled 10:45 PM meeting with journalist Edward R. Murrow was moved to past midnight. It was Roosevelt's last meeting as a peacetime President. The legendary newsman found the President sitting up in bed "in the semi-darkness, [his] ship models casting their shadows against the walls."[35]

Twelve hours later, President Franklin Roosevelt clutched the rostrum in the House of Representatives chamber before a joint session of Congress. "Yesterday, December 7, 1941," he began, "—a date which will live in infamy—the United States of America was suddenly and deliberately attacked by Naval and Air Forces of the Empire of Japan." With twenty-four hundred American dead and capital battleships at the bottom of a Pearl Harbor still aflame, the Commander in Chief's voice shook with indignation: "No matter how long it may take us to overcome this premeditated invasion, the American people *in their righteous might* will win through to absolute victory." When he concluded his six-and-a-half-minute speech with the words, "With confidence in our armed forces—with the unbounding determination of our people—*we will gain the inevitable triumph, so help us God*," the joint session erupted in cheers.

Thirty-three minutes later, Congress declared war on the Empire of Japan.

—•••—

When Anna Rosenberg was summoned to the White House on the Thursday after the attack, she decided to wear black in keeping with the occasion. She found a measure of buoyancy had returned to the Commander in Chief.

"When I walked in he looked up and said, 'Anna, we're going through a tough enough time without you going into mourning and wearing a hat like that.'"[36]

That afternoon, President Roosevelt signed the declaration of war against Nazi Germany and Fascist Italy.

———•••———

As Franklin Roosevelt's focus turned to war, Anna was finishing her presidential task of redirecting the energies of Mayor La Guardia and Mrs. Roosevelt, both of whom had embarrassed the White House as they sparred at the top of the Office of Civilian Defense. No memoranda survive that record Anna Rosenberg's efforts to persuade the two to resign. Scholar John Thomas McGuire attributes "the absence of such records . . . to the situation's political sensitivity."[37] Whether Anna dangled the carrot of more important future wartime roles or wielded the stick of the President's dismay at their mismanagement, it worked. In early 1942 both Fiorello La Guardia and Eleanor Roosevelt resigned their positions at the Office of Civilian Defense.

Neither Mayor La Guardia nor the First Lady blamed Anna for her role in their leaving the agency. La Guardia continued to pick Anna up at her apartment on weekday mornings when she was in New York for a bit of "uninterrupted chat." Indeed, Anna was "almost alone in having retained the Mayor's friendship since the start of his administration."[38] Though she was bruised by the episode, Eleanor Roosevelt became closer with Anna after this incident.

One reason was their shared distress over the President's controversial decision in the aftermath of Pearl Harbor to intern Japanese Americans away from the West Coast out of an irrational fear that they would offer succor to the enemy. While the First Lady was calling for tolerance toward Japanese Americans, Anna learned about life in the camps from one of her former staffers, a young man named Philip Schafer, who had been redeployed as a project supervisor at the camp in Eden, Idaho. The barracks were not yet constructed in the "ankle deep lava dust," lamented Schafer in his letter, yet the families were already arriving. "It's criminal that they are sent to us before we can care for them." A man had died of a stroke on the train to the camp, and Schafer attended the funeral in the desert where the sagebrush had been cleared. The Buddhist priest and mourners prayed and chanted "just as the sun set behind a faraway butte." The dead man, it was feared, was the "first of many who would die on the pilgrimage." On his final rounds that night, Schafer found that there "had been a slip" and that "the grave was still open."[39] At the edge of the desert, under the light of the full moon, he climbed out of his car, retrieved a shovel, and filled in the grave.

Anna shared the letter with Mrs. Roosevelt, noting that "even in these mad, hysterical days there are people who are making such a serious effort to carry out the principles of fair play and decency in which we believe."[40] After corresponding with "Mrs. Rosenberg" since 1928, it was following this exchange that Eleanor Roosevelt began addressing her letters to "Dear Anna," something she did until the end of her life.

⁂

In the weeks after the Pearl Harbor attack, Franklin D. Roosevelt pulled Anna ever closer as well. What had begun years before as a labor consultancy had broadened to include public opinion polling, acting as gatekeeper—a role formerly played by Missy LeHand—and making connections like a human switchboard. Rosenberg introduced young Nelson A. Rockefeller to the Boss and suggested creating a U.S.–Latin American agency to better safeguard American security interests with the coming of the war.[41] Roosevelt established the Office of Inter-American Affairs and named Rockefeller as its first chief. Admiring his liberal qualities, Anna also helped Lyndon Johnson navigate into the Roosevelt orbit.

Anna's deft handling of two major problems in 1941 and early 1942, one related to civil rights and the other to civilian defense, cemented her reputation as an official and unofficial power broker. Most importantly, as "an intimate companion and unofficial presidential advisor," she filled the work-and-play void in the President's inner circle.[42] "FDR purred at her gay flattery" and responded to her "subtle persistence," reported one White House insider. When Anna left the President's study "wearing another pert hat, a big gust of Presidential laughter" rang down the corridor.[43]

Anna Rosenberg was the confidante of the greatest American of the era, and the national press took notice. During the New Deal years, she had been profiled by the Sunday *New York Times* and in the *New Yorker*, but beginning in 1942 Anna was featured in pieces in *Time*, the *Saturday Evening Post, Harper's Bazaar*, and *Vogue* and appeared in numerous others. The Associated Press sent Adelaide Kerr to interview her, and the *New York Times* again dispatched S. J. Woolf to speak with her, and again his flattering drawing of her graced the Sunday pages of the nation's most prestigious newspaper.

Publishers and editors were drawn to her for the same reasons as the President, Mayor La Guardia, congressmen, industrialists, labor leaders, and union rank and file. Not only could she "oil the squeaks . . . in the machinery of government," but she did so as "a charming brunette" in a "smartly tailored suit."[44] She is "a logical woman . . . decisive, executive," with a "thick streak of reformer [that she] carefully disguises." She is the rare woman "who meets men politically as an equal," and those men, even if they won't talk to each other, "will always talk through attractive Anna Rosenberg."[45] A reporter visiting Anna's office watched in awe as she picked up one of her twin phones. "Take it easy," she told the caller. "I'm seeing the President tomorrow. We'll clear it up then." *That would be the President of the United States*, noted the journalist.[46] Beneath a flattering full-page photo of Anna wearing a pinstriped suit, white gloves, and a charm bangle inscribed with New Deal alphabet agencies, "WPA, CCC, NRA," *Harper's Bazaar* described her as capable enough to hold "important defense jobs," while wearing hats that are "intentionally spectacular and gay . . . they distract everyone, except her pet dachshund, Pretzel." The Associated Press described her as "smart" and "businesslike," yet "warmly sympathetic," and found her in person to be "much younger and prettier."* She was a "mystery woman" to Washington gossips, as divisive as "Tabasco sauce" to the *New York Times*, and to the *Saturday Evening Post* she was "a half pint of dynamite . . . a bundle of perpetual motion and electric intensity . . . incapable of leaving anybody unmoved."[47]

Anna Rosenberg was having a moment.

The rather more sober *New Yorker* called her a "close friend of Roosevelt's" and lauded her "protean activities" in early 1942. One of the varied activities that Anna added to her schedule that year as never before was her own public writing. Some things were meant to be done quietly,

---

* Adelaide Kerr, "Titles and Work and More Work," AP, May 5, 1942. Kerr noted that AR was "much younger and prettier than her pictures."

and some things needed a public discourse. The role of American women during wartime was the issue to which Anna Rosenberg added her own voice. Seventy-seven days after the attack on Pearl Harbor, this wife of a veteran and mother of a soon-to-be soldier knew instinctively that this global conflict would be different from all others. "War is no longer confined to trenches and battlefields," she explained. It would be up to the nation's women to "keep things going, no matter what happens . . . to take the men's places in the shops and factories. . . . They must carry on when those they hold dearest are fighting." Much would be expected of the daughters, sisters, mothers, and wives in the Second World War.

"The morale of a nation depends upon its women."*

---

* Quotes are from S. J. Woolf's piece "Trouble-Shooter," *New York Times Magazine*, February 22, 1942. Anna went on to formalize these thoughts in a series of writings. See, e.g., "Women in National Defense," *Journal of Educational Sociology* 15, no. 5 1942"; "Women on the Job," *New Masses*, December 8, 1942; "Social Security and the National Purpose," in *The Family in a World at War*, ed. Sidonie Matsner Gruenberg (UK: Harper & Brothers, 1942); and "War and American Women," *Free World* 7 (June 1944). Note: In December 1942 Anna was part of a symposium for the left-leaning *New Masses* magazine for which she wrote "Women on the Job." Other editorials were penned by a U.S. Congressman, the U.S. Labor Department, the vice-chairman of the War Production Board, the attorney general of California, and a professor of sociology at New York University. Because it appeared in *New Masses*, Congressman Martin Dies used this as evidence of Anna Rosenberg's communist leanings. See *New Masses* special edition, December 8, 1942.

CHAPTER ELEVEN

WAR IS AN "ALL-OUT" BUSINESS

On the evening of February 23, 1942, more than 60 million Americans—80 percent of the total possible audience—turned on their radios to hear President Roosevelt address the nation. Across the country, mothers shushed children while fathers spread world maps on kitchen tables to follow along as the President discussed the progress in the far-flung war. George Washington's birthday was celebrated that Monday, so the President began with an analogy between the War of Independence and America's situation in the two months after the Japanese surprise attack had brought the country into the war against the Axis Powers. "General Washington and his Continental Army were faced continually with formidable odds and recurring defeats," Roosevelt explained. "Supplies and equipment were lacking." Like the Continental Army, the U.S. Armed Forces had suffered early defeats, "from Hitler's U-boats in the Atlantic as well as from the Japanese in the Pacific . . . and we shall suffer more of them before the turn of the tide.

"This is a new kind of war," he explained to the radio audience. "It is different from all other wars of the past. . . . It is warfare in terms of every continent, every island, every sea, every air-lane in the world." Washington's men faced musket balls and cannon shot, but American and Allied forces faced motorized armies that could rip through enemy territory with alarming speed, deadly submarine attacks, and high-altitude bombers that could strike across vast areas of the globe.

To win such an all-encompassing war, the nation must "build up production—uninterrupted production—so that [the United States and its allies] can maintain control of the seas and attain control of the air." What FDR was calling for was "not merely a slight superiority, but an overwhelming superiority. "We can lose this war only if we slow up our effort or if we waste our ammunition sniping at each other," he warned. Victory, the President continued, "requires tremendous daring, tremendous resourcefulness, and above all, tremendous production of planes and tanks and guns and also of the ships to carry them."

By the time Roosevelt concluded his second wartime speech with a quote from Thomas Paine—the same words George Washington employed in December 1776 to rally his troops for a nighttime crossing of the icy Delaware River to attack the Hessians at Trenton—it was clear to the nation that this war would be won or lost on shipyards and factory floors as much as battlefields. There could be no "summer soldier or sunshine patriots"; all Americans would need to pull together and trust in the promise that "the harder the sacrifice, the more glorious the triumph."

The *New York Times* called the speech "one of the greatest of Roosevelt's career," and it was hailed across the nation and by America's allies. But there was a sobering reality embedded in FDR's rousing address. The numbers of ships, aircraft, tanks, and other tools of war needed for victory were staggering. The Commander in Chief promised 60,000 aircraft in 1942, 125,000 more in 1943, 120,000 tanks in the same period, 55,000 anti-aircraft guns, and 16 million deadweight tons of merchant shipping. "The figures reached such astronomical proportions that human minds could not reach around them," the *U.S. News* reported. "Only by symbols could they be understood; a plane every four minutes in 1943; a tank every seven minutes; two seagoing ships a day."

The President's promises took many by surprise. "I was with him the day he said we would build 50,000 planes in twelve months," Anna recalled. "I was dubious and told him so. He shook his finger at me, one of the few times he ever did, and said: 'Anna, remember this: There isn't anything the American people can't do when they make up their minds to do it.'"[1]

Anna shared FDR's conviction that this was a new kind of war. Like Roosevelt, she knew that America's contribution to victory would be in the production of arms as much as their use on the battlefield. She wrote:

> Our entire concept of national defense has been altered drastically. The old conception of warfare as a struggle for

supremacy between two groups of armed men has completely disappeared. In its place has come the realization
that war, or preparation against the dire danger of war, is
an "all-out business." It calls for more than a mass output
of guns, ammunition, tanks, and airplanes. Today, total
defense consists of the funneling of the entire resources of
a nation—physical, moral, and spiritual—into one basic
program.[2]

World War II was a global contest and for the United States to achieve
victory, extraordinary measures were necessary. Women would have to
take nontraditional jobs in arms factories and in the military.

Like Roosevelt, she also knew that labor unrest could not be allowed
to continue into wartime, when striking workers or stubborn owners
could cost lives overseas. At Anna's suggestion, in January 1942 Roosevelt established the War Labor Board to arbitrate labor disputes to
maintain wartime industrial productivity, and made her its Secretary. In
February Anna and FDR convened the board's first council with labor
leaders William Green, Philip Murray, and Sidney Hillman. Besides the
mechanism for avoiding strikes and walkouts during war, they discussed
hiring elderly Americans and complying with the President's mandate to
hire Blacks into defense industries.

The need for the nation to devote itself totally to war was acute in the
winter and spring of 1942. The day after FDR's address to the nation, a
Japanese submarine attack off the coast of California replaced the President's remarks as the top headline in the afternoon papers. The threat
to America's West Coast was but one sword thrust of Imperial Japan in
its duel for the entire Pacific. The Imperial Japanese Army had overrun
British Singapore and the Dutch East Indies, from which the United
States obtained 90 percent of its crude rubber, and was marching on
the Philippine Islands, an American-backed commonwealth. In March,
Far East Commander General Douglas MacArthur and his family were
evacuated from the Philippines to avoid capture, and on April 9 the garrison on the Bataan Peninsula fell to the Japanese. Worse still was the
news that the defenders had been forcibly marched seventy miles in the
tropical heat, without adequate water, and enduring wanton executions
along the way. Many months later newspaper casualty lists could only

guess at how many of the nearly twelve thousand Americans taken prisoner had survived the Bataan Death March.

The situation was no better in the European Theater, where the German dictator was predicting the collapse of Soviet Union during that summer's campaign. Russia was teetering, and so was Great Britain. On March 12, Prime Minister Churchill cabled Washington demanding "drastic action" to expand the number of ships used to convoy men and matériel across the Atlantic. The threat of American arms in the hands of the Allies didn't faze Germany. Nazi propagandists derided FDR's speech as "fantastical." Hitler scoffed, "What is America but beauty queens, millionaires, stupid records, and Hollywood?"

To produce these tools of war, President Roosevelt created the War Production Board, headed by Don Nelson, a business executive. Nelson was given vast powers, "including purchasing, contracting, specifications and construction . . . requisitioning, plant conversion, and the financing thereof; and the issuing of any directives . . . he may deem necessary or appropriate." The conversion to a wartime economy meant everything from mosquito netting made by lingerie makers to armor-piercing shells forged by an erstwhile pinball-machine factory to jeeps and tanks made by Detroit's automobile companies. "The economic power vested in me," wrote an awed Nelson, "was potentially greater than ever held by any other civilian, except a wartime president."

Nelson was among the many officials who were "startled and alarmed" when he heard Roosevelt's production goals. "He staggered us," Nelson recalled. "None of our production people thought that this volume was possible. . . . We thought that the goals set by the president were out of the question." Unfortunately, unlike Anna, Nelson never overcame his skepticism, and he allowed the scope of his task to overwhelm him. "As interpreted by me . . . it was not the one-man job conceived by the president." In short, Don Nelson was in over his head. Throughout 1942, output failed to meet schedules. There were competing claims to resources from civilian concerns and the military. Then the branches of the armed forces fought among themselves for their priorities. By the summer of 1942, Secretary of War Henry L. Stimson criticized Nelson for "not taking the steps which the War Department thinks should be taken to allocate raw materials so as to minimize shortages.

"Nelson has a lot of weak men around him," Stimson continued, "none of whom is competent to face and handle this vital problem." To Supreme Court justice and Roosevelt adviser Felix Frankfurter, Nelson was "an utterly weak man incapable of exercising authority." Edward A. Locke, Nelson's assistant chairman, admitted his boss "took much too long to reach a decision."

As the War Department feared, there were shortages of items vital to the war economy: aluminum, petroleum, rubber, meat, and sugar. Making matters worse was the inflexibility of management and obstreperousness of labor leaders. "The labor situation," wrote Eleanor Roosevelt, was in "appalling confusion," and "the public was fed up."[3] By August, infighting and conflicting public statements among officials led President Roosevelt to issue a public statement ordering an end to the bickering. The *New York Times* reported the President's candid anger: "Officials divert to quarrels with each other time and energy they ought to be devoting to fighting the enemy." This was just the type of "sniping" FDR had warned against in his February radio address.

Industrial production was off to a worrying start, in large part because the first quarter of 1942 had passed without a comprehensive wartime labor plan. "For months, ideas and plans for manpower mobilization have floated across the White House desk," *Time* reported, only "to sink out of sight in the president's 'dead basket.' The clear-cut necessity for such mobilization had been sidetracked by the usual scramble of power politics and by the president's reluctance to set in motion such an upheaval."[4] Numbed by his fear of a compulsory labor draft, FDR had failed to take any action whatsoever on manpower.

To jump-start presidential action, Anna attended a series of secret meetings with Supreme Court Justice William O. Douglas, budget director Harold Smith, and veteran adviser Sam Rosenman. The quartet emerged with a plan for President Roosevelt to centralize the nation's wartime labor needs. Nine days after the American surrender at Bataan, FDR established the War Manpower Commission. The WMC was responsible for carrying out programs and policies "to assure the most effective mobilization and maximum utilization of the Nation's manpower in the prosecution of the war." In its announcement, the White House made clear that "manpower" included "woman power" as well. Anna and the other planners

recommended that Roosevelt name Paul V. McNutt to chair the WMC—
it was a decision they would come to regret.

The "manpower" commission divided the nation into twelve regions;
the directors of each region would work to harmonize labor among the
defense industry, agriculture, and the armed forces. Anna was appointed
Director for New York, the nation's most populous state and the home of
New York City, the most important defense site in the country. The only
woman head among the twelve, Anna had to flip her commuting pattern, spending four days in New York and two days in Washington, where
she often conferred with the President. Nevertheless, she maintained her
presence in the capital. "Her perky hats," recalled a White House insider,
remained "a conspicuous part of Washington's wartime foliage."[5]

Sundays were always spent at home in New York City, "the one day
every week I live," she told *Independent Woman*, "the rest of the time I
work."[6] Pulling a recipe from the kitchen drawer, written in Hungarian by her mother or grandmother, Anna would make beef consommé,
chicken paprika, and a plum cake. Classical music playing softly from
the radio, a bottle of Hungarian Tokaji wine, and a cigarette or two
would add to her weekend relaxation.

The day of rest was well deserved. Whether she was in her office
in the East Wing or her headquarters in New York or commuting
between the two, she was always working. "Anna Rosenberg at work
is an exhausting sight," wrote Karl Detzer in his profile for *Independent Woman*. "The three telephone lines into her office are busy constantly. Her conversations are rapid fire. At the same time she reads
memos, conduct interviews, instructs her assistants, jots down notes.
Her tempo would kill most men within a few weeks." Similarly, in
the time S. J. Woolf was in her office "[s]he received a telephone call
from a Cabinet officer in Washington, another from a labor leader, still
another from the head of a large corporation. A secretary came in with
a letter that required an immediate answer and the answer was dic-
tated at once. An assistant came in to discuss a building program in an
upstate town." Woolf went on: "She receives about 100 telephone calls
a day, gets out 30 or 40 letters, and sees 20 or 30 people between 9:30
and 6:00 . . . [and does it all] with an easy dispatch."[7] A young woman
reporter was similarly awed by Anna, who seemed to be able to do it all:

"Mrs. Rosenberg keeps her home in order, her kitchen running well, her lipstick smooth and her hair waved."

Anna's efficient delegation, capacity for hard work, and track record of success was not matched by Paul McNutt, a longtime bureaucrat who had headed so many federal agencies, one Washington correspondent suggested he be addressed as "'Mr. Governor-Administrator-Director-Chairman McNutt' and be sure you leave nothing out." McNutt was a handsome midwesterner with copious amounts of whitish-blond hair. His attractive wife was known for risqué comments such as the one she made on conserving gasoline during wartime: "[Couples] should drive less and park more."

It seemed that McNutt had his eye on the future instead of on the current crisis. McNutt's ambition turned off those close to Roosevelt, who felt the handsome Hoosier was angling for a presidential run in 1944. McNutt was criticized for making political speeches during wartime, a practice that led Harry Hopkins to conclude he should not head the critical labor agency, "since he was running for office." To others, McNutt came off as a lightweight. Undersecretary of War Robert P. Patterson dismissed both Don Nelson and McNutt as "second line men." Patterson's superior at the War Department, Henry Stimson, was even more cutting: McNutt had "more ambition than brains."

As with war production, labor problems arose in the summer of 1942. The fact that skilled industrial workers continued to be drafted as privates and ensigns created critical labor shortages, which was worsened by worker absenteeism. Anna's investigators found that one in six workers missed work, "nursing babies and hangovers," and began preparing a comprehensive report to combat the problem. Job-hopping among workers imperiled defense contracts, as did the intransigence of owners unwilling to negotiate with unions, thereby causing strikes. When Sewell Avery, the chairman of retail giant Montgomery Ward, ignored FDR's directive that he bargain with the union, he was literally removed from his office by a platoon of soldiers with fixed bayonets.

The refusal of many unions and owners to abide by Executive Order 8802 and hire Black Americans further diminished the labor pool. "Despite the present emergency," read the report of a special commission,

"Negroes are still excluded from employment in many vital concerns." The result was a "mad scramble for workers."[8]

The labor problem was nationwide. Baltimore, Detroit, the Buffalo–Niagara Falls industrial region, Los Angeles, and San Francisco all lacked sufficient workers. The West Coast, however, had a unique set of problems that made it the priority. Relatively undeveloped industrially before the war, the West Coast had blossomed into a key war production center. Twenty-eight percent of all ship production came from shipyards in Los Angeles, San Francisco, Portland, Oregon, and Seattle. A substantial portion of all ship repair work was performed there, and bomber and fighter plane production was located on the coast. But there was an excessive turnover and absentee rate due to inadequate housing, transportation, and childcare and recreation facilities. It was an area with a heavy migration of workers, and there were no substantial labor reserves. All these problems threatened the fulfillment of critical contracts for the Army, Navy, and Allied governments.

The decision to place McNutt as head of wartime personnel also cost Anna the friendship of labor leader Sidney Hillman, who had coveted the post. Hillman blamed Anna for not pushing his candidacy hard enough with President Roosevelt. When someone leaked to the press that in addition to her government salary of $7,500, Anna's business brought in $28,000 annually, Anna privately blamed Hillman.[9] She had raised her profile, but Anna found that life in the goldfish bowl of the nation's capital and the high-stakes game of palace politics came with a price. The flip side of being hardworking "Seven-Job Anna" was that critics claimed she couldn't possibly do enough to earn such sums. Her retainers from Macy's and the Rockefellers were a huge sum in 1942, nearly a half-million dollars today, and Anna's finances made front-page news around the country. A congressional investigation ensued and, while there was no prohibition against her outside work, the episode was a green light for those looking to vent against her. "The headlines which have made Mrs. Rosenberg powerful," wrote the *Saturday Evening Post*, "are also to blame for her unpopularity."[10] Cleared by Congress, but remembering the imbroglio that cost Eleanor Roosevelt her civilian defense post, Anna offered to resign or cancel her private contracts. President Roosevelt told her neither was necessary, but Anna decided to close her New York office and forgo her private earnings for the duration of the war—a decision that further enhanced her standing with Eleanor Roosevelt, who lauded her for putting her "very special talent . . . at the disposal of the government during the war years—without pay."[11]

While the issue passed from the mainstream newspapers, it was given just enough oxygen in broadsheets printed in garages to keep the fires burning among the bigots and anti-Semites looking to justify their biases. Professional hatemongers from Los Angeles and the Midwest heaped scorn on the immigrant Jewish woman New Dealer, but Anna's enemies were sometimes closer than she knew. "Sure, she's a chiseling bitch," remarked a White House aide privately, "but she's our bitch."[12]

By the summer of 1942, Americans could be forgiven if they had forgotten the President's encouraging radio message from February. In the Pacific, the last U.S. garrison in the Philippines had fallen. Japanese power, now threatening Australia, was at its zenith. On the continent of Europe the German Sixth Army was pummeling Stalingrad, and in North Africa the great German panzer commander, Erwin Rommel, had rolled through British Egypt and sat triumphantly atop his tank turret at El Alamein. In June, Chief of Staff of the U.S. Army General George C. Marshall wrote that the "losses by submarines off our Atlantic seaboard and in the Caribbean—now threaten our entire war effort. I am fearful that another month or two of this will so cripple our means of transport that we will be unable to bring sufficient men and planes to bear against the enemy." Like Washington's Continental Army over a century and a half earlier, the battlefield defeats were compounded by a lack of supplies.

The military tide finally began to turn at the Battle of Midway, June 4–7, 1942, when a code-breaking coup from Naval Intelligence combined with the selfless courage of Navy dive-bomber pilots to send four aircraft carries of the Imperial Japanese Navy to the bottom of the Pacific, some thousand nautical miles northwest of Honolulu. It was "the first decisive defeat suffered by the Japanese Navy in 350 years," but it would be many months before the scope of that victory was widely appreciated.[13]

Likewise, the tide of war production began quietly to turn in September 1942 due in large part to the efforts of Regional Director Rosenberg. When her headquarters at 11 W. 42nd Street opened on Friday,

September 18, 1942, Anna told the assembled press that the two main problems were an overabundance of labor in New York City and a shortage upstate and elsewhere. There were 370,000 registered workers in New York City available for defense jobs—a pool of workers one-tenth the entire population of Chicago, nearly one-half of Boston, over half of Pittsburgh, and greater than the entire population of Seattle and Portland, Oregon. The question was where to move them in order to achieve the goals of mobilization.

Anna well knew the affinity "the Boss" had for his Navy and that to him shipbuilding labor was paramount. Earlier that year, she had been present in FDR's private office and witnessed the dressing-down he gave Emory S. Land over the inefficient use of merchant vessels in ferrying military supplies. The newspapers reported: "Mrs. Anna Rosenberg, White House advisor who in recent weeks has become in effect de facto Secretary of Labor," had been present as the President bitterly complained, "The present situation is far from satisfactory. It must be bettered at once." According to the reports, the "muddled state of the vital shipping situation [was] now the sourest spot in the war picture."

Anna's role seemed to be at odds with the official Labor Department. When *Collier's* ran a piece on Frances Perkins, "The Woman Nobody Knows," the authors blamed Anna for seizing "chances to usurp power and influence which rightfully belong to the Secretary of Labor."[14] This ignored FDR's propensity to create offices with redundant jurisdictions. "He relished giving different people overlapping assignments and letting them compete for governmental resources and his continued support."[15] In this competitive environment, a "kind word for Miss Perkins" from the President was "exceedingly rare" and when she was "pilloried as incompetent, and worse . . . no adequate defense has been forthcoming."[16] FDR may have concluded that the enmity of organized labor for Secretary Perkins and her "often-contentious relation with Congress" made it necessary to create a parallel domestic labor apparatus and to place the leadership in the hands of someone better equipped to get labor leaders and lawmakers to listen.[17]

That person, of course, was Anna Rosenberg, and she began solving the two problems at once. The unemployed New Yorkers would go the West Coast shipyards where they were desperately needed. Moving decisively, Rosenberg negotiated an agreement with the son of industrialist Henry J. Kaiser and the U.S. Employment Service, whereby Kaiser Shipbuilding would send agents to New York to sign up workers. Preparing quickly, Edgar F. Kaiser set up company offices in New York in September 1942.

By 5:00 AM on Wednesday, September 23, workmen were already lining up at the Kaiser office on the docks of Manhattan. By 10:00 that morning, the line of two thousand men extended three docks, each seeking an interview with a Kaiser agent. Once hired, the workers would be taken across country to Portland, Oregon (population 340,000), on special trains carrying six hundred workers each, fare fronted by the company, and housed in company barracks for $13.50 per week. By that afternoon Kaiser had his first trainload of workers.

This frantic hiring continued for several days until Anna received a troubling report from Charles Johnson, a civil rights activist. The shipbuilders' union was not allowing Blacks to join the union, so the only jobs they could get were as road pavers, menial laborers, and painters. Anna was furious. If she had to stand to her full height of 5'3" and wave her arms on the tracks at Penn Station, no further trains of workers were heading west.

Immediately halting the program, Anna summoned Edgar Kaiser and the union leader, Tom Ray, to New York. This was where the chameleon-like Anna was at her mediating best, able to "bulldoze, cajole, or charm."[18] On one side of the table was Mr. Kaiser, whose company was at the forefront of hiring Blacks—he would get the soft touch. On the other side was the rough, recalcitrant union leader, who had complained to a reporter from New York's *P.M.* daily that he had been getting "heat [from] Mrs. Rosenberg." The pressure from Anna was warranted. Ray had embarrassed the Roosevelt administration, telling the *Oregon Journal*, "Hell, I'm no dynamiter . . . but I'm opposed to having the colored working side by side with white women down in the holds of a ship." Sitting at the head of the conference room table was Anna, who, when pushed, could use language that could "make a longshoreman blush." As no notes were kept of the meeting, it is impossible to know if she made Mr. Ray blush, but when the situation demanded it she could "out-scream even the most leather-lunged labor leader." Her "poking, prodding, pleading, [or] ordering" worked. The next day *The Oregonian* reported "Mr. Ray Relents"; the "labor despot . . . bowed to . . . the government authorities." Three days after the meeting, Anna restarted the recruitment, and thousands of New Yorkers, Black and white, followed that first train.

Kaiser specialized in building Liberty Ships, which were used to transport troops and cargo. The ships were built to a standardized design, with some 250,000 parts prefabricated throughout the country in 250-ton sections and welded together at the shipyards. Built for just under $2 million, each could carry 2,840 Jeeps, 440 tankers, or 230 million rounds of rifle ammunition. Liberty Ships were the answer to Churchill's plea for help and to Roosevelt's call for "tremendous production of planes and tanks and guns and also of the ships to carry them."

Kaiser's first Liberty Ship, *Star of Oregon*, launched on September 27, 1941, after 131 days of construction. Once the thousands of East Coast workers were on the docks, a new record was set. The keel of the *Robert E. Peary* was laid on a Sunday; it set sail four days, fifteen hours, and twenty-nine minutes later. When a woman who had been asked to christen a ship out of Portland arrived too late, a dockworker shouted, "Just keep standing there, ma'am, there'll be another one along in a minute."[19]

When the *Robert E. Peary* set sail, Anna Rosenberg was on the other side of the continent, standing in the concourse of Grand Central Station. She was meeting Mayor La Guardia for a ceremonial unfurling of a giant service flag recognizing the city's railroad men who had transferred their service in wartime railroads to the armed forces.[20] As the twenty-five-foot red, white, and blue flag fluttered down from the North Balcony, the crowd cheered and some wept. As the luminaries noted that day, the New York Central System sent 11,098 men to shoulder arms— more than half of a full-strength infantry division. Under the magnificent dome, Anna was filled with pride thinking of the New Yorkers helping win the war on the docks of the West Coast, in the factories of the Northeast, and on the battlefields of North Africa and Guadalcanal.

CHAPTER TWELVE

THE BUFFALO PLAN

The more WOMEN at work, the sooner we WIN!
—U.S. Employment Service poster, 1943

In the fall of 1942, Anna turned her focus to the acute worker short-falls in Buffalo–Niagara Falls, a major defense hub where labor inefficiency threatened the trinity of aircraft production, shipbuilding, and ordnance contracts. Because it was located on the Buffalo River and the Great Lakes, Buffalo could receive raw materials and component parts, such as Minnesota iron ore and Detroit diesel engines. It was also a railway hub with a large hardworking industrial population who could manufacture the arms and send them easily on to East Coast ports for shipment overseas. Since 1940, the federal government had invested $5 billion in over one hundred companies in and around Buffalo. The region's workers toiled in steel mills and marine engine factories, cranked out Curtiss-Wright P-40 fighters for Great Britain's Royal Air Force, and shipped hundreds of Bell Airacobra pursuit planes to the desperate Soviet Air Force. They made "howitzer shells, steel armor for ships, machine guns and ammunition . . . diesel-powered invasion barges, parachutes, medical and hospital equipment, weather recording equipment, rubber rafts, uniforms, marine engines, firefighting equipment, amphibious cars, Army cots, pontoons, and TNT."[1] "I need not remark on the significance of the City of Buffalo in the war effort," President Roosevelt wrote Buffalo Mayor Joseph J. Kelly in August 1942; "in that task, I am sure . . . the citizens of Buffalo will unite."

After making several visits to the region to gather information on the growing labor shortage crisis, Anna reported to President Roosevelt at the White House. "He would ask me about specific plants and how much they were turning out . . . FDR always wanted to know what

131

was going on in the field." When he was told the news that plants were running behind, Buffalo was declared a "labor shortage area." FDR installed Rosenberg as the Labor Czar of Buffalo. The city was in desperate need of eighty-three thousand laborers—roughly the population of Little Rock, Arkansas. Anna and her team set up offices in room 5 of the State Office Building on Court Street in Buffalo. The first hearing with city leaders was Thursday, October 1. At 2:30 PM, the crowded room was "charged with doubt [and] antagonism" at the "unwarranted intrusion of Washington bureaucracy." Anna took the chair and spoke of her commitment to hear from all stakeholders in getting the Niagara frontier back on track. "I want to hear everyone capable of speaking about the situation."[2] By the time the meeting ended, what had been "bewildering" to local leaders was in the adroit hands of a labor expert. "There was no doubt on the part of anyone . . . that Mrs. Rosenberg was in command of the situation."[3]

From there Rosenberg's team began inspecting the defense plants and inquiring at a granular level of detail how the shortages could be mitigated. Her team gathered information on wages, hours, utilization of labor, training, as well as transportation, housing, childcare, and discrimination. Her management style helped her be successful. "I delegate a tremendous amount of work," she told the Associated Press' Adelaide Kerr in 1942. "I go out in the field and see what's going on, so that I know what people are talking about. But after that I delegate authority." She liberally credited her staff, which included Lillian Poses, one of the first women to graduate from New York University's Law School: "Their batting average is just as high as mine. You can get a lot done if you give other people credit for what they do. People want credit and they deserve to have it."

What was immediately clear to her team was that more women could help. "We know modern wars are fought on two fronts and that the battlefront and the production front are inseparable," Anna wrote; "you cannot remove eleven million men from the production front and expect the vacuum they leave behind to arm them. When the men have gone, women must move into the factories to take their place."[4]

At first, Buffalo had tried to attract women with a series of half measures. *Time* reported that the city "fumbled with numerous catch-as-catch-can makeshifts" such as building "a cozy Cape Cod cottage . . . in downtown Buffalo to give [women] a cozy place in which to sign up." Once under Rosenberg's control, the "proper recruitment of women" was strictly enforced, which meant hiring in the sequence of single women, married women without children, and, as a last resort, married women with children.

Hiring women was complicated by the gender norms of the time. In *Free World* magazine, Anna wrote of the need to "convince their husbands [and] batter down the stubborn pride of men who feared the loss of self-esteem and loss of community prestige [when] their wives go to work."[5]

Besides the resistance of their husbands, fathers, and brothers, women workers also had to surmount the obstacle of inadequate childcare. A four-year-old in California was found with matches, trying to light the family's gas stove. Such reports pained Anna, a working mother who was used to "[staying] up late at night waiting until every door was closed and every light was out to make sure that every member of my family . . . are safely in . . . I have a particular feeling for the fear and the worry of the mothers and fathers." In the completed report on worker absenteeism that was called a "masterpiece" by veteran Washington insider Bernard Baruch, Anna and her team cited the inadequacy of community facilities as one of the leading causes of absenteeism among women. "When women come into war plants, their schedules as housewives and mothers are disrupted if community facilities are not available." Without "proper childcare . . . involuntary absences must result." For the working mothers of Buffalo, Rosenberg and the War Manpower Commission converted Depression-era buildings to day-care centers and built recreation rooms, canteens, and cafeterias. Markets and essential services were ordered to stagger hours to accommodate women at the end of their shifts, and companies were instructed to provide ample check-cashing services, to obviate the need to cash checks at the tavern.

Recreation, too, was vital. For workers on the second shift, from 4:00 PM to 1:00 AM, movie houses ran films until five o'clock in the morning, and boating excursions launched at 2:00 AM. For the "graveyard shift," which started after midnight and ended at seven or eight o'clock in the morning, picnic grounds were opened, with tables and benches, a female attendant, and open fireplaces.

In December 1942, when she learned that toy prices had skyrocketed due to wartime shortages of materials, Anna persuaded Jack Straus, the president of Macy's, to take losses in the toy department so that war workers could afford doll carriages, wagons, and toy soldiers. Morale was critical, explained her report, whether one was "fighting with a gun, or fighting with the tools of production."

Just as she knew that enlightened management could prevent strikes, so could transparent foremen lift wartime morale. "Life behind the walls of a factory," she wrote, was as difficult and mystifying for inexperienced women as warfare was for the rookie soldier.[6] To boost morale, managers needed to explain the importance of the work to the greater cause.

The moves worked: by June 1943, there were two hundred thousand women making bombs and fuses, in airplane hangars or canneries, freeing up men for the heavier work at the steel mills and shipyards. As they arrived at the munitions plants at midnight and clocked in to their "owl" shifts, so they could be home in time to see their children off to school in the morning, the women of Buffalo were driven by a desire to fight back at the enemy. The war against Nazism, Anna wrote in a 1942 piece titled "Women on the Job," "strikes at the very heart of all a woman lives for—the home."

> I think that what outrages the American women most is the attempted total obliteration of the family unit under fascism and Nazism. Wherever these forms of government have been set up, they have with cold deliberation ruthlessly set about to destroy the dignity of the home and family, and to substitute for it the cold patronage of the state. Children are taught that they belong not to the family but to the state.[7]

So despite the late hours, the arduous work, and the 30 percent gap in pay with men, the women of Buffalo punched in and punched back. They were, Anna concluded, "helping to preserve the American family—its independence, its security, its hope of the future."

At one plant, Anna watched a young woman punching out tiny screws on a machine. "Monotonous, isn't it?" Anna said gently.

"It certainly is," she said wearily.

"Have you any idea what the screws are used for?"

"No," she said, "but I've wondered."

Anna linked the girl's arm in hers and said, "Come join me and we'll find out together."

After following along the entire manufacturing process, they made their discovery: the tiny screws were part of the fighter pilot's gunsight.[8]

Anna watched the girl's expression change from boredom to satisfaction.

This young woman and thousands like her made Anna immensely proud. "When you have walked as many miles through factory and foundry," she wrote in June 1944, "[seeing] the competence and confidence and spirit of hundreds of thousands of American women . . . youngsters in slacks and bobby socks and grandmothers in slacks and bandana . . . doing the tremendous work of war production, you can have only one proud opinion—American women are doing a magnificent job."[9]

Minority workers, underutilized due to persistent prejudice, could alleviate the pressure if only companies would hire them. At open meetings, luncheons, and dinners, Anna impressed upon the labor leaders, management, and Chamber of Commerce officials that minority hiring would alleviate the shortage. While some city officials didn't like it that she and her staff "injected themselves into such collateral matters as . . . discrimination," Anna, according to Buffalo historian Mark Goldman, "refused to tolerate the prejudicial hiring policies that had been for so long a part of local industry. In countless speeches to community leaders she insisted that they overcome the city's labor shortage by making maximum use of women and other minorities." This was not merely an expedient to Director Rosenberg. The *Buffalo Evening News* quoted her exhorting audiences that "the people of Buffalo must realize that minority groups just don't exist anymore. There must be no closing of doors to people because they are members of minority groups."

Rosenberg appealed to Black women at the bottom of the economic ladder to join the workforce, as doing so would lead to greater social equality. "As you advance you must fortify and solidify your gains," she counseled in a piece for *Opportunity: The Journal of Negro Life*. "Constant prodding" helped create "unprecedented opportunities for the city's minority groups," reported the *Buffalo Evening News*. After employing "only a handful" of Black workers in 1942, aircraft maker Curtiss-Wright had 1,492 Black workers on the payroll, 940 of them women, by June 1943. Bell Aircraft employed another nine hundred. Her work on behalf of the Black community in the Niagara district was consistent with Anna's commitment to civil rights. She had brokered Executive Order 8802 in 1941; insisted that Pacific shipyards hire Black workers in 1942; and was seen as an ally by Black leaders such as Paul Robeson, future Congressman Adam Clayton Powell, and Clarence Mitchell, Jr.

Buffalo's physically disabled population pitched in. By 1943 the *New York Times* reported over twenty-seven hundred disabled men and women were employed by the defense contractors, among them "footless truck drivers, one-handed machinists, one-armed engine mechanics, deaf card punchers, and several operators of overhead cranes who had artificial legs." Working closely with a disabled President she venerated, Anna shared FDR's belief that the exigencies of war would lead to greater social equality for those on the margins. Local high school hours were moved up so that boys could take part-time shifts after school as part of what was billed "The Double Duty Plan." Such work, while important, must not interfere with education, Anna told the Associated Press at the start of the school year in September 1943. "The young people of New York State have made tremendous contributions in war production this summer," she counseled. "They must return to school during the academic year because their education is an investment not only for themselves, but for the nation."

Rosenberg's total control over the mobilization efforts of Buffalo had alleviated, but not totally eliminated, the city's worker shortages. By 1943 the problem wasn't so much a lack of workers, as a lack of worker stability. The issue was that the city's aircraft plants—the "glamor jobs" according to the Buffalo papers—had higher rates of pay and better working conditions. Machinists and mill hands would jump to Bell Aircraft or Curtiss-Wright. This internal mobility, while good for workers, threatened the city's overall ability to manufacture the tools needed for war. In 1943 *Time* reported that the city's heavy industries were imperiled by "widespread labor pirating, sucking workers from the heavy work and low pay of the steel mills, shipyards, etc., into the pleasanter surroundings and high wages of the aircraft plants."[10] Such pirating put soldiers at risk: the United States relied on twelve thousand tons of steel per day for tanks and railroad cars.

Besides the job-hopping, companies that could afford it would stockpile workers to create their own labor reserves. As a result, other manufacturers suffered. In a single want ad in 1943, National Biscuit, which made K rations, the high-calorie food bar for paratroops and other mobile units, was forced to advertise for "packers, checkers, wrappers, porters, [and] truck greasers." Anna began formulating a solution to the job-hopping and stockpiling of workers—one that, while necessary, was sure to be met with resistance.

While Anna was tackling Buffalo's last remaining problems, FDR's patience with "second line men" Donald Nelson and Paul McNutt was finally giving way. In May 1943, without disbanding their agencies or firing either man, the President established a separate agency that in essence took away their powers. The Office of War Mobilization (OWM) was an independent government agency to coordinate America's mobilization efforts. President Roosevelt selected James F. Byrnes to direct the office.

Byrnes' powers over the war economy were vast and he would need able assistance. FDR tried to persuade the elder financier Bernard Baruch, a close friend of Anna's, to a home-front leadership post, but Baruch demurred. FDR subsequently named him as a special adviser to the OWM, where his experience in running the American economy in World War I would be valued.

A month after Byrnes took charge at the OWM, Anna instituted her emergency solution in Buffalo: the Controlled Referral Plan. The plan was based on two principles: 1) unemployed male workers could only get jobs at the plants with the most pressing need, and 2) workers could only change jobs with permission from central planners. To prioritize needs, representatives of the War Production Board, the War Manpower Commission, and the Army rated plants according to their contribution to the war effort on a scale of one to four, with one being the most vital. The U.S. Employment Service then referred available labor to plants rated one, then two, and so forth. Anna's plan placed a numerical cap on the number of workers in any given plant, which stopped the stockpiling of skilled workers, and surplus workers were sent to other plants. These efforts, combined with uniform childcare and the hiring of women and Blacks, came to be known as the Buffalo Plan.

Much depended on the success of the Buffalo Plan. If the plan failed, compulsory national service would become necessary. As Bernard Baruch warned, "The only alternative . . . is a national service act for the drafting of labor." Indeed, a frustrated and worried FDR threatened to sign a "Work-or-Fight" law mandating that either a civilian work at an essential job or be "deprived of civilian status and drafted." Opponents lambasted such a law as un-American. Theodore F. Green, Democratic Senator from Rhode Island, spoke for opponents of the law when he rejected the idea as "applying a totalitarian form of government to our democracy." And to Anna, such a law would be contrary to the very reason Americans were fighting. In her essay in the 1942 collection *The Family in a World at War*, she wrote of the need to safeguard the people's "spiritual resources":

> We chart our war program in terms of monthly output
> of horsepower, machine guns, freight carloads, [and] steel
> capacities. We cannot chart defense in terms of measured
> units of morale and spirit. But it would be tragic indeed if
> we did not recognize that those things, too, are of equal
> importance to the national war effort. They are the things
> which make a free people appreciate freedom and arouse in
> them the determination to perpetuate that freedom.

What *Time* called the "Rosenberg Plan" had in just a few months' time "brought order out of chaos." Tens of thousands of workers were sent to where they were needed most and kept there. Heavy industries got the men they needed and were able to get back to production schedules. By September 13, 1943, the *Buffalo Courier-Express* reported:

> Heavy industry plants here have returned to . . . output
> schedules under the plan's operation. The Buffalo-Niagara
> area obviously proved a worthy "guinea pig" in the exper-
> iment to solve the country's manpower problem. The eyes
> of the nation were watching the results of our referral

plan. . . . It now appears headed for adoption in every critical labor area in the country.

Buffalo was a proud city. "Production for war had become the primary
measure of achievement," wrote Mark Goldman, the Buffalo historian,
"and by these standards, Buffalo had done remarkably well. People were
proud of the part the city had played in making the United States the
'Arsenal of Democracy.'" Planes made in the city were celebrated for
attacking the Luftwaffe's Messerschmitts over the skies of North Africa.
Newspapers crowed about the Curtiss-Wright P-40 "lung[ing]" at Japanese ships and "plaster[ing]" them. Bell, Chevrolet, Westinghouse, and
Curtiss-Wright all received the coveted Army and Navy "E" award for
excellence. The citizens of Buffalo, wrote Dudley Irwin, the historian of
the Buffalo War Council, had "submerged all political, religious, race
and class distinctions" and had "united in one great community" to meet
"the challenge of total war." The Buffalo Plan had worked.

In September 1943, James Byrnes grafted Anna's Buffalo Plan onto
Seattle; San Francisco; Los Angeles; San Diego; and Portland, Oregon,
where, according to OWM historian Herman Miles Somers, it was
"enthusiastically received."[11] In the words of historian Roger Daniels,
its adoption by West Coast defense plants "solved the manpower issues
in that region." The plan was subsequently rolled out nationwide. In
March 1944, *Time* reported, "as regional War Manpower commissioner,
[Anna] has done a first-rate job in New York. There she evolved the 'Buffalo Plan' that became the national model for the manipulation of manpower shortages, from Connecticut to California." To Roosevelt scholar
Roger Daniels, Anna Rosenberg's plan was the "major achievement"
of the War Manpower Commission, its success "due to her skills and
insight." "If America had turned a corner in stabilizing its labor supply
McNutt neither received nor deserved praise for the accomplishment.
Anna Rosenberg . . . had fashioned the Buffalo Plan."[12] As he had done
before, Roosevelt had created a parallel, competing apparatus to solve a
vexing national problem. "The story went around Washington," Eleanor Roosevelt reported, "that the Secretary of Labor had been bypassed,
that [Frances Perkins] could not handle the situation, and that it had
been taken from her."[13] Secretary Perkins could not have been pleased by
national articles like "Anna Rosenberg Tackles Job of Recruiting Women

to Meet Labor Shortage" or when Washington bureau chiefs explained, "from the informed it is learned that Anna Rosenberg . . . carries more weight with Mr. Roosevelt than any of his labor advisers. It is understood she is not afraid to talk up to the President, to disagree with him, and he seems to like her for it."[14] Secretary Perkins surely would have felt the wrath of FDR if she publicly complained about her rival, but that was not her style. Instead, Perkins did what she could to erase Anna Rosenberg from the insider history of the war years by omitting mention of her in her 1946 memoir, *The Roosevelt I Knew*. Years after leaving government service, when she sat for a series of interviews with Columbia University's Oral History Office, Frances Perkins finally allowed herself to vent her animosity toward Anna Rosenberg with a series of cutting remarks and insinuations, some of which are quoted herein.

President Roosevelt had been right to place such confidence in the American people during the dark early days of the Second World War. They were better than the mere "sunshine patriots," he had referred to in his February radio address, and their "tremendous resourcefulness" in factories, shipyards, and aircraft production hangars resulted in "tremendous production." The U.S. military economy had pounded out "a fantastic statistical litany" by war's end, according to historian David Kennedy: 5,777 merchant ships, 1,556 naval vessels, 299,293 aircraft, 634,569 jeeps, 88,410 tanks, 2,383,311 trucks, 6.5 million rifles, 40 billion bullets—a "stupendous Niagara of numbers."[15] By way of explanation, historian Bruce Catton gives this analogy: "Say that we performed the equivalent of building two Panama Canals every month with a fat surplus to boot; that's an understatement, it still doesn't begin to express it all, the total is simply beyond the compass of one's understanding. Here was displayed a strength . . . to which nothing—literally nothing, in the physical sense—was any longer impossible."[16]

Achieving the "overwhelming superiority" of arms that President Roosevelt had called for had required contributions from millions of war workers, labor unions, corporate managers, and industrialists. Civilian men, women, and even children sacrificed so that planes made in Buffalo and ships made in Portland could be used against America's enemies across the worldwide map of the war. But the gargantuan task would not have been possible without the extraordinary efforts of Anna Rosenberg. From her position at the War Manpower Commission, she had boldly taken hiring away from the private sector and placed it in the hands of central planners. Hers was, *Time* reported, "the most sweeping federal mobilization action ever taken in an American city."[17]

After the war, when Anna received the Medal for Merit for "exceptionally meritorious conduct in the performance of outstanding services to the United States," President Harry Truman cited Anna's contribution to the Arsenal of Democracy when he wrote "the Buffalo Plan became a nation-wide program without which the necessary manpower for war production would not have been obtained."[18]

That was not the only accolade contained in the citation.

CHAPTER THIRTEEN

ASK NO QUESTIONS

[Building an atomic bomb] can never be done
unless you turn the United States into one huge factory.

—Physicist Niels Bohr

———

Since secrecy is so damaging to solidarity, the mere possession
of a secret gives rise to the suspicion of disloyalty.

—Edward Shils, *The Torment of Secrecy*

———

There is a tide in the affairs of men,
Which taken at the flood,
leads on to fortune.
And we must take the current when it serves,
Or lose our ventures.

—British Prime Minister Winston Churchill to President
Roosevelt on the eve of his 1943 visit to Hyde Park,
quoting Shakespeare's *Julius Caesar*

A meeting that would change the course of human history took place in October 1940 between President Roosevelt and Alexander Sachs, the director of the Lehman Corporation and an amateur scientist. The subject was alarming. According to two preeminent German Jewish scientists who had fled the Nazis, Hitler's progress on splitting the atom—and creating a new superweapon—was reaching a critical phase. Sachs handed the President an article by Leo Szilard titled "Instantaneous Emissions of Fast Neutrons in the Interaction of Slow Neutrons of Uranium," which boiled down how rare metals could be converted into massive amounts of exploding energy. Sachs also presented a letter written by Albert Einstein stating that "a single bomb of this type could destroy an entire city."

"Alex," said the President, thus enlightened, "what you are after is to see the Nazis don't blow us up?"

"Precisely."

By the beginning of the Second World War, physicists in the belligerent nations knew that atomic physics could lead to a bomb of unprecedented destructive power. The element uranium was the key to turning the theory into weaponry. Smashing a uranium atom with a neutron releases energy, and the neutrons from one smashup stimulate other breakups, and on and on. The "chain reaction" would result in unimaginable destructive power. Developing this knowledge into a bomb was complicated by the fact that only a rare part of the uranium atom would react like this. If the isotope 235 could somehow be separated from the element's other two isotopes, a Ping-Pong ball of uranium 235 would be equal to thousands of tons of TNT.[1]

In typical Roosevelt fashion, the meeting with Sachs concluded with decisive action. To finance what would become the Manhattan Project, a secret appropriation was made to the Bureau of Standards, and an advisory committee was assembled comprising scientists and military officers. When the military officers balked that such an outlandish weapon could exist, Pa Watson was ready for them.

"The Boss wants it, boys. Get to work."[2]

The Manhattan Project was the code name of the ultrasecret effort to build the world's first atomic bomb. The massive undertaking required 130,000 workers, from physicists and chemists in university laboratories to blue-collar workers in vast secret cities purpose-built for bomb making. From the hidden ridges of Appalachia to the Pacific Northwest, from the heart of Chicago to the desert of New Mexico, the clandestine work was carried out at the astronomical cost of $2 billion. Guiding the project was "the world's greatest concentration of scientific genius," all of them "focused on the single task of creating a practical atomic weapon." Racing to develop humanity's first atomic bomb before the Nazis became the most fateful secret in the history of the nation.

The brain and nerve centers of the Manhattan Project were the University of California, Berkeley and the University of Chicago. Under the direction of the brilliant Robert Oppenheimer, Berkeley was the epicenter for theoretical physics in the United States. For a year, physicists, chemists, and engineers in Berkeley's radiation lab used a particle accelerator to determine if plutonium would be fissionable like uranium. In 1940 they discovered a new element that could act as an alternative to uranium 235. They named it plutonium. The Metallurgical Laboratory at the University of Chicago was to design a viable method for plutonium production that could fuel a chain reaction.

Enriching uranium and producing plutonium are "Big Machine" physics, requiring massive mechanical contraptions: calutrons, cyclotrons, centrifuges, reactors, and huge underground lakes of cooling water. To convert the blueprints of the Rad Lab and the Met Lab into a weapon, the Army Corps of Engineers built secret atomic reservations with "astonishing speed."[3] Hidden in the ridges and valleys of the Appalachian Mountains, Oak Ridge, Tennessee, was chosen as the site where uranium would be enriched. More than 250 buildings dotted the hidden valley: chemistry laboratories, plants for water distillation and sewage treatment, shops, a service station, warehouses, cafeterias, gatehouses, locker rooms, a paymaster's office, a foundry, a generator building, and eight water-cooling towers.[4] When work commenced in December 1942 there were seventy thousand workers—not one knew they were working to isolate a specific isotope from a chunk of rare earth metal for conversion into a superbomb.

The fruits of the Rad Lab work resulted in the construction of a similarly vast atomic district near Hanford, Washington. The site had a long construction season and abundant water for hydroelectric power, and, like Oak Ridge, it was isolated. The seclusion of Oak Ridge and Hanford served to hide the work, as well as limit potential for espionage, while protecting population centers in case of accidental discharge of intense radiation. The sixty thousand Hanford workers were spread over nearly one thousand square miles across the northern desert. At the heart of the massive plutonium production site was the so-called B reactor.

As with West Coast shipbuilding, the Manhattan Project required an influx of workers from the cities of the Northeast. From the WMC office at 11 W. 42nd Street in New York City, Anna Rosenberg sent ten thousand New Yorkers to Tennessee and Washington State. Electricians, carpenters, and bricklayers heeded the call, as did chemists, chemical engineers, and physicists. None were told what it was they were building.

"At no time were the workers told what kind of tasks lay ahead of them, but they were informed that the work was . . . highly confidential."[5] "No one took me in on the secret," Anna reported. "I just knew that men were needed. So I got them."[6]

Perhaps it was best that the commission lacked details of the assignments. The 130,000 people at the two production locations worked behind barbed-wire fences under a strict regime of secrecy. There technicians, engineers, and scientists lived in "sparse environments [that] had many of the trappings of a monk-like existence," with dormitories separated by gender. Military police and the FBI were on constant alert for espionage. The merest suspicion would launch an investigation.

At the university labs, not only were workers kept in the dark; they were summarily let go at sixty- or ninety-day intervals. "A substantial number of workers" at the University of Chicago were working on a "key phase" of the bomb (we now know it was a particle accelerator). As the scientists reached "a certain stage of the experiment," those without security clearances were laid off with no explanation. It was necessary, recalled Rosenberg, as "one of them might put two and two together" and figure out the nature of the lab's mission. The dismissed workers were rightfully resentful. They had been let go with no explanation and no justification. As was their right, labor organizers petitioned for a union election in accordance with the National Labor Relations Act. Such an election would lead to publicity and public explanations that were "impossible to make." A similar conundrum unfolded at Berkeley's radiation lab. For the handful of people in the United States who knew the scope of the Manhattan Project, such publicity must be avoided at all costs.

When the top scientist of the project, Robert Oppenheimer, found out about the unionization effort, he alerted his superior, General Leslie Groves, who in turn notified Secretary of War Henry L. Stimson. On August 17, 1943, an unnerved Stimson fired off a letter to President Roosevelt. "The situation is very alarming," he concluded.

The New Deal had supported unions, but national security was at stake. Both the scientists and the workers were "privy to classified information, skills and equipment . . . the processes they controlled were particularly vulnerable to disruption or damage" in case of strikes.

The withdrawal of labor would imperil an essential project of national defense. At Oak Ridge, it was estimated that it would take three hundred days to produce sufficient enriched uranium for a single bomb core.[7] A work stoppage could drag the war deeper into 1945, or even 1946, with more and more deaths each day. Viewed by some conservative members of Manhattan Project management as "harbors of destabilizing political subversion," unions might even be a gateway to espionage.[8] Whether these worries were legitimate or unfounded, Americans workers' rights were enshrined in law. They could form unions, they could not be laid off or terminated without cause, and they could strike if necessary.

The first attempts to defuse the union efforts were delay tactics and clumsy strong-arm maneuvers such as threats to draft the organizers into the Army or exile them to lonely outposts. One unionizer, the physicist Dr. Giovanni Rossi Lomanitz of the radiation lab, was told his deferments were to be stripped, he was to be reclassified as 1A, and he would be ordered "to report for induction [into the Army] in ten days."[9] Both in Chicago and California, these threats failed to stop the organizers. In September and again in October, Secretary of War Stimson wrote FDR. The unionization activities were "dangerous not only to security but to the speedy completion" of the work on "the most important phases of uranium fission." "You will remember," he concluded, "the seriousness of this danger and the extreme urgency of action."[10] Upon receipt of the October letter, FDR summoned "Mrs. Fix-It."

When Anna walked into the President's study, he handed her the letter from the Secretary of War discussing the atomic bomb project. Anna was in on the secret.[11]

"You've got to talk to Phil Murray," directed FDR. "There can be no union. There can't be any strikes at the University of Chicago."

"What do you mean there can't be any strikes?"

"You will have to tell him he'll have to take my word for it, that this is a matter of national security."[12]

——◆◆◆——

It was a negotiation that Anna never forgot, "because it was so hard." Not only did she have to go up against the imposing Scottish-born leader of the Congress of Industrial Organizations, but she lacked her typical avalanche of data, having just the promise of the President. As he sometimes did, FDR gave Anna no specifics; it simply had to be done. "Find a way to do it," he told her. What Roosevelt was asking her to do ran contrary to her advice to clients that they increase transparency, that they reach out to workers as partners. If there was mutual trust rather than antagonism, union leaders could better control their members. When Eleanor found out about Anna's task, she said, "How can you go to Phil Murray and ask him to do this without any good reason?"[13] It was a question Anna was asking herself.

After securing a meeting with Mr. Murray, Anna walked the short distance from her office in the East Wing to the headquarters of the CIO. She knew Phil Murray well, and she also knew the tough former steelworker would stand up for the men and women he represented.

"Look, Phil," she said, "I've never asked you to lay off organizing anybody, anywhere. Isn't that right?"

"That's right," said the tall, balding Scot, in his slow, deep voice.

He was aware of the layoffs at the University of Chicago, so she got right to the point.

"You have to stop it."

Murray peered over his wire-rimmed glasses, his bushy eyebrows furrowing. The words took their time coming out.

"I know of no reason for doing so."

"The President assured me it was absolutely necessary for national security. War Department orders are to 'maintain a secrecy beyond that of any other project.'"

"Why?"

Anna, who had seen Stimson's letter, leveled with Murray.

The labor leader thought for a moment.

"You are asking me to do a tough thing." He paused. "But I'll do it."

"Okay. And Phil—lay off Berkeley. Ask no questions."[14]

---•••---

When the rank and file heard that the estimable Philip Murray had agreed to the extraordinary demand, they realized that the request had come straight from the top. The organizers had underestimated "the power that was going to be lined up against us. There were far more far-reaching consequences than any of us might have dreamed."[15] To Anna, the reason Murray assented was because over ten years FDR "had built up such a backlog of faith and trust with [labor leaders] and the rest of the labor movement, that he could make such requests."[16] As the go-between who patched FDR directly through to labor leaders, it had been Anna who had quietly gotten word to the steelmakers and autoworkers, garment workers and teamsters, that "mandates . . . would be interpreted generously," that they would be treated fairly by the administration.[17] These confidential assurances, combined with Roosevelt's understanding of labor, won concessions. As Anna described it:

> He was fair with the labor leaders—fair in the sense that he did not always press them to gain a point, even though it was badly needed. He explained to me that he knew the limitations under which labor leaders function. They "have to go back to the members," and it would be unfair to them to . . . weaken their prestige with their own people. But when necessary he did ask, and he got cooperation . . . at crucial and even desperate times.[18]

Anna, too, had leveled with labor for nearly two decades. The most fateful secret in the nation's history was safe.

The atomic bomb was not the only national security secret in the summer of 1943.

In August 1943, British Prime Minister Winston Churchill crossed the U-boat-infested North Atlantic on the camouflaged battle cruiser HMS *Renown* for a covert meeting with the American President. Armed sentries stood outside the conference room in Québec's Château Frontenac where President Roosevelt, General George Marshall, and the Chiefs of Staff met with the Prime Minister and his military attaché. The so-called Quadrant Conference was a "showdown" between the Allies over the inevitable invasion of Nazi Europe. Having been expelled from the Continent by the Wehrmacht, the British were "fatigued and defeatist," in the estimation of Secretary of War Stimson. After nearly four years of war "their hearts," Stimson told Roosevelt, "are not in it." As a result, the British were gun-shy about the audacious plan to invade occupied France with a massive amphibious assault. The Americans, by contrast, "stood six-guns blazing, eager for combat."[19] After three days of face-to-face discussions across a narrow wooden table, the sides agreed on the "Strategic Concept for the Defeat of the Axis in Europe"—Allied forces would cross the English Channel the following May, secure beachheads, and from there take the battle to the Germans across France and into the Third Reich itself. Deeply immersed in history both ancient and modern, Winston Churchill no doubt realized that the invasion—code-named Operation Overlord—would be the largest combined land and sea operation conducted since the invasion of Greece by King Xerxes of Persia in the spring of 480 B.C.[20]

Related discussions between the two leaders and their staffs in Washington mostly settled the issue of who would lead the Allied invasion. Here, too, the Americans got their way. The Supreme Allied Commander must be an American. America's top soldier, U.S. Army Chief of Staff George C. Marshall, was the obvious candidate. But taking the architect of the worldwide war effort away from Washington to take a theater command was worrying to FDR. If not Marshall, General Dwight D. Eisenhower, a protégé of Marshall, would take command of Overlord. Making the decision difficult for Roosevelt was his realization that if successful, the Supreme Allied Commander would be immortalized as a great war hero, the face of the Second World War for generations to follow. Could he take that away from Marshall?

Regardless of who led it, FDR, Churchill, and the Combined Joint Chiefs of Staff knew the success or failure of Operation Overlord would come down to the ability to supply war matériel to the twenty-six to thirty divisions slated to storm the beaches of Fortress Europe. The United States, with its greater production capability and larger population, would not only supply the arms but would add three to five additional divisions per month, some sixty thousand to one hundred thousand men. An armada of thousands of ships, landing craft, and transport aircraft would be needed. But even if they could hold the beaches, in the opening days of the assault, with no ports yet secured and no safe harbor, how would it be possible to maintain supply lines from ships bobbing offshore in mined and unpredictable seas? In a "solution so fantastic" the German authorities would never have guessed it (and indeed did not), the Allies planned to bring their own harbors with them across the English Channel. Dozens of scuttled ships, and huge concrete sections each nearly a football field in length called Mulberries, would be assembled by a crew of ten thousand men. The breakwater would allow for reinforcements to follow the troops as they fought from the sand and cliffs into the maze-like hedge country of Normandy.

The confidential Overlord plans made, the next topic was the ability of the United States to step up war production to meet the needs of the invasion eight months hence.* In attendance at the Washington sessions was Anna Rosenberg, who had been commuting between Buffalo and the White House. Bernard Baruch, who, like Anna, resided at the Shoreham Hotel when he was in the capital, was also present. Baruch was Churchill's "finest American friend," their relationship going back to World War I, when the financial whiz served the Wilson administration by running the U.S. wartime economy in 1917 and 1918. Churchill had been Minister of Munitions in Britain then, where he made a good show of visiting arms-manufacturing areas like Sheffield and Manchester but was poor at labor relations. Armament production requires labor, not just steel and coal, and fortunately Roosevelt had his experts in industry and labor in attendance. Bernard Baruch, now an elder statesman, was adviser to the Office of War Mobilization, and Anna Rosenberg was an officer of the Labor Victory Board and a director of the War Manpower Commission.

If the heavy industries that made steel and ships were operating at anything less than full bore due to labor shortages, Roosevelt knew, the margin between the success or failure of Operation Overlord, already slender, would shrink even more. Before lunch at the White House on September 8, 1943, the handsome, white-haired Baruch was in conversation with the Prime Minister—Churchill's "shoulders hunched forward like a bull's" and an eight-inch Corona cigar clenched between his teeth—when President Roosevelt wheeled in.[21] "Everybody around me," said FDR, interrupting, "is in favor of conscription of labor except you, Bernie."[22] While conscription was not favored by "everybody," FDR was

---

* While there were no minutes kept of the meetings in Washington and subsequently at Hyde Park, a sheaf of papers sent to Roosevelt by Churchill prior to the Prime Minister's visit indicates that war production was one of the topics.

being pushed to sign such a law by elements in the military, anti-labor Republicans, and some conservative Democrats. While Roosevelt touted the law as egalitarian, critics saw through that argument. "The democracy of national service," said labor historian Nelson Lichtenstein, "was always akin to that of the barracks and the regiment, where all shared equally in their unfreedom."[23] Nevertheless, FDR was willing to appease those in favor of national service, and so he pushed on. Knowing the headwinds such a Draconian law would face on the Hill, would Baruch be willing to publicly endorse the idea?

Bernard Baruch had a number of reasons to reject Roosevelt's request: forcing people into essential war work was anti-Democratic and perhaps unnecessary. Since its launch in June, Anna Rosenberg's plan was alleviating the labor shortages in the Buffalo-Niagara arms district. If it worked and could be scaled up, there was no need for a costly political battle over a "work-or-fight" law. Anna, too, was against such a law. The Democratic way would be to persuade the unions themselves to keep members from laying down their tools. Armed only with trust and good faith, she had persuaded tens of thousands of workers at the atomic sites to forgo their legal right to unionize. "Having to deal with many labor matters for the President," she told Baruch in private, she would be put in "an embarrassing position" if there was even the appearance that she was part of the mechanism crafting the conscription law.[24] Decades of trust could go up in smoke. To his credit, FDR didn't let Bernie Baruch's coolness to his conscription remark foul the mood. Cocktail hour was coming up.

It is unclear whether Winston Churchill had met Anna Rosenberg prior to this White House visit, but he knew of her from Baruch, who had praised her talents in a letter to the Prime Minister. As Eleanor was on an inspection tour in the South Pacific, entertaining Churchill was left to FDR, Anna, and the White House staff. It was not an easy task. Mr. Churchill could be exhausting: rooms had to be shuffled to accommodate his idiosyncratic habits; he was given to bathing at "unsuitable" times and walking the halls in his bathrobe. "One of his keenest physical pleasures," according to one Churchill biographer, "second only to alcohol, was submerging himself in . . . hot bathwater."[25] Worse still, he would dictate letters to his male secretary wearing nothing but a bath towel, or, sometimes, just a cigar. Finding the Prime Minister in this state on one occasion, President Roosevelt had to beat a "strategic retreat in his wheelchair." "The Prime Minister of Britain," Churchill said gleefully, "has nothing to conceal from the President of the United States."[26]

In order to remain lively for his guest, Franklin Roosevelt was compelled to go beyond his usual one or two drinks. The Prime Minister's drinking habit got Anna into hot water. "When I brought [Churchill] a Brandy," Anna recalled, FDR scolded her. "You should have known better. He drank it all up."[27] During the late-night discussions the brandy "disappeared steadily and many a cigar burned to ashes."[28] In spite of his oddities and appetites and their differing political views, Roosevelt was fond of the old Tory. In Churchill's company, Roosevelt, who was used to dominating gatherings large and small, was content to listen, "fiddling with his pince-nez, doodling on a tablecloth with a burnt match, rubbing his eyes when the smoke from a Camel irritated them, throwing in the occasional question."[29] Anna was always amazed at FDR's morale-boosting ebullience, and she saw Churchill, too, was perfect for his moment in history. Their friendship, she said, "inspired the country to such emotion, and inspired our allies . . . [FDR] and Churchill loved each other."[30]

Compared to Québec, Washington was a steam kettle that August. Hats in hand and jackets thrown over arms, men walked deliberately, as if trying to conserve stores of energy that were running low. Dark stains under their arms, sweat dripping down their backs, they paused every block or so to mop their brows with handkerchiefs. Women took refuge under shady trees in parks, fanning themselves and their children, before gathering their things and moving on. Congress was in the final days of a two-month recess, and following the lawmakers, everyone who could do so fled the oppressive humidity of the capital for the mountains or the seaside.

Just after 10:00 PM on Thursday, September 9, President Roosevelt was taken in stealth to the secret section of track by the Bureau of Engraving and Printing, where he boarded the armored Pullman car for the overnight trip to Hyde Park. Code-named U.S. Car No. 1, the fortress-on-tracks had a half inch of nickel-steel armor and bullet-resistant

windows—blacked out, like the names of the cars, to shield FDR's
movements from a curious press. Traveling with him was Anna Rosenberg. Though days at Hyde Park were usually noted with a simple "H.P."
rather than the White House daily calendar with its multitude of visitors and meetings and fifteen-minute increments, Presidential Secretary
Bill Hassett was in one of the train cars reserved for staff. Despite the
promise of cooler air, it would be a working weekend. Congress was to
reconvene on Tuesday, and the President was working on his address to
update lawmakers on the progress of the of the war in Europe and the
Pacific and on the home front. Anna was to draft the National Labor
Act legislation with Sam Rosenman; thereafter they were to show it to
Bernard Baruch in an effort to convince him.

The overnight train arrived at Springwood on Friday morning,
and, after settling in, the President and Anna were joined for lunch by
Sammy the Rose. Also at Hyde Park that weekend was Daisy Suckley,
FDR's younger cousin and companion (and the biographer of Roosevelt's Scottish terrier Fala). Meeting Anna for the first time, Ms.
Suckley wrote in her diary: "Mrs. R is very bright, nice-looking, and
seems very nice, but she has a certain over-anxiousness . . . which is
probably from her being Jewish . . . the [President] says Mrs. Rosenberg
helps him and is *very* good."[31] After dinner Friday night, Bill Hassett
noted in his off-record diary that Sam Rosenman and his wife, Dorothy, said their goodbyes and headed to Backer Cottage on the estate.
Anna remained with FDR at Springwood.[32]

As night fell along the Hudson River, this momentous period in
the Anglo-American alliance was coming to a busy end. The Churchill entourage was arriving from Washington on Sunday. The Prime
Minister would be accompanied by his wife, Clementine; his daughter Mary; and five high-ranking military commanders. The Churchills
were celebrating their thirty-fifth wedding anniversary, so there would
no doubt be an extra round or two of toasts.[33] Anna was headed back to
Buffalo, New York, where her plan for efficient labor deployment was
showing results, and FDR was headed back to address Congress, but
without the national service act. "He changed his mind over the weekend," Anna reported to Baruch. She "did not work on the legislation at

all those few days . . . the President seemed to have other things to do."*
The Arsenal of Democracy would either stoke all its fires in preparation
for D-Day, or it would not. But the Buffalo Plan would be given time
to work, and Americans would not be drafted into factories.

On September 17, the President of the United States addressed the
Seventy-Eighth Congress and described the progress in the European war:
"We are striking devastating blows at . . . shipyards, munition dumps,
transportation facilities—which make it possible for the Nazis to wage
war. And we are hitting these military targets and blowing them to bits."

In the Pacific Theater, we were in for "a long and difficult fight. We
must be prepared for heavy losses in winning that fight. The power
of Japan will not collapse until it has been literally pounded into the
dust. . . . They may look to the north, to the south, to the east, or to the
west. They can see closing in on them, from all directions, the forces of
retribution."

Every bit as critical as the battles up the "leg of Italy or in the jungles
of the Southwest Pacific or in the clouds over China" was the sweat and
toil on the home front:

> Factories and plants and shipyards throughout the United
> States . . . are now working at full blast, turning out the
> greatest amount of war production in the history of the
> world . . . 15,000 planes [and] almost 5 ships a day. . . . It
> is becoming more and more evident that this is essentially
> a great war of production.

The congressional message also promised a further invasion of Hitler's
Europe. "The Congress and the American people can rest assured . . . the

---

* AR to Bernard Baruch, April 27, 1949, Baruch Papers, Princeton University
Library, NJ. This was not FDR's final flirtation with the national service
law. In his 1944 State of the Union address, he gave it his "unexpected
endorsement," catching union leaders off guard. As historian Nelson
Lichtenstein describes it, this led to labor leaders reasserting their authority
over the rank-and-file to tamp down strikes and to preserve postwar labor
power. The UAW president put it starkly: "Our union cannot survive if the
nation and our soldiers believe that we are obstructing the war effort." See,
e.g., Lichtenstein, *Labor's War at Home: The CIO in World War II* (New York:
Cambridge University Press, 1982), 185.

leaders and the military staffs of Great Britain and the United States made specific and precise plans to bring to bear further blows of equal or greater importance against Germany—with definite times and places for landings on the Continent of Europe."

By the time the Churchills were returning to London on the *Renown*, the world's first atomic bomb was in development at hidden sites across the nation, feints and ruses were being woven into the plans for the covert cross-Channel invasion of Hitler's Europe, and the arsenal that would feed those troops was on its way to reaching maximum output. Ten days after the President's address to Congress, *Time* reported "the Rosenberg Plan . . . has worked" in alleviating the "manpower shortage." "Heavy industries are getting the workers they need, [and] are back on production schedules."[34] With Bernard Baruch's support, the Office of War Mobilization immediately applied the plan to the West Coast.

As World War II entered its fifth year, Anna Rosenberg might have imagined the endgame: the advancing armies, the tidal wave of men and machines rolling through ruined cities and villages of France toward the heart of Nazi Germany.

What she could not have imagined is that she would be with them.

CHAPTER FOURTEEN

WARTIME MISSION

We few, we happy few, we band of brothers;
For he to-day that sheds his blood with me
Shall be my brother.

—Shakespeare, *Henry V*

———

See that Anna doesn't get hurt.

—President Franklin D. Roosevelt

In May 1944, Anna and her husband, Mike, took the ferry across the Hudson River to see off their son, newly commissioned Lieutenant Thomas J. Rosenberg. The young officer was headed overseas to the Air Corps. The couple said their goodbyes as Thomas boarded the train, but Anna could not bear to watch the train pull out. After driving in silence back to the ferry station, Anna saw soldiers crowding behind a rope barrier. They were wearing helmets and packs, and Anna knew where they were headed. Rolling down the window of the cab, Anna watched as commuters barely gave the boys a glance. They were the last home folks the boys would see for a long time, maybe ever, and no one seemed to pay them a glance. She told the cabdriver to stop.

Anna pushed her way to the edge of the rope, leaned over, and touched one of the young men. "Good-bye," she told him, and "good luck." The boy straightened and smiled; then other boys turned toward her, their faces brightening. She stood there waving, trying to catch every face, saying it again and again: "Good luck, boys!"

"Every one of them was my boy," she recalled, "and every one of them was some mother's boy."[1] Some time later, when her son's deployment made the news, a reporter asked, "Has he a lot of friends in Europe?"

"That's unimportant," she fired back. "He went over because he has a lot of enemies there."[2]

A month later Anna was among the millions of mothers across the country who joined President Roosevelt in his prayer on the first day of Operation Overlord, the Allies' gargantuan sea- and airborne assault on the Normandy coast. An article of faith for the German high command was that by denying the Allies the Atlantic ports from Bordeaux, France, to Antwerp, Belgium, any momentary success would be surrendered for lack of supplies. Hitler himself had ordered the coastal defenders to fight to the last man, to empty the last box of ammunition.[3] Knowing that his soldiers would encounter a fanatical enemy, the President led the nation in the D-Day prayer:

> Almighty God: Our sons, pride of our Nation, this day have set upon a mighty endeavor, a struggle to save the Republic . . . and to free a suffering humanity. Lead them straight and true; give strength to their arms, stoutness to their hearts, steadfastness in their faith. . . . Their road will be long and hard. For the enemy is strong. He may hurl back our forces. Success may not come with rushing speed, but we shall return again and again—by the righteousness of our cause, our sons will triumph.[4]

The Allied landings on June 6 gained the beachheads, but the road to the interior proved to be long and hard. Normandy was bocage country, small farm fields separated by earthen berms and topped with thick hedgerows that made ideal obstacles for an advancing infantry. Correspondent Ernie Pyle described it as "a war from hedgerow to hedgerow, and when we got into a town or city it was a war from street to street."[5] It was tough, but within days there was enough of a toehold to send in massive amounts of soldiers and matériel—and a presidential adviser.

Not long after D-Day, President Roosevelt summoned Anna Rosenberg: "Anna I want you to go overseas, visit all the troops, see what can be done maybe now even but above all see what they would like to do when they come home."[6] Her mission was to gather information on the short term and plan for the long term. "We spent several fairly long periods discussing what I was particularly to observe," she explained. FDR instructed Anna to look into the "little things [that] big men overlook." In their series of discussions, "he was quite specific in detailing such things as mail, recreation and study. He asked that I make certain to see and talk with all kinds and grades of men."[7]

But Roosevelt was also looking over the horizon:

> I know that in their homesickness and desire to get back to everything that is close and dear to them the country they picture in their minds is far better than the one that actually existed when they went away. We will have to do something about living up to that idealized conception.[8]

The President's detailed instructions were based on experience; FDR knew what Anna would encounter in a war zone. As a young man in the Navy Department, Franklin Roosevelt had visited the trenches of World War I on behalf of President Woodrow Wilson. As he told audiences in a 1936 speech, "I have seen blood running from the wounded. I have seen men coughing out their gassed lungs . . . I have seen children starving. I have seen the agony of mothers and wives."[9] Now, a generation later, the wheelchair-bound President was sending Anna Rosenberg on a similar mission. "He knew they were going through a strange and, for some of them, terrible experience . . . he felt deeply with the soldier and had a passionate desire to assist him."[10] With the defeat of Germany expected in 1944 or 1945, Roosevelt was "concerned by the need to reabsorb into civilian life the enormous numbers of servicemen." As Special Representative to the European Theater of Operations, Anna's task was "to recommend educational, vocational, and other programs to help servicemen find places in the civilian economy" upon their return.[11] What would these millions of men, who had grown up during the Great Depression and then been called to war, do when they disembarked in Boston, New York, Philadelphia?

The bureaucrats at the War Department were confounded by the request that a civilian woman be flown to the European Theater of Operations as a personal emissary of the President of the United States and be allowed to travel at will in a war zone. But plans were soon solidified.

"I envy you tremendously," the President admitted to Anna upon her

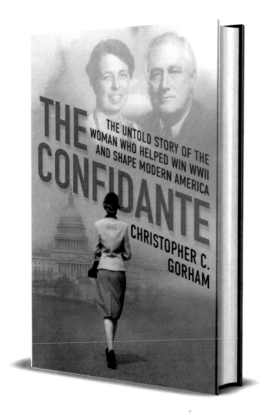

THE CONFIDANTE

THE UNTOLD STORY OF THE WOMAN WHO HELPED WIN WWII AND SHAPE MODERN AMERICA

CHRISTOPHER C. GORHAM

christophercgorham.com

departure. "You are doing something which above all things I would like to do myself."[12]

> General D. D. Eisenhower,   August 1, 1944
> Supreme Commander,
> Allied Expeditionary Force,
> European Theatre.
>
> Dear General:
>
> The President has asked Mrs. Anna Rosenberg to go to the European Theatre to get posted on soldier opinion with regard to demobilization and reentry into civilian life at the conclusion of the war. Mrs. Rosenberg . . . possesses rare ability on all phases of labor requirement and labor supply.
>
> She is a warm friend of mine and has been of extraordinary value in promoting war production here at home.
>
> I am sure that you will do everything possible to facilitate the achievement of her mission.
>
> [signed] Robert P. Patterson,
> Undersecretary of War[13]

The C-47 army transport carrying the President's representative touched down in London on Saturday, August 12, 1944, and Anna Rosenberg was whisked to meet General Eisenhower at Supreme Headquarters Allied Expeditionary Force (SHAEF).[14] Leafy Grosvenor Square provided a welcome respite from the heat wave that gripped London in the first few weeks of August. The fashionable area, so full of Yanks it was now called Little America, was also the home-away-from-home of the Supreme Allied Commander, who kept a suite at the nearby Dorchester hotel; its reinforced concrete was thought to be bombproof from Luftwaffe bombers.*

Dwight D. Eisenhower and Army Chief of Staff George Marshall had both been candidates for the Supreme Allied Command. At the end

---

* There he met Prime Minister Churchill; suite 104/05 is to this day known as the Eisenhower Suite.

of 1943, Eisenhower was promoted as it was thought that Marshall, who was overseeing the entire war, was too valuable and needed to remain in Washington. Anna had worked with General Marshall to solve personnel problems between industry and armed forces, and she knew the "Old Man" held Ike in the highest esteem.* Meeting General Eisenhower for the first time, Anna wore a Women's Army Corps uniform she had borrowed in Washington. Eisenhower was in dark olive officer's trousers, khaki shirt, and tie. The waist-length square-shouldered field jacket he was making famous as the "Eisenhower jacket" was nowhere to be seen on the hot afternoon. At fifty-three, Ike retained a good bit of the physique of the West Point athlete he had been three decades earlier. Wisps of sandy-gray hair crowned his oval face that was open and expressive. He lacked FDR's gift of easy chat, but he spoke freely and candidly, with many facial and hand gestures, in a voice that was somewhat higher than expected. As he had been asked to do by the War Department, Ike was a gracious and friendly host to Rosenberg in London, and, not surprisingly, the President's special emissary "soon charmed . . . Eisenhower and Walter Bedell Smith, Eisenhower's chief of staff."[15] Walter Smith, whom Anna called Beetle, was one of the two generals with whom she was to forge a particularly close bond while in Europe: the other was Omar Bradley, fondly known as "the G.I.'s General."

Anna's mission got under way when she visited the military hospitals in England, which reminded her of her work as a young nurse in New York a generation earlier. In late summer of 1944, London was besieged by a frightful new weapon: the V-2 rocket. The world's first ballistic missile, the "Vengeance Weapon," flew at supersonic speed and gave no audible warning to the civilians in its path. Even among the young, convalescing American soldiers nursing their own serious wounds, Anna sensed their palpable anger at the treacherous weapon that killed indiscriminately, and heard their promises to pay the Germans back. "In the blitzed villages of England, and when the buzz bombs came hard and fast at London, I heard American boys make that . . . vow."[16]

After the hospital visits and stops at Yank hangouts like the Red

---

*   Anna Rosenberg, oral history interview with Joe Frantz, 1973, during discussion of plants being "robbed" of skilled workers by the military.

Cross Club near Piccadilly Circus, Anna and her guide were ferried across the English Channel to the beaches where the deadliest fighting occurred on D-Day: Omaha and Utah. By mid-August, the bloody scenes of June 6 had been replaced by a massive supply operation to equip, clothe, and feed the four entire U.S. armies who were leading the liberation alongside Commonwealth and French troops. Shirtless, sunbaked soldiers of the "Com Z" units loaded crates onto an unceasing queue of canvas-topped trucks while minesweepers traversed the beaches.* Such large quantities of quartermaster items were landing ashore that civilians and prisoners of war were pressed into service alongside Army personnel. At long tables under the shade of huge tents, French schoolchildren wearing too-big U.S. Army shirts, jackets, and hats sorted socks into correct sizes. Among the hardest workers were Russian women whose families had been brought to Normandy by the Nazis as slave labor for roadbuilding and other heavy construction. The retreating Germans took the men but left the women behind. When the commanding officer of the depot expressed the fear that the work would be too heavy for them, they laughed, insisting that they be allowed to continue to help end the war. Their headscarves protecting them from the sun, they worked "diligently and uncomplainingly for long hours," salvaging a mountain of scrap tires to be turned into shoe soles and transforming a hill of torn shirts and raincoats into aprons, wiping rags, and typewriter covers. The spirit of the women so impressed Anna Rosenberg that she sent for an American journalist to observe the operations.[17]

From the beaches, the special mission took Anna on a path following the U.S. Army's axis of advance. The Second SS Panzer Division's stranglehold on the ancient Norman city of Saint-Lô, a strategic crossroads, had prevented the U.S. First Army under General Omar Bradley from accessing passable roads; without Saint-Lô, there would be no Paris, and without Paris, there would be no Berlin. Two weeks after General Bradley's men finally made their breakout, Anna witnessed the devastation wrought by the German occupiers. "No building was left standing," she reported that fall, "no streets, no roads, no houses." Surveying the rubble,

---

* Rear area known as Communications Zone, where communications and supply lines were established.

the American woman neatly attired in a military jacket, skirt, and cap was a welcome, motherly sight to three G.I.'s sitting "in the dust and dirt" of the city that came to be known as the "Capital of the Ruins."[18]

"You're from home. Thank God they can't do this to any town back there."[19]

From martyred Saint-Lô, Anna followed in the path the Allies were cutting in an easterly direction across northern France. Once in control of the road network and having broken through the crust of German defenses, the Allies trapped eighty thousand enemy soldiers in the "Falaise Gap." With Hitler forbidding a tactical retreat and U.S. Lieutenant General George S. Patton's U.S. Third Army racing to slam shut the enemy's escape hatch, Hitler's men were doomed.

As tank crews gave chase on the ground, German units that once had been the masters of Europe took flight in ones and twos into the maze of hedges. Overhead, Allied fighters and bombers had free rein; their twelve thousand sorties over the Falaise pocket destroyed eight infantry divisions and two panzer divisions.[20]

In the one hundred kilometers between Saint-Lô and Argentan, Anna was witness to the destruction of an entire German army. Over roads choked with burnt-out Wehrmacht equipment, Anna looked out at the smoking hulls of panzers, broken-down horse carts, and abandoned Citroëns sitting like giant tin snails. Mangled bicycles, ammunition boxes, and empty jerricans of petrol were strewn about the dusty roads, among broken and burned bodies.

The Falaise Gap was one of the most concentrated killing fields of the Second World War, and everywhere there was death. The bloated corpses of horses and cattle lay upside down, their limbs pointing skyward with rigor mortis, flies buzzing about the decaying flesh under the blazing August sun. German dead, including the smooth-faced child-soldiers of the Hitler Youth, lay in roadside ditches or splayed across the bonnets of their blackened jeeps and trucks, their bodies "swollen to elephantine grossness." What trees were left were "festooned [by] fragments of bodies."[21] A once-beautiful woman lay dead in the backseat of an abandoned Mercedes staff car.

Americans, too, lay among the dead, their equipment stripped by the desperate enemy. The smell of death was so pervasive that British

Spitfire and Typhoon pilots reported the stench reaching the cockpits of their aircraft. When General Eisenhower toured the Falaise area, he said the scene could only be described by Dante. "It was literally possible," reported the Supreme Allied Commander, "to walk for hundreds of yards at a time, stepping on nothing but dead and decaying flesh."[22]

Historians estimate that ten thousand Germans perished in the gap and fifty thousand were taken prisoner; perhaps twenty thousand escaped to the east to defend the gates of the Third Reich. The American units, many of them seeing their first combat, found it a merciless business. "When the Kraut quits, they'll quit—and not a minute before," observed one G.I. In a field hospital visit, Anna watched as a wounded American brought in a French child, "her body torn and shattered by a wood mine" left by the retreating Germans. "He cried, he cursed, he prayed," Anna said of the soldier. When a nurse took the child from his arms, he hissed: "I'll pay them back for this."[23]

That summer, Anna had even more reason to share the visceral feeling of hatred toward the Nazis when she learned that their evil reach had extended all the way to her circle of friends in New York. In June, Fiorello La Guardia's sister, the writer Gemma La Guardia Gluck, and her family were arrested by the Gestapo when the Nazis took control of Budapest. Held as a political prize on the orders of Adolf Eichmann and Heinrich Himmler, the family was deported to Mauthausen; then Gemma and her daughter-in-law were sent to the women's concentration camp at Ravensbrück near Berlin, with its "rabbit block" for diabolical medical experiments and gas chamber. Gemma La Guardia was held in a cell with a small window. "As I could sleep little," she wrote, "I watched the grim flaming smoke pouring out of the chimneys of the crematory."[24] Gemma survived, only to learn that her husband had been beaten to death by a drunk Nazi guard at Mauthausen.[25]

———•••———

Falaise was the final battle of Normandy. Free at last from the bocage, the Allies raced across the open plains toward the Seine River. On August 25, the French Second Armored Division and the U.S. Fourth Infantry Division liberated Paris. The City of Light was free for the first time since the terrible days of the débâcle in June 1940. To the soldiers, the deliriously happy Parisians "in their bright summer clothes" made "everything else in the world seem gray."[26] Women in dresses climbed up the turrets to kiss men with grimy faces, and children and dogs rode on the tanks, as young people bicycled alongside.

Anna and her guide arrived in liberated Paris shortly thereafter, where she was embedded with Lieutenant General John C. H. Lee and his Chief of Staff, General Everett Hughes. Lee had a monumental task: every day, each tank required more than one thousand gallons of fuel, and every division of twenty thousand soldiers needed thirty-five tons of rations and an even greater amount of ammunition. Nicknamed by his detractors "Jesus Christ Himself," General Lee was in charge of the hundreds of thousands of Com Z troops who maintained the vital communications and supply lines. A man of intense faith, he was the rare high-ranking officer who believed in racial equality; half of the nine hundred thousand Black servicemen then in Europe were under his command, and later in the war, when he ordered Black soldiers into combat alongside their white brothers to repel a German assault, his long military career was nearly ended.

After the hellish scenes in Falaise, Paris was heaven. Anna's brief stay at a "plush hotel" included a late night with General Lee, General Hughes, and one of Eisenhower's ordnance officers, who had three truckloads of cognac, some of which had made it into the hotel bar. General Lee showed Hughes a memo he had written to Eisenhower recommending that his supply troops wear regular field uniforms, including high boots and helmets. "I suggest you get the people to wear what they have—properly." Having seen the work at the supply depot at Omaha Beach done under the blazing sun, Anna told Hughes once Lee had departed well after midnight, "Lee can't be human." Before turning in for the night, Hughes, "tight on cognac," amused himself by coming up with an aphorism: "We want our wars wet but not wanton." He jotted it down in his notebook, and Anna's remark, too.[27]

With Paris in Allied hands, SHAEF moved to the Trianon Palace hotel in Versailles, a luxurious edifice at the edge of a vast woodland that had been the domain of Louis XIV. Two centuries after the Sun King, the grand hotel had housed delegates to the Versailles Treaty ending World War I, and later had been the playground of movie stars and playboys— Marlene Dietrich liked to relax there when working in nearby Paris. In

1940 the hotel became the headquarters of the Luftwaffe on the orders of Marshal Hermann Goering. Anna Rosenberg arrived at the hotel at the end of August, where she was met again by General Eisenhower and "Beetle" Smith. By that time, Anna had "impressed them with her ability, and dazzled them with her charm."[28]

From the comfort of the French capital, it was back to the foxholes and the reality of war in early September. By this time, Anna was traveling with Lieutenant General George S. Patton's Third Army, and she had traded the WAC uniform for Army trousers tucked into boots, a khaki shirt and tie, and a waist-length Eisenhower jacket. Her Sally Victor floral hats were a distant memory: as did everyone serving in the forward areas, she wore a helmet.[29] Since arriving in wartime France, she had followed in the path of the combat troops through "ankle-deep mud," across "mined beaches," down "shell-torn roads," and slept in "ruined villages."[30]

Upon sending her to Europe, the President had quietly instructed the Army to "see that Anna doesn't get hurt." This proved a major task to the officers assigned as her guides. "She wants to be where the fighting is thickest," Brigadier General Oscar Solbert reported. "She sleeps on the ground; she eats soldier food; refuses any comforts the men don't have."[31] The result, Eleanor Roosevelt later said, was Anna's "knowing more privates than anyone else."[32]

In her purse were her compact and lip rouge, a cigarette case, and a box of pencils; in her briefcase were notebooks in which she recorded her conversations with the servicemen. Her mission was to gather information on the present, as well as what the G.I. wanted to do following the world war. In the short term, whether it was Army chow, weapons, uniforms, or morale, Anna knew the Boss wanted to gather grassroots information, what his soldiers really thought. Like Eleanor Roosevelt on her dispatches, Anna knew to peek under the soup pot lid, to share the rations, to invite real talk, and to see behind the façade. As when he was Governor of New York, these field inspections informed FDR's presidential decision-making.

The President's emissary did not have the soldiers drawn up "to be reviewed by a V.I.P. stopping to ask a question here and there." As Anna saw her mission, "there was only one way to do this. That was to go to where the men were fighting, and this she proceeded to do, while the generals worried."[33] As they offered her a Chesterfield or a Lucky Strike—"Care for a smoke, Mrs. Rosenberg?"—they talked. There were the predictable complaints about the rations, too-small boots, and wet socks, but what Anna was learning about their dreams for the future surprised her. In the evenings, as the American Army traversed the Lorraine region of northern France that late summer and early fall, Anna looked at the pictures they pulled out of their helmets of their sweethearts, wives, and children, and she listened: "If I had a college education, I'd be a lieutenant now instead of a buck private."

Sharing C rations off the hood of a jeep, they told Anna about their hometowns and the characters that populated them; she heard: "What about the guys at home who kept the jobs? They'll be way ahead of me. I have no education."

Seeing the young men "as individuals, with names as well as the numbers on their dog tags, identities, with folks back home," she felt their yearning for home, their dreams for the future, and their fears.[34]

While the wisecracking, unshaven G.I.'s dreamed about the day they would take a seat in a college classroom, and the future beyond that, the immediate challenge was to survive. Their dreams rested on a sobering reality. "Over these men hangs the greatest question mark of all," explained Anna, "—*whether* they are coming home."[35] German snipers were everywhere, reported Ernie Pyle, "in trees, in buildings, in piles of wreckage, in the grass."[36] More fearsome still were the German Tiger tanks and deadly 88mm shells that had killed their comrades and untold numbers of civilians.

On August 30, the Third Army liberated Reims, the "capital of coronations" for French kings since the eleventh century. Just days after the Germans were driven out, Anna attended a ceremony in the sunlit Cathédrale Notre-Dame. In the elegant Gothic cathedral that had stood since 1211 and which still bore scars from the First World War, Anna watched an American unit receive bouquets of flowers from French orphans. "The [young soldier] standing beside me," she recalled," had "tears running down his cheeks." Holding his faded flowers, he turned to Anna: "They'll never make orphans out of the kids in Milwaukee."[37]

On September 4, Anna and her guide paid a visit to General Patton's command post at Châlons. Like Reims, the half-timbered city on the river Marne boasted a rich history. In June 451, Roman general Flavius Aetius fought Attila the Hun at the Battle of Châlons. Fortunately, the violence on the day of Anna's visit was much less serious. Patton had an English bull terrier named Willie, "a gregarious dog who had quite a way with women."[38] What occurred was recorded by General Patton in his diary: regarding Anna "in a very tight pair of slacks," Willie "was much outraged at her appearance." The general's dog "gently but firmly inserted his teeth into her leg. She took it in good part."[39] Equally at ease with generals and G.I.'s, to Patton's men Anna's presence was a welcome touch of home, but she also displayed a resilience the men respected. She waded through rivers in the dark, she warmed up in peasants' homes, and she ate K rations in the woods.[40] She was, in the words of the soldiers' weekly, "a 44-year-old blend of attractiveness and business who can be as appealing as a deb and as tough as a teamster."[41]

To the fighting men huddling in foxholes, she was the tangible link to their Commander in Chief. The soldiers, Anna recalled, would ask her to relay messages to President Roosevelt. "'Tell him for me . . . Tell him I said. . . .'—this with all the respect and affection in the world."[42] The connection between the men and the President was "one of the highlights of that trip," Anna explained. Two of Patton's soldiers told Anna they prepared FDR's meals when he had been at the Casablanca conference in 1943. "Would [you] be sure to tell the President how proud we were and how we will never forget it?"[43]

For the rest of September, Anna traveled with Patton's Third Army along "Liberty Road," as they fought for and freed village, town, and city. Valmy fell to the Americans, then Nancy, then the citadel of Verdun, to which millions of French infantry had marched along the Voie Sacrée toward the sound of guns and scenes of hell during the Great War. They were on the move, breaking down their tents so often that a couple of jokers said they'd "rather be with Ringling Brothers."[44] When they snatched a moment of R & R, Anna watched the young men scratch out short letters home, using ammunition boxes for writing boards.

The Army and its inspiring general with his pearl-handled revolver on his hip were closing in on Metz—a city whose steep granite hills had made it a pawn in the centuries-long Franco-German chess match.

From there lay the Siegfried Line and the frontier of Nazi Germany. On the approach to Metz, Patton became a victim of his own success. The general, whose credo was "We shall attack and attack until we are exhausted, and then we shall attack again," had raced across France for four hundred miles at such speed that he ran out of fuel.[45] The pause allowed the Germans to send reinforcements along with orders to fight to the last man. By the time the Third Army reached the city, it was a fortress. It was at the Battle of Metz that the Germans gave Patton his "first bloody nose." It was also Anna Rosenberg's closest call of the war. On their way to Patton's forward command post, she and her guide were so close to enemy territory that they were pinned down by German fire.*

———•••———

With the Third Army halted, Anna returned to England for another round of hospital visits to add to her study. From there, it was back home to the United States—six dozen filled-in notebooks in her luggage.[46] For six weeks, she had lived in a tent, eaten G.I. rations, and seen what the combat troops had seen. The generals prosecuting the war she now counted as friends: Eisenhower, "Beetle" Smith, Walton H. Walker, and "Georgie" Patton. But it was the ordinary G.I. who was at the heart of her mission. The American soldier in combat, she told an audience upon her return, "lived in foxholes, under fire, was wounded and returned to the front, [survived] on rations, crawled in the mud, had death constantly at his side, lost friends he loved, leaders he respected, saw cruelty, brutality, all the grim and dirty things that make war."[47]

---

* "Risky Promise," *Time*, November 5, 1951. Metz was also the city where Field Marshal Günther von Kluge, relieved of command during the Falaise battle and ordered to return to Berlin (and suspected by Hitler of being an accomplice in the July assassination plot), killed himself.

CHAPTER FIFTEEN

WHEN JOHNNY COMES HOME

You can't hide from death when you're in a war.

—War correspondent Ernie Pyle

*What was it that took a young combat veteran who was a
high school dropout and allowed him to serve in the House
of Representatives, even rising to become chairman of the
most powerful committee in the Congress? And the answer is
abundantly clear—the G.I. Bill.*

—Congressman Charles Rangel,
who first went to Korea in a segregated unit

What Anna Rosenberg discovered on the battlefields of France
also guided one of the most farsighted national policies in
modern American history: the G.I. Bill.

In June, before sending her on the wartime mission, President Roosevelt signed the Servicemen's Readjustment Act of 1944. FDR and most lawmakers agreed in principle that the nation must be prepared to reabsorb returning veterans and to avoid the embarrassment that followed World War I. After that war, returning soldiers were given a measly sixty dollars and a train ticket home.

In World War II, lawmakers on both sides of the aisle agreed on the need for a much more comprehensive response. As the Army fought through Nazi-occupied Western Europe and the Navy and Marines pressed the Japanese in the Pacific, policy makers at home wrestled with preparations for the return of the 12 million veterans who would be reentering an economy that had done without them for four years. The generation that Roosevelt predicted had a "rendezvous with destiny" had been adolescents and teenagers in the Great Depression; by and large they had never seen the inside of a college classroom nor held the keys of home ownership. There was much speculation. Would the Depression return at the cessation of the war and its massive production? Would veterans be better served by vocational training or an academic education? There was little consensus among the stakeholders in industry, labor, the federal government, the American Legion, or college professors. One Republican Congressman decried the "crafty effort of so many different groups to use the war for the reorganization of the world."[1] Lawmakers balked at the twenty-dollar weekly allowance for vets while they sought employment, claiming it would sap their will to look for a job. The *New Republic* opined that just a fraction of eligible veterans would make use of the readjustment bill, whatever its provisions.[2]

The education provisions were especially fraught. Professors testified that G.I. Joe could not compete with Joe College. Harvard President James Conant complained that campuses would be "flooded" by "the least capable among the new generation."[3] If college tuition was offered, should it be reserved for "persons of exceptional ability or skill" or to all veterans?[4] The threat that state and local control over education was to be taken over by the federal government led Mississippi Congressman John Rankin, a notorious bigot and red-baiter, to declare, "I'd rather send my child to a red schoolhouse than a red school teacher."[5] As a result, the education provisions of the initial bill were watered down; in some cases, even to "discourage veterans from flocking to colleges and universities."[6]

Since 1943, President Roosevelt had promised a benefits package to veterans, but, as historian Glenn C. Altschuler points out, FDR did not play a significant role in the contours of the bill. The bill he signed in June 1944 had begun on "hotel stationery"; it was a "temporary expedient" that had been "cobbled together."[7] But politically, it made sense. The President "claimed paternity for a measure his administration had neither introduced nor steered through Congress." It is also clear that Roosevelt shared with nearly everyone the idea that "satisfactory employment," not educational opportunity, was the key feature of the law.

The direction of the G.I. Bill changed the day after Anna Rosenberg returned to the United States from her wartime mission. Due to a storm, her flight to New York was diverted to Washington. Once on the ground she called the President, and he asked to see her the following morning to report on her findings. "I told him when I returned. They want a chance to better themselves, to go to school."

"These men all talk of wanting some education," she reported to the President. "Men who never thought of a college education were saying to me 'I could have been a lieutenant now if I'd gone to college.'"[8] After she recounted the soldiers' deep anxieties over education once they returned to civilian life, Roosevelt "lit up." "Yes, that's what we have to do," he said. "We've got to see that they get education when they come back. Sit down with [budget director Harold Smith] and Sam Rosenman, his counsel, and come up with something." Just days after her meeting with President Roosevelt, Anna was the only woman on a panel discussing the returning veteran. "He wants to get an education," she explained, "to be a doctor, a dentist, or a chemist, or an engineer. He wants to stake a claim in the America for which he was ready to give his life."[9]

Recalling the evolution of the G.I. Bill for Diane Sawyer in a televised 1982 interview, Anna explained that FDR "had an informal way of doing things. He didn't have a long study of it; he understood the feeling of the men immediately and he acted on it. That's how he was." President Roosevelt would not live to see it, but the 1945 amendments, nearly all of which related to education and training, transformed the G.I. Bill into an "opportunity bill." Flawed due to its lack of inclusiveness for Black veterans—something Anna would fight for after the war—the G.I. Bill is "without question, one of the largest and most comprehensive initiatives ever enacted in the United States."[10]

Upon her return from the battle zone Anna stayed in her apartment for four consecutive days, making more than four hundred long-distance phone calls at her own expense to deliver messages to the families of the men she met on the battlefield.[11] "Hello, Mrs. Brown, I have a message from your Charley. He sends you his love, and says to pet Rover for him. I saw him in Europe a week ago, and Mrs. Brown, he looks wonderful; he's gained seven pounds." In her notebooks, Anna had jotted down "small intimate details about each soldier, something important to a wife or mother."[12] The soldier who kept a photo of his wife in his hat; the one who yearned to know if his baby was a boy or a girl; the one who was growing a moustache.[13] If her speeches and interviews from these weeks are any indication, she also passed along to the mothers and fathers "the gratitude of this nation" to these "magnificent" young American soldiers. "The good nature, the selfless spirit" they displayed was reflected in "the faces of the liberated people of France." These parents' sons would return home with "new skills, greatly matured, and capable of far greater and better jobs."[14] Besides the phone calls, Anna wrote a "hair-curling letter" to one soldier whose mother complained he was not writing home. Thereafter, the G.I. wrote home regularly and sent carbon copies to Mrs. Rosenberg.[15]

───── ••• ─────

Franklin Delano Roosevelt had commenced his remarkable string of election victories in November 1928, and now, sixteen years later, he stood to be the only American President to be elected to a fourth term. But the domestic and international upheaval through which he had navigated his nation had taken its toll. FDR was visibly ill. By this last election, Roosevelt "was being treated for hypertension and congestive heart disease, exacerbated by 40 years of smoking. His color was poor; he looked gaunt, haggard, and much older than his 62 years."[16] Prior to the 1944 presidential election, there was a call among Democratic Party elite that Vice President Henry Wallace should be replaced in case FDR died in office. Although Wallace was popular with rank-and-file Democrats, he held a smattering of odd beliefs and uncommon habits. His fad diets—including one of milk and popcorn—and his fascination with a Russian mystic made him an easy target for Republicans.[17] To replace him, the leading contenders were Jimmy Byrnes, whose wartime work as the Home Front Czar earned him the nickname "the assistant president," and Missouri Senator Harry S. Truman. In high-level discussions with Ed Flynn and others, Byrnes' opposition to a federal anti-lynching bill and his criticism of Walter White, head of the NAACP, were seen as deal breakers. The list was narrowed to one.

Roosevelt turned to Anna Rosenberg to deliver the bad news to Byrnes. Anna told historian David McCullough that she told FDR "she couldn't do that. If the President wanted Byrnes to know he had no chance, then the President would have to tell him himself." But as she knew, Roosevelt wouldn't do it. In his memoir, *All in One Lifetime*, Byrnes recounts that on July 6, 1944, Anna Rosenberg, "FDR's confidante," came to see him. Rosenberg told Byrnes that there were objections to his nomination because Blacks in New York would vote against the ticket.[18] For Byrnes, a loyal FDR supporter, the news must have been devastating. Despite her being the courier of this bad news, Byrnes maintained his affection and respect for Rosenberg; he would later come to her defense.

The other change in the Roosevelt administration involved Anna herself. Of the cabinet reshuffle, "the most persistent rumor" was that "Mrs. Anna Rosenberg would succeed Miss Frances Perkins" as Secretary of Labor.[19] That the two women engaged in the palace drama were so contrasting provided a feast for the press. *Time* magazine alliteratively speculated that "[t]rim, smart Anna Rosenberg" might replace "Perkins' unfashionable hats with modish millinery from Manhattan." The anti-Roosevelt *Chicago Tribune* made the same prediction. The President also received correspondence from the public urging him to make the appointment. Perkins had never been popular with the press during her twelve years heading the Department of Labor. Anna, meanwhile, had been shortlisted as a speaker for that summer's Democratic National Convention, she was viewed as FDR's chief labor adviser, and her national reputation was trending upward. Perhaps realizing that she faced the same fate as Jimmy Byrnes, Secretary Perkins had packed up her office, had the carpet cleaned, and reupholstered the furniture and was on the verge of leaving Washington for Maine when President Roosevelt asked her to stay on.[20]

Anna Rosenberg had declined the position.

Some historians speculate that Roosevelt did not actually offer her the cabinet position, or that Anna lobbied for it in vain.[21] Others hypothesize that she was too chastened by the 1942 congressional investigation to accept it, or that because she had transitioned to defense-related government work, she was unwilling to return to labor matters.

This conjecture ignores the reality of her situation by late 1944. According to her longtime friend Senator William Benton, after years of living on a government salary while keeping two homes and commuting weekly, Anna was "busted. . . . She had no capital and she had no office space."[22] Anna herself had explained in late 1943, "I haven't an ambition in the world to hold public office . . . when the war is over I'm going back to private practice and make some money."[23] The imperative to right her finances was also due in part to the fact that her son, Thomas, was to join her at the firm after the war. She needed to *have* a business for them to go back to.

After two years of forgoing her private earnings, by 1944 Anna was borrowing against her life insurance to pay taxes on income she was no longer getting.[24] She was too proud to say so, but when friends discovered she was struggling they were eager to help. Bernard Baruch made her a loan, and Senator Benton and Nelson Rockefeller agreed to each loan her $12,000 for future public-relations work, and Benton provided office space. Years later, Benton recalled his conversation with Nelson Rockefeller, whose long public career included the vice presidency in the 1970s. When Benton approached him to loan Anna the money, he said, "Bill, I want to tell you right now that everything I've amounted to here in Washington, everything I feel I've achieved here in Washington, I owe to Anna Rosenberg."[25]

What must have been the most difficult for Anna was saying no to the Boss. According to Senator Benton, "Roosevelt had offered her [the] cabinet position. He had offered her the ambassadorship to Moscow. She had a chance to run for [NYC] Mayor and U.S. Senator. She turned these things down." The question remains: How could Anna Rosenberg decline an offer from the man she venerated more than any other besides her own father? Anna knew that as a woman with her background in a cabinet post, she would risk the kind of abuse hurled against Frances Perkins, "the most thoroughly damned and abused public official."[26] By pressing Rosenberg into service as his "chief labor coordinator" and "domestic labor *majordomo*," the President had effectively sidelined Secretary Perkins. In the words of one scholar, "one must note that Rosenberg by 1942 seemed closer to the President than his Secretary of Labor."[27] Indeed, during the war, Washington insiders called Anna the "de facto Secretary of Labor." In a sense, Anna Rosenberg had already held the job, and, because she did so behind the scenes, she had worked out of range of her enemies. As Anna liked to say, "I'm not dumb, dollink."

Moreover, there was the fact that President Roosevelt was in his last term in office and he was in ill health, as Anna saw up close. She told John Gunther the doctors "never told R or Mrs. R how ill," but when she realized how badly off he was during his speech at the Puget Sound Naval Shipyard, she "raised hell." Her alarm was ignored: "no one thought he was mortal."[28] A future without FDR as her political champion would be a very different future. Anna said many times how difficult it was to say no to public service when asked. But with the end of the war and the end of the Roosevelt presidency in sight, this was one of the rare times Anna could decline.

Of the four hundred families Anna Rosenberg telephoned after returning from the battlefields of France, we can only speculate how many received a tragic telegram from the War Department that Christmas. On December 16, 1944, Hitler launched his last counteroffensive, through the dense Ardennes Forest of Belgium. The desperate gamble to break through the broad Allied front appeared to pay off, as panzer divisions overran thinly held American positions, creating a bulge in the Allied line. Low on fuel, needing to move at speed, and outraged that their Reich had been breached, German tanks ran over U.S. trenches, then twisted back over them to bury the men alive.[29] At Malmédy, after eighty-four Americans surrendered to a Waffen-SS unit after a brief battle, they were taken to a field and machine-gunned from a tank turret. American command urgently issued a warning to all soldiers:

> It is dangerous to at any time surrender to German tank crews, and especially so to tanks unaccompanied by infantry; or to surrender to any units making a rapid advance. These units have few means for handling prisoners, and a solution used is merely to kill the prisoners.[30]

In response, American troops granted the enemy no quarter. "Across a fifty-yard gap in the woods a white flag appeared," a soldier recounted, "a sergeant stood up and motioned the Germans to advance. About twenty men emerged out of the woods. After they had advanced closer to the line, the sergeant gave the command to open fire. No prisoners were taken."[31] The soldiers of the First U.S. Army bore the brunt of the Germans' winter offensive, code-named Watch on the Rhine, and those of the Third Army, who wheeled north from Metz, rescued many of their comrades, including the encircled 101st Airborne at Bastogne. Six weeks after it began, the Allied line was straightened, but at great cost.

The Battle of the Bulge was the deadliest of the war; of the 440,000 U.S. soldiers and sailors who perished in World War II, nearly one in ten died in the bitter six-week-long battle across an eighty-five-mile-wide stretch of shattered forest.

And the interior of the Third Reich lay ahead.

From the men who lived through the Bulge, as with those in all theaters of war, Ernie Pyle had a message to the American people: "Thousands of our men will soon be returning to you. They have been gone a long time and they have seen and done and felt things you cannot know. They will be changed. They will have to learn how to adjust themselves to peace." Pyle had seen the bitter aftermath of combat, as had Anna, who also gave voice to the Jacks, Bills, Franks, and Johnnies. The men still fighting overseas—"your son and mine"—questioned whether a "rushing, busy America [would] take the time to understand . . . what he has lived through?" She shared their anxiety that "normal, fun-loving" Americans, with "visions of tomorrow's profits," would rush headlong into peacetime and force him "to bury deep within himself the wounds he received, the horrors he saw."[32] Anna cautioned civilian audiences against this war-weariness. Was it only the soldiers "who lived with death" who must readjust for the postwar future? "Readjust himself?" she asked, "Or should *we readjust ourselves*? He has traveled a long, hard road. Can't we meet him halfway?"

To an audience in New York City on October 10, 1944, Anna recalled the pride she felt alongside America's soldiers, and her fervent hope for the postwar era:

> In the ports of England, on the beaches of Normandy, on the roads of Brittany, I have seen the might and strength and wealth of America. On battlefields, in hospitals, in lonely apple orchards, I have seen . . . the true brotherhood . . . learned in war's filth and blood.
>
> So I have come back with one prayer in my heart . . . that this same wealth and unity will be used in the same full measure for Johnny—when Johnny comes home from the wars.[33]

CHAPTER SIXTEEN

CASUALTIES OF WAR

*Beware the toils of war . . . the mesh of the huge dragnet
sweeping up the world.*

—Homer, *Iliad*

---

*I want you to know how I appreciate all you did. It was
unselfish work, much of it behind the scenes and without
recognition, but I know what it means and I know you did it
because of your belief in what was needed in this country.*

—Eleanor Roosevelt to Anna Rosenberg[1]

As he did every Saturday, ten-year-old Bobby Kaprielian of Water-town, Massachusetts, just outside Boston, took the Mount Auburn Street trolley to the Coolidge Theatre. Bobby took a seat. Before *Son of Lassie*, or *Tarzan and the Amazons*, or the latest Boris Karloff thriller, there was always a newsreel of the latest events in the world war. A triumphant trumpet heralded the latest wartime news as a stentorian voice-over described far-flung events. Since last fall, Bobby had seen a London double-decker in the crater of a buzz bomb, Russian tanks slicing ever deeper into Germany, and Kamikaze pilots circling a Navy destroyer. On this day, after the lights dimmed, Bobby was disappointed. Instead of battle scenes, the newsreel was of a diplomatic meeting in a place he'd never heard of: "Here on the Black Sea, near the city of Yalta on the Crimea, is the meeting place of the leaders of Britain, Russia, and the United States." The "Big Three" appeared one at a time: Marshal Stalin appeared in his tunic and bushy moustache, Churchill climbed down from the transport plane in a double-breasted camel coat, puffing a cigar . . . and—

There was an audible gasp in the theater as the audience saw their President.

In his beat-up gray fedora and Navy cape thrown over his shoulders, the gaunt Roosevelt was hardly recognizable.

"FDR looked terrible," Kaprielian remembers; "his cheeks were sunken, his eyes had dark circles underneath. He had been a big man, a large man, strong upper body, but he looked older, thinner, tired. I'll never forget the reaction in that theatre."[2]

What was revealed in movie houses across the nation in early February 1945 had been known to White House insiders for some time: the President was gravely ill. In offices with the doors closed, hushed conversations were held on FDR's decline. "He was not up to his onetime physical condition," remembered one staffer; "he was obviously very tired. . . . We were concerned about his health."[3] The President's secretary Bill Hassett, who traveled with FDR on the special presidential train to Hyde Park and Warm Springs, told a colleague, "He is slipping away from us and no earthly power can keep him here."[4] That the end was near was clear to columnist Walter Lippmann. "His estimate of the vital interests of the United States has been accurate and far-sighted," Lippmann wrote. "He has served these interests with audacity and patience, shrewdly and with calculation, and he has led this country out of the greatest peril in which it has ever been to the highest point of security, influence, and respect which it has ever attained."[5]

Days before departing for the Yalta conference, FDR celebrated his sixty-third birthday. His fourth inauguration meal had been modest: chicken salad, butterless rolls, and a simple cake, but before his long journey the First Family spent all its ration points and splurged on a rib roast for "Father."[6] The six-thousand-mile trek to meet Stalin and Churchill was the very opposite of the convalescence FDR needed. Anna saw the President just before he departed for Yalta. She was "horrified at the way he had deteriorated precipitously."[7] He complained to her that he couldn't sleep—something he had not previously complained to her about.[8] The war had taken its toll. "Most presidents are just nominally Commander-in-Chief," she later explained. "He really was Commander-in-Chief. He knew what was happening. He was involved in everything. Late at night he would call up to find out what the casualties were. He suffered it with them. He lived it with them."[9]

After ten days at sea the heavy cruiser *Quincy* that carried Roosevelt across the Atlantic Ocean docked at Malta; from there FDR was helped onto the *Sacred Cow*, the Douglas Skymaster that was the precursor to Air Force One, for the fourteen-hundred-mile flight to the Crimean Peninsula, escorted by six P-38 fighters. After the *Sacred Cow* landed at Saki, a Soviet car and driver took the American President "over the ravaged, snow-blanketed countryside, dotted with ruined buildings, and abandoned Nazi tanks. . . . Red Army men—and women—guarded the entire route with submachine guns nestled in their arms."[10]

At last they reached the Black Sea resort; after a long sleep in the Czar's bedroom at the Livadia Palace, an imperial summer home and former headquarters for the local Wehrmacht, Roosevelt, wearing his Navy cape now at all times, commenced his meetings with Soviet Premier Joseph Stalin and British Prime Minister Winston Churchill.[11] At issue was the fate of postwar Germany, the war in the Pacific, and the political future of Poland. On the latter subject, Stalin agreed to allow political freedom in Polish elections—one of many promises he never intended to keep. But Franklin Roosevelt was hardly in a condition to challenge the Soviet dictator. FDR's hands now shook alarmingly, and his inability to sleep at night left him depleted. "The last meeting [at Yalta], when he was very sick," Anna Rosenberg recalled, "Roosevelt would doze off; Stalin would stop talking until Roosevelt came to."[12]

Anna saw the President on the day he returned to Washington, after the odyssey of 13,842 miles. General "Pa" Watson had died on the journey, and Harry Hopkins was consigned to bed, "living principally on coffee, cigarettes, and paregoric" and too ill to make the ocean crossing home.[13] The death of Pa Watson came as a shock to the President, who relied on his aid intimately; according to Anna, "it showed him he was mortal."[14] FDR's weight continued to drop, but he "shrugged off his doctors' advice, skipped rest periods, and labored long into the night."[15] Much of this effort related to the ongoing war. "As President and Commander-in-Chief, he had definite responsibilities," explained Anna:

> But his devotion to the servicemen went far beyond that.
> It was a personal identification with them. I cannot imagine that any other President, functioning under the awful
> pressure to which Franklin Roosevelt was subjected,

would have found time to concern himself so intimately
with the service.

Just after noon on Saturday, March 24, 1945, Anna Rosenberg's
driver took her from the Shoreham Hotel to the White House, for
lunch with the President. As they looked from the sun parlor on the
third floor of the Executive Mansion, the few clouds on an unseasonably warm day gave way to full sun. The sunshine could not mask
the reality that the President was seriously ill. To Anna, he appeared
to have lost two inches of height.[16] Two days after his last lunch with
Anna, the group of Navy doctors who examined the President "dis-
tinctly did not like what they saw."[17]

Sick as he was, the work of winning the war and planning for the
peace continued: President Roosevelt wanted Anna to return to Europe
on a second wartime mission. As she described it, this second trip was
"to check up on the data and information I had gathered and see what
changes were necessary to bring them up to date . . . he felt that peace
was near and that the G.I. would have new anxieties and fears." Both
General Eisenhower and the President wanted her to return to work
on the demobilization process.[18] In addition to a "broad program of
education"—the G.I. Bill—"[FDR] sensed there would be a new mental and spiritual attitude which would require deep understanding and
guidance."[19]

"You know," President Roosevelt told Anna, "the reason I am especially anxious to find out about these things is that in the last few years,
instead of helping them build their personal futures, we have asked them
to concentrate on building the world's future. Now I want to do everything I can to help them build for themselves again."[20]

As the lunch came to an end, Eleanor came to fetch her husband.
They were departing for Hyde Park, and from there FDR was to go to
Warm Springs, Georgia, for much-needed rest before continuing across
the country to San Francisco for a conference inaugurating the United
Nations. President Roosevelt told Anna that before heading to San Fran-
cisco he would return to Washington to provide further instructions
on her trip. As he was being wheeled to the door, an aide handed the
Commander in Chief a decoded cable from his ambassador in Moscow,
Averell Harriman. Accusing the United States of working behind their

backs, the Soviets demanded an immediate end to talks then occurring between American negotiators and German officers for the surrender of Wehrmacht units in northern Italy.

FDR blew up, Anna recalled. Slamming his hands on the arm of his wheelchair, he boomed, "Averell is right! We can't do business with Stalin. He has broken every one of the promises he made at Yalta."[21] Anna later relayed the moment to historian John Toland. "As he banged the chair," she told Toland, FDR kept repeating: 'We can't do business with Stalin!'" The luncheon outburst witnessed by Anna was followed in subsequent days by a series of angry and accusatory letters between the American President and the Soviet Premier.

Roosevelt's eruption at the duplicity of the Russians presaged what would become the Cold War, but the lunch meeting was momentous for Anna as well. She was going back to wartime Europe as FDR's special envoy at a time when the world war was entering its final act. Days after U.S. newspapers carried the instantly iconic image of six Marines hoisting the American flag atop Japan's Mount Suribachi after a bitter battle, a miraculously intact bridge captured by a small but quick-thinking American force allowed Second Lieutenant Karl Timmerman of Omaha, Nebraska, to become the first officer of an invading army to cross the Rhine River since the age of Napoleon. The entire First U.S. Army followed him into Nazi Germany. Victory in Europe and the Pacific was at hand. The nation's attention would soon turn to its millions of servicemen and -women returning to civilian life, an undertaking at the forefront of the President's thoughts.

Franklin Delano Roosevelt made it as far as Warm Springs, to the simple six-room cottage not far from where he had rebuilt himself psychologically after contracting polio. It was here, thirty years before, where joyous calls of "Rosie"—the stricken children's nickname for him—offered audible proof of his deep empathy and inextinguishable buoyancy. Elected to the office of President four consecutive times, FDR had led the nation through depression and global war, and now he dreamed of a global peace and an America that would be "far better than the one that actually existed when [the soldiers] went away."[22]

On the afternoon of Thursday, April 12, 1945, Franklin Roosevelt sat in an armchair near the fireplace, reading the day's mail while having his portrait painted. He wore a suit and his Harvard necktie, with his Navy cape over his shoulders. Suddenly he put his hand to his head and complained of a "a terrific pain," before losing consciousness.

Two hours later, at 3:45 PM, the president was dead of a massive cerebral hemorrhage.

◆◆◆

In Washington, it was a beautiful spring day. Anna Rosenberg was chatting with White House aide Jonathan Daniels in his office—"the April outside my windows matched the hats she wore," Daniels recalled—when White House Press Secretary Steve Early came to the door. Anna got up to leave. "Sit down," Early said gently; "he is dead."[23] Early summoned Mrs. Roosevelt, who was having tea at the Sulgrave Club in Washington, back to the White House. Early, "Mac" McIntire, Jonathan Daniels, and Anna Rosenberg were there when Eleanor Roosevelt arrived. Her first words were: "I am more sorry for the people of the country and the world than I am for us."[24]

At 5:25 PM the Vice President arrived at the White House. Ushers immediately escorted Harry S. Truman upstairs to Mrs. Roosevelt's private residence. Putting her hand on his shoulder, Eleanor said, "Harry, the President is dead."

After a second's pause to take in the news, Truman said, "Is there anything I can do for you?"

"Is there anything *we* can do for *you*?" she replied. "For you are the one in trouble now."[25]

At 5:47 PM, Eastern War Time, Americans heard the awful seven letters "FDR dead."[26] In the soft light of that April afternoon, a "cloudburst of grief . . . descended on the country and the world."[27] In Okinawa, officers and men of the amphibious fleet were at breakfast when they heard the broadcast. In an Omaha pool hall, men racked up their cues without finishing their games and without a word walked out. In a Manhattan taxicab, the fare told the driver, who pulled over to the curb, bowed his head, and wept. A woman in Detroit expressed the personal shock of millions of Americans when she said, "It doesn't seem possible. It seems to me he will be back on the radio tomorrow, reassuring us that it was just a mistake."[28] In London the hour was midnight; the British Broadcasting Company's bulletin called it "the darkest night of the war."[29]

The next morning, Friday, Anna Rosenberg returned to the White House. The men "still looked shell-shocked . . . I could hardly see, I was crying so."[30] She carried a condolence letter to Mrs. Roosevelt from her nephew, a Navy ensign. "My generation, especially, owes an imperishable debt to [FDR's] memory," wrote the young sailor, "for rescuing it from fear and lack of purpose. . . . This debt we shall strive to repay by building that kind of world for which he lived and that kind of America for which he died."[31]

On Saturday mourners crammed into the Memorial Church in Cambridge, Massachusetts, for a service led by Willard Sperry, Dean of the Harvard Divinity School. "He died too soon," said the Dean, noting the tragic timing. "He had earned the right to see victory on land and sea and in the air. . . . He will live in the memory of generations to come as one with whom his own time had dealt, if not unfairly, at least austerely. He is a casualty of these costly years of war."[32]

To young Americans, from ten-year-old Bobby Kaprielian to Anna's nephew, Navy ensign John von Arnold, FDR's legacy was already forming. An editorial in the *Harvard Alumni Bulletin* described FDR through the eyes of the young: "He was a symbol, a cause, a reason, and an anvil of strength to youth. He was the only President this fighting generation had ever consciously known. It knew him well."

After assuming the presidency, Truman reiterated that Anna's mission was to go ahead as planned. "I hope you will carry out the mission entrusted to you by [FDR], and upon your return report to me."[33] In the Europe to which Anna Rosenberg was returning, events heralding the collapsing Nazi state were occurring rapidly. Several days after the U.S. Army breached the Rhine River, the Sixty-Ninth Infantry Division engaged in an all-night battle against a unit of fanatical Waffen-SS for Germany's fifth-largest city, Leipzig. A week after that, a small detachment from the U.S. Sixty-Ninth Infantry Division came under fire in the German town of Torgau, south of Berlin. An escaped POW told the Americans that it was Russians, not Germans, firing from the far side of the Elbe River. Lieutenant Bill Robertson and the three men of his patrol ducked into a destroyed apothecary. There they found red and blue powders, mixed them with water, and made a makeshift

American flag on a bedsheet. Lieutenant Robertson climbed a tower on their side of the bridge and began waving the flag from a window and shouting, "Cease fire; *Amerikanski*!" Moments later, he was crawling across a mangled bridge girder toward the Russian uniforms approaching from the other side. Just after four o'clock, the young American officer neared his Red Army counterpart and extended his hand. "Put it there," he said.[34]

Both American and Russian armies were making discoveries of a different, terrible sort that spring. Near the German town of Ohrdruf, the men of XX Corps under the command of Major General Walton H. Walker had followed "the stink of death" and came upon the first of several concentration camps. Walker immediately summoned medics, ambulances, Signal Corps cameramen, and even Supreme Allied Commander General Dwight D. Eisenhower. On April 12, Generals Eisenhower, Bradley, and Patton arrived via military aircraft to see for themselves the bodies "sprawled in the streets" and "covered with lice"; three thousand "naked, bony corpses lay in shallow graves." Emaciated prisoners shuffled among piles of bodies, some covered with lime and others partially incinerated on pyres. Eisenhower was aghast. "This is beyond the American mind to comprehend."[35] Bradley had no words, while General Patton walked off and vomited.

Back at Third Army headquarters, the long and terrible day for the three generals ended by learning that their Commander in Chief was dead.

Eisenhower seethed with anger at the German atrocities. He ordered all units not on the front line to tour Ohrdruf. Soon well-clothed and well-fed German civilians were digging graves and carrying corpses under the watchful eyes of armed American soldiers. It was imperative that the world know what had taken place. Ike cabled General George C. Marshall, trying to described what he witnessed:

> The things I saw beggar description. . . . The visual evidence and the verbal testimony of starvation, cruelty and bestiality were so overpowering as to leave me a bit sick . . . I made the visit deliberately, in order to be in a position to give first-hand evidence of these things if ever,

in the future, there develops a tendency to charge these
allegations merely to "propaganda."

The Supreme Allied Commander then dispatched a message to
Washington and London to quickly send prominent lawmakers, journalists, and editors, to come see the camps so that they could convey
the horrible truth about Nazi atrocities to the American public.

"I can state unequivocally," read the cable, "that all written statements up to now do not paint the full horrors."[36]

Within days, congressmen and journalists began arriving to bear
witness. General Eisenhower had told Anna Rosenberg of the camps,
and within a fortnight she arrived at Nordhausen—one of the first
Allied civilian women to see the horrors. Dora-Nordhausen was "a hell
factory worked by the living dead."[37] Prisoners at Dora carved man-
made caves, a "vast underground factory," in the Harz Mountains to
hide the assembly of the V-2 bombs.* They slaved in the cold, damp
tunnels until they died or were too weak, at which point they were sent
to Nordhausen, where "prisoners festered with little food and reduced,
but difficult, labor details."[38]

Of the four thousand souls at Nordhausen, "only a few could stand
on rickety, pipe-stem legs. Their eyes were sunk deeply into their skulls
and their skins under thick dirt were a ghastly yellow." Upon liberation, "some sobbed great dry sobs to see the Americans . . . others
merely wailed pitifully."[39] It was at this camp that Anna Rosenberg
arrived days after its liberation. She was dressed as she had been on the
previous mission in Army trousers, an Eisenhower jacket, and a khaki
cap and carrying a man's briefcase and her purse. Climbing out of the
jeep with her aide, she noticed two freshly dug trenches. The smell of
death lingered in the air.

---

* *North Africa Stars and Stripes,* on April 27, 1945, reported that "at
Nordhausen the Yanks found a V bomb factory where during the last 19
months over 20,000 foreign workers died of exhaustion and hunger. Most of
these were Poles. They were employed in making a vast underground factory
for the V bombs. Only a few were left of the 25,000 normally working in
the vast underground factories. These were so weak from starvation and
exhaustion that they could barely croak their names and reporters found it
impossible to interview them."

"I saw the survivors. Few could stand erect." A few women slowly approached her. Their emaciated bodies were covered in ragged striped uniforms. Seeing these half-dead, dazed figures stripped of everything compelled Anna to offer the women something, anything. "I groped in my purse for something and found I had a few lipsticks. I hesitated. How could I give lipsticks to people who were starving? Yet I had nothing else."

She was ashamed, she admitted, yet she offered the little metal case to a ragged woman who held it tenderly in her hands caked with dirt.

"The look that came over her face cannot be described. The lipstick was nothing, yet to this woman it was everything. It was the first thing she had owned in years. Everything had been taken from her. Even her name had been blotted out by the Nazi stamp, Juden."

Anna then gave away the contents of her purse to the women, which included a mirror, some papers, pencils, a comb, and a compact.

Anna saw their faces "light with happiness," but it was a scarring experience. She spoke of the camp only once publicly and "with the greatest feeling," sharing with a Jewish relief organization her interaction with the survivors, her feelings of shame and helplessness that she had had no clothes or food to give to them, and of the need to return to the victims their human dignity.[40]

Awful as they were, both Ohrdruf and Dora-Nordhausen were sub-camps of the major camp some kilometers away at Buchenwald. From London, newsman Edward R. Murrow heeded the call to witness the scenes there. Upon his return, he spent three days idle, wrestling with his rage, before filing his report, "Liberation of Buchenwald."

> Men and boys reached out to touch me; and they were in rags and remnants of uniform. Death had already marked many of them. . . . In another part of the camp they showed me the children . . . some were only six. One rolled up his sleeve, showed me his number. It was tattooed on his arm. The others showed me their numbers; they will carry them till they die.
>
> I pray you to believe what I have said about Buchenwald. I have reported what I saw and heard, but only part of it. For most of it I have no words.

The hundreds of pairs of children's shoes that he saw in a huge pile at Buchenwald Murrow could not bring himself to mention.*

———◆◆◆———

Further inhumanity and death would have occurred if not for the U.S.-Soviet linkup on the Elbe River on April 25 that cut in half Hitler's thousand-year Reich after a dozen years. Days later, with the Red Army closing in, the Führer committed suicide in his command bunker. A week later, German Chief of Staff General Alfred Jodl was flown from northern Germany to Reims, France, in an American C-47 transport plane with a pinup model painted on its fuselage. Jodl, the nominal leader of Nazi Germany at that moment, and his aide-de-camp were escorted into a redbrick secondary school beside the railway tracks where General Eisenhower had established SHAEF. Twelve Americans, Britons, Soviets, and Germans and one French officer sat at the large rectangular oak table. Military maps hung across blue-green walls showed the state of battle on May 7, 1945: the zigzagging red line of the Western Allied forces, the pink line of the Soviets, and the yellow lines of international boundaries.[41] Eisenhower declined to attend the signing, because he outranked Jodl. In his stead, Walter Bedell Smith, Ike's Chief of Staff, accepted the surrender of Nazi Germany.

The war in Europe was over.

———◆◆◆———

The discovery and liberation of the concentration camps altered the course of Anna Rosenberg's second wartime mission. The first priority for the Allies was to repatriate the displaced as quickly as possible. The refugees were held in Assembly Centers, based on nationality and segregated from the general public to prevent the spread of disease and to provide food and medical care. Because Jews and non-Jews, victims and collaborators, were thrown together, tensions festered and sometimes turned deadly. Reports and warnings from chaplains, soldiers, journalists, and

---

* Joseph E. Persico, *Edward R. Murrow: An American Original* (New York: McGraw-Hill, 1988), 228–30. Like Anna Rosenberg, after descending into the camp Murrow was compelled to give the survivors whatever was on his person. In Murrow's case, the pockets of his correspondent's jacket were stuffed with the previous night's poker winnings.

members of Congress culminated in President Truman's dispatching Earl G. Harrison, the Commissioner of Immigration and Naturalization, to Europe to arrange for the treatment and repatriation of Jews in Germany. On June 3, 1945, Truman cabled Anna Rosenberg, already in Europe, to do the same with French Jews. On June 13, she and her aide, Lieutenant Commander Fischer, met in Paris with chaplains Judah Nadich and Irwin Hyman. They discussed the issues facing French Jews, and a memorandum was prepared to take back to the President.[42]

The final report, called the Harrison Report, created separate camps for Jewish refugees, to avoid their living alongside former assailants, and assigned Jewish chaplains.[43] Herman Dicker, an Army chaplain who served in France and then Germany, later explained that the assignment of the chaplains "eliminate[ed] many of the obstacles caused by lack of mutual understanding" between displaced persons and American military authorities.[44] By the end of July 1945 more than 7 million displaced persons were repatriated to their home nations, where they attempted to rebuild shattered lives.[45]

After the meetings in Paris, it remained for Anna to talk again to the soldiers—the G.I.'s who had won the war and were dreaming of that big ship home. General Patton's Third Army was the occupying force in Bavaria, and the general himself was military governor of that state—home of the sought-after prize of war, Hitler's Eagle's Nest. After arriving there via a military transport, the proud soldiers showed the President's emissary into the elevator to the home, which was carved into a cliff. The elevator exited into a small lounge, which led into the modern kitchen of white tile and white enameled appliances with gleaming stainless-steel fixtures.

Anna stepped into the long dining room; atop the sideboard on one side was a smattering of well-used liquor bottles. At the end of the dining room, a few broad steps took Anna Rosenberg down into the Great Room, a mountain lookout thirty-five feet in diameter made of white limestone and supported by dark oaken beams nearly twenty feet high. Anna walked across the vast room to the large bank of windows and looked into the valley below. Beyond the lake that lay like an upward-facing mirror between two mountains and past the green river that flowed through the valley, Anna could see into Austria. The distant peaks across the valley were part of that ancient empire of her birth and banishment, and had been until recently part of a terrifying new empire that would have destroyed her and her loved ones. The elegant Budapest they had enjoyed as a family was gone. The city, like Hungary itself, had experienced a disastrous war and domination by anti-Semites, Nazis—and Communism soon to follow. The topography of her life was like a battle map—the mountains, plains, and ancient capitals of her early life had given way to an ocean, to an island, to a new world. Now the battle was over, the war was over, and she was going home.

On her way out, Anna lingered in the library off the Great Room, reading the German titles on the bookshelves. She picked up a copy of *Stars and Stripes* and read of an upcoming concert at the world-famous concert hall in Salzburg. She longed to go, but she couldn't.

She had a report to deliver to President Harry S. Truman.

CHAPTER SEVENTEEN

HOMECOMING

Alas! and now where on earth am I? What do I here myself?
—Homer, *Odyssey*

WASHINGTON, D.C., OFFICE OF SECRETARY OF WAR ROBERT PATTERSON,
OCTOBER 29, 1945

In her dark tailored suit, her hat a modern-art cloud of white perched on the back of her head, Anna clasped her white-gloved hands in front of her and beamed as Secretary of War Patterson pinned the Medal of Freedom on her jacket. Created as the civilian equivalent of the Congressional Medal of Honor by President Truman in July 1945, Anna received the honor at the personal request of General of the Army Dwight D. Eisenhower. President Truman cited her "exceptionally meritorious service which has aided the United States in the prosecution of the war against the enemy."* Anna Rosenberg's "exemplary" work in wartime Europe for the "welfare of our troops," on "problems related to displaced persons," and on "questions of . . . rehabilitation," was of "material value to the interests of the United States

---

* "Mrs. Anna Rosenberg Gets Freedom Medal," *New York Times*, October 30, 1945. In April 1952, President Truman amended the award to add Cold War language regarding NATO and other allies. Recipients thereafter "furthered the interests of the security of the United States or of any nation allied or associated with the United States." The award was expanded by President John F. Kennedy in 1963 to recognize a host of extraordinary civilian accomplishments. Since 1945 more than twenty thousand people have received the Medal of Freedom, including Andrew Wyeth, Walt Disney, Ella Fitzgerald, and Justice Earl Warren. The very first Medal of Freedom was awarded to a woman: Anna Rosenberg, for her wartime missions.

government."[1] Anna Rosenberg was the first American citizen, man or woman, to be awarded the Medal of Freedom.

Rosenberg's earlier efforts on the home front also aided the prosecution of the war in the Pacific. Less than three months before the award ceremony, a B-29 Superfortress built in a Boeing factory substantially staffed by American women dropped the world's first atomic bomb—a weapon built in part by workers sent to secret sites at Oak Ridge and Hanford by Anna Rosenberg, who was also entrusted with preserving the secrecy of the Manhattan Project. The Hiroshima attack on August 6 was followed three days later when a second B-29 dropped a plutonium bomb over the secondary target of Nagasaki. On the day formal surrender documents were signed aboard the USS *Missouri* in Tokyo Bay, September 2, 1945, 2 million people rushed to New York's Times Square. Children banged garbage pail lids and car horns rang as the delirious mass sang, danced, and drank while the ticker-tape confetti rained down.

The celebrations in New York, London, and Paris gave way to a sobering reality. In the aftermath of the Second World War, people all over the world needed to reconstitute their lives. Twelve million American service members needed to find their place in the U.S. economy and reconcile their combat experience with the postwar rush to return to normal. Europe's Jews and war refugees needed to reconstitute their stolen lives. Harry Truman had to emerge from the long shadow of FDR. For Black Americans, the fight for equal opportunity in wartime defense jobs became a springboard for a comprehensive movement for greater equality in American life. In debt and living in a rented apartment, her business moribund after years of government service, Anna Rosenberg needed to restart her career.

With the end of hostilities, Anna resigned from the War Manpower Commission, proud of the "truly unprecedented degree of cooperation" displayed by her staff in service to the war effort. "If the American people are told by their Government simply and truthfully what is expected of them and why," she wrote, "theirs is a wholehearted response."[2] With loans from Senator William Benton and Nelson Rockefeller, Anna Rosenberg was able to purchase her longtime apartment at 1136 Fifth Avenue, a stately fifteen-story building on the Upper East Side with balconies, wood-burning fireplaces, and views of Central Park. After years of near-constant commuting and living in a hotel, Anna finally owned a small piece of New York City. She made it her own: the living room, as described in a *Vogue* piece accompanied with several interior photos, was done in a "cool, impersonal grey-and-white," with a ceiling-height arched bookcase. Anna's "fresh, delicate" bedroom was green and white and "essentially feminine," the dressing table topped with a collection of French perfume bottles. Fresh-cut flowers were everywhere— white Easter lilies, white carnations, and pale roses.[3]

When her son, Thomas, mustered out of the Army as a captain and returned home to be her partner, Anna announced the opening of her permanent venture:

> *Anna M. Rosenberg,*
> *Consultant on*
> *Public, Labor, and Personnel Relations*
> *Announces*
> *The Opening of Offices*
> *at*
> *444 Madison Avenue, New York, NY*

Occupying a large executive suite on the twenty-sixth floor of an Art Deco tower in midtown, Anna enjoyed views of the Empire State Building and Grand Central Station. Clad in a white satin blouse, her jacket on the back of her chair, Anna was a dervish of activity, on the phone, conferencing with clients, and engaging with her staff of a half dozen. The Rockefellers and Senator Benton's *Encyclopedia Britannica* were her first clients; many more would follow. Like her apartment, the offices of Anna M. Rosenberg were decorated in a correct, feminine way: white walls, a deep blue carpet, and plush white sofa and chairs. A crystal chandelier hung overhead, illuminating the plaques, medals, and framed photographs of Presidents Roosevelt and Truman.

As she had done during the Roosevelt wartime years, Anna Rosenberg combined her political and business contacts into a potent behind-the-scenes policy-shaping force. Late in Roosevelt's presidency, Anna's closest friend, Mary Lasker, a powerful philanthropist and public health lobbyist, asked her to urge FDR to extend the fruits of wartime science and medical research into peacetime. The Office of Scientific Research and Development coordinated scientific and medical research during the war, but by the executive order that had established it, the OSRD was set to expire and be defunded. Rosenberg and Lasker prepared a memo examining how the federal government could continue medical research and how it might "declare war" on the deadliest diseases; the memo was sent to Dr. Vannevar Bush of the OSRD, who formalized the ideas into a report for President Truman.

"Scientific progress is an essential key to our security as a nation," Dr. Bush concluded, "to our better health, to more jobs, to a higher standard of living, and to our cultural progress." Upon the publication of the Bush report, Mary Lasker, who had never met Truman, asked Anna to arrange a meeting with the new President. Just weeks after the atomic bomb attacks on Japan, the charming and pretty wife of advertising millionaire Albert Lasker met with Truman in the Oval Office. Before turning to the issue of healthcare, Truman unburdened himself to Lasker, admitting to the younger woman "at great length his feeling of guilt about being in this office at all." Lasker remembered the President saying, "Oh, I feel so inadequate in this office," and that he felt "very diffident about sitting at Roosevelt's desk . . . he felt very tentative and apologetic about being President, even to a stranger like me." She was surprised when then President Truman started to justify the use of the atomic bomb, telling her, "You know by doing this, [General] Marshall told me, we saved the lives of 300,000 American men because that many men would have been killed in the landings on Japan." Lasker, who didn't agree with the use of the atomic bomb, kept her opinions to herself. "I could see," she remembered:

> that this was so much on his mind because to a complete stranger he was still justifying himself out loud. I came to the highest officer of the land to get something done about the health of the people. But he was excusing himself at that moment.[4]

Despite Truman's tentative mood, Lasker found him amenable to the national health bill. "He was interested in the general idea of health insurance," she later recounted, "because he had been a county judge and he had seen a lot of trouble in families, troubled for lack of money for medical care." Harry Truman was also motivated to see through unfinished projects of his predecessor. "I want to do everything that Roosevelt intended to do," the new President told Sam Rosenman. "I want to carry out everything he intended to do."

"If you send this message to Congress," Lasker promised Truman, "you will go down in history as the first President to show any interest in the health of the people of the United States. It will be the first such message, and it will be an historic act. Will you do it?"

"This statement seemed to move him, and he said he would go ahead with it."

On November 19, 1945, in his message to Congress, Harry Truman became the first president to call for a comprehensive national healthcare system:

> Medicine has made great strides in this generation—especially during the last four years. . . . In spite of great scientific progress, however, each year we lose many more persons from preventable and premature deaths than we lost in battle or from war injuries during the entire war.
>
> In the past, the benefits of modern medical science have not been enjoyed by our citizens with any degree of equality. Nor are they today. Nor will they be in the future—unless government is bold enough to do something about it.
>
> We should resolve now that the health of this Nation is a national concern; that financial barriers in the way of attaining health shall be removed; that the health of all its citizens deserves the help of all the Nation.[5]

After wending its way through committees in both chambers of the legislature, the National Science Foundation Bill, including federal funding for medical science, was passed by Congress on August 6, 1947. This initial investment by the federal government in the health of the nation's citizens reveals Anna Rosenberg's quiet, potent power. She gained access for Mary Lasker and lobbied members of Congress, and it was in the service of a policy she cared about deeply. Never before had the President and the federal government committed such resources to

Americans' health and welfare. As a result of this and subsequent congressional laws and federal grants, the National Science Foundation was established and the National Mental Health Act and the National Heart Act were passed, among dozens of laws regarding blindness, neurological diseases, dental health, and other maladies. Before Truman's bold action, "cancer was a word you simply could not say out loud," recalled Mary Lasker.[6] Although the disease took nearly two hundred thousand lives each year, the media did not discuss it, federal spending on cancer research was minimal, and scientists understood it much less well than infectious diseases. This changed dramatically in the latter half of the 1940s, with massive investment in the war on cancer. Research capability rose exponentially: the National Institute of Health expanded to include the National Heart Institute (1948), the National Institute of Mental Health (1949), and the National Institute of Neurological Diseases and Blindness (1950), each with the ability to award grants to researchers around the world. Between 1946 and 1961, the budget of the National Institutes of Health increased 150-fold, to $460 million. By the late 1960s, it had reached $1 billion. Today the National Institutes of Health comprise twenty-eight institutes and centers with a budget of over $25 billion.

In addition to her behind-the-scenes power brokering, Anna took on official duties, in this case dealing with veterans' issues. President Truman named her to the advisory board of the Retraining and Reemployment Administration. As with her earlier work with the Social Security Board, it was a task that dovetailed neatly with Anna's natural empathy, what author John Gunther called her "intense warm humanness."[7] While rebuilding her business was imperative, helping servicemen and -women rebuild their lives was the focus of Anna's political engagement from 1944 onward. "Veterans, not cabinets, are my chief interest," she told a reporter.[8]

At the state level, Anna opened the New York City Veterans Service Center, which she chaired. The purpose of the center, she explained to the *New York Times*, was "to make sure that the retired service man doesn't get that run-around—that he does get a good exit interview in which he is fully informed of all services which would help him and his family. If he cannot afford medical and psychiatric treatment there must be community facilities to furnish such treatment."[9]

The need to offer mental health counseling was a consistent theme of Anna Rosenberg after returning from her wartime missions. She had not only seen soldiers in battle but lived with a husband who never fully recovered from trench warfare of World War I. Josef Israels II of the *Saturday Evening Post* found Mike "a shadowy figure in the background of [Anna's] professional life," and historian Anna Kasten Nelson termed him a "quiet little man," but Anna knew the reason behind his demeanor.[10] Despite Anna's calls for mental health services for vets, in the 1940s there was little consensus that such care was necessary. Publications by the U.S. Surgeon General, the Navy Medical Corps, academic round-tables, psychiatrists, and other MDs all drew the connection between the trauma of combat and the need for counseling. Others saw it as a waste of resources or mocked it outright. William Moore of the conservative *Chicago Tribune* called such a program "New Deal coddling" and claimed Rosenberg was "teaching overseas soldiers how to live as they have always lived" and "fitting servicemen to come back to their own homes."[11]

While the *Chicago Tribune* was laughing off the need for psychological readjustment to civilian life, both professionals and soldiers themselves acknowledged the need. In his article "The Home-comer," the sociologist Alfred Schuetz observed that "when the soldier returns and starts to speak—if he starts to speak at all—he is bewildered to see that his listeners, even the sympathetic ones, do not understand [that his] experiences have rendered him another man."[12] For the untold numbers of veterans who did not have the words, Arch Soutar, who had fought in the North Africa campaign, spoke candidly for them in the *Saturday Evening Post*:

> I saw men die who shouldn't have died. [Upon returning] I didn't feel prepared mentally. . . . I was frightened by mounting confusion and indecision. Things were coming at me so rapidly . . . I wanted only to be left alone, to absorb, a little at a time, this bewildering thing called America, home.[13]

Reorientation counseling provided an opportunity for conservatives to refresh their attacks on New Deal activism, but there was far less disagreement when it came to the educational opportunities at the heart of the G.I. Bill. The promise of the law was in its first stages of fulfillment in 1945 and 1946 as hundreds of thousands of soldiers, sailors, marines, and airmen "stormed the academic beachheads previously reserved for children of privileged parents."[14]

Visiting the New York University campus in August 1945, journalist Edith Efron of the *New York Times* wrote that the nearly two thousand soldier undergraduates were the same as their civilian counterparts "save for the small golden eagle in their civilian lapels and a few tell-tale crow's feet around their eyes." The veterans were still "untensing," but Efron found the newly democratized NYU campus that summer "a thing of beauty." For the first time, higher education was open to working-class Americans, Polish Americans, Irish Americans, Italian Americans, and Jews. Even Harvard president James Conant, who had feared a post-war "flood" of the "least capable," came around; the G.I. Bill, he realized, ended the perpetuation of a "hereditary class of educated people."[15] In time, hundreds of thousands of engineers, doctors, dentists, nurses, teachers, scientists, accountants, lawyers, and clergy were added to the nation's professional ranks, and "Americans began to perceive the under-graduate and graduate degrees as gateways to the professions, the new route to the American Dream."[16]

The $14.5 billion investment paid off: the Labor Department esti-mated that the treasury profited from the G.I. Bill because the veterans' increased earning power resulted in more taxes.[17] As the cross section of college-educated vets began to "take their places as the economic and social leaders of the country," the course was charted for "the new mer-itocratic society."[18]

Nowhere in America revealed the new meritocracy more than New York City, home of the largest concentration of returned ex-soldiers and -sailors. In January 1946, dignitaries from the military and city of New York met at 500 Park Avenue to celebrate a quarter of a million veter-ans helped by the New York City Veterans Service Center. To the live radio audience on New York's WNYC, Anna Rosenberg introduced the 250,000th ex-serviceman, ex-sergeant George Loomis, who with the help of the center had found a job and was taking extension courses at Columbia. "I can learn while earning on my job," explained Loomis.

The auditorium burst into applause when the young man concluded, "I feel ready to go out on my own thanks to the boost given me and all the other veterans."[19]

The challenge of readjustment was made less difficult by the support offered to ex-soldiers like Sergeant Loomis, but unlike many leaders in veteran affairs, Anna Rosenberg realized that the obstacles for women veterans were in some ways greater. "Women are not being welcomed home as conquering heroines," she wrote in an editorial for the *Washington Post* in January 1946. "The returned warrior in folk myth is always the gallant knight for whom the fair lady waits in the tower." Rosenberg found that returning WACs were "likely to meet neglect as a result of civilian apathy and callousness."[20] Instead of helping each other assimilate, civilians resented the "swell in the surplus of marriageable women" and indulged in "petty snobbishness." Women veterans "have been disillusioned and discouraged by a cold reception from various women's groups." As one officer put it, "I discovered that it is best not to mention my army career due to the unfortunate stigma attached to the WAC."[21]

While service members enrolled in college courses, found jobs, purchased modest new suburban homes in places like Long Island's Levittown, and started families, Europe's Jews continued to suffer from deprivation. In one French orphanage, sixty children shared twenty pairs of socks, a single pencil was shared by five children, they had "no toys to lavish affection on," and yet they were "living in luxury compared to those in Poland, Germany, and other countries."[22]

To respond to this and other terrible stories coming out of the displaced persons camps in Europe, in October 1945 Paul Baerwald, the chairman of the Joint Distribution Committee, a Jewish humanitarian organization, wrote to Anna to enlist her leadership in the effort to provide refugees with much-needed supplies of clothing, shoes, medicine, and other items. Involved in Jewish philanthropy for two decades, Anna agreed without hesitation. On March 1, 1946, the "Supplies for Overseas Survivors" was launched with the hope of raising 20 million pounds of relief supplies for Jews remaining in Europe's displaced persons camps. Food, supplies, comfort items, and medicine would "supplement the basic relief which is the first essential for these [survivors] who must be kept alive," Anna urged her fellow New Yorkers. These items, she promised, would help victims of the Holocaust to "regain the strength and courage" to rebuild. "I can't speak in terms of supplies, in cases of baled goods, or pounds of clothing. I can only talk in terms of human life."[23]

Soon four hundred "Operation S.O.S." groups in New York City alone were collecting pink baby blankets, tins of fish, bars of soap, jars of coffee, and bolts of wool coat cloth. New York City led the way, but items poured in from "virtually every city in the U.S."[24] Fifty employees were needed to staff the conveyor belts of goods, where bins, boxes, and bales were loaded onto ships. Fifteen tons were shipped each day.[25] Over its three years, over 26 million pounds of supplies were collected and distributed to European Jews. In the battle for aid, according to one JDC member referring to the dramatic saving of the British Army by an armada of civilian boats, it equaled "100 Dunkirks."[26] In her work *Un Plan Marshall Juif,* French historian Laura Hobson Faure credits Anna Rosenberg's early involvement with French Jewish refugees in Paris for setting the stage for the unprecedented philanthropic outpouring between 1944 and 1954 during which more than $27 million was sent to French Jews. To Faure, this was the Jewish Marshall Plan.

The homecoming for Black veterans came with a sharp reminder that the nation they had served overseas still considered them second-class citizens. While perhaps 250,000 ex-soldiers enrolled in colleges in the North and West, Black vets were shut out of segregated colleges in the South.[27] In all regions, racial covenants written into the deeds of new suburban homes prevented them from enjoying the comforts of the "crabgrass frontier." Enrollment in Black colleges exploded, and many graduates became foot soldiers and leaders in the civil rights movement that girded itself as uniformed Black veterans returned home to a backlash of white men eager to remind them of the social order of the Jim Crow South.

In Washington, the civil rights efforts focused on desegregation of the armed forces, a goal that had been deferred in the aftermath of FDR's executive order mandating equality in defense work and establishing the Fair Employment Practices Committee to enforce it. At the conclusion of the war, political leaders debated whether the FEPC should continue as a government program. As one of the drafters of the executive order that created the FEPC, Anna Rosenberg was in the fight. Leading up the 1946 congressional vote on the bill, A. Philip Randolph thanked Anna for suggesting "ways and means to secure the enactment of [a permanent FEPC]," for helping select "members of the committee," and for her fundraising, which was "simply magnificent and extraordinarily wonderful."[28] Despite the efforts of Randolph and allies like Rosenberg, the bill was blocked by southern lawmakers.

Segregation in education and housing was a slap at the veterans who had served their country, but worse was the ghastly violence that maintained it. Just hours after being discharged from the Army in February 1946, Isaac Woodard, a Black Army sergeant on his way home to South Carolina after serving in WW II, was taken off a Greyhound bus after an exchange with the driver, who refused to let him off at a rest stop to use the restroom. Local police officers savagely beat Woodard, leaving him unconscious and permanently blind. In Monroe, Georgia, that July, two Black men, one a veteran just returned from the war, and their wives were ambushed by an unmasked band of twenty white men. As the two young men were being led into the woods, a member of the mob yelled that one of the Black women recognized him; the two women, shrieking in fear, were then dragged from their car. The four were taken to a secluded area and shot to death.[29] Although the perpetrators of the maiming and murders were widely known in their communities, no one was ever charged for the crimes.

In response to the violence, at the end of 1946 Harry Truman established the President's Committee on Civil Rights to investigate the status of civil rights in the country and propose measures to strengthen and protect them. When an old acquaintance from Kansas City complained about Truman's interest in advancing civil rights, the President responded:

> When mob gangs can take four people out and shoot them in the back . . . and nothing is done about it, [the] country is in a pretty bad fix. When a mayor and city marshal can take a negro sergeant off a bus in South Carolina, beat him up and put out one of his eyes . . . and nothing is

done about it, something is radically wrong with the system. I am asking for equality of opportunity for all human
beings, and, as long as I stay here, I am going to continue
that fight . . . if it ends up in my failure to be reelected, that
failure will be in a good cause.[30]

In May 1947, President Truman had an opportunity to do something
about it, when a presidential commission advised him to desegregate the
armed forces. The Compton Commission, named after the president of
M.I.T., Karl Compton, was a nine-member group of academic and business leaders tasked with studying universal military training for all men
of military age. Truman K. Gibson, Jr., a lawyer who had been raised in
the South and educated at the University of Chicago, was the commission's lone Black member; Anna Rosenberg its only woman. "Segregation should have no place in [military training]," read the commission's
final report. "Nothing could be more tragic for the future attitude of our
people, and for the unity of our nation."[31] The report was not the only
evidence attitudes were evolving that spring. Just weeks before, Jackie
Robinson, a second lieutenant during World War II and outspoken critic
of segregation, ran onto Ebbets Field in Brooklyn, becoming the first
Black Major League Baseball player.

While Dodgers fans cheered on No. 42, stubborn biases were tested
in the South. In April a mixed-race group of sixteen men from the
Congress of Racial Equality departed on the first Freedom Ride, heading south to test the Supreme Court's recent ban on segregation in
interstate travel. Knowing that a bill to desegregate the armed forces
would be stymied by southern lawmakers, President Truman decided
to part ways with many former congressional colleagues and use the
power of his office.

As a young man in Missouri, Harry Truman had seen segregation
and racial violence. He was a "captive of his times and his upbringing,"
according to Truman Gibson. "His famous penchant for salty language
encompassed terms rightly seen as awful slurs. Still he had a basic sense
of right and wrong, and he saw segregation as wrong."[32] As Truman's
close adviser Clark Clifford later reflected, "the wonderful, wonderful
development of those years was Harry Truman's capacity to grow."[33]
In the spring of 1947 Anna Rosenberg saw the President's evolution up

close. On May 29, 1947, Anna was awarded the Medal for Merit. With this honor added to the previously awarded Medal of Freedom, Anna was now the recipient of the "two highest decorations which may be conferred upon a civilian."[34] The citation noted her "untiring and unstinting devotion to her country."[35] President Truman used the occasion to call an impromptu meeting in the Oval Office with Anna, Sam Rosenman, and Truman Gibson.

The President addressed Sam Rosenman and Anna first: "You don't understand Jim Crow trains like [Mr. Gibson] and I do."

Motioning Gibson to his desk, "My namesake," he joshed. Then came a stunning revelation.

"I've been mulling over this issue of segregation. I'm going to take the bull by the horns. I'm going to help your people."

President Truman brought up the maiming of Isaac Woodard.

"This shit has to stop. Enough is enough," the President continued. "Dammit, I'm going to do something."

According to Gibson, President Truman went on to voice "his opinion that Black Americans should have equal access to the important institutions of society like school. Then he told us he planned to issue an executive order eliminating segregation from the armed services. He knew it wouldn't be popular. President Truman told the group candidly, 'My wife kept me from sleeping last night. She doesn't agree with my views on race.'"

In December 1947, the President's Committee on Civil Rights issued its report urging a host of civil rights measures, including a Civil Rights Division in the Department of Justice, federal laws against lynching, the abolishment of poll taxes, and a permanent Fair Employment Practices Committee. On February 2, 1948, without conferring with congressional leaders, President Truman delivered to Congress the first civil rights message ever delivered by an American President.

> We shall not . . . achieve the ideals for which this Nation
> was founded so long as any American suffers discrimi-
> nation as a result of his race, or religion, or color, or the
> land of origin of his forefathers. Unfortunately, there still
> are examples—flagrant examples—of discrimination
> which are utterly contrary to our ideals. Not all groups of

our population are free from the fear of violence. Not all
groups are free to live and work where they please or to
improve their conditions of life by their own efforts. Not
all groups enjoy the full privileges of citizenship and participation in the government under which they live. We
cannot be satisfied until all our people have equal opportunities for jobs, for homes, for education, for health,
and for political expression, and until all our people have
equal protection under the law. . . . I have instructed the
Secretary of Defense to take steps to have the remaining
instances of discrimination in the armed services eliminated as rapidly as possible.[36]

Delivering the civil rights message in an election year was a bold gamble by Harry Truman. That winter and spring there was "an angry outcry
on the Hill"; a segregationist lawmaker even called Truman's proposed
program a "lynching of the Constitution."[37] At the Democratic National
Convention that summer, a southern bloc of Democrats walked out on
Truman to establish the States' Rights Party. Twelve days after the stunt,
President Harry Truman kept his vow to fight for the cause of civil rights
when he signed Executive Orders 9980 and 9981, desegregating the federal workforce and the U.S. Armed Forces.

In the months leading up to the 1948 election, Harry Truman
faced a fractured Democratic caucus and challenges abroad. Not only
was Europe awash with the displaced, but its bomb-damaged cities
and continuing rationing and privation were a breeding ground for
local Communist parties. To counter this, the United States in June
1947 launched the European Recovery Program. The Marshall Plan,
as it was soon called, was a "Cold War grand strategy . . . that committed the United States to nothing less than the reconstruction of
Europe."

To administer the $12 billion recovery program, Truman turned to
a friend of Anna's, Paul Gray Hoffman, the top executive of the Studebaker car company who moonlighted for the State Department. After
he initially declined the post, Truman replied, "Well, Mr. Hoffman,
some of the best people we have in government have to be drafted. We
hope you'll prove to be one of them, and I am expecting you to say

yes."* Hoffman came around. The Marshall Plan rebuilt Western European economies, prevented German and Japanese industrial power from falling into the hands of the Soviets, and prevented political chaos.[38] "My work," said Hoffman, "was in the national interest . . . there was a gloomy future for our country unless Europe was restored."[39] The gargantuan relief effort earned General George C. Marshall a Nobel Peace Prize and is considered one of President Truman's crowing achievements.

In the summer before the presidential election between Truman and New York Governor Thomas E. Dewey, a new conflict arose in divided postwar Germany. On June 24, Joseph Stalin ordered a blockade of all railways, roadways, and waterways into Berlin in an attempt to pressure the Allies to abandon the city.[40] President Truman immediately dispatched two squadrons of B-29s to airlift supplies to the beleaguered Berliners. The months-long Berlin Airlift was a "global public relations triumph" that led the Soviet dictator eventually to call off the blockade.[41] The crisis was handled well by President Truman, but it portended a more dangerous phase of the early Cold War.

Harry S. Truman presided over a complicated postwar America arriving at a dangerous juncture in international affairs. Every act of Soviet aggression in Europe was followed by Republican calls that the administration was "soft on Communism." The anxieties of the bipolar world had bled into every town and city and set citizen against citizen. By the end of World War II, the Dies Committee had morphed into the House Un-American Activities Committee. By 1947 congressional investigators were rampaging around the country hounding college professors; Jewish intellectuals; and Hollywood

---

* Paul Hoffman told President Truman he would talk it over with his wife, but that afternoon Hoffman was asked by the press, "Have you been offered the post as [Marshall Plan] Administrator?" to which he jokingly replied, "What does the job pay?" "Twenty thousand dollars a year," came the answer. Hoffman parried, "It must be a good job."

At that moment a loudspeaker came on stating that President Truman had just announced that Paul G. Hoffman had just accepted the post as Marshall Plan Administrator. "In drafting me . . . Truman did as great a favor for me as one man can do for another. It opened my eyes to many things of which I was totally unaware and it was the beginning of my real education." (Paul G. Hoffman, oral history interview, Harry S. Truman Library)

directors, screenwriters, and actors, everywhere ruining careers, ending marriages, and causing suicides.

Facing the wrath of HUAC and its "vile-tempered [and] contemptible Republican chairman," Truman issued Executive Order 9835, requiring loyalty oaths and subjecting government employees to investigations, including FBI and HUAC files. Dismissal could be based on the flimsy "reasonable grounds," a phrase never defined.[42] Many careers were ended prematurely in this paranoid environment, while others that might have been stillborn were launched: in 1946 an undistinguished local judge named Joseph McCarthy was elected to the U.S. Senate.

As Republicans pressured Truman from the right, New Dealers such as Eleanor Roosevelt and Anna Rosenberg pushed him from the left, urging a return to bold governmental action. The challenge for Harry Truman was to chart a postwar course of his own while appealing to a Democratic Party that remained stamped with Roosevelt's imprint. For a moment in 1948, the challenge seemed too daunting. Whether he continued to feel ill at ease in the office held for so long by FDR or whether he feared a presidency of an American Caesar if Republicans were to nominate General Douglas MacArthur, Harry Truman privately reached out to Dwight Eisenhower and floated the idea of Ike running as President, with Truman as Vice President.

Ike declined, and "Give 'Em Hell Harry" was left bearing the standard of the Democratic Party in the 1948 election. Passing the days before the vote in his hometown of Independence, Missouri, Truman could barely listen to the radio, as prognosticators had him losing badly. Newspapers and magazines were no more sanguine. Bettors made Truman a 15-to-1 underdog. Gallup polling showed Dewey five points ahead, and the *New York Times* predicted a Dewey victory, as did the *Wall Street Journal*, *Time*, and *Newsweek*. Handsome Thomas Dewey was on the cover of *Life*, above text that read "the next president." On election evening, after returns started to come in, Truman tried to get some sleep. He woke up at midnight and switched on the radio: although he was up by over a million votes in the popular vote, NBC's political reporter maintained that he was "undoubtedly beaten." Truman turned off the radio and went back to sleep. At four o'clock in the morning, aides woke the incumbent President to tell him his popular lead was over 2 million votes. "We got 'em beat," he replied.[43] After celebrating with jubilant supporters at Kansas City's Muehlebach Hotel, Harry Truman boarded the train bound for Washington, D.C. At Chicago, the President posed for photographers holding up an early edition of the anti-Truman *Chicago Tribune*, delighting in its premature banner headline: "Dewey Defeats Truman."

Harry Truman had emerged from the shadow of FDR. In his planting the seeds of national healthcare and civil rights legislation, some of which would not bear fruit for years, Anna saw Truman evolve into a leader. "I had tremendous respect for him. He was a courageous man. He grew so in the office."[44] Her friend Mary Lasker echoed this, saying, "When he won on his own he took on all the majesty of the office, and he looked like a President, if anybody ever did. He was superb." The victorious Truman's mettle would be tested, as he returned to the capital to lead a nation beset by internal mistrust and menaced by foreign foes.

As Anna worked to steer policy from her point of access to President Truman, it is worth asking whether she would have preferred a more direct way: as an elected official herself. She thrived at the game of politics but made denigrating remarks about politicians. She abhorred time-eating bureaucracy but was adept at the long game of lobbying members of Congress. Fear of Communism and the patriarchal postwar society made hers a difficult era to run for office as an immigrant woman. Today it is easier to picture someone with her combination of patriotic duty and pride in women's ability as a candidate for U.S. Senate, or Governor of the Empire State, or other high political office.

In September 1949, it fell to President Truman to tell the nation that the Soviet Union had successfully tested an atomic bomb. Questions immediately arose asking how the Russians had developed the bomb so quickly, and the hunt for spies was on. A week later, the world's most populous nation, China, fell to Communist forces. On world maps pulled down in front of chalkboards in classrooms across the country, the red-colored regions of the world were now shockingly prominent, and the peril seemed to be spreading.

On the pages of New York City's papers, on its radio stations, and on black-and-white televisions, news of the growing immensity of the

Cold War was distressing. The gravitational pull of the worldwide conflict was warping Americans' trust in each other and pulling President Truman toward limitless defense budgets and illiberal acts like the loyalty program.

Now officially out of government, Anna was insulated from the tumult of politics. With her son at her side and a staff of a dozen assistants, Anna continued to revive and grow her labor-relations and public-relations business. Her commute now was just two and a half miles, to the doorman's welcome under the green and brass awning of 1136 Fifth Avenue. Sunday afternoons, as Mike stoked the fire, Anna chose china from her collection to set the table and arranged fresh-cut flowers throughout the apartment. Sitting at the head of the table in her elegant dining room, Anna enjoyed the company of her son and his glamourous young wife, Jane Wade, a fresh-faced cover girl from Kansas City. As the fire crackled in the living room, the family enjoyed the views of Central Park below, a riot of fall color and young couples pushing strollers. It was good to be home.

CHAPTER EIGHTEEN

GENERAL MARSHALL CALLS

A nna Rosenberg sat in the living room of her Fifth Avenue apartment, opening the day's mail. While she worked, she listened to WNBC's *Symphony Orchestra*, a program on which the great Arturo Toscanini of the New York Philharmonic conducted the network's radio orchestra. Dispatching the day's invoices, thank-yous, invitations, and letters, Anna wielded her pearl-handled letter opener like the baton of the great conductor. Just as the third movement of Beethoven's *Eroica* reached its triumphant conclusion and gave way to a Chevrolet jingle touting the new Bel-Air model for 1950, she arrived at a handwritten letter on Secretary of Defense stationery. As she knifed into the back of the envelope, the jingle went on: "Drive your Chevrolet / through the U.S.A. / America's the greatest land of all. . . ." She crossed the room to turn the radio off, then sat down, tucking a pillow behind her lower back.

"Dear Anna, will you consider an appointment as Assistant Secretary of Defense?" Despite the "sacrifice this would impose on you I hope you can see your way clear to do this. I am writing this in longhand so that no one in my office will know of the proposal. I have not discussed it with the President. Faithfully yours, Marshall."

———•••———

The course of events that led George Marshall to offer a civilian woman a top-ranking post in the Pentagon began on the morning of June 25, 1950, nearly seven thousand miles from New York City. At four o'clock that morning, in a drumbeat of a rainstorm punctuated by blaring bugles, three columns of North Korean forces rumbled across the 38th Parallel and invaded South Korea. The Communist forces, supported by China and the Soviet Union, outnumbered those of the Republic of Korea; at certain critical points along the battle line, ROK units were outnumbered by five or six to one. Not only did the North Koreans possess superior numbers of men; they had more artillery and more tanks, including the Russian T-34, the indestructible workhorse that German panzer leader Heinz Guderian ruefully admitted had blunted the Nazi assault on Moscow in 1941.

The invasion took the South Koreans completely by surprise. By June 27, ROK Army headquarters had abandoned Seoul, on the west coast of the thick reverse S that is the Korean Peninsula, for a location farther south. The American ambassador and his family fled, and American families living in Seoul were evacuated to a commandeered Norwegian fertilizer ship in Inchon Harbor, which then sailed for Japan.

Events in the United States unfolded rapidly: the United Nations Security Council responded by making U.S. President Harry S. Truman its executive agent tasked with restoring peace to the peninsula. Truman immediately appointed his senior military officer in the Far East, General of the Army Douglas MacArthur, headquartered in Tokyo, as commander in chief of the United Nations Command.

Just two days after the invasion, Truman ordered American naval and air forces into action to support South Korea. Ground forces would be the next logical step. Congress acted that same day: the Selective Service Act was extended for one year, and the President was authorized to mobilize the reserves as needed for the conflict. Notably, for the time, women in the service reserves could be mobilized.[1] Despite the overwhelming congressional support, Truman did not ask for a declaration of war, labeling the response as a "police action."[2] After just a few days of fighting, General MacArthur dismally estimated that the ROK Army had all but disintegrated. On June 30, U.S. ground forces from Japan were ordered into action in Korea.

Despite the quick military response, in the opening weeks of the war the North Koreans pushed the American and U.N. forces to the southeastern port of Pusan.* Though they were able to dig in and defend the Pusan Perimeter, American forces had a tenuous hold on just one corner of the Korean Peninsula. The shocking reverses of the first months of

---

* The southeastern port city is now known as Busan.

the conflict revealed the unpreparedness of the U.S. military. Bazooka shells wouldn't penetrate the Russian-built tanks; poorly trained Army troops "broke and ran under pressure, or were captured," and air support mistakenly attacked Army and Marine units.[3] President Truman responded: he sat in on National Security Council meetings, met with General Omar Bradley, the chairman of the Joint Chiefs of Staff, and reshuffled the leadership of the CIA, naming General Walter Bedell ("Beetle") Smith as director.[4]

Truman wasn't done. The military defeats and ill-preparedness reflected badly on Secretary of Defense Louis Johnson. "Johnson said we could lick the Russians," complained one admiral. "He didn't say anything about the North Koreans!" Besides his overconfident bellicosity, Johnson feuded with the State Department and had been unable to rein in General MacArthur, who chafed under civilian command like an American Caesar, contradicting President Truman by indicating that attacks on Communist China were on the table. Infuriated, Truman made Johnson send a letter to the general, advising him: "No one other than the President as commander-in-chief has the authority to order or authorize [military action on the Chinese mainland]."[5] Behaving like a "head of state," MacArthur continued to defy Truman and issue statements contrary to official U.S. policy on China.[6]

After forcing out Johnson, in September 1950 President Truman begged George Marshall, three months shy of his seventieth birthday and with a kidney ailment, out of retirement, calling him while he and his wife were vacationing at the remote Huron Mountain Resort in Michigan. To take the President's call, George Marshall drove miles over dirt roads to the telephone at the back of the general store. Locals gawked at the white-haired military hero replying again and again, "Yes, Mr. President. Yes, Mr. President."[7]

In Marshall, Truman sought "a symbol of stability in a volatile hour, the incarnation of past military victory," and the revered rebuilder of Europe.[8] Hailed by many as the nation's greatest soldier-statesman since George Washington, Marshall, like Washington, was "ruggedly handsome," stood tall, and commanded the respect of all around him. The Old Man, as he was affectionately known, could walk into a Georgetown cocktail party "in an ordinary gray business suit," and the roomful of "high-level U.S. and foreign dignitaries dressed to the collars in gold braid" would stop their chattering and be reduced to a respectful whisper. He was uniformly "venerated," a "man of history sitting behind that desk," and "able to command attention without seeking it."[9] To the President who called upon him, the general was "the greatest living American." Anna Rosenberg, who knew her share of prominent figures in peace and war, said of the general, "I think he was the greatest American of his time."[10]

On September 21, George C. Marshall took over as Secretary of Defense. His top priority was to rebuild the armed forces. In the half decade since the end of World War II, millions of soldiers and sailors mustered out, went to college, got jobs, married, bought homes, and had children. The much smaller Army still occupied Germany, Austria, and Japan. When the South Koreans proved no match for the Communist North, it became clear that the United States would have to quickly build up its military strength to avoid catastrophe in East Asia while meeting the demands of occupation. Reservists were called up, recruitment was accelerated, and congressional extension of the 1948 Selective Service Act added draftees. The result was that the Army was augmented by more than 25 percent to strength of over 1 million.[11]

To Marshall, this was grossly inadequate. What was needed was an army of 3.5 million, an "enduring system of national defense." Complicating matters was the fact that military personnel questions were handled by dozens of government agencies. General James F. Collins, a veteran of the Pacific war then working on personnel issues at the Pentagon, lamented the fact that more than fifty agencies had a hand in the decision-making.[12]

<hr />

Anna put the letter down on the coffee table. She had known General George C. Marshall since World War II, when he was America's top general and she was with the Office of War Mobilization. When she learned defense plants were being "robbed" of their skilled workers by the military, she discussed the issue with General Marshall.[13] The Old Man, Anna knew, considered problems from every angle before deciding. Anna had heard chatter from her network that Marshall had been considering her for the post since September, but here it was, in the general's handwriting. She surmised that Marshall was keeping his plan from Truman to protect the President and his party in the upcoming midterm elections, knowing the backlash that could follow the appointment of a civilian woman, especially one with her background, to a top-level position in the military establishment.

The President and General Marshall had been in the crosshairs of conservative anti-Communists since the end of the war, but the attacks multiplied in 1949, when the Soviets detonated their atomic bomb and China fell to the Communists. Truman's "softness" on Communism and Marshall's failed 1947 diplomatic mission to China were blamed for these twin shocks. The hard-right contingent found a powerful voice in February 1950 when Senator Joseph McCarthy, a Wisconsin Republican, made himself the standard-bearer of red-baiting, claiming without evidence that Truman's State Department was infiltrated by hundreds of disloyal officials.

As she considered Marshall's request, Anna was under no illusions. Her reputation as an FDR favorite and ardent New Dealer made her a foe of McCarthy and his congressional allies. As Anna later admitted in an interview with Joe Frantz, she had "everything" her opponents wanted in a target. Referring to the notorious case of French anti-Semitism that ripped apart French society a decade before World War I, Anna didn't want to become Marshall's "Dreyfus case."* Her fears were well-founded. As historian Stuart Svonkin explains in his study *Jews against Prejudice*, by 1950 Jewish leaders at the American Jewish Committee and the Anti-Defamation League harbored fears that "professional anti-Semites would use the anti-Communist campaign to spread the canard identifying Jews with communism."[14] Becoming a latter-day Captain Dreyfus was bad enough, but there was also the issue of her last name. Although she was not related to Julius and Ethel Rosenberg, the married couple arrested in the summer of 1950 for passing atomic secrets to the Russians, Anna's surname nevertheless carried negative connotations.

Because of this, Anna tried to dissuade Marshall. "I tried very hard to tell him all the reasons why I thought it might be difficult," she told journalist William P. Rayner. Marshall would hear none of it. It was

---

* Alfred Dreyfus was a French Jewish army officer falsely accused of treason.

Anna (*left*) and her sister,
Clare, as children.
Anna Rosenberg Hoffman Papers,
1870–1983, Schlesinger Library,
Radcliffe Institute,
Harvard University,
Cambridge, Massachusetts
(hereinafter Schlesinger Library,
Harvard Radcliffe Institute)

Anna with three generations
of her family, Budapest 1910.
Flanked by her grandparents
with Anna's parents, Sarolta
(not yet Charlotte) and
Albert (in hat), in back row.
Albert sailed for America
in May 1910.
Schlesinger Library,
Harvard Radcliffe Institute

Anna, seated left, and Clare, standing, at embarkation hospital in New York City during World War I, 1918. *Schlesinger Library, Harvard Radcliffe Institute*

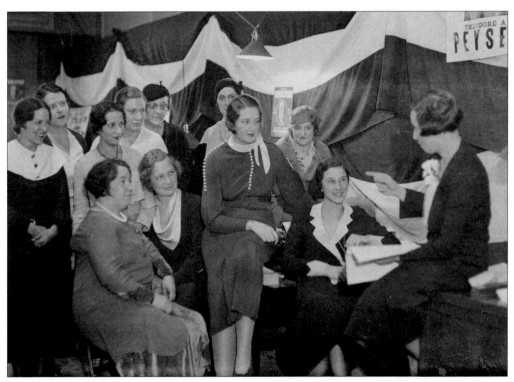

With Anna managing his campaign, Theodore Peyser was elected to the U.S. House of Representatives, 1932. *Schlesinger Library, Harvard Radcliffe Institute*

Portrait of Anna during the New Deal, possibly made in connection with her elevation to regional director of the National Recovery Administration in 1934. *Schlesinger Library, Harvard Radcliffe Institute*

Anna often found herself between Eleanor Roosevelt and Mayor Fiorello La Guardia. *Schlesinger Library, Harvard Radcliffe Institute*

As regional director of the Social Security Administration, Anna Rosenberg enlisted six million New Yorkers in a program that transformed their lives.
Schlesinger Library, Harvard Radcliffe Institute

Anna sponsoring the USS *Diphda* and
its crew as it launches on May 11, 1944.
A year later the ship was at the
Battle of Okinawa, part of the armada the
Japanese called "The Typhoon of Steel."
Schlesinger Library,
Harvard Radcliffe Institute

Anna in a light tank, 1944.
Schlesinger Library,
Harvard Radcliffe Institute

Anna during her mission as FDR's
Special Representative to the
European Theater of Operations in 1944.
Schlesinger Library,
Harvard Radcliffe Institute

On her wartime missions,
Anna made sure to check on
the wounded. This photo is with
an unidentified solider in 1945.
Schlesinger Library,
Harvard Radcliffe Institute

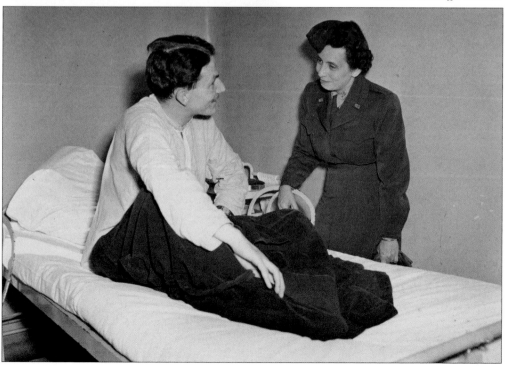

Anna with Major General Walton Walker near the front, Metz, France, September 8, 1944. Supporting General Patton's dash across France, Walker's fast-striking XX Corps was known as the "Ghost Corps."
Schlesinger Library, Harvard Radcliffe Institute

Anna Rosenberg with General Omar Bradley, France, 1944. Known as "the G.I.'s general," Bradley shared Anna's interest in the welfare of the ordinary soldier.
Schlesinger Library, Harvard Radcliffe Institute

Anna with General George S. Patton, near the front in Metz, France, September 1944. Anna and "Georgie" were fond of each other. Patton's dog, Willie, however, was not so nice to Anna.
Schlesinger Library, Harvard Radcliffe Institute

For her overseas missions during World War II, Anna Rosenberg became the first American citizen to receive the Presidential Medal of Freedom, here awarded by Secretary of War Robert P. Patterson on the recommendation of General of the Army Dwight D. Eisenhower. October 29, 1945.
Harris & Ewing, Harry S. Truman Library

Anna Rosenberg smiles at President Harry Truman as members of the Compton Commission look on. Sam Rosenman is behind Truman, and Truman Gibson stands behind Anna. Their work helped convince President Truman to desegregate the armed forces. May 29, 1947. *Harry S. Truman Library*

Anna Rosenberg often went head-to-head with powerful men, including Senator Lyndon Johnson, who called her "a true friend." *AP*

A familiar sight: Anna on the phone in the Madison Avenue offices of Anna Rosenberg & Associates, circa 1947–1950. *Schlesinger Library, Harvard Radcliffe Institute*

Anna M. Rosenberg being sworn in as Assistant Secretary of Defense, November 12, 1950. From left: Felix Larkin, General Counsel of the Department of Defense; General George C. Marshall; and Robert A. Lovett. *Harry S. Truman Library*

The Assistant Secretary of Defense
at her desk in room 3E-880,
the inner sanctum of the U.S. military
command, February 2, 1951.
U.S. Army, Harry S. Truman Library

Visiting with the men of
the Seventeenth Regiment,
Seventh Infantry Division,
near their command post
in Korea on October 23, 1951.
While at the Pentagon,
Anna Rosenberg insisted on
the integration of combat units
as well as on-base schools for
the soldiers' children.
*Schlesinger Library,
Harvard Radcliffe Institute*

Arriving in Korea for the start
of her second tour, November 1952.
*Schlesinger Library,
Harvard Radcliffe Institute*

Touring the Seventh Infantry sector
by jeep with the generals.
In cap is James A. Van Fleet,
Commanding General of the
U.S. Eighth Army and U.N. forces in Korea.
*U.S. Army Signal Corps,
enhancement by Erik Villard*

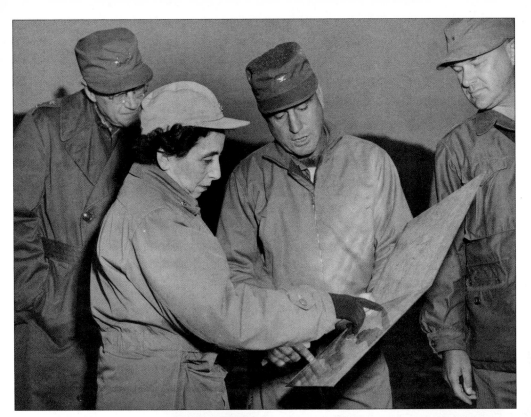

Anna stands with generals and map in 1952. Korea was a tough place to wage war. "Every ridge is a heartbreak," Anna reported.
Schlesinger Library, Harvard Radcliffe Institute

Anna with unknown sergeant in 1952. "The boys in Korea used to scrawl on the walls, 'Anna was here.' Was any woman ever paid greater tribute?"
— Senator William Benton.
Schlesinger Library, Harvard Radcliffe Institute

Anna at chow time with the troops.
Schlesinger Library,
Harvard Radcliffe Institute

After over two years at the
Defense Department, Anna bid
farewell to a Pentagon official
with this signed photograph.
She was self-conscious about
her handwriting and spelling.
Harry S. Truman Library,
Stohl, Ralph N. Papers,
Accession Number 97-1744

To Ralph Stohl.
With good wishes and
personal regards.
Anna M. Rosenberg.
The Pentagon.
1-7-53

President John F. Kennedy and Anna Rosenberg at Madison Square Garden, May 19, 1962.
Along with Arthur Krim, Anna was the cohost of JFK's forty-fifth birthday gala. *Photo by
Cecil Stoughton, White House photographer, John F. Kennedy Presidential Library and Museum, Boston*

President John F. Kennedy with Anna Rosenberg at the reception following the birthday gala
at Madison Square Garden. The only known photo of JFK and Marilyn Monroe was taken
at the same party. Composer Richard Adler is at left. *Photo by Cecil Stoughton,
White House photographer, John F. Kennedy Presidential Library and Museum, Boston*

Marilyn Monroe at the party
at the Krims' residence, May 19, 1962.
Photo by Cecil Stoughton,
White House photographer,
John F. Kennedy Presidential Library
and Museum, Boston

Anna with her grandson, Tommy, in 1960.
Schlesinger Library, Harvard Radcliffe Institute

his enemies, he told her, who would seek to use her appointment to "get back" at him. "I'm looking for a person with integrity and ability," the general assured Anna. "I don't care if it's a man or a woman."

By enlisting Rosenberg at the height of the Korean War and the opening of the era of McCarthyism, Marshall was risking his towering reputation as an international war hero and rebuilder of Europe in the hope that Anna would help him solve both short-term and long-term national security problems. Her mobilization expertise in World War II would be applied to the immediate problem: there were not enough service members in the armed forces. Defense spending cuts in the half decade following the end of World War II had resulted in a below-strength Army fighting in Korea. Moreover, because Anna was "on a first-name basis with official Washington," as reported by *Life*, she would be instrumental in securing congressional support for a standing force that was large enough and trained sufficiently to defend against future Communist aggression anywhere in the world. Marshall saw such a long-term policy as a national security necessity; Anna shared his fear that the draft alone was insufficient to meet the dangers of the rapidly expanding Cold War. Appointing Anna was, according to Marshall biographer Forrest C. Pogue, another example of the general's "disdain for political expediency." A colonel on Marshall's staff echoed this sentiment when he explained what motivated the Old Man: "What's good for the country was all he was after." As George Marshall admitted, appointing Anna Rosenberg would "be my biggest [mistake] or a stroke of genius."

As she was a civilian woman, the stakes were even higher for Anna. In the wake of Senator McCarthy's barging onto the national stage in February 1950, a congressional subcommittee was quickly formed to investigate his claims of subversion in the State Department. The first person to be investigated by the Tydings Committee was a woman, Dorothy Kenyon, a State Department official who, as a New York judge, had been an inspiration to a young Ruth Bader Ginsburg. Though she was exonerated by the committee in July 1950, Kenyon's decades-long career in public service was prematurely ended by McCarthy's baseless accusations.

The same fate befell State Department economist Marcia Harrison and international affairs expert Dr. Esther Brunauer—both of whom lost their positions. At a time when women made up a small percentage of government positions, a disproportionate 22 to 25 percent of files kept by House Un-American Activities Committee chief investigator J. B. Matthews targeted women. As Cold War scholar Landon Storrs explains, because women officials were often "pro-labor, pro-consumer, and pro–civil rights," red-baiters went out of their way to "harm careers of women in government, undercut the policy goals that many of them shared, and reinforce antifeminism in the wider culture."[15]

Indeed, as McCarthy and his allies were discovering, one easy way to rid government of progressive women was to label them as Communist. "The Communist utilization of women on a wholesale scale for revolutionary purposes," Matthews claimed in a speech, was evidence of the "diabolical cunning of the Communist conspiracy." In the first year of McCarthyism, the strategy of publicly questioning the loyalty of women in government was working.

In 1950 Anna Rosenberg was not only poised to be the most prominent woman in American government; she was second only to Eleanor Roosevelt as the most recognizable woman in American public life. She appeared atop polls asking readers who would make the best mayor of New York City, on best-dressed lists, and on popularity surveys. Many of those whose careers or lives had been ruined by allegations of disloyalty were liberal-minded women like Kenyon; others were Jewish, like economist Mary Dublin Keyserling; and still others, like Dr. Brunauer, had a foreign-born spouse or were themselves foreign-born. As Anna told Carl Borklund, editor of *Armed Services* magazine, "I was Jewish, an immigrant, [had] been a pro-labor worker, and was a woman. What could have been worse?" Anna knew that her reputation hung in the balance and if she failed, the path to power for women in general would become even narrower.

Not only was Anna risking her reputation in taking the Pentagon post; she was making a personal sacrifice. Before World War II had ended, Anna found herself borrowing from her life insurance and making ends meet with the help of loans from friends. By 1950 Anna had regained her financial footing. Taking the position at the Defense Department meant once again leaving lucrative private work and her social life in New York for a modest government salary and long hours in Washington, D.C.

Despite worries that she would become, as she put it, a "political football," Anna answered Marshall's call to return to public life. Senator William Benton said of his friend, she "accepted this appointment at such personal sacrifice" only "due to the great crisis we face."[16] Anna said of General Marshall, "When he asked me to come down to Washington, I couldn't say no."

———•••———

At five o'clock on the afternoon of Thursday, November 9, 1950, Secretary of Defense Marshall, bypassing the White House press office, quietly issued a press release appointing Anna M. Rosenberg as Assistant Secretary of Defense, pending presidential confirmation. The Senate was then in recess, so the date for her routine confirmation hearing in front of the Senate Armed Services Committee was set for November 29. General Marshall had tactically timed his press release late in the afternoon ahead of the somber Armistice Day weekend, but despite his caution, the appointment of Anna Rosenberg was picked up by right-wing radio star Fulton Lewis.

Although he is largely forgotten today, in the 1940s and 1950s Fulton Lewis, Jr., was a hard-right radio star with a rabid following. Every weeknight evening at seven o'clock, 16 million Americans tuned in to Lewis' program on the Mutual Broadcasting System, one of the "Big Four" with ABC, CBS, and NBC. With his program carried by five hundred radio stations, Fulton Lewis' career on the right-wing airwaves spanned three decades, between Father Charles Coughlin in the 1930s and Rush Limbaugh in the 1990s. Like them, Lewis was a "storm-center, a figure of great controversy."[17] A partisan commentator, Lewis supported limited government and keeping the United States out of World War II, and he opposed both FDR and Harry Truman. He was rabidly anti-Communist, proudly nativist, and was accused of being an anti-Semite. He loathed unions, opposed farm co-ops, and supported Senator Joe McCarthy until the bitter end. A 1987 editorial in the *Washington Post* referred to Lewis as "one of the most unprincipled journalists ever to practice the trade." His core audience never left him.

Anna Rosenberg provided an ideal target for Fulton Lewis. She was a middle-aged Jewish American woman, a foreign-born naturalized citizen, an urbane New Yorker, and a lifelong New Dealer. There was also the issue of her last name. To attack her would be to attack many of the things Lewis and his listeners loathed: immigrants, Jews, New Dealers, even Marshall and Truman, who had "lost" China to the Communists—all without saying those things. All Lewis had to do was label the Budapest-born Rosenberg a Communist. The day after her appointment, Fulton Lewis pounced.

At 7:00 PM on Friday, November 10, 1950, Lewis' listeners tuned in to hear "the voice with the snarl." "Good evening, ladies and gentlemen," Lewis began. Then he aimed his nightly diatribe at Anna Rosenberg. "The lady," Lewis growled, citing no evidence, "was linked to a Communist party cell." Dismissing her as "a sort of social worker," the radio star alleged that as a young woman Rosenberg had belonged to the "Communist clubs in and around New York City." The fact that she was born in Hungary did not escape Lewis' attention, nor did her "Jewish-sounding" name. Fulton Lewis predicted that in the Senate confirmation process Republican senators would ask her "why some years ago" she traveled in subversive circles. He concluded this initial attack with his signature signoff: "That's the top of the news as it looks from here."

Amplified by Lewis, Anna's appointment became a top news story during the three weeks before the Senate confirmation. The appointment of a civilian woman with Anna's background to a top military policy-making role at a critical stage in the Cold War was heralded by the media, discussed by public figures, and became a topic of conversation for ordinary Americans. "No woman had ever before held such a job in the manly precincts of the Pentagon," reported *Time*, describing Anna as "a 5'3" dynamo and a resolute wearer of outlandishly feminine hats which cover one of the shrewdest heads in public life."[18] To the *Chicago Tribune*, "Elevation of a woman to a vital position in the Defense Department [was] an example of the American tradition of opportunity for all."

Texas Congressman Ed Lee Gossett didn't see it that way, calling it "preposterous" that a "foreign-born female social worker" could handle a top position at the Department of Defense. "There are at least 100,000 native-born American men," claimed Gossett, "better equipped for this job than she is."[19] The imprimatur of a figure as estimable as General Marshall, however, assuaged the doubts of most Americans. Eleanor

Roosevelt marveled that "with the Army, Navy, Air Force, and Marine Corps, and the nation's leading industrialists and labor leaders to choose from, [George Marshall] wanted her to take charge of manpower."[20]

Within days of Fulton Lewis' broadcast, self-styled anti-Communist crusaders from every corner of the country joined anti-Semites in answering the call to attack Anna Rosenberg. The midwestern "Minister of Hate," Gerald L. K. Smith, had alerted his "fellow Americans" that "Anna Rosenberg, one of the most ominous and enigmatic figures in a secret [Jewish conspiracy]," now stood to be "the complete boss of the program of mobilization of American manhood."* These treacherous insinuations were not limited to the fringes of American society. Ignoring Rosenberg's qualifications, letters decrying Anna's gender, ethnicity, and loyalty poured forth from Los Angeles and Detroit, Baltimore and Dallas, and found their way to congressional offices and Senate mailboxes. Anna was a "magnet to draw together those seeking to destroy her."[21]

Despite the media noise and the shrill letter-writing campaign, Americans were fighting and dying in Korea, and work desperately needed to be done. At 11:00 AM on Wednesday, November 15, the day of the midterm elections, twenty-three people crammed into room 3E-880 of the Pentagon to watch history be made. At the center of the room was Anna, her nerves calmed somewhat by the presence of her son, Thomas, his wife, Jane, and trusty secretary Mrs. Phyllis Eckhoff. As top Army, Air Force, and Navy brass stood at attention, including General Omar Bradley and Marshall himself, Anna raised her right hand and swore to uphold the Constitution. With that Anna Rosenberg became the most powerful woman ever to serve in the United States military. "It is a great privilege in these serious times to be of some service," she said.[22] All that remained was the formality that her interim appointment be confirmed when the Senate returned to work.

At 7:45 the next morning, Secretary Rosenberg, carrying her purse and briefcase and wearing a tailored suit and high heels, pushed open the tall, heavy door of the Pentagon. Her new staff soon realized that

---

* Joseph and Stewart Alsop decried Smith as a "professional anti-Semite and tin pot amateur fascist" in their commentary on the situation, "Lesson in the Rosenberg Charges," *Washington Post*, December 17, 1950.

5:00 PM meant teatime, rather than leaving time, and after they went home in the evening Anna remained at work until late into the night. Translating General Marshall's objectives into a new program for 1951 meant Saturdays were full working days, as were half days on Sunday; on weekends, Anna "took over the Defense Secretary's kitchen to feed her staff."[23]

While Anna was putting in long hours at the Pentagon, elsewhere in the nation's capital, in hotel suites and congressional offices, her enemies were busily plotting. The field general of the smear campaign was Senator Joe McCarthy, whose office was the unofficial headquarters of the tawdry anti-Rosenberg brigade made up of amateurish private eyes and professional bigots. Second-in-command was Fulton Lewis, who sent his legman to Washington, D.C., to confer with McCarthy's men while he kept up his nightly radio blasts against the decorated public servant. Combining their considerable power, the radio star and the red-baiting Senator fanned the flames of anti-Semitism masquerading as anti-Communism. Their tactic was to take the most hateful rhetoric from the corners of America and polish it sufficiently to be debated in the U.S. Senate.

By November 29, the day of the vote on Anna Rosenberg's nomination as Assistant Secretary of Defense, every member of the thirteen-man Armed Services Committee—and President Truman—had received a letter or telegram denouncing Rosenberg. It is likely that most of the committee members saw the smears on Anna for what they were: rantings from the fringes of American society. The two known McCarthy allies on the Armed Services Committee, Senator Styles Bridges, Republican from New Hampshire, and Washington State's Harry Cain, may have seen things differently, but in the atmosphere of the Cold War the Democratic-led committee had no choice but to call in Anna Rosenberg and ask her to defend herself against the allegations. She would be the hearing's only witness.

At 3:45 that Wednesday afternoon, in room 212 of the Senate Office Building, Anna Rosenberg raised her right hand and was sworn in. After a series of background questions about her address, age, and arrival in America, the senators moved on.

"Where were you educated?" asked Chairman Richard Russell of Georgia.

"In New York City."

"Where?"

"The public schools of New York, and Wadleigh High School."

"Did you go any place after that?"

"No, I did not."

From there, the senators turned to the early years of her labor-relations career, when she was a young working mother. Between 1924 and 1928, she needed to earn money for her family because "her husband became ill after the birth of [their] son." "Consultant" was an "overrated term" for her, she said; it was her maternal obligation. These were modest jobs, she emphasized, some for as little as $35 per week—"part-time jobs" to pay the bills while her husband regained his health.

Responding to these questions, Anna employed a soft tone, what scholar Elizabeth A. Collins calls "feminine diminution." When trying to recollect a date, Anna said by way of apology, "I hope you will forgive me if I am a little bit nervous. This is my first experience, and if I am slightly nervous, please forgive me." Anna's demure responses were in keeping with other loyalty investigations of the era, when women "shaped their defenses," according to Collins, to "resonate with gender expectations . . . like wifehood and motherhood."

The committee members then asked Anna to describe her New Deal executive positions and her wartime mobilization work. After invoking President Franklin D. Roosevelt in connection with the wartime mission she made as his personal representative—one of three presidential missions to Europe for FDR—Anna explained that she had given up her private clients to take on the wartime post. "As you gentlemen recall, the War Manpower Commission was set up. [I was] a regional director. I remained with that Commission until 1945. On VE-day I left the government and went into my own business, where I have been ever since."

The members of the committee then asked her a series of questions about her business. "Who are your clients?" asked Chairman Russell, Democrat from Georgia.

"I know them by heart," began Anna. "The Rockefeller brothers."

Chairman Russell: "The what brothers?"

"The five Rockefeller brothers. John the Third, Nelson, David, Laurance, and Winthrop."

Russell: "Oh, yes."

Anna went on: Alfred Vanderbilt, John Hay Whitney & Co. and its principal Jock Whitney, philanthropists Albert and Mary Lasker, the Lazard Frères investment house and its president, André Meyer, Warner & Co. (now Pfizer Pharmaceuticals), Macy's department stores, I. Miller shoes, *Encyclopedia Britannica*, and concerns from perfumeries to breweries. "I am afraid, gentlemen," she said, wrapping up, "most of my clients are Republicans, and my fees are large."

Anna's shift to confidence and competence was deliberate, and risky. As Landon Storrs explains it, "female officials faced a . . . double-bind because [notions of] of femininity were incompatible with the wielding of power and expertise." But Anna's persona, described in the words of Anna Kasten Nelson as "blustery, hearty, and businesslike on the one hand, coyly feminine on the other," worked on powerful men. When she was regional director of the War Manpower Commission in World War II, Clarence Francis, the conservative chairman of General Foods, admitted Anna "had taken me into her camp." To Nelson Rockefeller, a Republican whose name was synonymous with capitalism, Anna was "brilliant, fair-minded, and extremely able."

The duality of her personality, a combination of straightforwardness and charm, gave Anna the freedom to display competence, entrepreneurial competitiveness, and even flashes of humor. When Senator Bridges, a known ally of McCarthy, asked her what type of beer one of her clients produced, Anna quipped, "The best, sir." During another exchange, a Senator asked her, "How close are you to Senator Symington?" Anna, whose daughter-in-law was Senator W. Stuart Symington's niece, answered, "Senator, if I were any closer, it would be a public scandal."

It is hard to imagine such repartee in the other hearings involving women, but Anna had worked with teamsters and longshoremen before becoming the nerve center of a network of leading businessmen, politicians, and military brass. She was, in the words of the late Professor Nelson, an "honorary man." Rather than regarding her femininity and ability as a double bind, Anna combined them into a one-two punch.

Questioning then drilled down to the substance of Fulton Lewis' on-air allegation that she had attended pro-Communist John Reed Club meetings in the 1930s. "I have never belonged to the John Reed Club," Anna stated flatly. "It was another Anna Rosenberg." While at the Social Security Administration more than a dozen years before, a sympathetic congressman had shown Anna the Dies Committee citation against her. "The person who was cited was not Anna M. Rosenberg," she explained. "I have always signed myself as Anna M. Rosenberg."

Prior to the hearing, Anna learned from the New York postmaster that there had been forty-six Anna Rosenbergs in New York at that time. Even Ben Mandel of HUAC had to admit that in New York, "Anna Rosenberg is a name like John Smith." What's more, it was known from the Dies Committee report that the Anna Rosenberg who attended the meetings in 1934 and 1935 had been a writer with the WPA's Federal Writers' Project. At that time Anna M. Rosenberg had been the nation's only woman regional director of the New Deal's National Recovery Administration. It was a simple case of mistaken identity.

Government salaries had been a line of attack against the other women targets, and so the fact that Anna was in line for a $15,000 per year government position gave her one last opportunity to read her audience. Senator McCarthy had opened his attack on Dorothy Kenyon by complaining that "this lady" received a $12,000 annual salary from the State Department. A witness in Mary Dublin Keyserling's hearing complained that Keyserling and her husband—also a government official—made five times his salary. Representative John Taber, a Republican from New York, called Keyserling a "parasite" on the federal payroll. By the time of Anna's hearing, such remarks, reflecting "both class and gender anxieties," according to Landon Storrs, were expected.

Anna was ready for it. When asked by Senator Millard Tydings of Maryland whether her stock holdings or clients would pose a conflict of interest, Anna was careful to not seem too eager for the position:

> Senator, if you do not mind, I would like to say something. I came down to Washington, I did not look for this job. I do not want this job. I came down here because General Marshall asked me. There is not another human being in the world for whom I would've done this. It is much

more difficult for me, a woman, because I cannot say to my husband and my family "Please move to Washington." So it is something I have done very reluctantly. I did it because I feel that everything I have, and maybe because I was not born in this country, I have an additional feeling of gratitude that everything I have I have got to put into this effort. There will never be any conflict because to me, my job will come first. I am a little bit sentimental on this point, and if I get a bit maudlin I hope you do not mind.

Far from taking advantage of a sizable government salary, Anna was taking a pay cut and upending her life out of a sense of loyalty to General Marshall and to her country. Nor was Anna half of a Washington dual-career power couple. Instead of following her husband into a government post, she was leaving her husband, sick with ulcers, behind in New York.

After her testimony, the committee members thanked Anna and excused her. Chairman Russell asked, "What is the pleasure of the committee on the nomination of Mrs. Anna Rosenberg?" Senator Lyndon Johnson was first to respond: "I move it reported favorably." One by one, the remaining senators followed suit. By the time Chairman Russell gaveled the close of the meeting at 4:55 PM, it had taken Anna only seventy minutes to convince all thirteen U.S. Senators on the committee of her fitness to serve.

CHAPTER NINETEEN

ENEMIES WITHIN

Oh, God, don't let me weaken. Help me to continue on.
And when I go down, let me go down like an oak tree
felled by a woodsman's ax.

—Anonymous quotation framed in the office
of Senator Joe McCarthy

———

INNOCENT BYSTANDER: *"I am not Cinna, the conspirator;*
I am Cinna, the poet."
THE MOB: *"Never mind, kill him for his*
name anyway!"

—Shakespeare, *Julius Caesar*

Establishing herself anew in Washington, Anna lived at the Shoreham Hotel as she had during World War II, not far from the leafy lanes and boutiques of Georgetown. Installed in a five-room suite, Anna began to reacquaint herself with life in the Capital. First she sent for some favorite objets d'art from her Fifth Avenue apartment to make the suite feel like home. French paintings on the walls comforted her, as did a porcelain Chelsea figurine on her desk topped in white leather. Large plants abounded, leaves glossy from her ministrations of mineral oil; a vase of pink roses stood on the long dining room table, with vases of white gladiolas elsewhere. The closetful of fine clothes, furs, and hats added to the luxury, but Anna would have little occasion to wear furs while in Washington this time around. Her social life in the capital had never matched that of New York City, but by working twelve- to sixteen-hour days at the Pentagon, Anna's social life nearly evaporated, the only rare indulgences being the National Symphony Orchestra at Constitution Hall or good Gallic cuisine at La Salle du Bois or Chez François.

Once Anna was confirmed by the Armed Services Committee by unanimous vote, all that remained was the formality of the full Senate vote. The day after the confirmation hearing, however, Senator Joseph McCarthy, who was not on the Senate Armed Services Committee, persuaded the Senate Minority Leader, Nebraska's conservative Kenneth Wherry, to postpone Rosenberg's full Senate confirmation. McCarthy then enlisted Congressman John Rankin, a notorious anti-Semite from Mississippi, and together they made haste.[1] On Friday, December 1, Rankin met with bespectacled retired businessman Benjamin H. Freedman, a character described by *Time* as "a peculiar and disgruntled zealot—a self-styled 'excommunicated Jew.'" The wealthy Freedman was a Holocaust denier and the financier of *Common Sense*, "a wild-eyed, anti-Semitic hate sheet." The four-page November issue, including a mail-order form for *The Protocols of the Learned Elders of Zion*, attacked Rosenberg, "who came from the heart of Eastern European Yiddish population" and whose record was filled with "subversive, pro-Communist activity."[2] In a perversion of the memory of Thomas Paine, Freedman mailed *Common Sense* to twenty-five thousand recipients, including all the names in the *Congressional Directory*, newspaper and radio columnists, and prominent Washingtonians.

Also present at the meeting was Gerald L. K. Smith, who sought to "keep the Zionist Jew from becoming dictator of the Pentagon." Following his meeting with two of the nation's most notorious extremists, Congressman Rankin took to the floor of the House Chamber, where he described Anna as "a little Yiddish woman from Austria-Hungary." In his speech read into the *Congressional Record*, Rankin went on: "The American people are aroused and indignant that this exalted position, one of the most powerful in the world, should be turned over to a foreign-born individual whose record for association with Communist organizations shows that she is unfit to occupy such a place of responsibility." If Rosenberg were to be confirmed, hyperventilated Rankin, "expect to see these Communists packed into our Defense Department by the thousands."[3] Echoing this diatribe was Congressman Clare Hoffman, who inserted into the *Congressional Record* an article by Smith dismissing Anna as "this Budapest Jewess." Because congressional debate is largely immune from libel laws, the Michigan

Republican's tactic was meant to give Smith's hateful rhetoric "maximum circulation."[4]

Over in the Senate, Joe McCarthy provided an audience to "Reverend" Wesley Swift, who had been a Ku Klux Klan organizer before establishing a church for white supremacists and whose public pronouncements included "All Jews must be destroyed."[5] Mrs. Rosenberg, according to the reverend, was not "only a Jewess, but an alien from Budapest with Socialistic ideas . . . with a well-known anti-Christian and pro-Communist record."

While McCarthy was hosting the good reverend, Texas Congressman Ed Lee Gossett squired Benjamin Freedman to the chambers of the Senate Armed Services Committee, where Freedman delivered the coup de grâce in the form of two anti-Rosenberg affidavits.[6] The first was signed by a former investigator for the Dies Committee claiming to have seen damaging information on Rosenberg in a leaked copy of her FBI file, and the other was a statement by a former Communist named Ralph De Sola, who claimed to have proof of Rosenberg's Communist ties and who was willing to testify against her.* The next day, December 5, acting chair Senator Richard Russell convened an executive session. Based on the sworn affidavits, the senators annulled their approval and voted to reopen the hearings on Anna Rosenberg.

McCarthy and the others plotters were triumphant. As they well knew, just the fact that a loyalty hearing was going to be held was enough to end careers. Like those of Dorothy Kenyon, Marcia Harris, and Esther Brunauer, it appeared that Anna Rosenberg's career would end in disrepute. "In this year of histrionics and hysteria," Anna said, "these accusations were very frightening and very bewildering."[7] Hoping to avoid indirectly besmirching General Marshall's career, Anna offered to resign. The Old Man would have none of it. "It was the only time I saw him get mad," Anna told Marshall's biographer Forrest Pogue.

---

* The FBI affidavit was signed by J. B. Matthews, the HUAC investigator for Congressman Martin Dies who had been pursuing Anna Rosenberg since the Sit-Down Strike in 1936–37. The FBI routinely opened files on government officials, and, in Anna Rosenberg's case, the file was voluminous due to her several government postings.

To obtain the FBI file himself, George Marshall invited Director J. Edgar Hoover to lunch. Marshall loathed Hoover. "Anna," he confessed, "I'd send for the devil if it would help get this cleared up."[8] The gambit worked: Marshall was able to privately review the file; the only outrage was how doggedly the Dies Committee and HUAC had tracked Anna's every interaction with groups they considered subversive, including civil rights organizations, consumer groups, and unions. To allow the loyalty hearing to go forward was risky, but Secretary Marshall would not bow to Joe McCarthy. "We will stick this out," he promised Anna.[9]

———— •••• ————

Friday, December 8, 1950, was a cold, raw day in the nation's capital, the unusually strong winds making it feel close to freezing. At eleven o'clock that morning, tall, slender Ralph De Sola, in a fedora and a gray double-breasted suit, strode into the Senate Armed Services Committee hearing room. Wearing wire-rimmed circular glasses, his black hair combed straight back, De Sola raised his right hand and was sworn in as the committee's first witness.

His testimony started off with claims that he recognized Anna Rosenberg from a brief encounter fifteen years in the past. De Sola claimed that he had spoken to Anna once at a John Reed Communist club meeting in 1935 and had seen her at four or five different meetings.* The committee was skeptical, given that Anna Rosenberg was a common name. How could he be sure that it was *this* Anna, Anna *M.* Rosenberg?

Senators then asked the witness multiple times to provide a physical description. How tall was she? How much did she weigh? What color was her complexion, her hair? What was the shape of her face? De Sola responded to the grilling, but Senator William Knowland of California seemed incredulous that De Sola had such a recollection of a person he had "casually met 15 years ago." The Senator insinuated that he was remembering her from newspaper photos rather than any Communist club meeting.

---

* John Reed was an American journalist and poet. After witnessing the Russian Revolution in October 1917, Reed wrote *Ten Days That Shook the World*, which made him a hero to American Marxists. After Reed died in Moscow of typhus in 1920, the cultural wing of the U.S. Communist Party conducted its activities through John Reed Clubs. Actor Warren Beatty portrayed Reed in the 1981 epic film *Reds*.

"And you remember talking to Mrs. Rosenberg on only one occasion?" followed up Senator Lyndon Johnson, in his measured Texas drawl.

"That is right." De Sola answered.

"And you remember how her voice sounded when you talked with her on that one occasion?"

"I think so."

Massachusetts Senator Leverett Saltonstall then wanted to know why, if De Sola had known Anna Rosenberg to be a Communist, had he kept quiet for a decade and half? Completely ignoring her war-related work at home that had been reported by every major newspaper and magazine in the country, De Sola reasoned that Rosenberg had been involved in "social work" in the Roosevelt administration and, accordingly, there had been no reason to sound the alarm. But now "I feel as if a Communist agent were as close as Mrs. Rosenberg to the Secretary of Defense, it would be . . . tremendously harmful."

By the early afternoon, De Sola's unconvincing testimony was leading to embarrassing surprises. Asked whether he had met with any members of Congress prior to testifying, De Sola admitted that he had been visited in his New York apartment late one night by two men who claimed to be from the Armed Services Committee:

> One of them, I think he stated he was from Senator McCarthy's office, [told me] that when I came down here, that is where I could leave my things and any messages that were coming for me, and that is what I did, at Room 254, Senator McCarthy's office. I went there this morning.

There was an astonished silence. Senator McCarthy was not on the Armed Services Committee. Was he tampering with a witness? The committee members were shocked at conduct so unbecoming of a member of the nation's highest legislative body.

By the time they took a recess at half past one, the committee had heard enough. They were ready to dismiss De Sola so he could make the four o'clock train back to New York. Anna, however, put an end to that plan. Chairman Russell, by way of offering her a chance to make an opening statement, asked Rosenberg, "Do you care to make any comment?"

After having painfully listened to De Sola for two and a half hours, Anna, "trembling with wrath" according to the *Chicago Tribune*, exploded.

> He is a liar and I would like to lay my hands on that man, Senator. It is inhuman what has been done to me in the past few days, and I am grateful to you people for the time you have spent; but I listened to the radio last night and my family listened and heard that I am charged with disloyalty.
>
> Now if this man is crazy or a Communist, I want to face him, Senator. I have never been a member of the John Reed Club; I have never been a Communist; I have never sympathized with Communists. I have spent my life trying to do something to help my country. I was ashamed . . . to have charges like that made against me. Forgive me, I know you have been here all day, but this has been a terrible ordeal for me.
>
> Please let me face this man.
>
> Please forgive me; maybe this is all wrong, but I plead with you, finish this. If you don't think I am fit to take this office, say so . . . I don't care what you charge me with, but not disloyalty, Senator. It is an awful thing to carry around with you.

This was a much different Anna from the one who appeared before the committee on November 29. To historian Elizabeth Collins, this "well-timed display of rage was perfectly pitched." While she was adept at shifting her persona depending on her audience or circumstance, since she was a teenage suffragette Anna was capable of outbursts of genuine anger when her core beliefs—women's right to vote, social equality, fidelity to democracy, and loyalty to America—were challenged. This was Anna's instinctive outrage at being labeled disloyal to her country by a character like De Sola. To journalist Fred J. Cook, "it was a cry from the heart."[10]

Emotions continued to run high once back in the hearing room. "My dear man, what in hell is the matter with you?" Anna demanded of Ralph De Sola. "I have never seen this man in my life," she told the committee.[11]

The Anna Rosenberg in the file had been a writer. "I have never been a writer," said Anna. What's more, she always signed her name as "Anna M. Rosenberg." In a bizarre exchange, De Sola challenged Anna to prove her innocence by producing the other Anna Rosenbergs, including the writer who attended the Communist meetings. Anna shot back: "It is up to *you* to have looked at them before you make such a serious accusation against me."

De Sola then countered: "I am far from convinced that you are not exactly who I think you are."

Anna fired back: "Mr. De Sola, I am not here to convince *you*." She continued, "I don't believe that any human being wants to do what you are doing purposely. You came into [this] room, and you said, 'This is the woman.' You never [even] looked at me. Do you know what you are doing to me?"

De Sola then looked her up and down: was she the same Anna Rosenberg as the one at the Communist club meetings fifteen years before?

"Would you mind standing up?"

"I will stand up!" Rosenberg shot back, glaring at De Sola. "Now tell me, am I the woman [from the Communist] Club?"

"Yes, she's it. I recognize her."

Time seemed to stand still. This was the face-to-face encounter that had ended so many careers in previous loyalty hearings. From the witness chair, Anna saw her home-state Senator Herbert Lehman attending the hearing although he was not part of the Armed Services Committee. He was in shock at the audacity of the lie and undone by the character assassination playing out before him, tears rolling down his cheeks.[12]

But there was no time for self-pity.

"What do you have to say to that?" Chairman Russell asked Anna.

"It's a goddamned lie!"

The hearing room suddenly went silent but for the scribbling pens and pencils of reporters. A moment later, echoing the earlier inquiry from Senator Saltonstall, Anna wanted to know why De Sola sat on this information for fifteen years, without telling anyone. He responded: "Because I am sorry to see that we have a Secretary of Defense who has to be assisted by a Communist. I am sorry for our country. If you had been put in a social security agency where it was at most a question of some sort of social work, social-welfare work, I would've said cynically to myself, 'Well, those people get there anyway and she can't do too much harm,' and—"

"Just a moment!" thundered the chairman, cutting off De Sola. "We will proceed in an orderly way!"

De Sola's chauvinistic remark that social work was women's work and unimportant turned out to be the last the committee heard from him. Anna, "trembling and choking with rage," according to the *Washington Times-Herald*, got the last word: "I would like to get on the record, Mr. Chairman, that I have never seen this man in my life."

After the day's testimony, a spent Anna was approached by Lyndon Johnson in the corridor. Anna had known Johnson since he came to Washington as a young congressman in thrall to FDR. It was the beginning of a thirty-five-year friendship and working relationship between Anna and LBJ. But at this moment, Lyndon Johnson was angry. Standing over her, he lectured her, "Don't you ever swear again! Do you realize what it means in the Bible Belt? And especially a woman! Don't ever use language like that again."

"Lyndon, someday when you're confronted with an accusation that staggers you, you will say it, too."

"I sure will," admitted LBJ, "but that's all right. I'm a man."[13]

———◆◆◆———

Ralph De Sola was on the train back to New York, but Friday's testimony left several questions unanswered: Who were the two investigators, one of whom claimed to represent Senator McCarthy? How large a role was McCarthy playing in all this? Was he the mastermind of the campaign against Anna Rosenberg, or was it Benjamin Freedman or Reverend Wesley Smith? Was it radio provocateur Fulton Lewis? And what was in that FBI file?

Regardless of who was behind the case against Anna, as Fulton Lewis crowed on his radio show that evening, there had a been a positive identification, and it was De Sola's word against hers.[14] When the hearings resumed Monday, December 11, a slate of witnesses were to corroborate De Sola's story.

———•••———

At this point the case against Anna began to unravel, beginning with the appearance of Helen Winner, De Sola's ex-wife. Her former husband, she said, was "sort of on and off unemployed."[15] Not only did he see-saw between jobs, but his "fanaticism" and "extremism" took him from ardent Communist to anti-Communist witness-for-hire.[16] Asked about De Sola's truthfulness, she hedged: "He is a truthful person, with some limitations . . . he believes what he says . . . it is an awfully difficult thing to explain."[17]

"Is he well-balanced?" asked Senator Lester C. Hunt.

"Is this going to appear some place? These are very hard things to say in a public hearing."

When the committee asked if De Sola was of "good, sound mind," Ms. Winner asked to respond off the record. She was thereafter dismissed.

De Sola's reputation for veracity took another hit when a coworker told the committee De Sola "time and again proved himself to be telling complete falsehoods . . . I wouldn't rely on any statement he made, under oath or otherwise." A former supervisor of De Sola's judged him to be "a person of extreme dishonesty who would stop at nothing for bits of notoriety in which he could stand out."

Fifteen ex-members of the John Reed Club denied ever knowing an Anna Rosenberg. Witnesses who were scheduled to appear went truant. "The odor of the affair," observed Eleanor Roosevelt, "got too bad for some of the witnesses who were supposed to appear against her."[18] Others changed their testimony; still others did more damage to their case. A woman named Marjorie Shearon, who had been fired as a low-level congressional staffer, spun a bizarre tale that Rosenberg was, along with President Truman, members of Congress, and leading Americans, part of "a gigantic conspiracy emanating from Moscow." In response, the letter of termination from the senator who fired her was read into the record: "It is my considered opinion that Mrs. Shearon is hysterical, psychopathic, and [a] completely untrustworthy individual whose testimony is deserving of absolutely no credence whatsoever." Long before her time was up, she, too, was dismissed. From the moment De Sola's testimony ended on December 8, the hearing had been digging up, in *Time* magazine's pungent phrase, "a veritable sea gull's nest of rotting political fish heads."[19]

By the end of Tuesday's hearing, after witness upon witness had blown holes in De Sola's story, it was clear the case against Anna Rosenberg was no more than "a flimsy tissue of lies."[20]

That evening, a number of politicians and prominent Washingtonians attended a dinner dance at the Sulgrave Club for the heiress of a prominent publishing family. The cheeky hostess sat two bitter enemies at the same table: Senator Joe McCarthy and the most influential syndicated columnist in the country, Drew Pearson. With his column appearing in six hundred newspapers, Pearson had written forty columns against McCarthy up to that point, including several alleging the Senator was a tax cheat. In response, McCarthy denigrated Pearson on the floor of the U.S. Senate, calling him a Communist tool, an agent of Moscow, all the while shielded by the cloak of immunity against libel and slander laws for senatorial pronouncements. Seeing Pearson take his seat across the table on what had been a long, deflating day must have curdled the Senator's already sour mood. "I'm going to tear you limb from limb," growled McCarthy by way of greeting, glass of whisky in hand. "Say, Joe," Pearson sniped back, "have you paid your income taxes yet? How long are they going to let you stay out of jail?" Then, according to Pearson, the Senator from Wisconsin called him "a God damned son of a bitch." Pearson rose to respond, but the wife of a Washington lawyer intervened: "Don't be a fool. Sit down! Can't you see he's been drinking?"[21] The two men retreated, but Pearson kept a wary eye on the Senator, who had a glass in his hand all evening.

As the party drew to a close, Drew Pearson went to the cloakroom. As he reached into his pocket for tip money for the coat-check girl, Joe McCarthy emerged from the shadows and Pearson felt a bear claw grab his shoulder. McCarthy "pinned my hands down," Pearson said, "swung me around, and proceeded to kick me in the groin with his knee." Just then Congressman Richard Nixon, a fellow red-baiter, walked in. McCarthy slapped Pearson hard across the face. "That one was for Dick!"[22] McCarthy then rumbled out into the night, later making a drunken call to a conservative journalist to brag that he'd kicked Drew Pearson "in the nuts."[23] "I thought he was going to kill him," said Nixon. The next month Pearson sued McCarthy for the injuries he sustained in the assault.

Twelve hours later, in the Senate Armed Services Committee hearing room, hundreds of letters were placed into the record praising Anna Rosenberg "in extraordinarily warm terms." The letters were from ordinary Americans as well as from General Eisenhower, CIA Director "Beetle" Smith, newspaper publisher Oveta Culp Hobby, elder statesman Bernard Baruch, former New Dealer James Byrnes, and the widow of Fiorello La Guardia—"everybody you ever heard of who was head of anything."[24] At four o'clock in the afternoon the next day, December 14, 1950, the committee voted unanimously to reapprove her nomination as Assistant Secretary of Defense. A week later, by overwhelming voice vote, the U.S. Senate approved Anna's nomination. Rather than besmirching Anna Rosenberg, the hearings, concluded Senator Benton, brought "to the attention of . . . the Senate, and to the country as a whole, [her] remarkable background and record . . . and extraordinary qualifications."[25] As she exited the Senate Office Building to head back to work at the Pentagon, reporters asked Anna for a comment. "I am proud of our Democracy," she replied.[26]

"When I got word," Anna told Marshall's biographer Forrest Pogue, "I rushed in [to Marshall's office]. He and the Joint Chiefs had their coats on. I was choked up." Breaking into tears, Anna told Marshall she has been confirmed as Assistant Secretary of Defense. General Marshall bent down and kissed her on the cheek. "That's wonderful, Anna. I know you've been through hell." Realizing he was getting too sentimental, the dignified old soldier straightened up and barked, "Now go home and fix your makeup. That's an order."

———•••———

In the aftermath of the hearings, Republican Senator Harry Cain sought a private conversation with Anna. "I was ready to attack you," admitted Cain, who had agreed to "carry the ball" for Senator McCarthy at the hearings. "I agreed to do it. Then I listened to you. And I just had the feeling that you were telling the truth, and I'm not going to do it." The denouement of the "spectacle of disgrace" sent its perpetrators fleeing. Benjamin Freedman distanced himself from the affair by "correcting his testimony" and offering to help Anna Rosenberg financially. Fulton Lewis was chastened by the head of his network and spent the next several months fending off accusations of anti-Semitism. McCarthy's legman, Ed Nellor, was rewarded by the Republican Party with a radio-TV director position; the hatemongers he wallowed with, Reverend Swift and Gerald L. K. Smith, slithered further underground, and Ralph De Sola skidded into obscurity.[27]

As for the FBI file—as George Marshall could have predicted—it turned out to be a dud. Shown the file by special permission granted by President Truman, a subcommittee of Senators Harry Byrd, Cain, and Hunt concluded, "There is not a word in the files to support any of the un-American charges alleged against Mrs. Anna M. Rosenberg." Rather than proving a nexus between Rosenberg and subversive organizations, the routine file kept on top-ranking government officials was "highly complimentary to the personal character, to the competence, capacity and to the loyalty" of Mrs. Rosenberg. Perhaps to atone for the needless damage the bureau had done to Anna's reputation, Director Hoover sent his agents on a nationwide search to locate the ex-Communist writer Anna Rosenberg who had attended the Communist meetings in Greenwich Village in the mid-1930s; they found her living in California.

Since Joe McCarthy barged onto the national stage waving his Big Lie that the Truman administration was teeming with Communists, McCarthy's string of cheap political wins in 1950 ended with Anna Rosenberg, who swung the first ax blow against the demagogic giant. Others would follow: Edward R. Murrow used the initial broadcast of his radio program *Hear It Now* to tell his nationwide radio audience "the character assassin has missed."[28] On the floor of the Senate, New York's Herbert Lehman supported Connecticut's William Benton as he accused McCarthy of "conduct unbecoming a member of the nation's highest legislative body."[29] For his part in the affair, McCarthy became linked to reactionaries, extremists, and crackpots; that he had been the puppet master of the sordid affair was crystal clear to contemporary observers:

> In Senator Joe McCarthy, the hate-peddlers found rallying
> point, a common hero. There was nothing strange about
> the political liaison, nothing contradictory when viewed

against the ragged tapestry of Joe's career . . . McCarthy had frequently used his office to further the aims of the gutter-crowd, but seldom so glaringly as in the 1950 [fight] over the appointment of Mrs. Anna Rosenberg as Assistant Secretary of Defense.*

During the first two weeks of December 1950, the drama unfolding in the Senate Armed Services hearing room had played out coast to coast, a battle in the Cold War culture war. Fulton Lewis continued his weeks-long assault over the airwaves, but on the radio and in newspapers, Rosenberg's defenders came forward. Syndicated columnists nationwide condemned the poisonous attack. Fedora-wearing Walter Winchell defended Anna, as did Marquis Childs, who decried McCarthy's "plot to smear and destroy Mrs. Anna Rosenberg."[30] Joseph and Stewart Alsop called the manufactured case against her an attempt to "tar and feather" Rosenberg, and even conservative columnist David Lawrence came to her defense. No one put it better than the Anti-Defamation League, which provided an early postmortem:

> In the jittery atmosphere of our day, aggravated by those who cynically played upon America's concern over the Communist danger . . . an accidental similarity of names . . . opened the way for a group of unscrupulous and irresponsible men to place upon the rack a public servant of unimpeachable reputation.[31]

The end of the ordeal was a relief to Anna, but there was hardly any time for her to regroup. The troops in Korea, spending their first Christmas on the cold, mountainous peninsula, badly needed trained reinforcements. That Anna was poised to send them help at the beginning of her career at the Defense Department was part of the battle. Unlike Dorothy Kenyon and the other women who were exiled from public life in the opening year of the McCarthy era, Anna Rosenberg had survived

---

* Jack Anderson, *McCarthy: The Man, the Senator, the "Ism"* (London: Gollancz, 1953), 309. Benton's charge was supported by another friend of Anna Rosenberg's, New York Senator Herbert Lehman. See Rosenberg, oral history interview with Wall.

the smear campaign and the ensuing investigation with her character and integrity intact. "The scurrilous attack on Mrs. Rosenberg," wrote Oregon lawmaker Maurine Neuberger in the *New York Times*, showed "that a woman can endure . . . abuse and yet emerge stronger and more respected for it."[32]

Far from feeling triumphant, Anna knew what the episode meant for her country. Two days before the full Senate vote, Anna wrote to Eleanor Roosevelt:

> I didn't believe that anyone who has lived the way I have and worked the way I have could be accused in such a way. . . . Maybe this nightmare that I've gone through will have one good result—that it will serve as a shocking example of what can be done to human beings who are trying to do an honest job. . . . Maybe it will wake us up to the fact that we have not only enemies without but very dangerous ones within.[33]

CHAPTER TWENTY

A WOMAN IS RUNNING THE ARMY!

A figure less military than Anna Rosenberg could scarcely be imagined. She is tiny—the tip of the bow of her pert little hat would hardly reach above the shoulder of a general.

—Eleanor Roosevelt, *Ladies of Courage*

THE PENTAGON, WASHINGTON, D.C.

Streaks of gray in her always-coiffed hair, a few lines beneath her makeup, Assistant Secretary of Defense Anna M. Rosenberg was an exotic newcomer in the male-dominated wilds of Pentagonia. Anna's bright silk blouses, chic suits, and "multi-colored back-of-the-head hats" provided colorful foliage in contrast to the olive drab and "austere blue" of the Defense Department.[1] The scent of French perfume was a novelty, as was as the sound of her battery of bracelets. "She came up here and jangled," marveled one Pentagon official; "those bracelets are like the bells of St. Mary's."[2] Military protocol was no match, reported the *New York Times*, for the "tiny, bright-eyed comet" of "fidgety energy" who looks like "a successful member of the afternoon bridge set." When a male staffer lectured her on the no-skirt rule, she shot back, 'Well, the pants rule hasn't been so hot.'" While other offices were emptying out for the day, Anna's was full of staff members for the five o'clock tea; jackets were unbuttoned or placed over the backs of chairs as Anna and her longtime assistant Phyllis, who had agreed to relocate to Washington, passed around a tray of cookies: "Take another one, *dollink*." As the staff took their cue from Anna's informality, the atmosphere of the office was "more reminiscent of Broadway than of the career military." Her staff of three young male consultants and three female secretaries, quickly baptized in "the Rosenberg technique of needling, cajoling, and enlightening," were soon affectionately calling her "Aunt Anna."[3]

George Marshall and Anna both recognized she was an anomaly. Although he never would have admitted it, the general worried whether Anna's decidedly nonmilitary style would play at the Pentagon. General Marshall, wrote Frances Levison in the *New York Times*, "has staked his reputation on her performance." Perhaps to insulate her from critics, the Old Man stationed her in the office next to his, 3E-880, the inner sanctum of the U.S. military command.

Once inside her office, visitors saw portraits of George Marshall and Bernard Baruch—two statesmen, one for the armed forces and one for the home front—in places of pride next to the photo of FDR. Her large desk was at the center of the room, which was lined with blue leather chairs. Next to the United States flag was the official flag of the Assistant Secretary: crossed arrows, an eagle, and four stars on a white field. "It's the only thing about me that's ever impressed my son," joked Anna. But beyond the flags, there were few signs of the military world. Paintings adorned the walls, including an oil of Vermont at maple-sugaring season, and potted plants and flowers abounded. Two "diplomas" were proudly framed behind her massive desk, one from a brewer's union, and one from a theatrical union; in large letters at the bottom, it read: "You are tops."[4]

General Marshall, who called everyone by their last name—"Vandenburg, Pace, Lovett!"—would saunter through the connecting anteroom into his neighbor's office several times a day to check on "Anna." Using her first name was an "unprecedented accolade," to which Anna responded by referring to her boss as "the General."[5] Although he left her "to handle her task in her own fashion," the General was "marvelously accessible" and "set out to help her make it a success."[6] Anna was at her desk on one visit early in her tenure when the General walked in and fixed her with a long stare. "Get her a chair that will fit her," he barked to an aide. "How do you expect her to make good judgments when her feet aren't on the ground!"[7] Marshall's paternal protectiveness soon gave way to an abiding confidence in Anna's ability to do the job. "He told me later that during that first meeting with the military leaders he had an aide stationed outside the door to let him know if I had any trouble and he should come to the rescue. I didn't. I took a very tough line."[8] As the number two person at the Defense Department, Anna Rosenberg was in charge of procurement, utilization, and policy-making regarding U.S. military personnel. She was, in the words of *Life* magazine, "far and away the most important woman in the American government, and perhaps the most important official female in the world."[9]

As for Anna, if she had doubts, they were quickly swept away by the expression of trust from her boss. "It wasn't an easy situation, and if it hadn't been for General Marshall, I don't know whether I'd have been able to do the job. He was a darling. . . . Before my first meeting with all the top generals and admirals, I felt that in order to be able to deal with them I would have to know exactly what my powers were. When I asked, General Marshall replied, 'Everything I can do, you can do.'"[10]

Anna was also buoyed by the hundreds of letters of support that followed her profiles in *Collier's*, *Life*, *Reader's Digest*, and other national magazines seizing on the petite-woman-at-the-Pentagon angle. "You certainly don't let any grass grow," wrote Nelson Rockefeller; "this is the perfect example of how you get things done." Other business leaders like Bernard Baruch added their voices in support. Hundreds of ordinary women complimented her on her post: "You carried the heart and loyalty of every woman with you," read one such letter. *Time* publisher Henry Luce wrote Anna, as did the editor-in-chief of Doubleday, who joined the chorus asking for her memoir. "If you'd write it for Doubleday that would please me, but what would please me the most is for you to write it." In off-the-record remarks, President Truman told the press, "I've never heard anybody brag on a person as the Secretary of Defense does on Anna."[11] General Marshall wasn't the only one pleased with Anna's work. The *Washington Post* cheered that "so great a responsibility [had been] entrusted to a woman," and a "so able a woman chosen to discharge it."[12]

The fact that Anna had a spacious office right next to General Marshall's rankled a few aides. "It was six times as big as McNeil's," remarked a veteran Pentagon hand; "it was big enough to hold a dance in there. It made her post appear as important as hell."[13] Such petty jealousies were well-known to Rosenberg. "The military people were very upset to have a woman come in and, in effect, be their boss," Anna explained. "They felt they were confronted by a natural antagonist."[14] To some, the new Assistant Secretary of Defense was the overly officious "Madame Bangles," clanging along the seventeen and a half miles of cavernous Pentagon corridors while generals, admirals, and their staffers hid.* Others were less witty in diminishing her because of her gender. "This little girl from New York," grumbled Truman adviser Joseph D. Keenan, "what's her name, Anna Rosenberg." A grunt accused of going AWOL complained to the Court Martial Review Board, "Rosenberg—she's telling the generals what to do. It's pretty bad when a woman is running the army!"[15] Even General James F. Collins, assigned to be Mrs. Rosenberg's executive assistant, had his doubts: "I had always been with the troops and tried to avoid the Pentagon. I told Anna I didn't want to be there . . . I didn't even bring my family to Washington. But after I got started, I got interested in what we were doing."[16]

Petty jealousy notwithstanding, Anna's grit and grace won over most critics. If the sexist remarks and latent resentment from some of the men in the Pentagon bothered her, she shrugged it off. "If you can't take it," she told Edward R. Murrow, "you don't belong in Washington. It's just an everyday affair."[17] Within days of assuming the highest position ever held by a woman in the U.S. military, Anna began translating General Marshall's vision for a Cold War military into reality. A profile in *Independent Woman* magazine found her at the head of a "big conference table, surrounded by military and civilian leaders, hard at work on her new job." The *New York Times* described her darting and zooming "up and down Pentagon halls and escalators," from conference to conference, bringing "differing points of view . . . to terms." Mornings were often spent studying material and preparing reports for congressional committees, afternoons saw her testifying before lawmakers, and most evenings she was back in her Pentagon office. When colleagues saw the hours she put in—sometimes to 10:00 PM, sometimes midnight, sometimes all-nighters—they were won over. "We had our squabbles," said General

---

* In 1983, after Anna's death, the Pentagon established a Women's Memorial Corridor, and Anna's grandson, Thomas P. Rosenberg, brought her bracelets to be included in the exhibit, which was hosted by Secretary of Defense Caspar Weinberger.

Collins, "but she was a worker . . . the job got done, and I don't think anyone else could have done it."

> Nobody bluffed her. If somebody told her the White House had said something, she'd say "Who in the White House? It's a big place." . . . If somebody changed his story on her, she'd say "wait a minute" and reach into that desk drawer and come up with a slip of paper with what they'd said on such and such a date.[18]

Ever practical, Anna did not let military bureaucracy slow her down. "Where procedure is concerned, ignorance is bliss," she told *Time*.[19] "She leaps upstream over sluggish Washington channels," reported the *New York Times*. "When all this is over," Anna explained, "there'll be no historic documentation of our work. I issue no memos. There's nothing around with eight copies. When I want something done I just call up a friend. . . . Before I came here I heard a lot about protocol, channels, red tape, the big brass, and all those other ogres of bureaucracy. I must say they haven't bothered me at all."[20] Perhaps because of her efficiency, Marshall quickly made Anna the Defense Department's point person with President Truman. Dispatching Anna on one such mission to the White House, the General instructed her, "Tell him it's politically dangerous, but would be good for the services. But don't overemphasize the good of the services. Just tell him what the situation is, not disguising the political danger." Anna did as she was told, but Truman shot back: "Please don't tell me what is politically dangerous and what is not. Just tell me what General Marshall wants because that's the way it's going to be."[21]

With only two links in the chain of command above her—General Marshall and President Truman—Anna was free to be demanding of those under her. When military old-timers gave excuses, Anna cut them off with a "sharp, loud 'Baloney!'" While some military men harbored "secret resentment, and sometimes not so secret," at being told what to do by a woman, others found a "tough little woman who has the spirit to answer back, to fight for her own case, and to parry with the best of them."[22]

Backed by Marshall's "granite confidence" and having quickly established herself as a force in the Defense Department, Secretary Rosenberg took as her first task streamlining personnel management. "The House Armed Services Committee had made a study that showed there were something like 54 agencies handling manpower and personnel," lamented General Collins. "Our manpower was all scattered around, and when Marshall saw the report he decided immediately he needed somebody to pull the whole thing together. He had known Anna when she was on the War Manpower Commission and felt she could do it."[23] Seeking to centralize military personnel, in April 1951 Secretary Marshall transferred to Rosenberg all Munitions Board functions relating to "manpower, industrial relations, and labor supply." In May the General abolished the Personnel Policy Board and put it under Rosenberg, and in June he did the same with the Civilian Components Policy Board. A number of citizens' committees were also directed to report through Rosenberg, including the Defense Advisory Committee on Women in the Services (DACOWITS) in August.[24] By mid-1952, Anna was the human resources department of the entire U.S. military. By the end of the year, her staff numbered 327 full-time military and civilian employees.[25]

The centralization of military personnel was part of Rosenberg's urgent task to increase the size of the armed forces. When the Korean War broke out, the armed services were "woefully unprepared to fight a war."[26] Post–WW II budget cuts took the armed forces from nearly 10 million men and eighty-nine divisions in 1945 to 591,000 and ten divisions in 1950.[27] Hardened WW II vets had been replaced by green recruits. Half of this diminished Army were serving overseas as occupation forces, where the relaxed atmosphere did little to establish combat readiness. Compounding matters was an antiquated reserve system that creaked to produce under-strength and subpar units. "It was nothing," Rosenberg said of the Army. "We had to build from scratch. We had no manpower. We had a reserve system which wasn't worth two cents. By the time you called up a reserve unit, the men were all too fat and too old, or had developed diseases. Nevertheless, we had to go ahead."[28] The deterioration of the nation's military readiness played out against the backdrop of a worsening international situation. To fight the Korean War, to contain Communist aggression, and to occupy Japan and West Germany, Secretary of Defense George Marshall demanded an army of 3 million or more.

Moving with alacrity, Assistant Secretary Rosenberg consolidated the various personnel agencies and began drafting policies for the short- and long-term readiness of the U.S. military. Within weeks of her Senate confirmation, General Marshall presented her recommendations for increased personnel to Congress. The draft age would be lowered from nineteen to eighteen, and the period of service would be extended from twenty-one to twenty-seven months. Concerns as to these changes were allayed by the fact that fewer WW II veterans, now fathers and home-owners, would be called back to duty. The defense bill also included a provision for long-term security in the distressed international atmo-sphere of the early Cold War: Universal Military Training. UMT was the Cold War version of an idea debated since the time of George Wash-ington and the citizen-soldier, a program in which all American men upon turning eighteen would receive six months of basic military train-ing before continuing with their education or career, while also form-ing a large civilian reserve cohort until the age of twenty-five.* "If war comes," Rosenberg cautioned a congressional committee, "it is likely to come with terrifying speed, and it may be directed at our own country as a first target."[29] A large, quickly mobilized force would lessen the threat. According to General Marshall, "a good standing army in America would have averted not only the Korean War but World War II itself."[30] But war had erupted and the U.S. military had been caught flat-footed. *Time* called the reserve system "ramshackle and disorganized" and the National Guard "wobbly, clique-ruled and riddled with politics." It was a system in need of "drastic overhauling" made ever more urgent "if war breaks out with Russia in the next year or two."[31]

While President Truman was in favor of the program, compulsory military training had many foes in Congress, who saw it as an unnec-essary and expensive check on Americans' freedoms. There was also the question of whether such training would be racially integrated—an untenable scenario to southern lawmakers. "If you can't sell it," Dwight

---

* "The citizens of America, from 18 to 50 years of age," wrote George Washington in 1783, "should be borne on the Militia Rolls, provided with uniform arms, and . . . accustomed to use them." When the UMT bill was sent to Congress, Anna Rosenberg phoned Senator Lyndon Johnson to tell him, "George Washington started it, and you finished it!" ("National Affairs: After 168 Years," *Time*, June 11, 1951.)

Eisenhower cabled Anna from Supreme Allied Headquarters in Paris, "no one can."[32]

For five months while the bill was debated, Assistant Secretary Rosenberg led the charge for UMT on Capitol Hill. She "systematize[d] the information, conciliate[d] the disputants, iron[ed] out the confusions," and drafted a workable program under which all grown men would give a period of service to their country. Senator Lyndon Johnson hailed her work as "the most comprehensive study ever made of manpower in America . . . the best job that's been done in Washington in twenty years."[33] Her proposal gained "the satisfaction of the military," and General Marshall sent her to persuade Congress. "He gave her work his blessing," reported the *New York Times*, "and relinquished to Mrs. Rosenberg the task of battling with the wolves."[34] In April 1951, Anna Rosenberg, "a powerhouse of both information and energy," articulated to Congress the need for UMT:

> We are faced today with a serious and threatening international situation. . . . The security of our nation requires that we have, in a constant state of readiness for combat, a much larger number of trained men than the country can afford or want to keep permanently under arms. . . . The democratic answer to this problem lies in a relatively small regular military establishment and an effective civilian reserve capable of swift mobilization in an emergency.[35]

The "democratic" nature of Rosenberg's national security solution portended its ultimate defeat. Mississippi Congressman John Williams demanded to know whether segregation would be maintained in the training program. When Rosenberg responded with a blunt, "No," another segregationist congressman complained "this measure is . . . an Anna Rosenberg *social integration* scheme."[36] In the end, the normally pro-military southern congressmen voted down the effort to institute UMT.

The defense bill President Harry Truman signed on June 19, 1951, did include Rosenberg's other policies, such as lowering the draft age to eighteen and a half, and lengthening the service commitment to twenty-four months. Not only did this increase the size of the armed forces, but it was made more equitable. All military enlistees were required to take the Armed Forces Qualification Test. Year after year, top-scoring examinees were poached by the Air Force and lowest-scoring soldiers went into the Army—which fed into the Army's argument that its high proportion of poorly qualified soldiers made segregated units necessary. To end this, Rosenberg proposed a recruit-sharing system, so that all branches would benefit fairly from the nation's top-level recruits.[37] Congress adopted her plan, and Secretary Marshall ordered the services to share low-scoring draftees proportionately, undercutting the Army's argument to remain segregated. Historian Morris MacGregor credits this policy change as the "single most significant contribution of the Secretary of Defense" to the integration of the armed forces.[38]

As she worked to square New Deal social equity with the national security policy of containment, Anna Rosenberg's next step was the recruitment of women. Rosenberg set out to obtain seventy-two thousand servicewomen by first asking Congress to remove the 2 percent ceiling on the strength of women in the regular forces. Congress complied. But in the years after World War II, recruiting women was especially difficult. The American public was tired of war. Korea was a "police action" rather than a true national emergency, and the war did not ignite the patriotism that drove the Greatest Generation. In the conservative fifties, there was little interest in seeing women in nontraditional roles and many women were uninterested in filling such roles. According to historian Judith Bellafaire, "The vast majority of American women of military age had marriage, not military service, on their minds."[39]

Despite the headwinds, a nationwide mission to recruit women set off in November 1951. In his annual Armistice Day radio address on the eleventh, President Truman opened the recruiting campaign: "There are now 40,000 women on active duty in the Army, Navy, Air Force, and Marines. In the next seven months we hope at least 72,000 more will volunteer for service. Our Armed Forces need these women. They need them badly."[40] Women of the Armed Services parades were held in Chicago, San Francisco, Atlanta, and other cities, culminating with a ticker-tape parade down Broadway in New York City. The National Advertising Council prepared and distributed thousands of newspaper ads, outdoor advertising signs, bumper stickers, and fact sheets to over fifteen hundred newspapers, magazines, and other media outlets as a public service to enhance the recruiting campaign. The theme was "Share Service for Freedom."

When she discovered that recruiters lacked suitable marketing materials, Assistant Secretary Rosenberg had surveys conducted and updated the marketing messages to recruit and retain women. The Army's "Procurement of Women" became Anna's "Recruitment of WAVES."[41] Articles like *Collier's* "The Girls Get Ready to Serve" appeared in the nation's magazines, and Anna deployed a top woman reporter from the *New York Herald Tribune* to "visit all the theaters in which women are serving and report on their activities."[42] The U.S. Postal Service issued a commemorative three-cent stamp, "Women in Our Armed Forces," and Hollywood obliged, releasing *Never Wave at a WAC*, a comedy in which a society princess and a pinup model become unlikely friends after joining the Army for very different reasons.*

Meanwhile, Rosenberg presided over the first meeting of the Defense Advisory Committee on Women in the Services, established by General Marshall at her urging. Made up of fifty prominent members, women college presidents, physicians, and philanthropists, DACOWITS would spearhead the nationwide recruiting campaign. The young women they recruited would be more than "typewriter soldiers"; they would serve as nurses and doctors, communications technicians, and intelligence analysts. The Assistant Secretary of Defense championed "womanpower" not because it freed up more "manpower," but because she believed serving in the armed forces would not only satisfy a military expediency but provide a path to greater social equality.

Anna had consulted President Truman when he signed the Women in the Armed Forces Integration Act in 1948, and she continued to draw the connection between service and sacrifice, equality and respect—a link at the heart of her own success. "Manpower isn't just men," she told a reporter, "it's human power—men and women . . . the

---

* Linda Witt, Judith Bellafaire, Britta Granrud, and Mary Jo Binker, *A Defense Weapon Known to Be of Value: Servicewomen of the Korean War Era* (Lebanon, NH: University Press of New England, 2005), 86 and 230. In the 1952 film, when character Jo McBain, played by Rosalind Russell, is asked for character references, the first name she gives is "Anna Rosenberg, Assistant Secretary of Defense."

old dividing line between 'a man's job' and 'a woman's job' is fast disappearing."[43] To another reporter she explained, "If this country is to have proper respect for its women, the women have to take a share of the responsibility."

For the first few months of the recruitment campaign, the efforts seemed to be paying off. "Overall strength in each of the [service branches] increased impressively."[44] By mid-1952, however, it was clear the campaign would not meet its goal. Colonel Mary Hallaren, director of the Women's Army Corps, later attributed the failure to "inexperience of women recruiters; parental objection; poor reputation of service women; and competition with civilian industry."[45] Despite falling short on numbers, the Korean War era campaign resulted in women serving in an unprecedented variety of roles in the services: administration, personnel, supply, communications, and intelligence. Today DACOWITS remains one of the Defense Department's most enduring advisory committees.

After a year and a half on the job, it was clear George Marshall's gamble on Anna had paid off. Entrusted with total control over the "seemingly insatiable service requests for manpower" and operating on three and four hours of sleep, Anna Rosenberg had delivered.[46] By April 1952, military personnel was consolidated and the combined armed forces was 1.7 million strong, on its way to 3.3 million by the end of the Korean War.[47]

Anna Rosenberg's capacity for hard work was matched by a human touch that was unprecedented at the top of the military establishment. As it had done in the New Deal and World War II, in 1951 the *New York Times* treated its readers to another feature on Anna in its Sunday magazine. In forming personnel policy that would affect millions, she was guided by the idea that she "must consider the effective use of American minds, skills and strength, and never forget the lives, hopes and futures of individuals. . . . Although we will talk of facts and numbers, never for one moment did those numbers become anything other than individuals to us."[48] Early in her tenure, Rosenberg returned to her office to a huge stack of mail. Her secretary Phyllis explained they were from the families of reservists complaining about being called back into service despite having seen combat in World War II.

"What are you going to do with them?" asked Anna.

"Oh, we have form letters for reply, Madam Secretary."

"There will be no form letters over my signature to people with great trouble. We will handwrite replies in the evenings after things are quiet." After five o'clock tea, Anna explained to her team that when they were informing relatives of a casualty or death, personalized letters were to be sent to the grieving families. "No husband was ever 'Section 3, Paragraph 2a' to his wife," she said. When Bernard Baruch's biographer Margaret L. Coit paid a visit, she was struck by Anna's empathy. "You felt her quality of compassion," wrote Coit, "that rare combination of intellectual sharpness and emotional warmth."[49] This combination of intellect and feeling won over critics. One male colleague remarked that "she has the ability to make instant decisions." Another observed, "There is nothing unfeminine about her. She loves men. She loves you." Echoing Bernard Baruch's comment to Winston Churchill about Anna having the mind of a man and the soft brown eyes of a woman, General Collins said "she has the mind of a businessman and politicians, and yet the graces of a woman."[50]

In cheering her nomination, the *Washington Post* had highlighted her "masculine forcefulness and toughness" in its editorial.[51] Such phrases were common in pieces on Rosenberg, but they were often followed by descriptions of Anna's feminine wardrobe and womanly characteristics. The truth was that Anna had an extraordinary ability to be a no-nonsense executive without masking her gender.

"Madam Secretary," complained a senator, "you have worn on your hats practically every state flower except mine."

"Your state flower is a sunflower, Mr. Senator. You can't wear a sunflower on your hat."[52]

When Ed Murrow suggested that her hats weren't very businesslike, she responded, "Why? Would you expect a man to look like a woman in a woman's world? I believe you can look like yourself wherever you are." Holding one of her hats in her hand, she resisted the suggestion that they were a drawback. "I think they help; they sort of divert people a little bit."[53] She did not let military decorum affect her management style. "Anna Rosenberg may have entered the Pentagon with jangling bracelets and heels that tapped on the corridor floors," explains one scholar, "but to many of her associates, she [was] an 'honorary man.'"[54] One of her prized possessions was an invitation to a men-only dinner in the capital: "Stag," read the invitation, "with the exception of Mrs. Rosenberg."[55] Her ribald sense of humor she balanced with a motherly sense of caring. Stylish but not too sexy, Anna avoided the scorn of women but was not so mannish that she turned off men. She was loved by her secretaries and men loved her. She was one of the girls and she was one of the boys.

While Anna Rosenberg was strengthening the size of the armed forces in the most democratic fashion possible, there was one military problem that could only be solved by the Commander in Chief: General Douglas MacArthur. The Supreme Far East Commander had brilliantly turned the tide of the Korean War with his daring landing at Inchon, behind enemy lines. Thereafter it was the Americans pushing the enemy northward, back toward the Thirty-Eighth Parallel.

But MacArthur's ill-considered public remarks painting President Truman and U.S. policy as timid were sowing confusion among U.S. allies, and sharpening the sword-rattling with Communist China and the Soviet Union. On December 1, 1950, MacArthur was asked by a reporter if the restrictions on operations against Chinese forces on the far side of the Yalu River were "a handicap to effective military operations." He replied that they were indeed "an enormous handicap, unprecedented in military history."[56]

Hawkish senators like Robert Taft, Republican of Ohio, as well as much of conservative America, saw MacArthur as a hero and believed his dark insinuations that America was being sold out by timid (if not traitorous) elements within. Taft was joined by others in Congress in calling for attacks on mainland China, even if it meant Russia's entry into the war. Truman, who wanted to avoid a war with Communist China and the nuclear-armed Soviet Union, issued a directive requiring all military officers and diplomatic officials to clear with the State Department all but routine statements before making them public, "and . . . refrain from direct communications on military or foreign policy with newspapers, magazines, and other publicity media."[57]

MacArthur continued to meddle in politics, complicating U.S. policy toward Communist China and Formosa (Taiwan), a U.S. ally. General MacArthur was carrying out "a public political campaign designed to discredit the President's policies and compel the White House to follow his own."[58] When MacArthur contravened Truman's directive and scuttled cease-fire talks the following spring, President Truman had no choice. At 1:00 AM on April 11, 1951, an emergency White House press conference notified the worldwide press that Truman had relieved MacArthur of command, "effective at once."[59]

The sacking of General Douglas MacArthur was seen as the reestablishment of civilian control over the military by the left, and by the right as an abdication of the responsibility to eradicate global Communism, even if it meant nuclear war with the U.S.S.R. That this was a firefight in the intellectual civil war of the early Cold War was immediately clear to Edward R. Murrow, who summarized the recall of the war hero two days later on his radio program *Hear It Now*:

> Most of us are agreed it is our duty and our destiny to defend the free world against aggressive world Communism. General MacArthur wanted to do it one way, the President, the Joint Chiefs of Staff, and a majority of Congress wanted to do it another way. The General was relieved of his command. The action has vastly encouraged our allies and divided this country.

The recall of the popular general was "perhaps the most convulsive popular outburst in American history and the severest test which civilian control of the military has ever had to face in this republic."[60] Drawn by the "heat and passion" of the moment, anti-Communists were joined by anti-Semites, and extremists eager to make a martyr of MacArthur and make war on President Truman, Defense Secretary Marshall, and Anna Rosenberg.

In the forty-eight hours after the sacking, 125,000 telegrams deluged the White House, twenty anti-Truman for every one defending the President. In countless towns the President was hanged in effigy, flags flew at half-mast or upside down, and angry signs were taped to windows: "To hell with the Reds and Harry Truman."[61] On the floor of the Senate, Joe McCarthy delivered a sixty-thousand-word screed against General George C. Marshall, calling him "incompetent," "timid," and "stupid," before labeling him a traitor in the war against Communism, a catalyst in "a great conspiracy, a conspiracy on a scale so immense as to dwarf any previous such venture in the history of man."*

On April 15, Representative Ed Lee Gossett retrieved from his congressional mailbox a copy of the extremist pamphlet *Common Sense*. The cover story was "MacArthur Victim of Invisible Government: Rosenberg-Lehman-Frankfurter Gang are Behind Dismissal of Greatest American Patriot; Truman is Just a Stooge."[62] Books like *The Iron Curtain over America* by John Beaty and *The Third Zionist War* by George W. Armstrong were rushed into print in 1951, seizing on the notion that Anna Rosenberg's career was all part of a grand subversive conspiracy. *The American Jewish World* noted the attendance of Senators Joe McCarthy and Robert Taft at a carnival held at a Maryland farmhouse where attendees witnessed a burlesque of Anna Rosenberg that was "in extreme bad taste" and "very raw."[63] An old confederate of Fulton Lewis, George Racey Jordan, who had accused Harry Hopkins of being a Soviet agent and who claimed to hold "no religious prejudice," told an audience that "some fellows . . . may have to come East and shoot a few people." Who was on Jordan's hit list? Supreme Court Justice Felix Frankfurter, FDR aide David Niles, and Anna Rosenberg.[64]

It was clear who was being blamed for the demise of the GOP's favorite soldier.

The MacArthur crisis further complicated Anna's mission at the Pentagon. President Truman mandated desegregation in 1948, but the Department of Defense had engaged in foot-dragging. By the outbreak of the Korean War in June 1950, the Army continued to be segregated, and action by the Senate was made impossible by the southern bloc. Under the leadership of Louis Johnson and George Marshall, the Department of Defense's interest in racial affairs was minimal. That changed with the Rosenberg appointment, when military personnel matters, including race, came under her jurisdiction. The new

---

* David M. Oshinsky, *A Conspiracy So Immense: The World of Joe McCarthy* (New York: Free Press, 1983), 197. George Marshall was put off by MacArthur's extreme vanity. During one wartime meeting, when MacArthur said, "My staff tells me—" Marshall cut him off, saying, "General, you don't have a staff; you have a court."

Assistant Secretary was "well-acquainted with integration leaders and sympathetic to their objectives," in the words of one military historian.[65] "I know I speak for many in the Senate," Minnesota senator Hubert Humphrey told Anna, "when I say that your presence in the Department of Defense is most reassuring."[66]

On the one side, liberal senators like Humphrey, Herbert Lehman, and William Benton were heartened by Anna's career-long dedication to civil rights. On the other side of the aisle were segregationist congressmen who could derail defense budget requests and who were smarting from the sacking of General MacArthur and amplifying his dark conspiracy theories. To show progress toward integration while avoiding retaliation from its opponents was, for Anna, a "delicate situation."[67]

With the Senate divided, Anna Rosenberg counseled Senator Lehman against further action in that chamber, vowing instead to do what she could within the Defense Department:

> I had told [Senator Lehman] that I would try very hard
> to do something, but I asked that they do nothing in the
> Senate. I felt that I could work it out, and work it out much
> better if it was done quietly and if everybody who would
> be in opposition to it wasn't alarmed . . . he said, "All right,
> we'll give you a chance to work things out."

With that, Secretary Rosenberg commenced a campaign of persuasion, in-person audits, and letter writing. First she had to convince her boss, George Marshall. "He was opposed to integration," she explained:

> But when I argued with him and accused him of being
> a stick-in-the-mud conservative, he said sharply that he
> had no political philosophy, that he belonged where it
> was right and didn't care whether it was conservative or
> liberal, and that he was ready to change his mind on any
> subject so long as he was given information to convince
> him. Well, I convinced him.[68]

Anna's arguments were based on "reasons of social justice and those of simple defense." A key factor on the defense side was performance reports of segregated units in Korea, such as the all-Black Twenty-Fourth

Infantry Regiment. The unit boasted a rich history, having fought in the Spanish-American War and produced individual heroes, including one decorated with the Medal of Honor. But segregated units consistently had underqualified leaders and less experienced men. In the first days of the war, the Twenty-Fourth had routed the Koreans at Yechon, but since then its battle record was "spotty" and field commanders came to recognize that Black troops "in mixed units did better in combat."[69] Like the mediator she was, Rosenberg, armed with data from the field, argued that integration would lead to better military performance. The importance of ending military Jim Crow "can't be underestimated," Anna argued; "it's a living example of democracy in action—the only answer to Communist propaganda."[70] Her position that integration was morally just and militarily efficient resonated with the Old Man, who thereafter ordered the use of Black troops in integrated combat units.* On July 1, 1951, General Matthew Ridgway, who had replaced MacArthur (and who personally opposed segregation), gave the order for "integration of Negroes into all units."

A year into Rosenberg's tenure, 300 of the 385 all-Black units had been integrated. By 1952 she was able to report to Senator Humphrey that "at the present time there is no segregation in the Navy or Marine Corps . . . integration has been accomplished in all [Army] training divisions and in replacement training centers throughout the United States." By mid-1953, the *New York Times* reported that "the Army's program of wiping out racial segregation is ahead of schedule and at least 90 percent of [Black service members] are serving in non-segregated units." By 1954, six years after President Truman signed Executive Order 9981 desegregating the armed forces, the Department of Defense was able to proclaim that the last segregated unit had been dispersed. Rosenberg's efforts were not limited to U.S. bases; by the time of the cease-fire on the Korean Peninsula in July 1953, combat units in the Far East, Europe, and Alaska had all been integrated.

The most stubborn resistance Anna faced on integration was not

* Leonard Mosley, *Marshall: Hero for Our Times* (New York: Hearst Books, 1982), 455–58. Anna Rosenberg recalls that after Marshall ordered the integration of combat units in Korea, "he had an off-the-record row with Eisenhower about it because [Ike] was against [it]."

from generals or admirals, but from the U.S. Office of Education. Congress had passed Public Law 874 in 1950, which forbade segregation of schools on military bases. By the end of 1952, as Anna forced the issue, all but a few base schools integrated in compliance with the law. The last holdouts were Fort Sam Houston and Fort Bliss in Texas; Fort Sill, Oklahoma; Fort Belvoir, Virginia; and Fort Bragg, North Carolina, where Black families were forced to live in a corner of the base called Fort Bragg's Harlem, and their children were bused off-base to Jim Crow schools. When a Black lieutenant demanded to know why his daughter could not attend school on the base, the heartbroken principal, Mildred B. Poole, could only reply that "it's because of the color of her skin."*

In January 1953, the U.S. Commissioner of Education, Earl McGrath, wrote a dissembling letter to Anna Rosenberg claiming "it may be the case that some local [schools] will be unable by reason of their own state law" to provide integrated schooling for Black children on the bases. Secretary Rosenberg would have none of the states' rights argument, firing back: "As you know, it has been the policy of this department to do away with discriminatory practices in the Armed Forces. I would appreciate your letting me know whether you consider it proper that children be required to attend a segregated school on a Federal installation . . . financed by Federal money."[71] The Education Department's allowance of segregated schools, she continued, violates "not only the policy of the Department of Defense but also contravenes the policy set forth by the President."[72] Under pressure from Secretary Rosenberg and with the courage of Principal Poole, the schools at Fort Bragg were integrated before those in nearby Fayetteville.

In his landmark study of race and the U.S. military, Richard M. Dalfiume concluded that by the time Rosenberg left the Defense Department in 1953:

> Segregation and discrimination were virtually eliminated from the internal organization of the active military.

---

* Because of her efforts to integrate the schools at Fort Bragg, Principal Poole was forced out of her job in 1956. She died in 1992, and in 2018 the Mildred B. Poole Elementary School opened on the base.

Integration and equal treatment was the official policy in such on-base facilities as swimming pools, chapels, barbershops, post exchanges, movie theaters, and dependents' housing as well as in the more direct areas of assignment and promotion. Military life had developed a unique interracial character unlike that found in the other major institutions of American society.[73]

Echoing this point, historian Morris MacGregor concludes, "that such a fundamental restructuring was completed in [so short a time], should be seen as a credit to the efforts of Assistant Secretary of Defense Rosenberg."

Rosenberg had assured Senator Lehman that in order to avoid a political battle with southern lawmakers, integration of the armed forces was best "done quietly" from within the military establishment. Her strategy worked: racial integration was accomplished "quietly, with little fanfare, and with surprising success."[74] A government report found that in Korea, racially mixed units were "equal to . . . all-white units in terms of efficiency, combat effectiveness, and bravery."[75] The U.S. military establishment, long a conservative bastion, had taken a socially just position ahead of civilian social practices. In time, the rest of the country caught up: on May 17, 1954, less than a year and half after the integration of Fort Bragg's schools, the U.S. Supreme Court rendered its unanimous decision in *Brown v. Board of Education*, desegregating *all* American public schools.

CHAPTER TWENTY-ONE

EVERY RIDGE A HEARTBREAK

To the Communists—Compliments of Anna Rosenberg
—Message scrawled on artillery shell
by members of the 955th Field Artillery Battalion

SEVENTEENTH INFANTRY REGIMENT HEADQUARTERS,
TOKKAL-LI, KOREA, OCTOBER 23, 1951

As the second winter in the Korean War approached, the battle line between American-led U.N. Forces and North Korean and Communist Chinese had established itself across the Korean Peninsula. The line began south of the Thirty-Eighth Parallel before snaking in a northeasterly direction 150 miles and terminating at the Sea of Japan. All along the way were impassable alpine ridges and steep, shadowy valleys. Along that line, units like the Seventeenth Infantry Regiment, nicknamed the Buffalos, had fought costly battles at places they knew as Pork Chop Hill and Triangle Ridge. Now, in the fall of 1951, the eastern third of the line was held by the U.S. Eighth Army. Its mission was to destroy North Korean and Chinese units that had held the heights to the north, including the strategically important hilltop ridges ringing the "Punchbowl"—the Haean Basin—just a few kilometers south of the Thirty-Eighth Parallel.

The Buffalos had just emerged from a weeks-long fight at Bloody Ridge when they received a prominent visitor: Assistant Secretary of Defense Anna Rosenberg.

———◆◆◆———

Rosenberg was "Aunt Anna" to her Washington staff, but she brought a mother's interest in the well-being of her main constituency: soldiers. Her keen regard for the soldiers and their families, she explained to a

Senate committee, was "because I belong to that sex which used to stay up at night waiting until every door was closed and every light was out to make sure that every member of my family are safely in. . . . I have a particular feeling for the fear and the worry of mothers and fathers."[1] In the Pentagon, many were in awe of her ability "to be as furiously concerned about the problems of a single soldier as about the recruitment of a division."[2] Much of Anna Rosenberg's focus while at the Pentagon was on lessening the personal hardships created by the huge expansion of the armed forces. Housing allowances for families of service members were earmarked, cost-of-living increases were adopted, and for front-line soldiers, additional combat pay was added.[3] "Anna Rosenberg," reported the *New York Times*, "became in a true sense the G.I.'s advocate at the Pentagon."[4]

Being their advocate on Capitol Hill was part of her job, as Anna saw it, but just as she had done in World War II, she wanted to talk to them in person *and* on the battlefield. "I want to see how the G.I.'s [are doing], what food and clothing they have, and to give any help we can," she told reporters. To get answers to these questions, in the fall of 1951, Secretary Rosenberg made her first tour of the front in Korea.

On the way she inspected the Alaska Air Command at Anchorage, where winds whipped at 120 miles per hour; and the icy Shemya Air Force Base thirteen hundred miles away at the far end of the Aleutian Islands; and conferred with the generals in still-occupied Japan. When Anna landed in Seoul following the three-and-a-half-hour flight from Tokyo, a reporter asked, "How many Black soldiers are fighting in Korea?" With a withering look she replied, "I don't know or care how many *Black* soldiers are here; as far as I'm concerned, there are only *American* soldiers."[5] With that she boarded a military transport bound for the front line. When the small prop plane landed on the gravel airstrip, Anna emerged wearing dark green officer's trousers tucked into high-topped paratrooper boots, a peaked khaki cap with a brass "U.S" pin, and a khaki field jacket, and around her neck a decidedly nonmilitary silk scarf. After shaking hands with the commanders, Anna led the men up a hillside away from the officers as Signal Corps cameras followed.

As artillery boomed in the distance, Anna gathered the men around. Black, white, and Latino faces peered in as the number two official in the U.S. military, a Jewish middle-aged woman, began digging into the practicalities of life at the front. "How's the food, boys? Come on, I want the lowdown." Out of earshot of the generals, Anna grilled the men on the food and the medical care, and were the uniforms adequate to the wintry conditions? The soldiers seemed happy with the rations, which Anna confirmed after peering under the pot lids and eating with the men in the mess tents. "They have the best food in the world," she reported. "I actually saw men have fried chicken right up at the front line."[6] Bantering with the Army cooks, Anna saw fresh vegetables, apples, oranges, and "for dessert there were canned peaches."[7] Instead of the mess hall, Anna went into the kitchen. Instead of the barracks, Anna went into the latrine. "When she made visits to American military bases around the globe, she made sure no one put up barriers between her and the troops."[8]

The soldiers spoke positively of their medical care. Just as FDR would have wanted her to do, she confirmed this by visiting the wounded and speaking to them at their MASH bedsides.* Despite a shortage of nurses she hoped would be shored up with the stateside women's recruitment campaign, Anna was pleased with the level of care. "The wounded have the most superb care," she confirmed. "I saw a man twenty minutes after he was wounded, evacuated . . . by helicopter. When I asked him if I could call his mother when I got back to the States, he smiled at me and said, 'I'll be there before you.' And he was."[9] Rosenberg's evaluation of the medical care was borne out by the low combat death rate and high percentage of soldiers returning to duty, statistics Doris Condit, a historian of the Korean War, cites as "supporting the claim."[10]

"If I ever came across a group of American boys who didn't gripe about something or other," said Anna, "I'd think something was seriously wrong." After returning from a mission, they appreciated the portable showers, the movie nights, and the prompt mail, but everywhere they asked Anna to send "USO girl shows."

---

* Mobile army surgical hospital. These field hospitals in South Korea inspired one of the most popular TV shows in American history, *M*A*S*H*, which ran from 1972 to 1983.

"It must be a terrible disappointment to you," Anna replied, "that only an old lady came out to see you."

"It's better than nothing," they cracked.[11]

No one griped about the winter field jacket, but footwear, the scourge of soldiers from the marching Roman legions to the First World War, was a serious problem. "I wanted to find out if the men were properly supplied with heavy socks and boot liners. It was so bitterly cold there and so many men had been coming back with amputated feet from frostbite. The men didn't want to complain. I made them show me their footlocker. I went to five different tents so no one man could be blamed." After discovering there was a shortage of both items, she called the responsible general in Tokyo. "I'll get on it in the morning," he told her. "No, General, you'll get on it right now. I'm waiting here until they arrive." As General Collins explained, "She fought a lot of fights like that. She really stood up for the soldiers and sailors."[12]

The main feedback she heard on the hillside, at the mess table, and in the medical tents was the longing to return home. The men wanted the "scoop." Anna told the troops of the new rotation policy, in which troops would be rotated home under a point system based on time at the front, and replaced after about nine months with fresh units. "No man in combat will spend a second winter in Korea." When one soldier said he'd been in Korea eleven months, she repeated, "No man in combat will spend a second winter in Korea."[13] Another young soldier learned Anna was from New York and asked, "I wish you would call my mother and my sister, if it's not too much." (Upon her return to the United States, Anna called Mrs. Angela Brienza of Brooklyn to say she'd seen her son John. "If I hadn't known he was from a city," Anna told her, "I would have thought he came from the Texas cow country. He looks that conditioned and tanned."[14])

When the new rotation policy was unfurled prior to her trip, Supreme Allied Commander Matthew Ridgway and Eighth Army's General James A. Van Fleet "winced," thinking it impossible, but by February 1952, Anna had kept her promise. Nearly a quarter-million service members from the Army, Navy, and Marines had been sent home, replaced by 225,000 fresh troops. Only 137 critical specialists spent the second winter of icy war in Korea.[15] Her rotation policy made her popular with the troops: she came in third place as Miss Wolfhound 1952, as voted by the Twenty-Seventh Infantry Regiment "Wolfhounds," barely bested by Doris Day and Marilyn Monroe.[16]

At Tokkal-Li, the fashion among the men of the Seventeenth Infantry Regiment was moustaches; the Buffalos considered themselves "the toughest outfit in Korea," and the facial hair made the young men look older and meaner. As the unit prepared for its push by digging foxholes in their new forward position and as artillery thundered in the distance, Anna talked with the troops. As soldiers Black and white alike gathered 'round and lit up cigarettes, Anna crouched among them, parrying with their one-liners. "They have to have good, deep foxholes," observed Rosenberg, who at points along the line carried a captured Russian-made submachine gun. "The enemy might be only 1,500 yards from us." Anna leaned in to listen as an allied ROK officer questioned a captured Chinese Communist.

The snowcapped ridges of the Korean Peninsula were a world away from the hellscape Anna remembered from Falaise, France, in 1944, but the toll of war was the same. The dead and wounded, orphans and widows, stretcher-bearers and prisoners of war. And the faces of the combat-fatigued. "They look as if they can take anything. And what they take sometimes is pretty tough," she wrote in *Collier's*. "I saw men who had gone through the hardest fighting and were just back from the front. They had that look you see only in the faces of men who have been there. It's a look I saw during the last war."[17] Knowing the long-term toll of combat from her work with veterans, Rosenberg emphasized spiritual support for the troops. Charles Carpenter, the first Air Force Chief of Chaplains, commented that aside from the Armed Forces Chaplains Board, Anna Rosenberg was the "greatest influence in the development of the chaplains' program in all the forces" and she "has been most helpful in strengthening the spiritual standards in the service. . . . Her emphasis, during her visits to all the areas in which military personnel are serving, has always been upon the necessity of maintaining spiritual and moral standards."[18]

While the chaplains and rabbis offered what comfort they could, the bloody peninsula took a toll on those serving, including Anna. She put on a brave face, but she knew the dangers that lurked over every ridge.

"[The] boys were joking and laughing with you, and you knew they were going up to the front, and you didn't know if they would ever come back. You yearned for them and you felt that every one of them belonged to you. Those were heartbreaking moments."[19] "One day I saw a group of about 80 men who had just been brought out of a Communist trap by a young first lieutenant, Stephen J. Patrick, from Bridgeport, Connecticut. He and his executive were the only officers in his outfit not killed or wounded. As he stood there talking to me, I could see the look of pride in the faces of his men. He was only a youngster and probably had never been in such a tight fix before, but he had what it takes to make a leader; and those men looking up to him—I could see it in their faces—would go through anything for him."[20]

By light aircraft, helicopter, and jeep, in the fall of 1951 and again in the fall of 1952, Anna visited U.S. troops along the 150-mile front line. Her time with the Twenty-Third Infantry Division was marked by the mauling the unit had taken at Heartbreak Ridge over a month of fighting. A badly wounded soldier, twenty years old, was helicoptered to the rocky field that served as a landing zone. As medics gave the soldier blood, he looked up at Secretary Rosenberg: "I know who you are," he said softly. "You're Anna Rosenberg. I read in *Stars and Stripes* that you were coming. My buddy owes me a quarter. I bet him I'd see you. I told him, wherever I am, the women follow." He made the wisecrack, Rosenberg said, to show he wasn't in pain, because "he saw in my face the heartache I couldn't hide."[21] He then fell unconscious. Secretary Rosenberg tracked his case while he recovered in Honolulu before returning home to Los Angeles.

"You can't know what Korea is like and you can't know what our men are like unless you see for yourself," she wrote in *Collier's*.

> Korea is the most rugged place I have ever seen. Every ridge is a heartbreak. . . . It's hard to imagine that men can fight and live in those mountains, especially when you recall that these same men a few months ago were the people you met in your daily life in America.[22]

They had left America as lawyers, clerks, farmers, and students, but in the mountains of Korea they had transformed into a cohesive fighting force.

Women serving in Korea—whether nurses, WAVES, or WACs—were not immune from the deprivations and dangers of war. The MASH setups were a new kind of field hospital, closer to the action, where medical staff wore combat fatigues, helicopters shuttled the wounded, and conditions were tough. Lieutenant Katherine Wilson was responsible for as many as six operating tables simultaneously, and at times worked until she was "nearly anesthetized by the fumes."[23] Captain Viola McConnell, recipient of the Bronze Star, described the conditions:

> It was the cold weather . . . that probably affected us more than anything. When an abdomen would be opened, steam would rise from the body. . . . Water was scarce and to scrub our hands for surgery water would drip, one drop at a time, from a handmade tank.[24]

The dramatic advances and retreats up and down the peninsula in the early stages of the war brought the enemy into close contact with women service members and nurses. The thirteen nurses in the first MASH unit found themselves in the midst of battle on the march to Pusan. The women "scrambled into a roadside ditch, while the battle flared all about them. . . . All through the night they huddled together for warmth in the cold roadside pit as machine guns and rifles hammered."[25] At sunup they attended the incoming wounded, saving many, but losing eight. But they had survived, and thereafter called themselves the Lucky 13. The chief nurse of the 8055th MASH, Captain Phyllis LeConte, said of the fluid battle lines, "It seemed we were never safe, never settled and all the while the casualties kept coming." In their history of women serving during the Korean War, Linda Witt and her coauthors recount "during the horrific first months, military women . . . were almost constantly under fire and on the move."[26]

While no American servicewoman or nurse died in Korea due to enemy fire, some were held as prisoners of war, and each branch suffered casualties. Eleven Navy nurses were killed when their plane crashed on takeoff from Kwaejon Island, and another one died as a result of the sinking of the USS *Benevolence*. Army major Genevieve Smith died in a plane crash in transit to her post as chief nurse in Korea. Three Air Force nurses also died. In all, three nurses received the Bronze Star, six the Commendation Ribbon, and ninety the Navy Unit Commendation.[27]

Whether civilian or military, American women in the Korean War served in an unprecedented breadth of roles. In 1950, 629 WAC personnel served in the Far East Command Headquarters. By 1951 their numbers had increased to 2,600, and they were rising in rank and moving into arenas formerly occupied only by men. Women headed wards in military hospitals in Japan and were senior noncommissioned officers in motor pools, mess halls, and post offices. Women could be found in administration, engineering, communications, and intelligence; they worked as censors, interpreters, draftsmen, weather personnel, and even aides-de-camp as far forward as Seoul.

For many women, serving in Korea was an ordeal to be borne before returning to civilian life. To others, the experience was transformative. "I came out of boot camp," recalled Jerry Robb, "thinking I was absolutely, really something . . . that is not such a bad thing to teach young women."[28] An American teacher working for the U.S. Air Force recalled, "working in Korea with the fellows fighting there proved to be the ultimate experience of my lifetime."[29] As the highest-ranking woman in Korea, Anna Rosenberg was a role model. When she visited the Women's Army Corps in Far East Command in Tokyo, she told them, "The very fine work you are doing out here is a credit to all women in America."[30] To reporters, she gushed, "I can say with great pride that the women in the services are contributing substantially to the great fight for freedom."[31]

In visiting the front lines and listening to the soldiers' problems, Anna also earned a reputation as "a G.I. heroine."[32] Before she left Korea, the colonel of the Seventeenth Infantry Regiment presented Secretary Rosenberg with a certificate, signed by the Adjutant General, naming her an "honorary Buffalo." Three privates from the Twenty-Third thanked her for her visit by gifting her four pheasants they had hunted that morning; a tough-looking sergeant gave her a bouquet of flowers: "These are from us to you." When the cannoneers of the 955th Artillery Battalion proudly produced a shell on which was painted: "To the Communists—Compliments of Anna Rosenberg," she quipped "I'd like to take it back with me. I have a couple of targets in Washington I'd like to use it on."[33] When she arrived back in Washington, she received a cable: "[T]he enlisted men of the 23rd Infantry Regiment have chosen you as our official pin-up girl."[34]

The gratefulness of the troops moved Anna. "One of the things that always got me was the fact that they thanked me for visiting them. They would say, 'We're grateful to you for coming up to see us.' Grateful to someone who comes up and spends a day or two! If a boy of eighteen or nineteen, who hasn't lived even half a life, can go to such places to serve his country, certainly a woman of my age can take the chance."[35]

Her morale-boosting visit had come at the right time. In mid-November, after a month of fighting "the most savage single action of the Korean War," the men of the Twenty-Third, using "bayonets and flame throwers and bare fists," rooted out the last Communist forces from their bunkers in Heartbreak Ridge. A week later, Anna Rosenberg was back in New York, where she delivered an impassioned speech as part of the women's recruiting drive. "The bleak and burned out hill [known as] Heartbreak Ridge . . . that's the hill that made me look at New York and the rest of America with a gratitude and with a new love. Like someone who's been blind and can suddenly see the beauty . . . to once again be in a city and in a country where citizens stand as free people, [who] look out at the horizon with peace and hope."[36]

That freedom, peace, and hope were paid for by the sacrifices of the men and women in the services was apparent to Anna. In February 1952, Anna Rosenberg's feature piece in *Collier's* came out. "This I Saw in Korea" is written not in the language of a Washington functionary, but in a familiar voice, worried for the young people in danger, and immensely proud: "I had the feeling as I flew home that if all the water I passed over was ink, and every blade of grass a pen, I still could not write enough to tell of the magnificence of our fighting men."[37]

In the months after her return to the Pentagon, Washington was anticipating a transfer of power after two decades in which a Democrat lived in the White House. Having served nearly two full terms as President, Harry Truman decided in March 1952 not to run again: "I have served my country long, and I think effectively and honestly." An upset win like he pulled off in 1948 was impossible to imagine. Truman's firing of MacArthur and the unsatisfactory stalemate in Korea made the incumbent deeply unpopular. Republicans expected to win the presidency in 1952, and Senator Robert A. Taft of Ohio became the leading candidate for the GOP nomination. Douglas MacArthur, craving power and itching to settle scores, was discussed as his possible running mate.

The prospect of a Taft-MacArthur ticket petrified moderate Republicans, who hoped to nominate their own war hero—the coolheaded centrist Dwight D. Eisenhower. In 1948 Ike had been discussed as a potential candidate for the Democratic Party—Truman himself even floated the idea of an Ike-Truman ticket. Eisenhower had declined that offer, but in the summer of 1952 he tendered his resignation as Supreme Allied Commander of NATO and returned to the United States from Paris in order to run for President as a Republican. His campaign vow to end the conflict in Korea upset Truman, who had seen Ike as a supporter of the containment action, and when Eisenhower failed to defend his mentor, George Marshall, against Senator Joe McCarthy's wild accusations, the once-warm relations between the two men became icy.

In the summer of 1952 Douglas MacArthur gave the keynote address at the Republican National Convention, but his man Taft was unable to withstand the moderates' support of Eisenhower. Ike and his running mate, Congressman Richard M. Nixon, would face cerebral Illinois Governor Adlai Stevenson in November's election. As American leaders, including Truman and Eisenhower, sparred over the external and internal threats of the Cold War, Anna prepared for her second inspection tour of U.S. military bases and the Korean front. It would be her last mission as the top woman in the Truman administration.

After stops at Anchorage and Far East Command in Tokyo, Anna spent a night aboard the USS *Missouri* off the northeast coast of Korea, before flying by Navy carrier plane to Seoul, where she had tea with South Korean President Syngman Rhee. Over the next several days Anna toured more than half the 150-mile front line across the peninsula, visiting with three infantry units, a Marine unit, and elements of the South Korean Army. Her jammed itinerary took her from prisoner-of-war camps to frontline positions to ships at sea. She "hedge-hopped" by light plane and helicoptered over Bunker Hill, which had replaced Heartbreak Hill as the bloody and contested prize. Inspecting a MASH unit, Anna met with the wounded and asked about their welfare and heard their gripes.

"Send us Marilyn Monroe!" a G.I. shouted as Anna's trip wound down. "That's all I've had requests for since I got here," Anna told reporters. Back in Los Angeles, the Hollywood star went on record saying, "I think Mrs. Rosenberg must have been joking. But, like all American women, I have the boys in Korea very much in mind, and would do anything to contribute to their happiness." Just weeks into her tempestuous marriage to retired Yankee great Joe DiMaggio, the twenty-seven-year-old Marilyn Monroe flew to Korea, where the leathernecks of the First Marine Division went mad as she sashayed onto the stage in a slinky black gown. Losing her voice during "Anything Goes," she gave a quick fluff of her blond hair as cheers rang through the Korean valley speckled with light snow.[38]

When Anna Rosenberg's second trip drew to a close, she squinted under the spotlights and told the assembled war correspondents, "I found the men in excellent condition, and that's what I was most interested in, their personal welfare."[39] Then she boarded the USAF C-121 *Constellation* that would take her to Tokyo, Manila, Saigon, Bangkok, Agra, New Delhi, Karachi, Saudi Arabia, Athens, Tripoli, and the Azores. By the time she reached Washington, she had flown 20,282 nautical miles, nearly the circumference of the globe.

The work continued at the Pentagon, reading and answering letters of gratitude from service members, their spouses, and their families. Typical was the letter from a mother from California thanking Anna for the "happiness you brought the boys and my son in Korea." She got letters from WAC officers and Navy nurses. "I do not hold a very high position in the Army," wrote Sergeant First Class Mildred Paradise, who offered "anything I can ever do to repay your kindness." Three sergeants from the 955th Artillery Battalion sent her a card, "To the One I Love." Inside, they wrote: "We realize this card isn't exactly appropriate, but it's the best we could get." Another sent her a photo of the wooden "Powder Room" sign they'd put up for her at the forward base. She got handkerchiefs and flowers, news clippings and the offer of a holiday ham. "As much as I appreciate your thoughtfulness," Anna replied to the grateful mother, "please do not send me a ham." As always, she responded personally to each letter. "She got letters from American servicemen all over the world," reported the *New York Times*, "and she followed them up. And servicemen's wives wrote to her. It all got answered."[40]

Anna had one final letter to write.

> Dear Mr. President:
>
> It has been one of the most rewarding experiences of my life to have had the privilege of working with General Marshall. . . . I am proud to say that I will leave my post with a sense of substantial accomplishment . . . in my work I have had the great personal satisfaction of being associated with some of the most devoted public servants—in uniform and out—in my thirty years [in government]. Unfailingly, in every major question of defense, your only criterion for reaching a decision was what is best for the country and what is best for the people.
>
> With deep respect, believe me,
> Anna

Anna Rosenberg left the Defense Department in January 1953, after compiling an excellent record of achievement in her twenty-six months. Being a woman in a male-dominated military establishment did not constrain her; rather, she felt a sense of liberation. "A woman is not bogged down with traditions and service customs which have accumulated over the years," she told a Kansas City reporter. "I refused to be bogged down, so went ahead and did what had to be done. Some were fearful, but others were relieved that things got done. Many say now that it is what they always wanted to do."[41] Perhaps the men, too, felt freer. Soldiers "find it easier to sound off to a woman than to a man."[42] When George Marshall asked Anna to join him at the Pentagon, he did so because he wanted the best person for the position, and she was. As Assistant Secretary of Defense during the first hot conflict of the Cold War, charged with reconciling military personnel expansion with civilian needs, Rosenberg had "the most important public task ever entrusted to any woman in American history."[43] In accepting her resignation, President Truman wrote by hand: "Dear Anna—you've done a whale of a job. There are no words adequately to express my appreciation.—H.S.T."[44]

In their time together, Marshall, "aided by Anna Rosenberg . . . oversaw the rebuilding of the depleted postwar armed forces, increasing military [strength] to 3.5 million men and women . . . enough to contain Soviet aggression in Europe and at the same time end the fighting in Korea . . . and they did it in less time than the mobilization Marshall oversaw at the beginning of World War II."[45] She was not the "dictator of the Pentagon" as her attackers feared, but instead insisted on fundamental democratic fairness in the military.

After years stalled on the beachhead of integration, Rosenberg led the service branches to seize the long-awaited victory on that front. Her efforts also lifted the 2 percent cap on women in the services, opened doors previously closed to military women, and established a permanent advisory legacy with DACOWITS. Due to her efforts, a G.I. Bill for Korean vets was passed into law. As the Truman administration's number one woman executive, she had crossed the globe to share the experiences of the men and women living on military bases and fighting to contain Communism.

By the time *Life* published a long photo-essay on Anna, "The Busiest Women in the U.S.," Anna had appeared on the covers and in the pages of America's leading magazines: *Time, Newsweek, U.S. News & World Report, Fortune, Look,* and *Collier's*. She was the subject of numerous articles in Jewish publications, as both the target of McCarthyism and the second-in-command at the Pentagon, and she appeared in *Paris Match* and Germany's *Der Spiegel*. She was invited to speak at colleges and universities and received honorary degrees from some of them, including Tufts University. Anna Rosenberg was at the apex of her long public career, and, like many others, Edward R. Murrow wanted to know: of all her positions and posts, which was the most gratifying assignment? "The most gratifying assignment I ever had was Assistant Secretary of Defense . . . you know on that job, really, everything you did touched the lives of people."[46] Korea may be known as the "Forgotten War," but Anna Rosenberg was fondly remembered by the soldiers who fought there. "She's the only person who ever stood up for us," a baby-faced corporal told war correspondent Jim G. Lucas. "Anna is a legend."[47] "The boys in Korea," reported Senator William Benton after his own inspection trip to the front line, "used to scrawl on the walls, 'Anna was here.'

"Was any woman ever paid greater tribute?"

CHAPTER TWENTY-TWO

DRAFTING EISENHOWER

I have been impressed by her keen thinking, her direct
and forthright attitude, and her outspoken interest in
Americanism and its perpetuation.[1]
—General Dwight D. Eisenhower

Anna walked into her corner office on the twenty-sixth floor of 444 Madison Avenue, took in the view of the needle atop the Empire State Building from one set of windows, and gently hung the little jacket that matched her black skirt over the back of her chair. In her impeccably correct executive suite, this was the only informal touch. The white-walled, bright blue-carpeted office was filled with plaques, medals, and autographed pictures of the U.S. presidents she served, Roosevelt and Truman. There was a signed photo of Eleanor Roosevelt, one of Bernard Baruch, and she had added a third "diploma" to the wall—Honorary Buffalo. Anna fidgeted with a vase of freshly cut roses, careful not to catch the billowy sleeve of her white blouse on a thorn, and sat down just as her secretary brought in her breakfast of decaffeinated coffee with a few vanilla wafers balanced on the saucer.

Life was good. After living for more than two years at the Shoreham Hotel, it was good to be back with her family and in her Fifth Avenue apartment with its views of Central Park. The solitary meals she had in Washington were forgotten when she and Mike entertained Thomas and his charming wife, Jane. The workdays spent among the generals and admirals seemed a long time ago as she watched her youthful staff dart about the office, a haven of creativity, handing her a file for this client or that. Thomas, her partner, had run the business well in her absence, and business was booming. There were lunches with Mater, who at eighty-five still traveled often to Europe, and Sunday games of bridge with her sister, Clare. There were trips to the hairdresser and her hat maker. A miniature dachshund Anna named Timothy completed the picture of domestic contentedness.

There was also work to do. Madison Avenue was where the leaders of American industry went to hone their messaging and to become more competitive in the postwar economy. Anna Rosenberg & Associates still counted on its long-term concerns like *Encyclopedia Britannica*, but the firm was attracting new clients. She also added movie studios to her roster as a result of her negotiating to bring first-run films to the G.I.'s in World War II and Korea. Her due diligence included treating her family to films like *Singin' in the Rain*, *The Caine Mutiny*, and *To Catch a Thief*, shown on a reel-to-reel projector in the living room after Sunday supper. While she didn't meet Cary Grant, the debonair retired cat burglar ensnared by Grace Kelly in the paradise of the French Riviera, she did meet several stars. In one contract negotiation in Hollywood, her opposite number was the actor Ronald Reagan, who, as union president of the Screen Actors Guild, had yet to fully embrace conservatism. "Ah," said Reagan by way of a greeting, "the stalking horse of the capitalists." "Listen, Mr. Reagan," Anna fired back, "do you want to trade a lot of bullshit or do you want to get this thing settled?"[2]

In 1953 the Studebaker automobile company hired her. Much smaller than Chrysler, Ford, or General Motors, Studebaker was known as a niche maker of high-quality cars. Under the leadership of Paul Gray Hoffman from the Great Depression until 1948, when he took over administration of the Marshall Plan, Studebaker produced "distinctive and innovative cars that won approval from buyers and experts."[3] Hoffman had been the company's star salesman in Los Angeles, a millionaire by the age of thirty-four, then its director of sales before becoming the chief executive. When he returned as chairman in 1953 he discovered during his five-year absence a series of corporate misadventures had brought the company to the verge of collapse.[4] He set out to save it.

Paul Hoffman hired Anna to turn Studebaker into a company "whose labor relations and market strategy conformed to industry leader General Motors."[5] If Studebaker could improve the "morale and goodwill of the working force," Hoffman believed, it would be an intangible that would translate to more sales. His faith in the wisdom of managerial transparency and worker satisfaction was a product of his brand of enlightened capitalism, rather than New Deal idealism, but it was one of the many things he had in common with Anna Rosenberg.

Like Anna, Hoffman had for decades combined private-sector success with behind-the-scenes government work, and like Anna, he employed pragmatism in the service of a larger vision. To *Time*, Hoffman was a "recognized power" beyond the scope of the auto industry.[6] Washington insiders handicapped Hoffman as a potential cabinet member, and the *Detroit Free Press* even suggested he was presidential timber. Although his family home was in California, Hoffman, like Anna, was a well-known power player in the New York–Washington corridor. His was a commuting pattern Anna knew very well: Hoffman would work five long days in New York or Washington before flying out to spend the weekends at his avocado ranch in Palm Springs. His wife, Dorothy, suffered from a heart condition, so Hoffman spent his workweeks on the East Coast alone.[7]

The friends who kept Hoffman company were the same circle of business leaders and powerful politicians who valued Anna's friendship, among them Henry Luce, the magazine magnate behind *Time, Life*, and *Fortune*; Beardsley Ruml, the former University of Chicago professor who was a top executive at Macy's; and Senator William Benton. Paul, like Anna, skewed younger than his age. One friend remarked, "[H]e was November in age, but March in spirit."[8]

Physically, Paul Hoffman looked the part of the C.E.O. He was tall and handsome, with neatly combed silver hair and chill blue eyes. Like many men of the era, he favored double-breasted suits and wore a gray felt fedora. The low-key Hoffman first met Anna Rosenberg during the early days of World War II when she was FDR's labor troubleshooter and Studebaker supplied the government with aircraft engines and amphibious vehicles. Both earned the respect of George C. Marshall in the war years, and both counted Bernard Baruch as a friend. Both served in the Truman administration: Hoffman as Marshall Plan Administrator and Anna as Assistant Secretary of Defense. Hoffman was an establishment figure with progressive tendencies, while Anna was a progressive respected by the establishment. They both had faith that government could and should work for all Americans. Anna came to know Paul better when she accompanied "Bernie" Baruch to dinners at Hoffman's Washington apartment.

So when the executive needed advice on the long-term survival of his company, he quite naturally turned to Anna Rosenberg. Studebaker, she told him, could distinguish itself by emphasizing its craftsmanship and quality in the era of mass production. "America," she explained, "has become a symbol of the biggest, the newest, and the shiniest—but not necessarily the best."[9] Soon the automaker adopted a new production code, and Studebakers featured the seal "We Stand Behind the Quality of this Car."[10] While Anna's sound advice on messaging and her overhaul of Studebaker's labor policies did not result in the long-term survival of the automaker—the last Studebaker rolled off the line in 1963—the friendship between Anna Rosenberg and Paul Hoffman altered the course of both their lives and had an enduring impact in American politics. Were it not for their counsel and support from the late 1940s onward, it is quite possible Dwight D. Eisenhower would not have been in a position to win the presidency and to save his party from its rabid right flank.

—•◆•—

To describe the importance of Anna's emerging friendship with Paul Hoffman, it is necessary to go back to Anna's relations with General Eisenhower during World War II and in the years afterwards. During her tours of Europe in 1944 and 1945, Anna had earned Ike's respect and admiration. In 1946, when Ike succeeded George Marshall as Army Chief of Staff and was making his first forays into politics, he sought Anna's advice on issues confronting the returned veteran. The two main points to emphasize, Anna counseled, were the responsibility of communities to the returning veteran and the raising of awareness as to the value of the vets' skills and qualities. In July the general told the citizens of Amherst, Massachusetts, "Just as the military developed the leadership . . . of our youth in battle, so now must you . . . produce the pattern of leadership that will best employ them in peace."[11]

The switchboard that was Anna Rosenberg made another connection in November, when she had the president of the Congress of Industrial Organizations, the powerful federation of unions, invite Eisenhower to be the featured speaker at the annual convention, held that year in

Atlantic City, New Jersey. It was Eisenhower's first major semi-political speech, and he enlisted Anna's help in its drafting. Ex-G.I.'s were performing remarkably well in colleges and universities, she knew, and they had other assets to bring to industry. "The men who held out at Bastogne . . . who clung to the beachhead at Anzio, and who fought through the jungles of the Pacific," Anna argued to Ike, possessed tangible and intangible qualities of leadership that would be a benefit to any company.[12]

Eisenhower, in turn, told the delegates on the evening of November 20, 1946, "The average veteran has developed in leadership, in initiative, in mental maturity and in self-reliance by reason of his service. He is a better citizen because he has borne his part in defending all citizens, and because he did so in a crisis that demanded full play for the best of man's virtues."[13] In the same speech Eisenhower endorsed the United Nations, championed increased prosperity for the American worker, and called for world peace. The audience "wildly cheered" as "a wave of enthusiasm for [Ike] as a Presidential candidate swept through" the convention hall.[14] The CIO speech marked a turning point in the transformation of Dwight D. Eisenhower from soldier to statesman. "It must be noted," observed syndicated columnist George E. Sokolsky "that every man whom Mrs. Anna Rosenberg has groomed has won a place of distinction."[15]

Anna continued to strengthen ties between Eisenhower and organized labor when he returned to civilian life in 1948 to serve as president of Columbia University, the next step of "the political education of General Eisenhower."[16] In the summer of 1948, as Truman's popularity waned, newspaper editorials suggested the Democratic Party nominate the popular war hero for a presidential run that fall. Anna sent the editorials to Eisenhower—the idea was a "darn good" one, she wrote.[17] Eisenhower disappointed many Democrats by not running in 1948, but he continued to test the waters. If too many days passed without a telephone call or a visit from Anna, Ike would complain: "I trust that this is only because you are busy—I would certainly hate to think that I have been listed in your black book."[18] When Anna was confirmed as Assistant Secretary of Defense, Ike complained, "[Y]our leaving New York has thrown a number of my personal plans into . . . a state of confusion."[19]

The next month would see another delay of Eisenhower's political plans when he was called back to Europe to command NATO forces as the war in Korea deteriorated. In 1951 and 1952, General Eisenhower and Anna Rosenberg remained in consistent contact on national defense matters such as universal training, rotating combat troops from Korea, and the ending, once and for all, of segregation in the U.S. military.

Meanwhile, the Draft Eisenhower movement continued to gain momentum across the country and its two political parties. As President Truman struggled with a stuttering economy and the impasse in Korea, Americans signaled their excitement for the popular general through "Volunteers for Eisenhower" and "Mothers Club for Ike." Wearing their "I Like Ike" buttons, they wanted an end to McCarthyism, firmer control of Communist expansion, a renewed and reinvigorated Republican Party, and an end to the Korean War. When President Truman decided not to run again in March 1952, "Democrats for Ike" calculated that supporting Eisenhower, who had announced he was a Republican, was the prudent course. Were a Republican to win, which appeared likely, wouldn't it be better if it were Eisenhower, a moderate internationalist, rather than isolationist Senator Robert Taft, who indulged the extremism of McCarthy and the paranoia of MacArthur?

Moderate Republicans, too, put pressure on Eisenhower. Paul Hoffman, a lifelong Republican, knew Senator Taft and disliked his "pedantic arrogance." The fear was Taft "might neglect American allies in Europe" and "imprudently lead the U.S. into a disastrous war."[20] What was needed was a strong American presence internationally in order to check Communism militarily, economically, and morally through programs like the Truman Doctrine, the Marshall Plan, and NATO. Carrying this message, Senator Henry Cabot Lodge, Jr., of Massachusetts and Paul Hoffman visited the general at NATO headquarters near Paris and urged him to run for president. To persuade Eisenhower, Hoffman "used flattery, appeals to duty, and a sense of practical politics." Showing Ike the Gallup polls indicating he could win, Hoffman told him he was beyond the control of "the boys in the smoke-filled rooms" and uniquely qualified to redeem the GOP while moving the country "away from an atmosphere of hatred and fear" and toward world peace.[21]

In November 1951, Paul Hoffman paid another call on Ike, this time in the privacy of Eisenhower's red-tiled villa at Marnes-la-Coquette, and the superlative salesman—"smooth as glass and as sharp if need be"—applied his best pitch. "What about your grandchild?" he asked the general. "Do you want little David to grow up in a world at war?" This time the general's reticence seemed to fade away; instead of declining, he sat there silently, thinking. When Hoffman returned to New York, he told his like-minded friends and colleagues in confidence, "We have a candidate."[22] Two months later, in January 1952, Dwight D. Eisenhower answered his "clear-cut call to political duty." He would be willing to accept the call of the American people to serve as their president. The January 21 issue of *Life* magazine, the one with the long photo-essay on Anna Rosenberg at work and home, featured the hero of the moment on the cover with the words "The Eisenhower Campaign Is Born."

One year after Paul Hoffman visited the general at his villa, Dwight David Eisenhower won in a landslide over Democratic candidate Adlai Stevenson. From Augusta, Georgia, the President-Elect cabled Anna, who was in Tokyo on her way to visit the troops in Korea: "I shall certainly do my best at the job."[23] The election meant not only a change of parties after two decades, but for Anna, it was her return ticket to civilian life. While Eisenhower praised Anna's work at the Defense Department, after his election the political cost of keeping a former New Dealer and Democrat in the Pentagon was going to be too much to ask. The Taft Republicans were urging Ike to "clean house . . . starting with Mrs. Anna Rosenberg in the Defense Department." There was also the "unfortunate coincidence of names." Arrested in 1950, the spies Ethel and Julius Rosenberg were to be sent to the electric chair later in 1953 for passing atomic secrets to the Soviets.[24] In helping get Dwight Eisenhower elected President, Anna was paving the way for her return to civilian life, to her pastel Madison Avenue office, and to her family and friends.

The national press no longer had "Little Anna at the Pentagon" as a daily subject, and her work with Eisenhower was done quietly, but Rosenberg remained a household name through the 1950s. Eleanor Roosevelt was the "world's most famous widow," a "head of state" abroad, everywhere a "symbol of hope, sanity and dignity."[25] In nationwide surveys, Anna was often paired with Mrs. Roosevelt as the most admired American women. If Eleanor was the custodian of the Roosevelt name, Anna was the keeper of the New Deal flame, the idea that seemingly intractable national problems can be solved effectively through well-conceived and quickly dispatched government action.

On Memorial Day, 1954, Anna was the featured speaker at the rose garden in Hyde Park, just steps away from FDR's gravesite. "In her excellent address," reported Eleanor Roosevelt, "she remind[ed] us of what he had stood for in his lifetime and what he still could inspire us to do if we remember his ideals and the way in which he tried to carry them out."[26] Unable to convince Anna to write her memoir, in her 1954 best seller, *Ladies of Courage*, written with Lorena Hickok, Eleanor Roosevelt devoted a glowing section to Anna. Perhaps more attuned to his own mortality following a serious health scare, in November 1955 President Eisenhower named Anna to the commission to plan the memorial to honor Franklin D. Roosevelt.[27]

In other ways, too, Anna was the New Deal conscience of the Eisenhower presidency. In her unofficial capacity, she continued to advise on issues related to labor and defense. The introductions Anna made with labor leaders paid dividends for Ike as his administration enjoyed imperfect but peaceful relations with organized labor. The federal minimum wage was increased to one dollar an hour, and both unemployment and workers' compensation coverage was expanded. Robust enforcement under the Fair Labor Standards Act led to wage restitution, and the number of companies ruled ineligible for government contracts rose from forty-three to seventy-four. Ike made a "conscientious effort to be fair and friendly in his dealings with organized labor," appointing a former pipe fitter as Secretary of Labor, although efforts to amend the anti-union Taft-Hartley Act failed. Favoring Rosenberg-style "preventative mediation" as a way to avoid strikes, the time lost to work stoppages declined as compared to during the Truman administration.[28]

The liberalism of the Roosevelt-Truman era was easier to adopt in the context of the Cold War, when Eisenhower and other Republicans "often praised unions for fighting Communism and lifting living standards to help them make the case that American capitalism was delivering more to workers than Soviet communism."[29] Recalling his premilitary days on a dairy farm, President Eisenhower told union members,

"I worked 84 hours a week on the night shift from 6 to 6, seven nights a week. . . . In the years since, unions, cooperating with employers, have vastly improved the lot of working men and women."[30] Referring not only to labor policy but to investments in Social Security, the Interstate Highway System, and education, biographer Stephen E. Ambrose claims Eisenhower "put a Republican stamp of approval on twenty years of Democratic legislation."[31]

In race relations, Anna's efforts at the Defense Department had helped make the armed forces one of the first sectors of American society to integrate. In her fight with Education Commissioner Earl McGrath over segregated schools on Army bases, Anna argued that the expenditure of federal funds made such segregation unlawful. In his column in the *New York Age*, Walter White credited Anna with working "to overcome the legal technicalities behind which segregationists operated" and urged President Eisenhower to continue her policy, which he did.[32] Asked by a Black reporter about segregated schools on military bases, Eisenhower set forth the position established by Rosenberg: "I will repeat it again and again: whenever Federal funds are expended I do not see how any American can justify legally, logically, or morally discrimination. . . . If there are any benefits to be derived from them all should share, regardless of such inconsequential factors as race or religion."

Eisenhower went on to appoint Earl Warren to the Supreme Court, completed the desegregation of all federal property, including Washington, D.C., and signed into law the Civil Rights Act of 1957. When Arkansas Governor Orval Faubus allowed a violent mob to prevent nine Black students from attending Little Rock's Central High School, President Eisenhower dispatched the 101st Airborne Division to escort the children into the school and to each and every class, which they did for the entire school year. "When he had to," concludes biographer Stephen Ambrose, "he acted decisively" on civil rights.[33]

While Anna was happy to work behind the scenes, Paul Hoffman hoped to leverage his foreign policy experience into the role as Secretary of State in the Eisenhower administration. To raise his profile and to set forth his plan for dealing with Stalin and with the Soviet Union, he had published a slender manifesto: *Peace Can Be Won*. Hoffman's basic premise was that Truman had failed to realize, until it was too late, that Stalin's "manifest destiny was world domination."[34] In the chess match with the Russians, Hoffman argued, we were always a few moves behind. The Secretary of State position went to John Foster Dulles, but Hoffman remained a praetorian guard for Ike and was made a delegate to the United Nations, specializing in foreign aid.

By working to prepare and persuade Dwight Eisenhower to run for president, Anna and Paul Hoffman were among a group of influential figures who prevented power from falling into the hands of the hard-right wing of the Republican Party. In 1954 the symbol of the divided party and the divided nation, the man whom Hoffman called a political "profiteer" of the Cold War, fell from his pedestal. In the spring of that year, Senator Joe McCarthy locked horns with Edward R. Murrow on the CBS TV program *See It Now*. In an extraordinary deviation from the media's self-imposed rule against editorializing, Murrow, staring into the camera, challenged his fellow Americans to stand up to the demagogue:

> The line between investigating and persecuting is a very fine one, and the junior Senator from Wisconsin has stepped over it repeatedly. . . . We must remember always that accusation is not proof and that conviction depends upon evidence and due process of law. . . . This is no time for [those] who oppose Senator McCarthy's methods to keep silent.

Murrow's challenge seemed to embolden pro-democracy forces, which began to assert themselves. Several weeks after performing his accusatory act on *See It Now*, McCarthy's young staffer Roy Cohn got the senator into a public fight with the Army over a request for preferential treatment for G. David Schine, a close friend of Cohn's. Forty-five million Americans watched the Army-McCarthy hearings on ABC that spring. With Cohn at his side, McCarthy produced doctored evidence, interrupted repeatedly, pontificated, and made crude personal attacks. On June 9, the attorney for the Army, Joseph Welch, an older man with a folksy manner, had heard enough. As McCarthy assassinated the character of a young lawyer from Welch's firm, Welch took his glasses off and leaned forward to cut off the assault. Seemingly on the verge of tears,

Welch demanded of McCarthy: "Have you no sense of decency, sir, at long last? Have you left no sense of decency?"

Moments later, when Welch deferred to the chairman to call the next witness, the gallery burst into applause. The public unveiling of McCarthy as a boor and a bully was followed the next month when he was finally censured by his colleagues in the U.S. Senate. The first strike against McCarthy had been Anna Rosenberg's spirited defense against his spurious attack in December 1950. The final blow that felled McCarthy was delivered four years later by the Republican Senator from Maine, Margaret Chase Smith.

The middle of the decade was a trying time for Anna Rosenberg. In August 1955, Anna received the news that her mother had passed away while on holiday in Santa Margherita, Italy. The next month, President Eisenhower suffered a major heart attack while in Denver, Colorado. By the time he was released from the hospital, the presidential election was only one year away, and whether Ike would run for a second term was in doubt. As 1955 turned to 1956, Eisenhower remained silent as to whether he would run for his second term later that year. As a leading figure in Democratic politics, Anna joined Mrs. Roosevelt, Herbert Lehman, and others in supporting her party's candidate, Adlai Stevenson. If he were to win, the rumor was Anna would be named Secretary of Labor. At the end of February 1956, however, Ike announced he would run again, and there was an air of inevitability for a second term. While she was outwardly for Stevenson, the relationship she had with "Dear Ike" was a mutual admiration going back to the war years, and Anna was pragmatic enough to see the benefits of a "modern Republicanism" continuing to invest the future of the nation from its position in the center of American politics.

After thirty-seven years of marriage, in 1956 Anna separated from Mike Rosenberg. With its long absences and with Anna as the primary earner, the Rosenbergs' marriage had always been an uncommon one. Anna's close proximity to powerful men had, at times, excited gossip; one such bit of chatter involved Anna and Walter "Beetle" Smith. While Anna's correspondence with Smith is warm, there is no evidence they were anything more than good friends. Given her discretion, it is not surprising Anna left no clues as to why she chose this moment to separate. Her timing may have had to do with her being out of official government service, where leaving her marriage would have fueled speculation. She was also spending more time with Paul Hoffman, both at Studebaker corporate offices and in New York, where he maintained his own apartment while his wife remained in California.

Even while married to Mike, Anna came across to some observers as "unattached," and her life continued much as it had always done.[35] She remained in the Fifth Avenue apartment, kept company by her miniature dachshund. She spent time with her circle of friends who either lived in New York or kept apartments in the city. She lunched with Eleanor Roosevelt and mentored Nelson Rockefeller, spending hours with him at a conference table going over his speeches.[36] The work paid off in 1958 with his election as Governor of New York. Anna paid visits to Bernard Baruch when he was in the city and vacationed at his property, Hobcaw Barony, in South Carolina. Anna traveled with Mary Lasker, now a widow, to her villa in Boca Raton, and to Paris and the South of France. She kept in contact with William Benton and flew to Los Angeles, where she stayed with Danny Kaye and made Chinese food with his wife, Sylvia.

In New York, Anna was point person for the city's new beautification efforts, midwifed an agreement on a potentially crippling transit strike, and began appearing at public events with Mr. Hoffman. One such event was a night cruise for charity aboard the French liner *Liberté*, during which passengers dined on *coupe glacée Romanoff* and Caspian caviar, and which returned the couple to port in the wee hours the following morning.[37]

<hr />

On October 20, 1959, under a radiant fall sky, two hundred mourners gathered at Fort Myer Chapel at the edge of Arlington National Cemetery to pay their respects to George C. Marshall. The architect of victory in the Second World War, international war hero and statesman, and recipient of the Nobel Peace Prize, the Old Man had been a mentor to Dwight Eisenhower and, later, to Anna Rosenberg. In the early days of her time at the Pentagon, she complained about having to wear the identification badge because it put holes in her jackets.

Her complaint made General Marshall wonder if anyone ever actually looked at the badges. As an experiment, he had Anna wear his name badge and he wore Anna's. This they continued until the day he left the Pentagon for retirement. For a few years at least, Anna consoled herself, Marshall and his wife had been able to tend to their beloved rose garden.

General Marshall had planned the state funeral of President Roosevelt and wanted nothing so elaborate for himself: no memorials, no eulogies, just a gravesite at Arlington National Cemetery. After lying in repose at the Washington National Cathedral, his body was taken to Arlington. At the chapel prior to the private family service, President Eisenhower sat next to ex-President Truman, and Anna Rosenberg sat nearby, in her black hat of mourning, tears running down her cheeks. "General Marshall," said Harry Truman, "was a man of the greatest ability. . . . He was a man of honor, a man of truth, and a man of greatest ability. He was the greatest of the great in our time." Echoing these superlatives, Anna said, "I do not think there was ever . . . a greater soldier, a better statesman, and a greater human being."[38]

Two months later, Anna found herself again on the front pages of the *New York Times*, when she mediated a transit strike in New York City. The nation as a whole saw her in action when she appeared as a guest on Edward R. Murrow's popular TV show, *Person to Person*. The innovative program sent CBS cameras to the homes of famous figures, while Murrow interviewed them from back at the studio. Elizabeth Taylor was a guest, as was Marilyn Monroe. Hollywood royalty Brando, Bogart, and Bacall were featured. Senator John Kennedy and his wife, Jackie, appeared on one episode, and Harry Truman on another. The Rat Pack—Frank Sinatra, Dean Martin, and Sammy Davis, Jr.—all appeared, as did artists such as Duke Ellington and John Steinbeck. Now it was Anna Rosenberg's turn in the spotlight.

Black cases stenciled with "Columbia Broadcasting System" were piled high in the kitchen of Anna's apartment on the Upper East Side of Manhattan near Central Park. Stepping over wires and cables that ran across the living room carpet, the TV crew scurried about making final preparations. The relative chaos that beset her tasteful home was amplified by the muffled barking of Timothy, unhappily confined to the kitchen. The producer directed Anna to sit on her sofa and face the main camera, pointing to three other film cameras sitting on tripods. Two efficient young women appeared on either side of Anna to check her makeup and then disappeared. A boom with a microphone at the end was pushed toward her. "Mrs. Rosenberg, say something, if you would, so we can get levels."

A moment later, looking into the monitor, Anna recognized the Broadway actor and Kent cigarette pitchman Bob Wright. The live telecast opened with his persuasive baritone: "I think we have just about enough time to light a cigarette before we visit our first guest. I'll be lighting a Kent, of course." The producer flashed five fingers, then four; then . . . Edward R. Murrow was on the screen introducing her: "Mrs. Anna M. Rosenberg was once described by Bernard Baruch as blessed with the mind of a man and the soft, brown eyes of a woman. During the past twenty-five years she has used these talents plus extraordinary energy to prove that a woman's place is in any job that has to be done at the city, state, or national government." Mrs. Rosenberg's service of "great distinction," Murrow went on, earned her "the country's highest civilian awards."[39] Then he introduced his TV audience to Anna's well-appointed living room, where she sat in an armchair.

The legendary newsman, whose dispatches from London during the Second World War made him a household name, was dapper as always in a gray flannel suit, white shirt, dark tie, and pocket square. His dark hair and eyebrows punctuated a slender face; his deeply furrowed brow and steady gaze at the camera conveyed seriousness. The overall impression was of "a casting director's ideal . . . of a famous war correspondent." Handsome as he was, it was his voice that most people recognized. His was a voice that "punched through," that made "twenty-six" sound like "the most important declaration ever made by man."[40] As he sat in the CBS studio, wisps of smoke rose into the picture from the ever-present cigarette he cradled in his left hand. Then the voice:

"Evening, Mrs. Rosenberg."

"Good evening, Ed."

After chitchat about Anna's upcoming trip to Europe, the CBS newsman asked Anna about her time at the Pentagon. It was the most gratifying position of her long career, she said, but also heartbreaking "when I had to put down that thousands of men had to be called into service. To me they were not numbers; they were each individuals, the son of someone or the husband of someone, someone dearly loved."[41] She talked about the time Fiorello La Guardia locked her in City Hall; how she missed FDR's sense of humor; and her deep respect for George Marshall, "a man who truly believed in women." Cameras followed as Anna showed Murrow and his viewers room after room, full of chintz and silk, cushions and crystal. They discussed her love of flowers and frilly hats. "I learned long ago not to comment on a woman's hat," deadpanned Murrow.

Anna talked about her girlhood dream of becoming a "scientific gardener," surrounded by flowers. Of her father and mother, she said "they are the ones who made me feel that no matter what you do, no matter how much you serve your country, you can never repay [it] for the freedom and opportunity." And she recalled the encounter she had with the board of aldermen as a teenager, when she appeared before them to complain that the girls of Wadleigh didn't have enough desks to attend school at the same time.

"I realized the power of politics."

"Anna," said Murrow, tapping his cigarette, "you have quite a book to write someday."

CHAPTER TWENTY-THREE

HAPPY BIRTHDAY, MR. PRESIDENT

At this stage, it appears that for women the New Frontiers are the old frontiers.

—Columnist Doris Fleeson

Oh, you're one of those feminists!

—JFK to a female newspaper reporter who asked him to compare his wife, Jacqueline, to Eleanor Roosevelt.

Columns of sunlight angled into Eleanor Roosevelt's large town house at 55 E. 74th Street, on Manhattan's Upper East Side. Monday, September 26, 1960, was a pleasant early fall day. After a busy afternoon, the former First Lady had invited a small group of women, including Anna, to watch the nation's first televised presidential debate. That evening they watched Republican Vice President Richard M. Nixon debate Democratic Senator John F. Kennedy from a soundstage in Chicago. The Vice President's gray suit blended with the set on the black-and-white television, and his uncrossed legs and fidgety hands gave the appearance of a man not entirely comfortable under TV lights. In contrast was Kennedy's sharply tailored dark suit and steely, straightforward gaze. As the moderator introduced the two candidates for the 1960 presidential election, Nixon was in profile, looking over at the younger Massachusetts senator, whose eyes remained on the camera. Kennedy delivered his opening remarks first and concluded by harkening back to the "rendezvous with destiny" phrase FDR used in his 1933 inauguration. "I think our generation of Americans has the same rendezvous," Kennedy went on. "The question now is: Can freedom be maintained under the most severe attack it has ever known? I think it *can* be. And I think in the final analysis it depends upon what we do here. I think it's time America started moving again."

At the Democratic National Convention in Los Angeles that summer, the well-financed and well-connected Kennedy secured the nomination. One of his first acts after becoming the nominee was to pay a visit to FDR's widow in order to win her support. Kennedy spent a day with Mrs. Roosevelt in Hyde Park, and afterwards Eleanor told Anna, "My final judgment now is that here is a man who wants to leave a record— perhaps for ambitious personal reasons as people say—but I think I am not mistaken in feeling he would make a good President if elected."[1]

In 1961, as President Kennedy pointed the way for his domestic agenda, the New Frontier, American women seemed poised to take the next step toward a greater share of public policy–making. Mrs. Roosevelt, Anna, and Mary Lasker agreed to fundraise for Kennedy, but they expected JFK to reciprocate by placing women in positions within the administration, even the cabinet, as had been the case with FDR, Truman, and Eisenhower. As one historian puts it, by 1960 "the contributions of women during World War II made many believe that the nation owed them a share in the ideals of justice and equality, some gesture of recognition in the particular form of legislation—an equal rights amendment to the Constitution or, less radical, an equal pay law." The expectation was that JFK would continue this "growing reliance upon qualified women for high public posts." Eleanor Roosevelt suggested Kennedy talk to Anna Rosenberg.[2]

Democratic National Committee veteran Clayton Fritchey echoed this idea, telling JFK, "[W]e have no Madam Perkins, or Anna Rosenberg . . . whose names became household words. . . . Today there are no really famous women serving in government."[3] President Kennedy did not heed the advice. He failed to appoint a single woman to his cabinet and named a scant few in policy-making roles. Instead of household names making far-reaching policies for the entire nation, the Kennedy women appointees toiled in obscure corners of the federal government, as customs collector for Portland, Maine, as superintendent of the Denver mint, or as minister to Bulgaria.[4] Democratic committeewoman Margaret Price complained that "the absence of professional women in any staff capacity in the Kennedy entourage has led to the impression that his is an all-male cast."⁵ Party official Emma Guffey Miller wrote Kennedy to tell him of her "grievous disappointment . . . that so few women have been named to worthwhile positions." When Kennedy had a presidential aide send the reply, Miller was further infuriated.⁶

While her talents remained untapped, Anna Rosenberg joined Mary Lasker for a trip to the South of France. The two women stayed in the luxurious colonnaded Villa Fiorentina in Cap Ferrat, with its large private park overlooking the sun-kissed Mediterranean and its two swimming pools. One evening Mary invited Gérald Van der Kemp, the curator of Versailles, to dine with her and Anna. After aperitifs, dinner was served on the terrace while a real-life version of *To Catch a Thief* was quietly unfolding upstairs in the villa. By the time dinner had ended, Mary discovered that $120,000 of jewelry was gone, as was Mr. Van der Kemp's key to his apartment in Versailles. The harried French flics finally tracked down the leader of the jewelry thieves, a handsome blond Russian known as "le beau Sacha."⁷ The cat burglar was not the only one who saw only dollar signs when Mary Lasker and Anna Rosenberg were in town. To the Kennedy men, Anna and Mary were "the New York fat cats."⁸

After returning from France, Anna flew to Los Angeles for board meetings and from there made a quick trip into Mexico to obtain a divorce. At the time, most U.S. states were "at-fault" jurisdictions that required extensive proof and time-consuming court review. People with means, including many Hollywood stars, opted instead for the easier and less costly "Mexican Divorce," following directions from the Burt Bacharach hit of the same name, which promised listeners they could "leave their past behind" with a quick trip south of the Rio Grande.

———— • • • ————

Anna did so, following the path trod by the likes of Johnny Carson, Elizabeth Taylor, and Marilyn Monroe.

Anna may have been disappointed to be seen as a donor rather than a driver of decisions, but as a loyal and important figure within the party she took on the role with her typical relish. Early in 1962 Anna planned a massive fundraiser for the Democratic Party and its popular, young leader. The President's forty-fifth birthday was coming up in May, and what better way to celebrate it than a star-studded gala at Madison Square Garden? After enlisting the deep-pocketed Arthur Krim, the head of United Artists film studio, Anna and her co-chair went about securing the cream of American show business.

Saturday, May 19, 1962, was an unseasonably hot day. After peaking above 90 degrees, the sunset finally brought some relief, but as the 17,500 guests found their seats in Madison Square Garden, it remained stuffy. Among the guests at the Birthday Salute were JFK's brother Robert; the Mayor of New York City, Robert F. Wagner, Jr., and his wife. Paul Hoffman, who had been a widower for a year, was there, as was Vice President Lyndon Johnson, who had been invited at Anna's insistence. It was perhaps not entirely surprising that it was left to Anna to invite LBJ. The Kennedy-Johnson partnership was a marriage of convenience, rather than a trusting working relationship. JFK needed support from southern Democrats, which Johnson could deliver, but the younger Kennedy did not hesitate to exert his authority over Lyndon Johnson. "Kennedy never said a word of importance in the Senate and he never did a thing," complained Johnson, "but somehow . . . he managed to create the image of himself as . . . a youthful leader who would change the face of the country."[*] In the words of Doris Kearns Goodwin, "It was not easy [for Johnson] to apprentice himself to a backbencher nine years his junior." While LBJ was there, perhaps reluctantly, notably absent at the event was the president's wife. Jacqueline Kennedy remained at the Kennedy country house in Virginia, where she was a last-minute entry in an equestrian event.[†]

As the lights dimmed in the arena, actor Peter Lawford, the president's brother-in-law, opened festivities as master of ceremonies. Comedian

---

[*] Selverstone, ed., *A Companion to John F. Kennedy* (UK: Wiley, 2014), 152, and Doris Kearns Goodwin, *Lyndon Johnson and the American Dream* (New York: Harper & Row, 1976), 163. The enmity between LBJ and Robert Kennedy was such that each man would devolve into profanity when discussing the other.

[†] Gossip columns at the time suggested a JFK-Monroe affair. To Kennedy biographer Robert Dallek, "numerous phone calls listed in the White House logs from Monroe to Kennedy suggest something more than a casual acquaintance" (*An Unfinished Life: John F. Kennedy, 1917–1963* [Boston: Little, Brown, 2003], 580–81).

Jack Benny warmed up the crowd for a set of jazz tunes by the regal Ella Fitzgerald. A dance troupe was followed by Anna's friend, entertainer Danny Kaye, then leading man Henry Fonda. Sitting right next to Anna, the President took in the entertainment with a bemused grin.

At the end of the gala, it was time for the headliner. "Mr. President," Peter Lawford announced, "Marilyn Monroe."

The stage remained empty, save the lonely grand piano. Moments passed as the crowd chattered in the dark. With a nervous laugh, Lawford stalled for time: "A woman about whom . . . it truly may be said . . . needs no introduction . . . let me just say . . . here she is!" The drumroll sounded; the audience quieted down, fanning themselves with their programs. Still, the screen siren failed to appear.

Life magazine photographer Bill Ray recalls the moment: "[B]oom, on comes this spotlight. There was no sound. No sound at all. It was like we were in outer space." As the light tracked her, the thirty-five-year-old platinum blonde was in no hurry, taking geisha-like steps to the podium mic. She was literally sewn into her skintight dress, one she called "skin and beads," with a white mink wrap slipping from her bare shoulders.* Lawford put his arm around her to help her take off the wrap: "Mr. President, the *late* Marilyn Monroe." "There was this long, long pause," remembers Bill Ray, "and finally, she comes out with this unbelievably breathy, 'Happy biiiiirthday to youuuu,' and everybody just went into a swoon."[9]

The party then moved to Arthur and Mathilde Krim's luxury town house at 33 E. 69th Street. Official White House photographer Cecil Stoughton captured JFK as he mingled with the stars: Harry and Julie Belafonte, Shirley MacLaine, Diahann Carroll. Kennedy posed for photos with Anna Rosenberg and the Krims, and taken that night was the only known photo of Marilyn, Bobby, and JFK together.

Vice President Johnson, remembered Arthur Krim, was uncharacteristically quiet and reserved, not knowing many people in the New York society scene. Off in the corner, his hands in his pockets, Johnson felt

---

* In 2016, the gold rhinestone dress became the "world's most expensive" when Ripley's Believe It or Not! acquired it at auction for more than $5 million. By agreement with Ripley's, entrepreneur and tastemaker Kim Kardashian wore the dress to the 2022 Met Gala.

"culturally inferior" to the Kennedys and was "sorely conscious of being seen as an outsider" among the artists and intellectuals, like bow-tied Kennedy adviser Arthur Schlesinger, Jr., who chatted up Marilyn Monroe. "I do not think I have seen anyone so beautiful," Schlesinger remembered, "but one felt a terrible unreality about her, as if talking to someone under water, receding into her own glittering mist." Seventy-seven days after her whisper-song to the President, Marilyn Monroe died of a drug overdose, leaving unfinished her final film, *Something's Got to Give.*

It had been a blockbuster event, and Anna may have been grateful for its success. She may also have thought she could have done more. Given her patriotic inability to turn down leaders who sought her skills, it seems likely Anna would have taken a position in Kennedy's cabinet if offered. It was not, and we can only speculate as to how Anna felt at this moment. For three presidencies spanning two decades, she could walk into the White House or phone the President with ease. Now she was seen as a big-money donor. Not only that, but there was a whisper of impropriety to the evening marked by the notable absence of Jackie Kennedy and the overt sexuality of Monroe's performance. If Anna was underappreciated that evening, she may have consoled herself in the knowledge that Lyndon Johnson now knew the immense power of fundraising, even over the course of a single day spent among the elites of New York City.

Two months after the Kennedy gala, Anna was the center of attention at her own joyous event. On Thursday, July 19, 1962, Anna sat under the hair dryer at Julius Caruso's salon on Park Avenue while dictating to her assistant Phyllis responses to a large batch of mail. Then Anna's driver drove her to the Unitarian Church of All Souls on Lexington Avenue and 80th Street. That afternoon Anna and Paul Hoffman, seventy-one, were married in front of fifty guests. Newspapers noted it was Anna's sixtieth birthday.[10] As the chamber orchestra played Mendelssohn's "Wedding March," the bride entered the New England–style chapel in an ice-blue satin dress with a bolero jacket embroidered with tiny pearls and a matching tulle casque hat. On her manicured hand shone a vintage Florentine diamond ring. Anna's sister, Clare, was matron of honor, and Senator William Benton was best man. Thomas attended, as did five of Hoffman's seven children.[11]

In the brief sermon befitting a second marriage, the Reverend Walter Donald Kring remarked on the political differences of the two notables he was marrying. The couple, he said, "will not always agree with each other, for even in marriage they must preserve their individuality. Their differences must not divide them but unite them and make their lives richer in meaning." The newspapers picked up on the fact that the word "obey" was omitted from the wedding vows. To reporters, Anna gushed, "Every time of your life can be a happy one!" and the beaming groom exclaimed, "At least 200 people have told me how wonderful Anna is, and anyone who wants to say how wonderful she is can say it again. I love to hear it!"[12] Paul and Anna then departed for their honeymoon at Lake Como, Italy.

That fall the sun glistening off Lake Como was but a memory. On a gloomy Saturday afternoon in November 1962, Anna stood again in the hemlock-rimmed rose garden of the Roosevelt family estate. Together with family friends, old New Dealers, heroes of the war, foreign dignitaries, and U.N. delegates, she paid her respects as Eleanor Roosevelt was laid to rest next to her husband. Standing side by side, hats in hand, were Presidents Kennedy, Truman, and Eisenhower. Vice President Lyndon Johnson stood nearby, as did Adlai Stevenson and New York Governor Nelson Rockefeller. Next to the politicians were the Roosevelt children and their spouses. The Reverend Gordon Kidd gave the eulogy: "In the death of Eleanor Roosevelt the world has suffered an irreparable loss. The entire world becomes one family orphaned by her passing."[13] A first sergeant from the West Point Band lifted the bugle to his lips as rain began to fall. As "Taps" rang out in the ancient river valley, Anna wept, her black-gloved hand squeezing Paul's.

With Mrs. Roosevelt gone, Anna became more outspoken in her attempts to see the doors to top public and private positions open for women. The lack of influence and access to the Kennedy White House meant she had to take the message public. "Women have one particular thing to contribute," she told journalist Godfrey Sperling; "besides all their technical knowledge, they have a great talent for human relations." She continued, "There has been progress. But it is not fast enough. Here are 50 percent of the people who are not participating sufficiently in the activities of their country. It is a great waste."[14] To another reporter, she pointed out there were only thirteen women in Congress and seven of them were widows who inherited the positions after their husbands died in office. There were "less than a handful of women in policy-level positions." "I do not advocate opportunities for women just because they are female. I gladly leave that to the professional women's rights advocates. But if she has the necessary wherewithal, her sex should not be held against her."[15]

———◆◆◆———

On Friday, November 22, 1963, the audience settled into Boston's magnificent redbrick Symphony Hall. The weekly lunchtime concert was to be Rimsky-Korsakov's suite from his opera *Le Coq d'Or*, conducted by Erich Leinsdorf. Since Lyndon Johnson had offered him a life in America rather than returning to Nazi Austria back in 1938, Leinsdorf had enjoyed a career as one of the world's great conductors. The concert was carried live on Boston radio. As the elegant musician walked across the stage, the audience fell silent, eager for the concert to begin. "Ladies and gentlemen," he began in his heavily accented English, "we have a press report over the wires—we hope it is unconfirmed, but we have to doubt it—the President of the United States had been the victim of an assassination." Gasps and cries echoed through the august hall, which was just a few miles from JFK's birthplace. The conductor then led the musicians in an impromptu version of the funeral march from Beethoven's Third Symphony as the grief-stricken men and women in the seats above stifled sobs.

In concert halls, movie houses, on car radios, and on television, Americans across the nation learned the terrible news that afternoon. On CBS, a bulletin interrupted the soap opera *As the World Turns*. At 2:40 PM anchor Walter Cronkite was handed the wire report and, removing his glasses before looking into the camera, said: "From Dallas, Texas, the flash apparently official . . . President Kennedy died some thirty-eight minutes ago." Swallowing hard, Cronkite needed a moment to compose himself. His voice cracking, he continued: "Vice President Johnson has left the hospital in Dallas, but we do not know to where he has proceeded."

From Parkland Hospital, the Vice President had been raced to Love Field, where he was urged to board Air Force One to return to

Washington to be sworn in. The jet remained on the tarmac, broiling under the bright Texas sun, as Johnson refused to return to Washington without Mrs. Kennedy. A federal judge was then summoned to the airfield. Less than two hours after the deadly gunshots rang out at Dealey Plaza, Lyndon Baines Johnson stood next to Jackie Kennedy in her pink Chanel suit flecked with blood. He raised his right hand as Judge Sarah Hughes swore him in as the nation's thirty-sixth President.

CHAPTER TWENTY-FOUR

A TRUE FRIEND ACROSS ALL THESE YEARS

Anna is a fighter, a good person to have on your side—an intellectual with a heart.

—Lady Bird Johnson

Within weeks of his sudden ascension to the presidency, Lyndon Johnson met with Anna Rosenberg at the White House. While the location of the meeting was new, their friendship was not. In 1937, before Lyndon Johnson was elected to Congress, Anna recognized him as a "real liberal" and made a campaign contribution of $500. Johnson never forgot the gesture and often told the story of how Anna's generosity "saved the election."[1] From the late 1930s onward, they championed and implemented FDR's bold social legislation, Johnson in Congress and Anna in New Deal agencies. Anna saw much of Franklin Roosevelt in LBJ, and Johnson valued Anna much as FDR had done—as a confidante who combined expertise and friendship, wise counsel and quiet discretion.

In the fifties their "deep mutual respect" matured into an enduring friendship. From his perch on the Senate Armed Services Committee, Lyndon Johnson saw Rosenberg's mettle up close during the McCarthy smear campaign. Johnson's wife, Lady Bird, recalled how the "ugly mood of the country manifested itself" with the attack on Anna. "She was immediately jumped on by the communist scare folks as having been a member of the Communist Party. Lyndon espoused her cause . . . he liked ability, and patriotism, and she had both of those . . . in high degree. And she was tough." Lyndon, Lady Bird said, "became a great admirer of hers. She was one of the smartest, toughest, most interesting people who crossed our path and remained a lifelong friend. . . . She really won him over."[2] Having Lyndon Johnson as a defender and admirer was important to Anna. "When the chips were down and you needed Lyndon, he was there. He was there as a Senator; he was there as a friend."[3] As she told Mary Lasker, "You'll never get anywhere in the Congress unless you get Lyndon Johnson on your side."[4]

As Assistant Secretary of Defense fighting to improve the experience of ordinary G.I.'s, Rosenberg had often butted heads with Johnson, who kept a keen eye on military spending. "He was not easy to convince," Anna said. "You had to bring facts to him."[5] Despite their differences, Johnson had been impressed when she appeared before Congress and he commended her work at the Defense Department. As a senator he singled her out for praise on universal training, calling her work "the best job that's been done in Washington in twenty years."[6] Her intelligence and persistence were consonant with his view of the capability of women. "He really always felt that lots of women were as smart as lots of men," explained Lady Bird. "He did not labor under any delusions that they were necessarily gentle, velvet creatures."[7] Working with women like Anna Rosenberg "convinced him it was possible and desirable . . . for women to play a greater role in the economic and political life of the nation."[8]

At their meeting in January 1964, Anna discussed with the President "better utilization of women in the business world and government."[9] Action on this front would be a deviation from the JFK regime, but while Johnson sought continuity of his predecessor's initiatives, such as civil rights, this was one area where Kennedy had failed, and where real action would be welcomed. LBJ suffered by comparison to Kennedy, who was the "romantic and glamourous symbol of a hoped-for new era."[10] Putting women in policy-level positions, Rosenberg argued, would not only correct course but enhance Johnson's image.

"After that [meeting]," reported Anna, "he took off like a rocket on the job." In fact, the launch was that same day. Liz Carpenter, Mrs. Johnson's Press Secretary, was waiting for the White House elevator that afternoon when the President stepped off: "Anna Rosenberg tells me that we need more women in government . . . be at the cabinet meeting tomorrow." There would be no commissions to consider philosophical questioning. The pragmatic thrust at the heart of the

Johnson-Rosenberg working relationship was on full display as the President directed his cabinet:

> I want every manager in government . . . to take note of this untapped resource. The day is over when the top jobs are reserved for men. In the baskets on your desks, if you'll go back and look, you'll find there are a lot of women who've been asking for elevation. I want you . . . to get some of them moving.[11]

The machinery of the executive branch cranked to life. Aides "pressed departments and agencies for action, kept a count of the numbers of women appointed and promoted, and maintained a list of women qualified for government service."[12] When he caught someone foot-dragging, the President gave him the "Johnson Treatment," standing over him, pointing his finger in his chest, demanding in his Texas drawl, "Do you have any women in top jobs at your agency?"[13] Once he had inspired his staff, the master politician's next step was to seize the public-relations victory. Pledging to end "stag government" and reminding the country that it could not continue to waste half its human resources, on January 29, 1964, President Johnson announced a campaign to hire fifty women to top government posts. Johnson, Anna recalled, was "never reluctant to give a person credit for something," and newspapers freely acknowledged her role as the prime mover of the initiative in articles like "Anna Rosenberg Hoffman Inspired LBJ to Recruit Women" and "Put Bug in President's Ear, Then He Appointed Women."[14]

That year Anna was honored at the White House with the Eleanor Roosevelt Political and Public Service Award. "Anna Rosenberg has contributed outstandingly in many ways to public service and to many public causes," said President Johnson at the ceremony. "Her brilliant mind, her versatile talents, and her generous spirit have meant much to the nation, to her city, and to her fellow men." In remarks described by Lady Bird as "most touching," Anna, hands and voice trembling with emotion, credited her career in public service to "Mrs. Roosevelt . . . the greatest believer in the ability of women—her influence on [FDR] opened the door for women in government."[15]

Through the spring of 1964 the President, at agency meetings and news conferences and in speeches around the country, spoke of the need to end the "waste of woman-power." By the end of the summer, over sixteen hundred women had been promoted or appointed at level GS 12 and above, including two ambassadors, the Assistant Secretary of Agriculture, and the first women to ever serve on the Atomic Energy Commission, the Interstate Commerce Commission, and the Board of Directors of the Import-Export Bank.[16] "It is better to have many women in important jobs," Anna said proudly, "than one woman in a cabinet position as a symbol."[17]

For a leader whose power had always derived from Texas and Washington, the women-in-government effort helped raise his national profile, which was vital in the early days of his presidency. Johnson was estranged from his home state, as it had been the site of the slaying of JFK. Powerful as he was in the corridors of Washington, Johnson was not a widely known figure outside the Beltway. As Senate Majority Leader, LBJ had "purposely avoided the limelight" in the Capitol in order to build his power from within the chamber. As Vice President, Johnson shied away from the spotlight, convinced the Kennedy coterie wanted it that way. "You're the Vice President," chided Anna. "Get national publicity!"[18] But Johnson lacked the glamour and urbanity of Kennedy. He was plainspoken and could come off as crude, more homespun than Harvard. To win in 1964, Johnson needed new bases of support from which to launch himself as a truly national figure.

New York City was the capital of American media, as well as a wellspring of Democratic voters and donors. In the summer before the election Anna hosted a private luncheon for the President at the 21 Club attended by the top echelon of the city's media empires. "People were curious about Lyndon. People like Bill Paley [head of CBS], people from the *Times*—they really didn't know him." LBJ, who knew reporters, but not the owners who employed them, was in top form. "I never heard him better," Anna said. "He was relaxed. He was open." The newspaper and TV people, like Roy Howard of the Scripps-Howard newspapers, told Anna, "God, we didn't know how good this man was, how able." "They went away enchanted," Anna recalled.[19] In August, Johnson continued to curry the favor of powerful media figures when he made a trip to Syracuse University to open the communications center named after publishing magnate S. I. Newhouse.*

Nobody knew New York's powerful labor leaders better than Anna, and as Johnson toured New York that summer she was there as he received a terrific reception from the International Ladies' Garment Workers' Union; the women had all left their workshops to come see him. "I've never seen crowds like it," Anna remembered. "Old-timers, who really knew what it meant [to have] an American president who cared for them . . . Lyndon was moved by it."[20] Johnson attended the annual Al Smith Dinner, spoke before the American Bar Association, and opened the 1964 New York World's Fair in Queens, speaking on his commitment to civil rights and enlisting foot soldiers for his "War on Poverty." Lyndon and Lady Bird were guests of Anna and Paul Hoffman and hobnobbed with the Krims and Mary Lasker. "I worked very hard in New York State," Anna said, recalling the months leading up to the election.[21]

The civil rights bill then wending its way through Congress was at the heart of Johnson's domestic agenda. On this issue, Anna ran interference at the President's urging, just as she had done for "the Boss." Rosenberg called off attacks from the left that Johnson was moving too slowly on civil rights, convincing influential patrons like Mary Lasker to hold their fire, while persuading newspapers like Dorothy Schiff's *New York Post* to stand down. As a seasoned mediator, Anna knew what was facing the President:

> He was a master politician and a master tactician. He knew exactly what he could get and what he couldn't get from the Senate. . . . And he knew that to get passage of any real civil rights bill, he had to make some compromises.

---

* In September, the so-called Daisy ad ran on television; the Madison Avenue–produced spot showed a little girl in a sunlit field plucking petals from a daisy. As she counts the last petal, a mission control–style countdown begins: "Ten, nine, eight, seven . . ." The nuclear mushroom cloud is then reflected in the girl's eye. A masterpiece of negative political advertising, the ad sought to exploit the fear of GOP candidate Barry Goldwater's Cold War extremism.

Anna's intervention helped, but congressional compromise, LBJ's strong-arm tactics, and the moral weight of his office were all needed to get the Civil Rights Act to the President's desk. After four months, Senate liberals broke the filibuster by southern lawmakers and President Johnson signed the bill into law on July 2, 1964.

A generation before, when Anna had urged President Roosevelt to end discrimination in wartime defense hiring, the nation had taken a step toward racial equality. A decade later, as the top woman in the Truman administration, she had worked to end segregation in the armed forces and on U.S. military bases worldwide. In her career she had met with civil rights leaders, sympathetic lawmakers, and presidents willing to take executive action. This was the moment they had been working toward. The Civil Rights Act wasn't just presidential power, it was federal law; it wasn't limited to one sector of American society; it was nationwide. By mandating racial integration of all facilities receiving federal funding and all places of public accommodation, the law marked "a definitive end to the brutal . . . system of segregation that existed in the South since the turn of the century: 'white' and 'colored' water fountains, schools, and medical facilities; whites-only swimming pools, movie theaters and restaurants; [and] legally permissible discrimination in the workplace."[22] Jim Crow had never been just a series of racist laws; it was a code of conduct, a way of life where white men removed their hats for white women, but not Black women; where Black girls were forbidden by shopkeepers from trying on the dresses they wished to buy; and where Black men were called by first names (or worse).

President Johnson's commitment to civil rights was not political expediency; it was real. "I had many talks with him [on civil rights]," Anna recalled. "I was convinced . . . I knew he wanted to get things done. I knew he was a superb—I hate to use the word—politician [but] I don't think I truly realized what this man really would do when he had this enormous power."[23] Anna could be forgiven for not forecasting the extent of Johnson's efforts: not since Abraham Lincoln had a President done so much for Black Americans.[24]

———◆◆◆———

President Johnson had guided the nation through the trauma of the Kennedy assassination, while making his own mark as a leader. As the election approached, LBJ was seen as a champion of civil rights and an able commander in the fight against poverty. When the GOP nominated Arizona Senator Barry Goldwater, seen as a hard-right extremist, the path was cleared for a Johnson victory in the fall. That November the relationship built between the tall Texan and the Empire State paid off. Johnson became the only Democratic presidential candidate in history to carry every single county in the state of New York. Johnson took all five boroughs of New York City, the first presidential candidate to do so since FDR in 1936. Even Staten Island, the most Republican of the boroughs, voted for Johnson—the only Democrat to win over the islanders in nearly thirty years. Landslide Lyndon was back.

Less than two years after he'd stood in the corner of the Krims' town house, an outsider in Kennedy's shadow, Lyndon Johnson had a base of political support in New York, he had trusted advisers there, and he and Lady Bird enjoyed a circle of social friends. Never before had Anna had a relationship with a President and First Lady *together*. Spending time in the company of a President together with Paul Hoffman, rather than alone, was another unique experience for Anna. Lady Bird Johnson was struck by how they complemented each other. Recalling her time with Anna and Paul after a dinner at the couple's Sutton Square town house, the First Lady gushed:

> They are both so smart, give so much to living, and love it. . . . The evening ended with a series of toasts. . . . A very nice toast about me from Anna. I liked it because she used the word "useful." I want very much to be. And for once I was satisfied with myself, because I felt it. . . . There are some evenings that deserve the title of brilliant. This one was.[25]

The press delighted in making an issue out of the fact that Anna was a veteran New Dealer and her husband a lifelong Republican, but at home there was mainly consensus. "We're in agreement on most things," reported Anna. "We're both busy people; we lecture each other on working so hard and both of us go on doing it."[26] Paul was the director of the United Nations Special Fund, and after Studebaker closed down for good he busied himself with his avocado ranch, the family business based in Indianapolis, and as a trustee of Kenyon College.

With LBJ in the White House, Anna returned to the prominence she had enjoyed through the presidencies of FDR, Truman, and Eisenhower. A joke made the rounds in Washington that Anna could pick up the phone and say, "Get me the Senator! Get me the Governor! Get me the President! . . . Someday she'll pick up her phone and say, 'Get me God!'"[27] Anna Rosenberg had come full circle.

Lyndon Johnson's similarities to FDR were not lost on anyone. "He was very proud of his relationship with President Roosevelt," Anna explained. "If I would bring to his attention something on which the President [Roosevelt] would like action, he would go all out. . . . When I told him a complimentary story about himself by President Roosevelt, he would make me repeat it saying, 'You sure he felt that way?' He was very, very proud of his relations with [FDR]."[28] To another interviewer, Anna said Johnson "adored Roosevelt" and "wanted to have some of that aura."[29] In 1961, after the Vice President sent her his autographed photo, Anna wrote back: "I am putting it next to the picture of the man both you and I loved—President Roosevelt. This ought to tell you what I think of [you]."[30]

Both leaders saw in the presidency the power to help Americans down on their luck. Franklin Roosevelt's empathy came from his struggle with polio; Johnson's came from seeing deep poverty in Texas as a young man. As Anna described it:

> You could always trace back the terrific impressions made upon him in his youth. When he talked about education, he would talk about when he was a teacher; he would talk about the one room school. When he put up a fight on poverty, he would talk about his mother carrying pails of water to the house. He would talk about the kids he taught who didn't have any breakfast, who didn't have any lunch.*

If Lyndon Johnson found himself in a position to do so, Anna knew, he was determined to fix what he saw as the issues bedeviling the nation: "When he was leader of the Senate, certainly when he was president, by

---

* Anna Rosenberg, oral history interview with Joe Frantz, 1973. LBJ remembered, "My mother had to lug pails of water every day from the well. I'm going to see that no woman has to do that again."

God, he was going to correct the wrongs he knew existed."[31] Like the New Deal before it, Johnson's Great Society launched a number of programs to improve the quality of the lives of the most vulnerable Americans. From Head Start for disadvantaged preschool children to Medicare for senior citizens, the Great Society reflected Johnson's "conviction that government should unlock potential for individuals while recognizing that individuals owe core obligations to each other."[32]

Sharing this conviction, Anna did her part, reprising for LBJ the role she had played for Roosevelt of "going up and talking to the men on the hill." For anti-poverty laws, civil rights, education, and medical research, Anna wrote letters, made phone calls, and went to Capitol Hill. "If you had enough information and conviction, you talked to the people in Congress who happened to be concerned with that particular matter. I was concerned with social legislation. I did a lot of that for President Roosevelt." For President Johnson, too: when a piece of legislation came up that Anna was interested in and Johnson favored, he told her "now you better see some of your friends in the Congress to see that they line up for it."[33]

President Johnson also consulted her on legislation. When he signed the Medicare bill into law he presented her with one of the pens. "I have quite a few pens from him given at the signing of a bill," Anna recalled. "I know you worked hard on this," Johnson would say, or "this was your idea," or "Remember, you gave me that idea." After working behind the scenes for decades, women, including Anna, were getting their due. "I would be very embarrassed," Anna confessed, "because there would be a congressman there who thought it was their idea."[34] Continuing their decades-long efforts on national healthcare, Anna and Mary Lasker convinced President Johnson to support cancer research—their work culminated in the National Cancer Act of 1971.

Just as she had helped Roosevelt hone his message with polling, Anna coached Lyndon Johnson on his public speaking. "What do you think of my talk?" he'd ask.

> "Be a little lower key, make people feel you're talking to
> them." I used to tell him about Roosevelt's fireside chats
> on radio. I would get in the taxi the next morning and the
> driver would say "Roosevelt said to me." They didn't feel it

was a speech to the country; it was a speech to an individual. I used to tell Lyndon "talk to one person. Think of just one person, and talk."[35]

On Sunday, March 7, 1965, civil rights leader Reverend Martin Luther King, Jr., and over five hundred supporters were attacked while marching from Selma to Montgomery to register Black Americans to vote. After the demonstrators crossed the crest of the bridge, one hundred feet above the Alabama River, they were set upon by police and state troopers, some mounted on horseback and all armed with billy clubs. Televised images showed men and women, many fallen to their knees, being beaten by helmeted troopers wearing gas masks as clouds of tear gas swirled. Americans saw Amelia Boynton, one of the organizers of the march, beaten unconscious and being dragged away from further attack, and learned that a white Unitarian minister from Boston named James J. Reeb, who had gone to Selma in solidarity with the marchers, had been brutally beaten to death by white vigilantes. The racial violence of Bloody Sunday made headlines around the world.

On Monday, March 15, 1965, President Lyndon Johnson denounced the bloodshed and galvanized voting rights supporters across the nation. Standing at the rostrum before a joint session of Congress, at 9:02 PM the President opened with the words: "I speak tonight for the dignity of man and the destiny of democracy." The President's address, broadcast nationwide, continued: "At times history and fate meet at a single time in a single place to shape a turning point in man's unending search for freedom. So it was at Lexington and Concord. So it was a century ago at Appomattox. So it was last week in Selma, Alabama." Vowing to take swift action, Johnson declared, "On Wednesday I will send to Congress a law designed to eliminate illegal barriers to the right to vote." Echoing Martin Luther King, and the anthem of the civil rights movement, President Johnson ended with "We Shall Overcome."

On the day he sent the voting rights bill to Congress, Johnson received a letter from Anna. "I listened to your speech with overwhelming pride," she began; "as I listened to you I had the feeling that all Americans were taller and could walk with their heads up and their eyes focused towards your great dream. People all over the world will understand the fundamental greatness and goodness of this country." To Anna, the speech was Lyndon Johnson's finest moment. "As a president," she told an interviewer, "he was superb domestically; he really got this country on the road to doing things that are making a vital difference. . . . No president ever used the power of the presidency more beneficially, or better, for the worthwhile things, than he did."[36]

At home, the hectoring between Anna and Paul on their intense work habits resulted in a mutual decision. Anna was in her mid-sixties and Paul was older by a decade, and it was time to slow down and enjoy life. In July 1965, the couple purchased a twelve-room country estate in the leafy village of Katonah, in New York's Westchester County. The colonnaded portico and the white brick exterior gave the stately two-story home the air of a miniature White House.

On summer weekends, the couple relaxed by the pool and dined on the patio rimmed with enormous terra-cotta urns and their shady plants while classical music from the nearby Caramoor Music and Art Center was carried by the soft summer breeze through the trees. While Anna remained a meticulous dresser when at work ("Clothes are important," she told a woman reporter from the *Boston Globe*, "and as you get older the more time you should take in their selection"), at Katonah Anna was more likely to wear a caftan or a brimmed sun hat to match her canvas sneakers, Capri pants, long-sleeved work shirt, and gardening gloves.[37]

With its library, billiards table, gardens, and riding paths, Katonah was a haven. Anna's grandson, Tommy, remembers it as "magical." "I was the only grandchild. She pampered me tremendously." Anna's sister, Clare, was also a regular visitor. The two sisters would challenge other pairs to games of bridge. When the sisters lapsed into Hungarian during the games, another winning hand usually followed.[38] When Anna and Mary Lasker went to Katonah, they had Anna's driver, Mr. Gibbs, take them to their favorite hamburger stand on Route 22, where they happily indulged.

While Anna was finally able to tend her long-dreamed-of rose garden, she remained at the ready as a sounding board and adviser to LBJ. Despite the host of social legislative accomplishments of the Great Society, the Vietnam War bedeviled Johnson. As in the Korean War, the question was how to determine the most equitable format for the thousands who would serve in combat. "I'm responsible for the lives of the men," he told Anna. Johnson, she said, was "very, very heartbroken about the casualties in Vietnam. He would go down to the operations room at all hours to get the news. He felt the responsibility for those men himself."[39]

In trying to decide who should face the danger, Johnson "struggled for a fair method to determine who should go to war when all do not go."[40] The President was particularly distressed that Black young men were fighting and dying in disproportionate numbers compared to the more affluent, whose sons avoided service through college deferments. In 1966, with the draft law set to expire in July of the following year, President Johnson initiated the National Advisory Commission on Selective Service. The commission, which sought a more equitable way to distribute the burdens of military service, was a diverse group that included a civil rights activist, the president of Yale, the publisher of *Ebony* and *Jet*, the publisher of the *Houston Post*, a theologian, a judge, and Anna Rosenberg Hoffman.*

The group suggested significant changes to the selective service system. To ensure random selection, they urged a lottery system; they suggested weakening the discretion of local draft boards to exempt or defer (the boards were mostly white); and they voted to end college deferments. In the end, two of the three measures were watered down. Draft boards would keep their discretion, but two hundred Blacks, Hispanics, and Native Americans would be named to the boards. Johnson kept the discretion to end graduate school deferments, but Congress continued the deferments for college enrollees. This did little to allay Johnson's concern that the draft was "coddling . . . the affluent middle and upper classes." LBJ took what action he could: in February 1968, he ended most graduate school deferments, with the exception of medical, dental, and divinity students. "The thickness of daddy's wallet" should not determine whether one suffered in the jungles of Vietnam.[41] There is no doubt that had the commission's three main recommendations been

---

* President Johnson's involvement even extended to approving the committee's staff members, insisting that the commission's attorney be Charles Rangel, a Black lawyer and a veteran of the Korean War, for which he was awarded the Bronze Star.

enacted, the toll of the Vietnam War would have been borne more evenly among America's social classes.

Making the torturous decision of who would face a tour of duty in Vietnam was one of the President's last acts. He had risen from the dusty schoolhouse in Cotulla, Texas, to the pinnacle of American power, but the war that divided the nation was too much. On Sunday, March 31, 1968, at 9:40 PM, Lyndon Baines Johnson peered into the camera from his desk in the Oval Office and told the American people, "I shall not seek, and I will not accept, the nomination of my party for another term as your President."

• • •

In the thirty years they had known each other, as Lyndon Johnson ascended from congressman, to senator, to Majority Leader, to Vice President, and finally to President, Anna Rosenberg championed his rise and supported Lady Bird. So Anna was especially saddened by LBJ's decision to not seek reelection. The relationship between Anna and Lyndon Johnson was summed up in his uncommonly emotional response to Anna's letter after the Selma March: "We have worked through many causes together, and there is no judgment I value more highly than yours. No letter you will ever write will ever mean more. Bless you for being a true friend across all these years."[42]

THE LAST NEW DEALER

In the years and decades after World War II, the men and women who guided the nation through Depression and war began to leave the scene. It is not an overstatement to say that the efforts of Roosevelt's New Dealers saved democracy by winning the war, and preserved capitalism by championing policies that elevated millions of Americans into the middle class.

The last reunion of the old New Dealers took place on June 25, 1975. That evening the men and women who had followed Franklin Roosevelt's buoyant leadership met at the City University of New York. Over a dinner of poached sole and roast leg of veal with mushrooms and wine sauce, the old gang reminisced. Averell Harriman recalled the dark days of 1933: "Ten cents an hour was the order of the day and people had nothing to eat." Another remembered the quarter-million marchers in the National Recovery Administration parade. Former Mayor of New York Robert F. Wagner, Jr., boasted, "My father was one of the architects of the New Deal." Arthur Schlesinger, Jr., made toast after toast, and Anna Rosenberg shared her story of wearing a black hat to the White House after Pearl Harbor. They were all immensely proud of being part of those dramatic days, and they missed their leader: Franklin Delano Roosevelt, whose smile had meant as much as a meal to struggling Americans. "In times of crisis," the president's eldest son said, America would find someone like FDR, "to put us back on the road to the future."

In the last decade of her life, Anna Rosenberg Hoffman worked to keep the ideals of the Roosevelt era alive. After Paul died in 1974, she was an executive for the Eleanor Roosevelt Institute, and she coordinated efforts to see FDR memorialized on the National Mall.* Widowhood did not sap Anna of her voice. When President Ronald Reagan called for program cuts and smaller government—in essence a reversal of the New Deal—Anna maintained in newspaper and TV interviews that it was the responsibility of government to take decisive action to combat the nation's problems. She reiterated her belief that groups of Americans owe each other a responsibility, and that Black Americans and American women were due a greater share of social equality. The doorways to opportunities "are still shut tight in most places" for women, she wrote in her essay "A New Look at Woman's Work." As for her own career, she modestly credited luck but also said, "I never tried to be anything but what I was. . . . You don't have to be like a man to succeed. If you know your stuff, you'll be alright."[1]

Despite her frailty following treatments for lung cancer, in early spring of 1983 Anna asked Mr. Gibbs to drive her to Katonah. It was a glorious late-spring day. After Mr. Gibbs had settled into his apartment, Anna called him to the kitchen: the rose garden beckoned. Mr. Gibbs linked his arm with hers as he helped her through the fragrant corridor of red, pink, and white flowers. He held her by the elbow as she paused to gingerly pinch a pale green stem or caress a newly bloomed petal. Step after step, they walked slowly and in silence, feeling the heat of the sun. The soft breeze that rustled the rosebushes carried with it a melody from the Spanish Courtyard at Caramoor; it was a piece by Brahms.

In the decade he worked for Anna, the rules of Cleotha Gibbs' employment were two: (1) don't be late, and (2) show up having read the front page of the *New York Times*. "Her Bible," according to Mr. Gibbs. Over the years, as they made the hour-long commute between the city and the country, as they drove the city's parkways and crossed its bridges, as they toured every town and hamlet in Westchester County or sat in traffic on Sixth Avenue, Mrs. Hoffman and Mr. Gibbs would discuss the top news stories, from the twists and turns of Watergate, to the Iran hostage crisis, to the attempted assassination

---

* While Anna did not live to see it, her last task for "the Boss" bore fruit: on September 16, 1991, work commenced on the Franklin Delano Roosevelt Memorial; it opened on May 2, 1997.

of President Reagan. Although Mr. Gibbs knew of her background in Washington and the presidents she worked with, Mrs. Hoffman didn't discuss the past. There was no talk of Lyndon Johnson, Dwight Eisenhower, or Harry Truman. The only president she talked about was Franklin Roosevelt.

The New Deal was in danger of being rolled back, she fretted.

The one hundredth anniversary of FDR's birth was coming up soon, she announced.

Sure, there was inefficiency, she would say, but without government programs like Social Security, Americans would be worse off. . . .

She told Cleo the Pearl Harbor hat story. She told him about being scolded by Eleanor for pouring martinis in the rubber plant. She told him how the taxi drivers in the midst of the Great Depression responded to FDR's fireside chats.

But one day, Anna revealed something quite different.

"He used to send me love letters."

"Mrs. Hoffman?" Cleo raised an eyebrow.

"President Roosevelt, *dollink*," she replied. "He used to send me love letters. Every day.

"An envelope would arrive at my hotel, straight from the White House."

She paused for a moment.

"Of course, I had to burn them."[2]

Mr. Gibbs took a peek in the rearview mirror. Anna was gazing out the rear passenger window.

They drove on.

—•••—

On May 9, 1983, in the heart of the city that had adopted her as a child of immigrants three-quarters of a century earlier, Anna died.

To prepare its obituary, the *New York Times* called Owen Blicksilver, a young public-relations professional who worked for Anna's firm and who acted as the family spokesperson. When I interviewed Mr. Blicksilver for this book, he described Mrs. Hoffman with great affection as a loyal, fair-minded, approachable, and hardworking boss. In his years with her he'd heard bits of Anna's past and had, of course, seen the photos of presidents in her office, but knew little of what she did in World War II or her time as Assistant Secretary of Defense.

"She liked me because I really didn't understand who she was."[3]

Anna's personal discretion was just one reason her remarkable life in service to her country faded from collective memory.

Anna Rosenberg *was* famous, at least during World War II and for a decade afterwards. From her first profile in the *New Yorker* in the late 1930s until the middle of the 1950s, she appeared in *Collier's*, *Fortune*, *Life*, *Look*, *Newsweek*, *Reader's Digest*, the *Saturday Evening Post*, *Time*, *U.S. News & World Report*, Germany's *Der Spiegel*, and *Paris Match*. For a decade and a half, Americans voted her at or near the top of countless lists of the nation's brainiest and most admired women (often finishing second to her friend Eleanor Roosevelt). Anna was second to none when it came to style, appearing on numerous best-dressed lists. "I wear the same suits as last year," she told *Time*, "only a little more shiny."[4] On television, she appeared on NBC's *Meet the Press* and CBS' *Person to Person*. She was a regular on mid-century radio. The *New York Times* first ran a story about her when she was a teenager in 1917, and Anna Rosenberg appeared in the pages of that paper for the next seven decades, until her obituary ran on May 10, 1983.

Besides the name Rosenberg, sexism and ethnic prejudice are certainly among the reasons Anna's story slipped through the cracks of history. She was a Jewish woman operating in spheres almost exclusively dominated (and later chronicled) by men. Rather than take credit for the ideas she proffered, Anna was content to remain in the background. Whether advising presidents, her private clients, or military leaders, Anna was the unseen hand. Hers was a soft power, exerted indirectly, which complicated efforts to measure her place in history.

In spite of her discretion, Anna made a captivating story line for the nation's media. Her striking appearance was often the focus of the articles. A *New Yorker* profile from 1938 paints her as a petite "coquettish" woman with "brown, bobbed hair and an attractive, pert face." Two decades later, in the pages of the *New York Times*, she was a "pint-sized hurricane" who fancied "hats, bangles, and a wide variety of French perfumes." The countless stories in between never failed to remark on the anomaly of so feminine a figure wielding so much influence in such male domains. Making her appearance the focal point obscured Anna's accomplishments. At the moment she commenced her pivotal role at the top of the Pentagon during the early days of the Cold War, the *New York Times* story was titled "Dynamo in Bracelets." Anna Rosenberg was a public-relations expert, but when it came to herself she did not court the press; the press courted Anna. "I want to be regarded as a public official. The fact that I am a woman plays no part." She didn't care to discuss her "favorite color" or recipes or other "foolish questions," but the media gave her a platform.[5] To the extent she responded to the attention, it was in the service of issues important to her or to credit someone she admired. It was never about her.

Anna's lack of formal education is yet another reason her star dimmed. In America then as now, where one went to school can confer power and prestige. Frances Perkins attended the University of Pennsylvania's Wharton School of Economics and Columbia University. Those Ivy League institutions promote Perkins as the woman who inspired the New Deal. Rather than the posh transatlantic accent taught in the era's boarding schools and *thee-ah-tah* classes, Anna spoke all her life with a slight Hungarian accent, tinged with a bit of the Bronx. For the woman who was a critical asset to Roosevelt during the war years, there is no college or university that can proudly claim her and maintain her memory. While she was not insecure, Anna's lack of credentials bothered her throughout her life and was one of the reasons she did not promote her story. "My consciousness of how little I know," she admitted in an address at Yeshiva University, "has caused me to spend my life in thrall to all of those who have mastered the learning of the arts and sciences."

Anna had other reasons to not seek greater fame. In 1954 she refused Eleanor Roosevelt's urging that she begin work with a biographer. She turned down major publishing houses seeking her memoir. She never wavered. "That's a book that will never be written," she countered Edward R. Murrow, who urged her to put her story on paper. Her very devotion to Franklin Roosevelt was at the heart of this refusal. Anna "learned the valuable lesson of never repeating an intimate White House conversation" and found the avalanche of so-called me-and-FDR memoirs distasteful.* "I'm never going to write a book, and thank God, I've stuck to that. Everyone who comes out of Washington writes a book."[6]

For Anna Rosenberg, the telephone was her device of choice, not the typewriter. Whether she was in the New York City subway solving a strike or in Korea visiting the troops, Anna wanted to be in the field rather than at a desk. Never good at spelling, her syntax sometimes scrambled, Anna didn't consider herself a writer. "I believe that writers ought to write books and not amateurs," she told Murrow. Though she was a public person, there was no diary and no daily appointment calendar (at least not in writing). "When this is all over," she stated flatly, "there'll be no historic documentation of our work. I issue no memos."[7]

She also wanted private things kept private. Jimmy Roosevelt, the president's eldest son, also planned a memoir. He was something of a playboy, hopping from job to job, crashing sports cars, and otherwise embarrassing his parents. Anna had no respect for his dissipating ways. Jimmy repeatedly asked Anna for her letters from his father, and she repeatedly refused. Rather than see her private correspondence with FDR in Jimmy's hands, Anna burned most of the letters. Whether it was matters of national security, delicious bits of Washington gossip, or something else, President Roosevelt trusted Anna to keep what they discussed in his second-floor study in confidence.

Though we do not have the private correspondence between Anna and FDR, there is a treasure trove of material. By closely examining her papers at Harvard's Schlesinger Library and cross-referencing those with others at the FDR Presidential Library and Museum; the Truman,

---

* By the time Eleanor recommended the biographer, nearly everyone who had worked closely with Roosevelt had published a memoir: Frances Perkins (1946), Jimmy Byrnes (1947), Ed Flynn (1947), Mike Reilly (1947), Henry Stimson (1947), Jim Farley (1948), Cordell Hull (1948), Henrietta Nesbitt (1948), Robert Sherwood (1948), Grace Tully (1949), William Leahy (1950), and Sam Rosenman (1952). Elliott Roosevelt had published a memoir of his father in 1946, and Eleanor Roosevelt herself came out with *This I Remember* in 1949. Henry Morgenthau and Harold Ickes told their "me-and-FDR" stories in serial articles for magazines. Even FDR's dog Fala cashed in: in 1942 Charles Scribner's Sons published *The True Story of Fala,* authored by Daisy Suckley, Roosevelt's younger cousin and companion, and her ghostwriter.

Eisenhower, and Johnson collections; dozens of libraries from Ann Arbor to Yale; and long-forgotten magazine articles and newspapers, a dramatic narrative history emerged. Hers is the story of what one extraordinarily driven citizen can do for democracy in war and peace. Her talent, hard work, and devotion to duty helped defeat the forces of fascism abroad and modernized the lives of millions here at home. We take for granted Social Security, women in the military, and cancer research. Yet forging government support for those things took years of effort. "The things that make life . . . more than bearable," Anna explained, "are the things that make a nation great."[8] Anna Rosenberg knew the war generation dreamed of returning to an America better than the one they'd left, and she was a fighter for that promise. She is also an example for us today. Anna never took democracy for granted—a lesson for our own time as we face foreign autocrats and home-grown demagogues. "I'm not a crusader or a reformer," Anna said, "but there are a lot of things happening you just cannot sit by watching idly. I decided to do something about it."[9]

In her paper on Anna Rosenberg's time at the Defense Department, the late scholar Anna Kasten Nelson lamented the fact that other women did not follow Rosenberg in top military posts in the 1950s and 1960s. The precedent she set as a woman at the Pentagon was almost "entirely forgotten," according to Nelson, and so Anna Rosenberg became a "pioneer with no followers."[10] It is true the Eisenhower-Kennedy years did not match those of FDR-Truman in terms of women in high government or military positions, but Anna Rosenberg's impact on national policies and their implementation continues to this day. Her talent, hard work, and devotion to duty improved the lives of millions of Americans. What was vitally important to her—expansion of government services, racial integration, the democratization of the armed forces, veterans' care, and medical research investment—has all been incorporated into our way of life.

In the middle of the Great Depression, Anna appeared before a gathering of nervous New Yorkers to explain how the Social Security program worked. Anne H. Hinckley, a young librarian at the talk, was so moved by Anna's opposition to selfishness and greed and by the new era she represented, she wrote a poem in her honor. "One small, pale crusader," she wrote, had given her hope. "Thank God, I caught the flame / I can be fine."

A half century later, another woman reflected on what Anna Rosenberg meant to her. In her June 1984 *New York Times* column, Ann P. Harris made a promise to the new generation of American women:

> We saw women playing an active role in government and politics, speaking up and being listened to on important issues of the time. Eleanor Roosevelt, Frances Perkins, Anna M. Rosenberg [were] our role models. . . . When the new generation of young women is looking for role models, they'll be there, just [like] Eleanor, Frances, and Anna.[11]

Acknowledgments

Much of this book was written during the worldwide COVID-19 pandemic, when safety protocols at libraries meant they were closed entirely or partially before reopening (and closing and reopening again). It was only due to the extraordinary efforts of archivists and library professionals that my research was allowed to progress on schedule. My sincere thanks to Sarah Hutcheon, Jennifer Fauxsmith, Diana Carey, and Laurie Ellis of Harvard University's Radcliffe Institute of Advanced Studies; Director Paul Sparrow and Patrick Fahy of the Franklin D. Roosevelt Presidential Library in Hyde Park, New York; Melissa Davis, Director of Library and Archives at the George C. Marshall Foundation in Lexington, Virginia; and the archivists at the Harry S. Truman Presidential Library, as well as those at the presidential libraries of Dwight D. Eisenhower, John F. Kennedy, and Lyndon B. Johnson. This book would not have been possible without the Boston Public Library Interlibrary Loan specialists, who consistently delivered hard-to-find material. My thanks to Nora Dolliver of the New York Public Library and to the staff of Columbia University's Oral History Project. I owe thanks also to Kira Thompson, Local History Librarian of the Poughkeepsie Public Library District; to Megan and Rick Prelinger, who operate a fine library in San Francisco; and to Christin Monaghan and Suzanne Harde of the Zaccheus Wright Memorial Library at Westford Academy in Westford, Massachusetts.

I am fortunate to work with an agent as patient and insightful as John Rudolph of Dystel, Goderich & Bourret LLC. Without him, I would not have been welcomed into the family at Kensington/Citadel. There, the project was in the good hands of editor in chief Michaela Hamilton, editor Liz May, copy editor Barbara Wild, production editor Sherry Wasserman, and the book design and publicity teams.

I thank those who gave their time for interviews. Owen Blicksilver

315

and Cleotha Gibbs both shared marvelous memories of what it was like to work with and to know Mrs. Rosenberg. Her grandson, Thomas P. Rosenberg, spoke movingly of the time he spent with her and made it possible to imagine Anna's beautiful home and gardens in Katonah. My thanks to Robert Kaprielian, Korean-era Army veteran and pillar of Watertown, Massachusetts. Through Bob, I was able to meet and to discuss my book with Andrew Rudalevige, Chair of the Department of Government and Legal Studies at Bowdoin College. I was also honored by the time given to me by Andrew Kersten, Dean of the College of Arts and Sciences at the University of Missouri–St. Louis, in discussing labor issues during World War II. Missy LeHand's biographer, Kathryn Smith, was invaluable.

My gratitude to those who read early chapters and drafts: Judy Fox, Mark Chesak, Don Hayes, Colleen O'Brien, Eric Lausch, Will Reeves, and especially Randy Baidas, whose support of my endeavors goes back very far indeed. I owe thanks to Michael Amundson of PBS' *Nova* for consulting on the details of filming for television, and filmmaker John MacGibbon, for his book trailer. Thanks to Steven Cohen, Senior Lecturer at Tufts University, and to my colleagues at Westford Academy, both in and out of the History Department, who provided encouragement throughout the project, particularly Stephen Scully, Adam Ingano, and Jack Holbrook. Further thanks are due to authors Nancy Werlin, Heather Dune Macadam, and most of all Stephen Puleo, whose enthusiastic feedback on my very first pitch was the spark that ignited Anna Rosenberg's return to the historical discussion.

I am obliged to the more than one thousand students I've had the pleasure of getting to know in my Modern American History course; engaging teenagers at 7:35 in the morning requires storytelling chops, so to the extent I have succeeded in bringing this remarkable woman back to life, it is because of them. In particular, I shall always be grateful to Breila O'Malley, whose interest in learning more about Anna Rosenberg led us to her papers at Schlesinger Library. Thanks also to the sisters MacKenzie (I hope one day to pick up a book by Lauren M.), Alexandra Ryan, Cristina Haraty, Julia Craffey, and Sophia Sloan, whose love of books was a great benefit to the one you are holding.

The encouragement of family during the writing of this book

nourished me. My heartfelt thanks to Gregory and Judy Gorham, who supported me in their time of personal loss; to Phil Hayes and to Nancy and Glen Traylor. No one's support meant more than that of my wife, Elizabeth, my first reader. Her keen eye and insight were invaluable. Over many, many dinner conversations, she helped me realize what this story could become.

This book is dedicated to her.

Notes

PROLOGUE: THE EAGLE'S NEST

1. See Walter Bedell Smith Reference for AR in FBI File, 1950.
2. S. J. Woolf, "Trouble-Shooter," *New York Times Magazine*, February 22, 1942.

1. ROMAN CANDLE

1. "Critical Time for Shirtwaist Strike," *New York Times*, December 15, 1909.
2. "150 Strike Waifs Find Homes Here," *New York Times*, February 11, 1912.
3. "The Waiters' Strike," *New York Times*, June 1, 1912.
4. "400,000 Cheer Suffrage March," *New York Times*, November 10, 1912.
5. Peter M. Judson, *The Hapsburg Empire: A New History* (Cambridge, MA: Belknap Press of Harvard University Press, 2016), 333–35.
6. *Person to Person* TV show, 1959.
7. *Person to Person* TV show, 1959.
8. Anna Rosenberg letter to Joseph Kover dated July 1, 1970.
9. Alvin H. Goldstein, "She Deals in Man Power," *St. Louis Post-Dispatch*, September 28, 1942.
10. Albert Lederer Naturalization Petition, National Archives and Records Administration.
11. "20,000 March in Suffrage Line," *New York Times*, October 28, 1917.
12. Josef Israels II, "Mrs. Fix-It," *Saturday Evening Post*, October 1943.
13. S. J. Woolf, "A Woman Sits in Judgment for NRA," *New York Times*, March 31, 1935.
14. *Person to Person* TV show, 1959.

2. THE TAMMANY INSTINCT

1. Josef Israels II, "Mrs. Fix-It," *Saturday Evening Post*, October 16, 1943.
2. Eleanor Roosevelt and Lorena A. Hickok, *Ladies of Courage* (New York: G. P. Putnam's Sons, 1954), 204.
3. See, e.g., Elisabeth Israels Perry, *Belle Moskowitz: Feminine Politics and the Exercise of Power in the Age of Alfred E. Smith* (Evanston, IL: Northeastern University Press, 2000).

4. Roosevelt and Hickok, *Ladies of Courage*, 205.

5. Josephine Van de Grift, "Women Promoters on Political Stage, Says Gov. Smith's Premier," *Buffalo Times*, August 13, 1923.

6. Meilan Solly, "What the First Women Voters Experienced When Registering for the 1920 Election," https://www.smithsonianmag.com/history/what-first-women-voters-experienced-when-registering-1920-election-180975435/, July 20, 2020.

7. See, e.g., James Aloysius Farley, *Behind the Ballots: The Personal History of a Politician* (New York: Harcourt, Brace and Company, 1938), 28.

8. See, e.g., William E. Leuchtenburg, *The Perils of Prosperity, 1914–1932* (Chicago: University of Chicago Press, 1993).

9. Karl Detzer, "Little Anna Goes to Washington," *Independent Woman*, January 1951.

10. Richard O. Boyer, "Middlewoman," *New Yorker*, April 23, 1938.

11. Boyer, "Middlewoman."

12. Boyer, "Middlewoman."

13. Israels, "Mrs. Fix-It."

14. *Jewish Telegraphic Agency*, November 21, 1934.

15. Israels, "Mrs. Fix-It."

16. Israels, "Mrs. Fix-It."

17. Detzer, "Little Anna."

18. Detzer, "Little Anna."

19. S. J. Woolf, "A Woman Sits in Judgment for NRA," *New York Times*, March 31, 1935.

20. Jacqueline McGlade, "Establishing Mediation as Enterprise: The Career of Anna Rosenberg," *Business and Economic History* 25, no. 1 (Fall 1996): 244, and Richard Norton Smith, *On His Own Terms: A Life of Nelson Rockefeller* (New York: Random House, 2014), 130–31.

3. THE BUSIEST WOMAN IN NEW YORK

1. Elisabeth Israels Perry, *After the Vote: Feminist Politics in La Guardia's New York* (Oxford: Oxford University Press, 2019), 210.

2. Josef Israels II, "Mrs. Fix-It," *Saturday Evening Post*, October 16, 1943.

3. "Miss Government," *Brooklyn Daily Eagle*, November 15, 1925.

4. James Aloysius Farley, *Behind the Ballots: The Personal History of a Politician* (New York: Harcourt, Brace and Company 1938), 42.

5. Farley, *Behind the Ballots*, 77.

6. Farley, *Behind the Ballots*, 42.

7. David Montgomery, "Thinking about American Workers in the 1920s," *International Labor and Working-Class History*, no. 32 (Fall 1987): 4–24.

8. Jacqueline McGlade, "Establishing Mediation as Enterprise: The Career of Anna Rosenberg," *Business and Economic History*, 25, no. 1 (Fall 1996): 245.

9. See, e.g., McGlade, "Mediation."

10. Anna Rosenberg Hoffman Papers, 1870–1983; Box 4: Rosenberg & Associates, Inc., annual reports, 1923–1970; 83-M162–84-M65, Schlesinger Library, Radcliffe Institute, Harvard University, Cambridge, MA (hereinafter ARH Papers, Radcliffe Institute).

11. Richard O. Boyer, "Middlewoman," *New Yorker*, April 23,1938.

12. "A Tribute to Anna Rosenberg Hoffman," ARH Papers, Radcliffe Institute.

13. McGlade, "Mediation," 245.

14. "Sentence for Anna," *Time*, March 6, 1944.

15. "Anna M. Rosenberg—She Sells Intuitions," *Fortune* 50, no. 5 (1954): 74.

16. Elizabeth A. Collins, "Red-Baiting Public Women: Gender, Loyalty, and Red Scare Politics" (unpublished doctoral dissertation), University of Illinois at Chicago, 2007.

17. "Sentence for Anna," *Time*, March 6, 1944.

18. S. J. Woolf, "A Woman Sits in Judgment for NRA," *New York Times*, March 31, 1935.

19. Adelaide Kerr, "Dynamic Anna Rosenberg Is a Top-Flight Labor Counselor," *Des Moines Register* (IA), November 19, 1950.

20. Woolf, "A Woman Sits in Judgment."

21. Boyer, "Middlewoman."

22. Cary Reich, *The Life of Nelson A. Rockefeller: Worlds to Conquer, 1908–1958* (New York: Doubleday, 1996), 246.

23. Reich, *The Life of Nelson A. Rockefeller*, 227.

24. Steve Holroyd with David Litterer, "The Year in American Soccer—1926," https://soccerhistoryusa.org/ASHA/year/1926.html.

25. Martha Neumark, "Lights of New York" column in *The Sentinel: The American Jewish Weekly* 95, no. 13 (September 27, 1934), and *Jewish Daily Bulletin*, June 3, 1926.

26. Victor Riesel, "America's Busiest Woman," *HYC*, October 14, 1942.

27. Anna Kasten Nelson, "Anna M. Rosenberg, an 'Honorary Man,'" *Journal of Military History* 68, no. 1 (January 2004): 133–61.

28. Richard Norton Smith, *On His Own Terms: A Life of Nelson A. Rockefeller* (New York: Random House, 2014), 129.

29. Leonard White "My Father and I," *New York Times*, June 1946.

30. Boyer, "Middlewoman."

4. THIS MAN ROOSEVELT

1. *New York Herald Tribune*, October 9, 1928.

2. See, e.g., Marion Dickerman and Kenneth S. Davis. *Invincible Summer: An Intimate Portrait of the Roosevelts, Based on the Recollections of Marion Dickerman* (New York: Atheneum, 1974), 16.

3. James Aloysius Farley, *Behind the Ballots: The Personal History of a Politician* (New York: Harcourt Brace, 1938), 66–67.

4. Farley, *Behind the Ballots*, 66–67, and Kenneth S. Davis, *FDR: The New York Years, 1928–1933* (New York: Random House, 1985), 9.

5. John Gunther, *Roosevelt in Retrospect* (New York: Harper & Brothers, 1950), 84–86.

6. Davis, *FDR: The New York Years*, 33.

7. Davis, *FDR: The New York Years*, 35.

8. Davis, *FDR: The New York Years*, 32.

9. John Thomas McGuire, "The Historical Presidency: In the Inner Circle: Anna Rosenberg and Franklin D. Roosevelt's Presidency, 1941–1945," *Presidential Studies Quarterly* 45, issue 2 (June 2015): 396–406.

10. Jacqueline McGlade, "Establishing Mediation as Enterprise: The Career of Anna Rosenberg," *Business and Economic History* 25, no. 1 (Fall 1996): 244.

11. McGuire, "Anna Rosenberg and Franklin D. Roosevelt's Presidency."

12. *New York World*, September 28, 1928.

13. Richard Breitman and Allan J. Lichtman, *FDR and the Jews* (Cambridge, MA: Harvard University Press, 2013), 34–35.

14. Eleanor Roosevelt, *This I Remember* (New York: Harper & Brothers, 1949), 47.

15. Dickerman and Davis, *Invincible Summer*, 26.

16. See, e.g., October 17, 1928, speech in Binghamton, New York.

17. Davis, *FDR: The New York Years*, 48–49.

18. Davis, *FDR: The New York Years*, 37.

19. McGlade, "Mediation," 244. See also "Dynamo in Bracelets: Anna Marie Rosenberg," *New York Times*, December 29, 1959 (as Governor, FDR "often consulted her"), and Lynn Hudson, "The Confident Confidante: Anna Rosenberg Hoffman," *50 Plus*, August 1981 (as Governor he "consulted her frequently on labor matters").

20. McGlade, "Mediation," 244.

21. McGlade, "Mediation," 244.

22. "People: Women at Work," *Time*, January 29, 1951.

23. Terry Golway, *Machine Made: Tammany Hall and the Creation of Modern American Politics* (New York: Liveright Publishing, 2014), 244–46.

24. See Anna Rosenberg oral history interview with Joseph Wall, Oral History Research Office, Columbia University, July 18, 1958.

25. Davis, *FDR: The New York Years*, 38.

26. Davis, *FDR: The New York Years*, 38.

27. Davis, *FDR: The New York Years*, 38.

28. Rosenberg, oral history interview with Wall, 1958.

29. Davis, *FDR: The New York Years*, 45.

30. Davis, *FDR: The New York Years*, 46.

31. Davis, *FDR: The New York Years*, 46, citing Perkins memoir.

5. ACTION IN ALBANY

1. Kathryn Smith, *The Gatekeeper: Missy LeHand, FDR, and the Untold Story of the Partnership That Defined a Presidency* (New York: Touchstone, 2016), 94.

2. Lynn Hudson, "The Confident Confidante: Anna Rosenberg Hoffman," *50 Plus*, August 1981, 56–59.

3. Richard Norton Smith, *On His Own Terms: A Life of Nelson Rockefeller* (New York: Random House, 2014), 130–31.

4. Smith, *On His Own Terms*, 130–31.

5. John T. Bethell, "Frank Roosevelt at Harvard," *Harvard Magazine*, November 1, 1996.

6. See, e.g, *New York Daily News*, July 12, 1930.

7. For the state of relations among Anna and Eleanor's friends at this time, see Anna Rosenberg, oral history interview with Thomas Soapes, FDRL, 1977, and the section on Anna in Eleanor Roosevelt's *Ladies of Courage*, 198–205.

8. Susan Ware, *Beyond Suffrage: Women in the New Deal* (Cambridge, MA: Harvard University Press, 1981), 130.

9. Rosenberg, oral history interview with Thomas Soapes; Anna Rosenberg interview with Diane Sawyer of *CBS Morning News* on centenary of FDR's birth, January 30, 1982.

10. Richard O. Boyer, "Middlewoman," *New Yorker*, April 23, 1938.

11. Jackson, Robert H. *That Man: An Insider's Portrait of Franklin D. Roosevelt* (New York: Oxford University Press, 2004), 7.

12. Kenneth S. Davis, *FDR: The New York Years, 1928–1933* (New York: Random House, 1938), 158–59.

13. Davis, *FDR: The New York Years*, 158–59.

14. Davis, *FDR: The New York Years*, 158–59.

15. Final Report of the Temporary Emergency Relief Administration, June 30, 1937.

16. Davis, *FDR: The New York Years*, titles to chapters 7 and 8.

17. FDR radio address from Albany, April 7, 1932.

6. A NEW DEAL

1. Jacqueline McGlade, "Establishing Mediation as Enterprise: The Career of Anna Rosenberg," *Business and Economic History* 25, no. 1 (Fall 1996): 245.

2. James Hagan died on March 4, 1929, in tony Palm Beach, Florida.

3. McGlade, "Mediation," 245.

4. McGlade, "Mediation," 245.

5. McGlade, "Mediation." 244.

6. *New York Evening Journal*, September 15, 1934; *Brooklyn Daily Eagle*, September 18, 1934; and *New York Times*, September 18, 1934.

7. *Brooklyn Daily Eagle*, September 18, 1934.

8. *Democrat and Chronicle* (Rochester, New York), December 8, 1934.

9. *New York Evening Journal*, November 21, 1934.

10. S. J. Woolf, "A Woman Sits in Judgment for NRA," *New York Times*, March 31, 1935.

11. Woolf, "A Woman Sits in Judgment."

12. Woolf, "A Woman Sits in Judgment."

13. Anna Rosenberg, interview with Diane Sawyer of *CBS Morning News* on centenary of FDR's birth, January 1982.

14. McGlade, "Mediation," 245.

15. ARH Papers, Radcliffe Institute.

16. "La Guardia Blasts Court's NRA Ruling," *Daily News* (New York), May 29, 1935.

17. Grace Robinson, "Steel and Dry Goods to Keep NRA Wages," *Daily News* (New York), June 4, 1935.

18. "Wage Cut Complaints Deluge NRA Office," *Brooklyn Times Union*, May 31, 1935.

19. "Slate Woman for WPA Czar," *Daily News* (New York), September 26, 1935.

20. Marion Dickerman and Kenneth S. Davis, *Invincible Summer: An Intimate Portrait of the Roosevelts, Based on the Recollections of Marion Dickerman* (New York: Atheneum, 1974), 134–35.

21. Rosenberg, interview with Diane Sawyer.

22. A comment made the rounds that Felix Frankfurter was a one-man recruiting office for the New Deal.

23. Frank Costigliola, "Broken Circle: The Isolation of Franklin D. Roosevelt in World War II," citing Thomas Corcoran, *Rendezvous with Democracy*, unpublished autobiography (written with Philip Kopper), chap. 10, p. 13, Box 587, Corcoran Papers, Library of Congress.

24. David McKean, *Tommy the Cork: Washington's Ultimate Insider from Roosevelt to Reagan* (Hanover, NH: Steerforth Press, 2004), 96.

25. Anna Rosenberg, oral history interview with Joe Frantz, 1973.

26. Robert Dallek, *Lone Star Rising: Lyndon Johnson and His Times, 1908–1960* (New York: Oxford University Press, 1991), 169.

27. Erich Leinsdorf, oral history interview, LBJL, and Robert A. Caro, *The Years of Lyndon Johnson*, vol. 1, *The Path to Power* (New York: Vintage, 1982), 481–82.

28. See FDR's daily calendar for that date, FDRL.

29.   Robert M. Hutchins and Mortimer J. Adler, eds., *The Great Ideas Today 1966* (Chicago: Encyclopedia Britannica, 1966), in which appears Anna Rosenberg's essay "A New Look at Woman's Work."

30.   Frances Perkins, *The Roosevelt I Knew* (New York: Viking Press, 1947), 294.

31.   Elliott Roosevelt and James Brough, *A Rendezvous with Destiny: The Roosevelts of the White House* (New York: G. P. Putnam's Sons, 1975), 131.

32.   "Ruling Elates Champions of N.Y. Wage Law," *Daily News* (New York), March 31, 1937.

33.   Dickerman and Davis, *Invincible Summer*, 103.

34.   Roosevelt and Brough, *Rendezvous*, 172.

35.   Richard O. Boyer, "Middlewoman," *New Yorker*, April 23, 1938.

36.   Charles Grutzner, "World Troubles Rest on 'Miss Government,'" *Brooklyn Daily Eagle*, November 15, 1936.

37.   Grutzner, "World Troubles Rest on 'Miss Government.'"

38.   Anna Rosenberg, "Social Security and the National Purpose," in *The Family in a World at War*, ed. Sidonie Matsner Gruenberg (New York: Harper & Brothers, 1942).

39.   Elsie Elfenbein. "An Interview with Anna M. Rosenberg," ARH Papers, Radcliffe Institute.

40.   Rosenberg, "Social Security and the National Purpose."

41.   Rosenberg, "Social Security and the National Purpose."

42.   Rosenberg, "Social Security and the National Purpose."

7. HYDE PARK

1.   Sidney Fine, *Sit-Down: The General Motors Strike of 1936–1937* (Ann Arbor: University of Michigan Press, 1969), 144.

2.   Kathleen McLaughlin, "Sees No Violence in the Strike Riots," *New York Times*, June 10, 1937.

3.   Howard, J. Woodford, *Mr. Justice Murphy: A Political Biography* (Princeton, NJ: Princeton University Press, 2015), 174.

4.   Marion Dickerman and Kenneth S. Davis. *Invincible Summer: An Intimate Portrait of the Roosevelts, Based on the Recollections of Marion Dickerman* (New York: Atheneum, 1974), 4.

5.   Frances Perkins oral history, 386.

6.   Frances Perkins oral history, 425.

7.   *Person to Person* TV show, 1959.

8.   Frances Perkins oral history, 430–35.

9.   Frances Perkins oral history, 430–35.

10.   Frances Perkins oral history, 430–35.

11.   Elliott Roosevelt and James Brough, *A Rendezvous with Destiny: The Roosevelts of the White House* (New York: G. P. Putnam's Sons, 1975), 27.

12. Roosevelt and Brough, *Rendezvous*, 201.

13. Emily Herring Wilson, *The Three Graces of Val-Kill: Eleanor Roosevelt, Marion Dickerman, Nancy Cook and the Place They Made Their Own* (Chapel Hill: University of North Carolina Press, 2017), 160.

14. Anna Rosenberg, oral history interview with Joe Frantz, 1973.

15. Lynn Hudson, "The Confident Confidante: Anna Rosenberg Hoffman," *50 Plus*, August 1981.

16. Frances Perkins oral history, 436–38.

17. Ted Morgan, *Reds: McCarthyism in Twentieth-Century America* (New York: Random House, 2020), 186.

8. THE INNER CIRCLE

1. Eleanor Roosevelt, *It's Up to the Women* (New York: Frederick A. Stokes, 1933), 189–204.

2. Elliott Roosevelt and James Brough, *A Rendezvous with Destiny: The Roosevelts of the White House* (New York: G. P. Putnam's Sons, 1975), 239.

3. Joseph E. Persico, *Edward R. Murrow: An American Original* (New York: McGraw-Hill, 1988), 155 and 165.

4. Alfred B. Rollins, Jr., ed., *Franklin D. Roosevelt and the Age of Action* (New York: Dell, 1960), 247–48.

5. FDR Personal Letters, 1928–1945, FDRL, 967–68.

6. Public speeches of FDR.

7. Persico, *Edward R. Murrow*, 165.

8. Frank Costigliola, "Broken Circle: The Isolation of Franklin D. Roosevelt in World War II," *Diplomatic History* 32, issue 5 (November 2008): 685.

9. Costigliola, "Broken Circle", citing Thomas Corcoran, "Rendezvous with Democracy," unpublished autobiography (written with Philip Kopper), chap. 10, pp. 15–19, Box 587, Corcoran Papers, Library of Congress.

10. Costigliola, "Broken Circle," citing Walter Trohan, *Political Animals* (Garden City, NY: Doubleday, 1975), 136–37.

11. Frank Costigliola, *Roosevelt's Lost Alliances: How Personal Politics Helped Start the Cold War* (Princeton, NJ: Princeton University Press, 2013), 72–73.

12. Roosevelt and Brough, *Rendezvous*, 170–71.

13. Costigliola, "Broken Circle," *Diplomatic History*, 678.

14. David McCullough, *Truman* (New York: Simon & Schuster, 1992), 298.

15. Anna Rosenberg, oral history interview with Joseph Lash, 1969.

16. *Chicago Tribune*, October 16, 1947.

17. See Walter Bedell Smith Reference for AR in FBI File, 1950.

18. Joseph Lelyveld, *His Final Battle: The Last Months of Franklin Roosevelt* (New York: Alfred A. Knopf, 2016), 161.

19. FDRL PPF 8101, AR to FDR, December 13, 1938.

20. FDRL PFF 8101.

21. Eleanor Roosevelt, *This I Remember* (New York: Harper & Brothers, 1949), 48.

22. Rosenberg, interview with Diane Sawyer of *CBS Morning News* on centenary of FDR's birth, January 1982.

23. Anna Kasten Nelson, "Anna M. Rosenberg, an 'Honorary Man,'" *Journal of Military History* 68, no. 1 (January 2004): 136.

24. Rosenberg, interview with Diane Sawyer.

25. Roosevelt and Brough, *Rendezvous*, 226.

26. Marion Dickerman and Kenneth S. Davis, *Invincible Summer: An Intimate Portrait of the Roosevelts, Based on the Recollections of Marion Dickerman* (New York: Atheneum, 1974), 129–30.

27. Rosenberg, interview with Diane Sawyer.

28. Frances Perkins oral history, 441.

29. John Gunther Papers, AR File, Hanna Holborn Gray Special Collections Research Center, University of Chicago Library.

30. Lynn Hudson, "The Confidant Confidante: Anna Rosenberg Hoffman," *50 Plus*, August 1981.

31. "Tribute to ARH," ARH Papers, Radcliffe Institute.

32. Statement of Senator William Benton, *Congressional Record*, December 21, 1950, *Congressional Record: Proceedings and Debates of the Congress* (Washington, D. C.: U.S. Government Printing Office, 1950).

33. William D. Hassett, *Off the Record with FDR, 1942–1945* (New Brunswick, NJ: Rutgers University Press, 1958), xv.

34. Anna Rosenberg, oral history interview with Joe Frantz, 1973.

35. John Gunther papers, AR file.

36. Rosenberg, oral history interview with Joseph Lash.

37. Frances Perkins oral history interview, 444.

38. Eleanor Roosevelt and Lorena A. Hickok, *Ladies of Courage* (New York: G. P. Putnam's Sons, 1954), 187.

39. Roosevelt and Hickok, *Ladies of Courage*, 204–5.

40. Nelson, "'Honorary Man,'" 135.

41. John Thomas McGuire, "Between Two Eras: Anna Rosenberg and the Maintaining of the Alternative View of Public Administration, 1941–1945," *Administration and Society* 51, no. 2 (February 1, 2019): 242.

42. Roosevelt and Hickok, *Ladies of Courage*, 204–5.

43. Roosevelt and Hickok, *Ladies of Courage*, 188, and David Brooks, "How the First Woman in the U.S. Cabinet Found Her Vocation," *The Atlantic*, April 15, 2015.

44. Roosevelt and Hickok, *Ladies of Courage*, 190, and Dickerman and Davis, *Invincible Summer*, 39.

45. Jerry Kluttz and Herbert Asbury, "The Woman Nobody Knows," *Collier's*, August 5, 1944.

46. Brooks, "How the First Woman in the U.S. Cabinet Found Her Vocation."

47. Hannah Steinkopf-Frank, "Frances Perkins: Architect of the New Deal." *JSTOR Daily*, July 8, 2020.

48. Brooks, "How the First Woman in the U.S. Cabinet Found Her Vocation."

49. "A Tribute to Anna Rosenberg Hoffman," ARH Papers, Radcliffe Institute.

50. Josef Israels II, "Mrs. Fix-It," *Saturday Evening Post*, October 16, 1943.

51. "A Reporter at Large: Strike," *New Yorker*, October 15, 1938.

52. *Current Biography*, 1943.

53. Roosevelt and Brough, *Rendezvous*, 26.

54. Roosevelt and Brough, *Rendezvous*, 26.

55. Hassett, *Off the Record with F.D.R.*, 140.

56. Roosevelt and Hickok, *Ladies of Courage*, 190–91.

57. Roosevelt and Hickok, *Ladies of Courage*, 190–91.

58. "A Tribute to Anna Rosenberg Hoffman," ARH papers, Radcliffe Institute.

59. Margaret L. Coit, *Mr. Baruch* (London: Victor Gollancz, 1958), 669.

60. Frances Perkins oral history, 439–441.

61. Frances Perkins oral history, 439.

62. Frances Perkins oral history, 439–445.

63. Rollins, *Franklin D. Roosevelt and the Age of Action*, 86–87, citing John Gunther.

64. Roosevelt and Brough, *Rendezvous*, 261.

65. Betty Houchin Winfield, *FDR and the News Media* (New York: Columbia University Press, 1994), 219.

66. FDR May 16, 1940, Message to Congress.

67. FDR fireside chat, May 26, 1940.

68. Rosenberg, interview with Diane Sawyer.

69. Roosevelt and Brough, *Rendezvous*, 277.

70. Cantril to AR, May 20, 1941, and Public Opinion Polls File, FDRL.

9. SIGN IT, MR. PRESIDENT!

1. John A. Salmond, *A Southern Rebel: The Life and Times of Aubrey Willis Williams, 1890–1965* (Chapel Hill: University of North Carolina Press, 1983), 174, and David M. Kennedy, *Freedom from Fear: The American*

People in Depression and War, 1929–1945 (New York: Oxford University Press, 1999), 767.

2. Doris Kearns Goodwin, *No Ordinary Time: Franklin & Eleanor Roosevelt: The Home Front in World War II* (New York: Simon & Schuster, 2013), 247.

3. Goodwin, *No Ordinary Time*, 246–47.

4. Goodwin, *No Ordinary Time*, 246–47.

5. Goodwin, *No Ordinary Time*, 247.

6. Salmond, *Southern Rebel*, 172.

7. Lerone Bennett, Jr., "The Day They Didn't March," *Ebony*, 1977.

8. Ted Morgan, *FDR: A Biography* (New York: Simon & Schuster, 1985), 593–95.

9. Goodwin, *No Ordinary Time*, 248–49.

10. Bennett, "The Day They Didn't March."

11. Bennett, "The Day They Didn't March."

12. Bennett, "The Day They Didn't March."

13. Kennedy, *Freedom from Fear*, 767.

14. James MacGregor Burns, *Roosevelt: The Soldier of Freedom* (New York: Harcourt, Brace, Jovanovich, 1970), 123.

15. See, e.g., Harvard Sitkoff, *A New Deal for Blacks: The Emergence of Civil Rights as a National Issue* (Oxford: Oxford University Press, 1978).

16. Salmond, *Southern Rebel*, 175.

17. Bennett, "The Day They Didn't March."

18. Doris Weatherford, *American Women during World War II: An Encyclopedia* (New York: Routledge, 2010), AR entry.

19. Bennett, "The Day They Didn't March."

20. Memo from FDR to Harry Hopkins, September 1942.

21. John Gunther, *Roosevelt in Retrospect* (New York: Harper & Brothers, 1950), 81 and 65.

22. "Profiles: Early Voice III—the March," *New Yorker*, December 16, 1972.

23. Salmond, *Southern Rebel*, 175.

24. "Profiles: Early Voice III."

25. Goodwin, *No Ordinary Time*, 251.

26. Kennedy, *Freedom from Fear*, 767.

27. Bennett, "The Day They Didn't March."

28. Goodwin, *No Ordinary Time*, 251.

29. "Profiles: Early Voice III" and AR oral history interview with Joseph Lash, 1969.

30. Rosenberg, oral history interview with Joseph Lash, 1969.

31. Bennett, "The Day They Didn't March."

32. Office in East Wing near that of James Byrnes comes from David McCullough interview with ARH. See David McCullough, *Truman* (New York: Simon & Schuster, 1992), 298.

33. Rosenberg, oral history interview with Joseph Lash.

34. Joseph Rauh added "national origin" in response to a comment made by Wayne Coy, a White House aide: "Hey, Joe, if we're doing this don't forget the Poles."

35. Andrew E. Kersten, *Labor's Home Front: The American Federation of Labor During World War II* (New York: New York University Press, 2009), 258.

36. Editorial *New York Amsterdam News*, July 5, 1941.

37. *California Eagle*, October 23, 1941.

38. Bennett, "The Day They Didn't March."

39. Kennedy, *Freedom from Fear*, 767.

40. "Profiles: Early Voice III" (author Jervis Anderson was the Jamaican-born biographer of A. Philip Randolph).

41. *Current Biography*, 1943.

42. S. J. Woolf, "Trouble-Shooter," *New York Times Magazine*, February 22, 1942.

43. *San Francisco Examiner*, March 26, 1972.

44. Woolf, "Trouble-Shooter."

45. Bennett, "The Day They Didn't March."

46. Woolf, "Trouble-Shooter."

47. Christopher C. DeSantis, ed., *The Collected Works of Langston Hughes: Fight for Freedom and Other Writings on Civil Rights* (Columbia: University of Missouri Press 2001).

48. Roger Daniels, *Franklin D. Roosevelt: The War Years, 1939–1945* (Champaign: University of Illinois Press, 2016), 333.

49. Anna Kasten Nelson, "Anna M. Rosenberg, an 'Honorary Man,'" *Journal of Military History* 68, no. 1 (January 2004): 138.

10. MRS. FIX-IT

1. Alvin H. Goldstein, "She Deals in Man Power," *St. Louis Post-Dispatch*, September 28, 1942.

2. Anna Rosenberg, oral history interview with Joseph Lash, 1969.

3. Joseph P. Lash, *Eleanor and Franklin* (New York: W. W. Norton, 1971), 640–41.

4. Lash, *Eleanor and Franklin*, 641.

5. Thomas Kessner, *Fiorello H. La Guardia and the Making of Modern New York* (New York: Penguin Books, 1991), 492–501.

6. Lash, *Eleanor and Franklin*, 641.

7. Rosenberg, oral history interview with Joseph Wall, 1958.

8. *Person to Person* TV show, 1959.

9. Rosenberg, oral history interview with Lash.

10. Anna Rosenberg oral history with Lash; see also Roger Daniels, *Franklin D. Roosevelt: The War Years, 1939–1945* (Champaign: University of Illinois Press, 2016), 262, and Doris Kearns Goodwin, *No Ordinary Time: Franklin & Eleanor: The Home Front in World War II* (New York: Simon & Schuster, 2013), 280–81.

11. Rosenberg, oral history interview with Lash.

12. Lash, *Eleanor and Franklin*, 640–41.

13. Jonathan Daniels, *White House Witness, 1942–1945* (Garden City, NY: Doubleday, 1975), 7.

14. Rosenberg, oral history interview with Lash.

15. Anna Rosenberg, oral history interview with Thomas Soapes, 1977, FDRL, and Goodwin, *No Ordinary Time*, 324.

16. Anna Rosenberg, interview with Diane Sawyer of *CBS Morning News* on centenary of FDR's birth, January 1982.

17. Goodwin, *No Ordinary Time*, 15.

18. Goodwin, *No Ordinary Time*, 629.

19. Rosenberg, oral history interview with Soapes, and Daniels, *FDR: The War Years*, 262.

20. Rosenberg, oral history interview with Soapes.

21. Elliott Roosevelt and James Brough, *A Rendezvous with Destiny: The Roosevelts of the White House* (New York: G. P. Putnam's Sons, 1975), 72, and Goodwin, *No Ordinary Time*, 629.

22. Rosenberg, oral history interview with Soapes.

23. AR–ER correspondence, 1935–45, FDRL.

24. AR–ER correspondence, 1935–45, FDRL.

25. Roosevelt and Brough, *Rendezvous*, 48.

26. Rosenberg, interview with Diane Sawyer and oral history interview with Joe Frantz, 1973.

27. Rosenberg, oral history interview with Lash.

28. Rosenberg, oral history interview with Soapes.

29. Chester L. Cooper, *In the Shadows of History: Fifty Years behind the Scenes of Cold War Diplomacy* (Amherst, NY: Prometheus Books, 2005), 35–40.

30. Roosevelt and Brough, *Rendezvous*, 299.

31. Roosevelt and Brough, *Rendezvous*, 301.

32. See, e.g., *New York Times*, November 26, 1941.

33. Roosevelt and Brough, *Rendezvous*, 302.

34. Roosevelt and Brough, *Rendezvous*, 304.

35. Joseph E. Persico, *Roosevelt's Secret War: FDR and World War II Espionage* (New York: Random House, 2001), 136.

36. Lee Dembart, "New Dealers and Historians Recall Glory at Reunion," *New York Times*, June 25, 1975.

37. John Thomas McGuire, "The Historical Presidency: In the Inner Circle: Anna Rosenberg and Franklin D. Roosevelt's Presidency, 1941–1945," *Presidential Studies Quarterly* 45, issue 2 (June 2015): 402.

38. Josef Israels II, "Mrs. Fix-It," *Saturday Evening Post*, October 16, 1943.

39. Letter to AR from P. Shafer, in AR–ER correspondence, 1935–45.

40. AR–ER correspondence, 1935–45; FDRL.

41. "Profiles: Best Neighbor-II," *New Yorker*, April 18, 1942.

42. McGuire, "Anna Rosenberg and Franklin D. Roosevelt's Presidency."

43. Daniels, *White House Witness*, 134 and 280.

44. S. J. Woolf, "Trouble-Shooter," *New York Times Magazine*, February 22, 1942.

45. "Seven-Job Woman," *Vogue*, 1942.

46. "Sense and Sensibility," *Junior League Magazine*, April 1942.

47. Woolf, "Trouble-Shooter," and Israels, "Mrs. Fix-It."

11. WAR IS AN "ALL-OUT" BUSINESS

1. *Look* magazine, April 1952.

2. Anna Rosenberg, "Women in National Defense," *Journal of Educational Sociology* 15, no. 5 (January 1942): 287–92.

3. Eleanor Roosevelt and Lorena A. Hickok, *Ladies of Courage* (New York: G. P. Putnam's Sons, 1954), 193.

4. "U.S. at War: Manpower, Unlimited," *Time*, April 27, 1942.

5. Jonathan Daniels, *White House Witness, 1942–1945* (Garden City, NY: Doubleday, 1975), 38.

6. Karl Detzer, "Little Anna Goes to Washington," *Independent Woman*, January 1951.

7. S. J. Woolf, "Trouble-Shooter," *New York Times Magazine*, February 22, 1942.

8. Dean J. Kotlowski, *Paul V. McNutt and the Age of FDR* (Bloomington: Indiana University Press, 2015), 347.

9. Josef Israels II, "Mrs. Fix-It," *Saturday Evening Post*, October 16, 1943.

10. Israels, "Mrs. Fix-It."

11. Roosevelt and Hickok, *Ladies of Courage*, 199.

12. Daniels, *White House Witness*, 38.

13. Elliott Roosevelt and James Brough, *A Rendezvous with Destiny: The Roosevelts of the White House* (New York: G. P. Putnam's Sons, 1975), 315–16.

14. Jerry Kluttz and Herbert Asbury, "The Woman Nobody Knows," *Collier's*, August 5, 1944.

15. Thomas E. Cronin and William R. Hochman, "Franklin D. Roosevelt and the American Presidency," *Presidential Studies Quarterly* 15, no. 2 (Spring, 1985): 281.

16. Kluttz and Asbury, "The Woman Nobody Knows."

17. John Thomas McGuire, "Between Two Eras: Anna Rosenberg and the Maintaining of the Alternative View of Public Administration, 1941–1945," *Administration and Society* 51, no. 2 (February 1, 2019): 241.

18. Israels, "Mrs. Fix-It."

19. Leonard Arthur Sawyer and William Harry Mitchell, *The Liberty Ships: I History of the "Emergency" Type Cargo Ships Constructed in the United States during World War II* (Centreville, MD: Cornell Maritime Press, 1970).

20. *Central Headlight* 3, no. 11, November 1942.

12. THE BUFFALO PLAN

1. Mark Goldman, *City on the Edge: Buffalo, New York, 1900–Present* (Amherst, NY: Prometheus Books, 2010), 134.

2. Hilton Hornaday, "Labor and Industry Deeply Impressed by Mrs. Rosenberg," *Buffalo Evening News*, October 24, 1942.

3. Buffalo Chamber of Commerce, "Daring Young Woman," October 24, 1942.

4. Anna Rosenberg, "War and American Women," *Free World* 7 (June 1944).

5. Rosenberg, "War and American Women."

6. Rosenberg, "War and American Women."

7. Anna Rosenberg, "Women on the Job," *New Masses*, December 8, 1942.

8. Bernard Simon, "Lady in the Pentagon," *National Jewish Monthly*, May 1951.

9. Rosenberg, "War and American Women."

10. "Manpower: The Buffalo Plan," *Time*, September 27, 1943.

11. Herman Miles Somers, *Presidential Agency: OWMR, The Office of War Mobilization and Reconversion* (Cambridge, MA: Harvard University Press, 1950).

12. Dean J. Kotlowski, *Paul V. McNutt and the Age of FDR* (Bloomington: Indiana University Press, 2015), 357.

13. Eleanor Roosevelt and Lorena A. Hickok, *Ladies of Courage* (New York: G. P. Putnam's Sons, 1954), 194.

14. Adelaide Kerr, "Anna Rosenberg Tackles Job of Recruiting Women to Meet Labor Shortage," *Louisville Courier-Journal*, September 29, 1942, and Theodore C. Alford, "Washington Correspondence," *Kansas City* [Missouri] *Times*, May 4, 1942.

15. Comer Van Woodward and David M. Kennedy, *Freedom from Fear: The American People in Depression and War, 1929–1945* (Oxford: Oxford University Press, 1999), 230–31.

16. Stephen Puleo, *Due to Enemy Action* (San Francisco: Untreed Reads, 2012), citing Bruce Catton.

17. "Manpower: The Buffalo Plan."

18. ARH Papers, Radcliffe Institute.

13. ASK NO QUESTIONS

1. Richard J. Overy, *Why the Allies Won* (London: W. W. Norton, 1995), 235.

2. Elliott Roosevelt and James Brough, *A Rendezvous with Destiny: The Roosevelts of the White House* (New York: G. P. Putnam's Sons, 1975), 245–46.

3. Stephen M. Younger, *The Bomb: A New History* (New York: HarperCollins, 2009), 16.

4. Richard Rhodes, *The Making of the Atomic Bomb* (New York: Simon & Schuster, 1986), 488.

5. "10,000 from New York Worked on Atom Bomb," *New York Times*, August 9, 1945.

6. Karl Detzer, "Little Anna Goes to Washington," *Independent Woman*, January 1951.

7. Rhodes, *The Making of the Atomic Bomb*, 488.

8. Sean F. Johnston, "Security and the Shaping of Identity for Nuclear Specialists," *History and Technology* 27 (2011): 2, 123–53.

9. Interview of G. Rossi Lomanitz by Shawn Mullet, August 18, 2002, Niels Bohr Library & Archives, American Institute of Physics, College Park, MD.

10. Letter from Sec. of War Stimson to FDR, October 29, 1943, PSF Files, R-General, FDRL.

11. Anna Rosenberg, oral history interview with Thomas Soapes, 1977, FDRL.

12. Rosenberg, oral history interview with Soapes, and "He Shared Our Lives," *New Republic* special edition, April 15, 1946.

13. Rosenberg, oral history interview with Soapes.

14. Rosenberg, oral history interview with Soapes, and "He Shared Our Lives."

15. Interview of G. Rossi Lomanitz by Shawn Mullet, August 18, 2002, Niels Bohr Library & Archives, American Institute of Physics, College Park, MD.

16. Rosenberg, "He Shared Our Lives."

17. Nelson Lichtenstein, *Labor's War at Home: The CIO in World War II* (New York: Cambridge University Press, 1982), 78.

18. Rosenberg, "He Shared Our Lives."

19. Overy, *Why the Allies Won*, 141.

20. Victor Davis Hanson, *The Second World War: How the First Global Conflict Was Fought and Won* (New York: Basic Books, 2017).

21. Elliott Roosevelt and James Brough, *A Rendezvous with Destiny: The Roosevelts of the White House* (New York: G. P. Putnam's Sons, 1975), 293.

22. Bernard Baruch to AR, Baruch Papers, Princeton University Library.

23. Lichtenstein, *Labor's War at Home*, 183.

24. AR to Bernard Baruch, April 27, 1949, Baruch Papers, Princeton University Library.

25. Roy Jenkins, *Churchill: A Biography* (New York: Farrar, Straus and Giroux, 2001), 712.

26. Roosevelt and Brough, *Rendezvous*, 306.

27. Anna Rosenberg, interview with Diane Sawyer of *CBS Morning News* on the centenary of FDR's birth, January 1982.

28. Roosevelt and Brough, *Rendezvous*, 294.

29. Roosevelt and Brough, *Rendezvous*, 293.

30. Rosenberg, interview with Diane Sawyer.

31. Geoffrey C. Ward, *Closest Companion: The Unknown Story of the Intimate Friendship between Franklin Roosevelt and Margaret Suckley* (New York: Simon & Schuster, 2012), 237.

32. William D. Hassett, *Off the Record with F.D.R., 1942–1945* (New Brunswick, NJ: Rutgers University Press, 1958), 201.

33. Hassett, *Off the Record with F.D.R.*, 201.

34. "Manpower: The Buffalo Plan," *Time*, September 27, 1943.

14. WARTIME MISSION

1. Anna Rosenberg, "War and American Women," *Free World* 7 (June 1944).

2. *Honolulu Advertiser*, June 6, 1944.

3. *Report by the Supreme Commander to the Combined Joint Chiefs of Staff on the Operations in Europe of the Allied Expeditionary Force, 6 June, 1944 to 5 May, 1945* (Washington, D.C.: Government Printing Office, 1945).

4. Samuel Rosenman, ed., *The Public Papers and Addresses of Franklin D. Roosevelt, 1944–45*, 152–53.

5. Ernie Pyle, *Brave Men* (New York: Henry Holt, 1944), 398.

6. Anna Rosenberg, interview with Diane Sawyer of *CBS Morning News* on the centenary of FDR's birth, January 1982.

7. Anna Rosenberg, "He Shared Our Lives," *New Republic* special edition *A First Appraisal by Those Who Knew Him*, April 15, 1946.

8. Rosenberg, "He Shared Our Lives."

9. President Franklin D. Roosevelt, August 15, 1936, in Chautauqua, NY; Speeches of President Franklin D. Roosevelt, 1933–1945; Collection FDR-PPF: Papers as President, President's Personal File, 1933–1945, FDRL; National Archives and Records Administration.

10. Rosenberg, "He Shared Our Lives."

11. Anna Kasten Nelson, "Anna M. Rosenberg, an 'Honorary Man,'" *Journal of Military History* 68, no. 1 (January 2004): 140.

12. Rosenberg, "He Shared Our Lives."

13. Letter dated Aug. 1, 1944, from Patterson to Eisenhower from AR documents from DDE Presidential Library.
14. Supreme Headquarters Allied Expeditionary Force.
15. Nelson, "'Honorary Man.'"
16. *New York Herald Tribune*, October 22, 1942.
17. "Nov 29, 1963, Quartermaster Supply European Theater of Operations in World War II, Office of the Chief of Military History Special Staff," U.S. Army Historical Manuscript File.
18. A title given by Irish playwright Samuel Beckett.
19. *New York Herald Tribune*, October 22, 1942.
20. Carlo D'Este, *Decision in Normandy* (Old Saybrook, CT: Konecky & Konecky, 1994), 431–32.
21. D'Este, *Decision in Normandy*, 431–32.
22. Dwight David Eisenhower, *Crusade in Europe* (Garden City, NY: Doubleday, 1948), 306.
23. *New York Herald Tribune*, October 22, 1942.
24. Gemma La Guardia Gluck, *Fiorello's Sister: Gemma La Guardia Gluck's Story* (Syracuse, NY: Syracuse University Press, 2007), 77.
25. Gluck, *Fiorello's Sister*, 113–14.
26. Pyle, *Brave Men*, 459.
27. David John Cawdell Irving, *The War between the Generals* (London: Allen Lane, 1981), 275.
28. Nelson, "'Honorary Man.'"
29. See photo of Anna Rosenberg with General Walton H. Walter, September 9, 1944 near Metz, France.
30. *New York Herald Tribune*, October 22, 1942.
31. Karl Detzer, "Little Anna Goes to Washington," *Independent Woman*, January 1951.
32. Doris Weatherford, *American Women during World War II: An Encyclopedia* (New York: Routledge, 2010), 398.
33. Eleanor Roosevelt and Lorena A. Hickok, *Ladies of Courage* (New York: G. P. Putnam's Sons, 1954), 200–201.
34. Roosevelt and Hickok, *Ladies of Courage*, 200–201.
35. *New York Herald Tribune*, October 22, 1944.
36. Pyle, *Brave Men*, 373.
37. *New York Herald Tribune*, October 22, 1944.
38. Kathleen Kinsolving, *Dogs of War: The Stories of FDR's Fala, Patton's Willie, and Ike's Telek* (Washington, D.C.: WND Books, 2012).
39. George Patton, *War as I Knew It* (New York: Houghton Mifflin Company, 1995), 126.
40. Carol Taylor, "Lady Dynamo," *New York World Telegram*, April 3, 1945.
41. *Yank* magazine, British edition, November 1944, 16.

42. Rosenberg, "He Shared Our Lives."

43. Rosenberg, "He Shared Our Lives."

44. Pyle, *Brave Men*, 397.

45. For Patton quote see obituary, "Patton's Career a Brilliant One," *New York Times*, December 22, 1945 and D'Este, *Decision in Normandy*, 468–69 for fuel issue.

46. "Busiest Woman in the U.S.," *Life*, January 21, 1952.

47. *New York Herald Tribune*, October 22, 1944.

15. WHEN JOHNNY COMES HOME

1. Glenn C. Altschuler and Stuart M. Blumin, *The G.I. Bill: A New Deal for Veterans* (New York: Oxford University Press, 2009), 58.

2. Altschuler and Blumin, *The G.I. Bill*, 72.

3. Michael J. Bennett, *When Dreams Came True: The G.I. Bill and the Making of Modern America* (London: Brassey's, 1996), 133.

4. Bennett, *When Dreams Came True*, 132.

5. Bennett, *When Dreams Came True*, 159.

6. Altschuler and Blumin, *The G.I. Bill*, 81.

7. Bennett, *When Dreams Came True*, 135, and Altschuler and Blumin, *The G.I. Bill*, 82.

8. Lynn Hudson, "The Confident Confidante: Anna Rosenberg Hoffman," *50 Plus*, August 1981.

9. "Texts of the Addresses at Times Hall on U.S. Programs for Demobilization and Rehabilitation," *New York Times* October 10, 1944.

10. Altschuler and Blumin, *The G.I. Bill*, 83.

11. Eleanor Roosevelt and Lorena A. Hickok, *Ladies of Courage* (New York: G. P. Putnam's Sons, 1954), 200–201, and Doris Weatherford, *American Women during World War II: An Encyclopedia* (New York: Routledge, 2010), 398.

12. Karl Detzer, "Little Anna Goes to Washington," *Independent Woman*, January 1951.

13. Carol Taylor, "Lady Dynamo," *New York World Telegram*, April 3, 1945.

14. "Texts of the Addresses at Times Hall," *New York Herald Tribune*, October 22, 1944, and *Yank* magazine, November 1944.

15. Detzer, "Little Anna."

16. John T. Bethell, "Frank Roosevelt at Harvard," *Harvard Magazine*, November 1, 1996.

17. Alex Ross, "Uncommon Man: The Strange Life of Henry Wallace, the New Deal Visionary," *New Yorker*, October 7, 2013.

18. James F. Byrnes, *All in One Lifetime* (New York: Harper & Brothers, 1958), 221.

19. "Cabinet Reshuffle Due," *New York Daily News*, November 9, 1944.

20. Roosevelt and Hickok, *Ladies of Courage*, 194–95.

21. Ted Morgan, *FDR: A Biography* (New York: Simon & Schuster, 1985), 675.

22. Senator William Benton oral history interview, Columbia University, 1968.

23. Josef Israels II, "Mrs. Fix-It," *Saturday Evening Post*, October 16, 1943.

24. Roosevelt and Hickok, *Ladies of Courage*, 203.

25. Senator Benton, oral History interview, and Cary Reich, *The Life of Nelson A. Rockefeller: Worlds to Conquer, 1908–1958* (New York: Doubleday, 1996), 400–401.

26. Jerry Kluttz and Herbert Asbury, "The Woman Nobody Knows," *Collier's*, August 5, 1944.

27. John Thomas McGuire, "Between Two Eras: Anna Rosenberg and Maintaining of the Alternative View of Public Administration, 1941–1945 " *Administration and Society* 51, no. 2 (February 1, 201): 241.

28. John Gunther Papers, Hanna Holborn Gray Special Collections Research Center, University of Chicago Library.

29. Antony Beevor, *Ardennes 1944: The Battle of the Bulge* (London: Viking, 2015), 158.

30. Beevor, *Ardennes 1944*, 162.

31. Beevor, *Ardennes 1944*, 235.

32. Anna Rosenberg, "He Shared Our Lives," *New Republic* special edition, April 15, 1946, and *New York Herald Tribune*, October 22, 1942.

33. "Texts of the Addresses at Times Hall."

16. CASUALTIES OF WAR

1. ER to AR, November 10, 1956, in ARH Papers, Radcliffe Institute.

2. Author interview with Robert Kaprielian, July 2021.

3. Eben A. Ayers, White House press officer, oral history interview, HSTL.

4. William D. Hassett, *Off the Record with FDR, 1942–1945* (New Brunswick, NJ: Rutgers University Press, 1958), 327.

5. Ronald Steel, *Walter Lippmann and the American Century* (Boston: Atlantic-Little, Brown, 1980), 300.

6. Elliott Roosevelt and James Brough, *A Rendezvous with Destiny: The Roosevelts of the White House* (New York: G. P. Putnam's Sons, 1975), 393.

7. John Gunther, *Roosevelt in Retrospect* (New York: Harper & Brothers, 1950), 365.

8. Gunther, *Roosevelt in Retrospect*, 365.

9. Anna Rosenberg, interview with Diane Sawyer, 1982.

10. Roosevelt and Brough, *Rendezvous*, 396. FDR's daughter, Anna Boettiger, accompanied the President on the Yalta trip.

11. Roosevelt and Brough, *Rendezvous*, 405.

12. Rosenberg, interview with Diane Sawyer, 1982.

13.   Roosevelt and Brough, *Rendezvous*, 396. Paregoric is used to treat diarrhea.

14.   John Gunther Papers, AR File, Hanna Holborn Gray Special Collections Research Center, University of Chicago Library.

15.   Roosevelt and Brough, *Rendezvous*, 405.

16.   Gunther Papers, AR File.

17.   Gunther, *Roosevelt in Retrospect*, 374.

18.   Anna Rosenberg, "He Shared Our Lives," *New Republic* special edition, "A First Appraisal by Those Who Knew Him," April 15, 1946.

19.   Rosenberg, "He Shared Our Lives."

20.   Rosenberg, "He Shared Our Lives."

21.   Joseph Lelyveld, *His Final Battle: The Last Months of Franklin Roosevelt* (New York: Alfred A. Knopf, 2016), 304, and John Toland, *The Last Days* (New York: Random House, 1966), 272 and notes on p. 611. Details of this conversation, says Toland, came directly from Anna Rosenberg.

22.   Rosenberg, "He Shared Our Lives."

23.   Jonathan Daniels, *White House Witness, 1942–1945* (Garden City, NY: Doubleday, 1975), 280, and John Gunther Papers, AR File, Hanna Holborn Gray Special Collections Research Center, University of Chicago Library.

24.   John Gunther, *Roosevelt in Retrospect* (New York: Harper & Brothers, 1950), 376.

25.   David McCullough, *Truman* (New York: Simon & Schuster, 1992), 342.

26.   McCullough, *Truman*, 345.

27.   AR Memorial Day remarks, 1954, in ARH Papers, Radcliffe Institute, and Gunther, *Roosevelt in Retrospect*, 376.

28.   AR Memorial Day remarks, 1954, in ARH Papers, Radcliffe Institute.

29.   John T. Bethell, "Frank Roosevelt at Harvard," *Harvard Magazine*, November 1, 1996.

30.   Lynn Hudson, "The Confident Confidante: Anna Rosenberg Hoffman," *50 Plus*, August 1981.

31.   Letter to ER from John von Arnold, April 13, 1945, ARH Papers, Radcliffe Institute.

32.   Bethell, "Frank Roosevelt at Harvard."

33.   HST to AR, April 1945, ARH Papers, Radcliffe Institute.

34.   Christopher C. Gorham, "The Handshake That Ended the War," werehistory.org, April 25, 2018.

35.   John Toland, *The Last 100 Days* (New York: Random House, 1966), 376–77.

36.   *Atrocities and Other Conditions in Concentration Camps in Germany*, 79th Congress, 1ˢᵗ Session, S. Doc. No. 47 1945).

37. Al Newman, "Nordhausen: A Hell Factory Worked by the Living Dead," *Newsweek*, April 23, 1945.

38. Robert H. Abzug, *Inside the Vicious Heart: Americans and the Liberation of Nazi Concentration Camps* (New York: Oxford University Press, 1985), 30–31.

39. Newman, "Nordhausen," cited by Abzug in *Inside the Vicious Heart*.

40. Press release from Joint Distribution Committee, "Mrs. Anna Rosenberg Urges Contributions for Survivors," March 1946, and Proceedings of the National Federation of Temple Sisterhoods, 32d, 33d, and 34th Annual Reports, the 16th Biennial Assembly, November 1, 1943, to October 31, 1946, held at Cincinnati, Ohio, March 3–6, 1946.

41. Lara Marlowe, "A Forgotten Surrender." *Irish Times*, May 7, 2005. According to Marlowe, the room where the surrender was signed has been untouched since May 1945.

42. Alex Grobman, *Rekindling the Flame: American Jewish Chaplains and the Survivors of European Jewry* (Detroit: Wayne State University Press, 1993), 71.

43. Ronit Yael Stahl, "God, War, and Politics: The American Military Chaplaincy and the Making of a Multireligious Nation" (dissertation submitted in partial fulfillment of the requirements for the degree of Doctor of Philosophy [History], University of Michigan, 2014).

44. Stahl, "God, War, and Politics," 217–18.

45. "The Harrison Report, United States Holocaust Memorial Museum, accessed May 9, 2022.

17. HOMECOMING

1. "Mrs. Anna Rosenberg Gets Freedom Medal," *New York Times*, October 30, 1945.

2. AR to Paul McNutt, August 19, 1945, National Archives.

3. "Seven-Job Woman," *Vogue*, 1942.

4. Mary Lasker interview, Oral History Research Office, Columbia University, 142–43.

5. President Harry S. Truman Special Message to the Congress on the Nation's Health Needs, April 22, 1949.

6. Mary Lasker oral history interview, Columbia University, 142–43.

7. John Gunther, *Taken at the Flood: The Story of Albert D. Lasker* (New York: Harper & Row, 1961), 253–54.

8. "Mrs. Rosenberg Spikes Cabinet Tale," *Morning News* (Wilmington, DE), November 17, 1944.

9. "State 'Complacent' to Mrs. Rosenberg," *New York Times*, February 8, 1944.

10. "Quiet little man" is from Josef Israels II, "Mrs. Fix-It," *Saturday Evening Post*, October 16, 1943; "shadowy figure" is from Anna Kasten Nelson, "Anna M. Rosenberg, an 'Honorary Man,'" *Journal of Military History* 68, no. 1 (January 2004).

11. William Moore, "Urges Troops to Be Trained for Civilian Life: Mrs. Rosenberg, FDR Aide, Discloses Plan," *Chicago Tribune*, October 5, 1944.

12. Alfred Schuetz, "The Homecomer," *American Journal of Sociology* 50, no. 5 (March 1945).

13. Arch Soutar, "Home Coming Isn't Easy," *Saturday Evening Post*, December 16, 1944.

14. Glenn C. Altschuler and Stuart M. Blumin, *The G.I. Bill: A New Deal for Veterans* (New York: Oxford University Press, 2009), 76.

15. Michael J. Bennett, *When Dreams Came True: The G.I. Bill and the Making of Modern America* (London: Brassey's, 1996), 240–41.

16. Altschuler and Blumin, *The G.I. Bill*, 86–87.

17. Bennett, *When Dreams Came True*, 242.

18. Bennett, *When Dreams Came True*, 251–52.

19. "NYC Veterans Care Center 250,000th Veteran Served Ceremony, Jan. 24, 1946," audio courtesy of the NYC Municipal Archives, WNYC Collection. WNYC archives id: 69329; Municipal archives id: LT438.

20. Anna Rosenberg, "The Girls Come Home," *Washington Post*, January 24, 1946.

21. Helen G. Brown (former lst Lt WAC), "Adjustment of Problems of College and Non-College WAC Veterans" (M.A. thesis, Stanford University, 1947).

22. Proceedings of the National Federation of Temple Sisterhoods, 32d, 33d, 34th Annual Reports, the 16th Biennial Assembly, held at Cincinnati, Ohio, March 3–6, 1946.

23. Press release from JDC, "Mrs. Anna Rosenberg Urges Contributions of Comfort Items for Jewish Survivors in S.O.S. Collection of Relief Supplies," March 1946.

24. "JDC Accomplishes Its 'Operation S.O.S,'" *New York Times*, April 13, 1949.

25. "JDC Ships 15 Tons Overseas Each Day," *New York Times*, May 3, 1946.

26. "JDC Accomplishes Its 'Operation S.O.S,'" *New York Times*, April 13, 1949.

27. Elizabeth Anne Wheal, Stephen Pope, and James Taylor, *Encyclopedia of the Second World War* (New York: P. Bedrick Books, 1989), 182.

28. Asa Philip Randolph to AR June 10, 1946, and July 3, 1946, and telegram from APR to AR September 6, 1946, Asa Philip Randolph Papers, Library of Congress.

29. "Murder in Georgia," *New York Times*, July 27, 1946.

30. Truman K. Gibson, Jr., and Steve Huntley, *Knocking Down Barriers: My Fight for Black America* (Evanston, IL: Northwestern University Press, 2021), 225.

31. Jon E. Taylor, *Freedom to Serve: Truman, Civil Rights, and Executive Order 9981* (New York: Routledge, 2012), 72–76.

32. Gibson, *Knocking Down Barriers*, 225.

33. David McCullough, *Truman* (New York: Simon & Schuster, 1992), 589.

34. "Medal for War Services Given to Mrs. Rosenberg," special for the *New York Times*, May 29, 1947.

35. "Medal for War Services Given to Mrs. Rosenberg."

36. Harry S Truman, "Special Message to the Congress on Civil Rights," February 2, 1948, Public Papers of the Presidents of the United States, January 1 to December 31, 1948 (Washington, D.C.: U.S. Government Printing Office, 1964), n. 20.

37. McCullough, *Truman*, 587–88.

38. *Glens Falls Times* (New York), February 13, 1965.

39. John Lewis Gaddis, *The Cold War: A New History* (New York: Penguin, 2005) 33–34.

40. Gaddis, *The Cold War*, 33–34.

41. McCullough, *Truman*, 551–52.

42. McCullough, *Truman*, 705–10.

43. Lynn Hudson, "The Confident Confidante: Anna Rosenberg Hoffman," *50 Plus*, August 1981.

18. GENERAL MARSHALL CALLS

1. Linda Witt, Judith Bellafaire, Britta Granrud, and Mary Jo Binker, *A Defense Weapon Known to Be of Value: Servicewomen of the Korean War Era* (Lebanon, NH: University Press of New England, 2005), 65.

2. Bevin Alexander, *Korea: The First War We Lost* (New York: Hippocrene Books, 2004), 42.

3. Carl W. Borklund, *Men of the Pentagon: From Forrestal to McNamara* (New York: Frederick A. Praeger, 1966), 96–99.

4. Melvyn P. Leffler. *A Preponderance of Power: National Security, the Truman Administration, and the Cold War* (1992; repr., Lexington, MA: Plunkett Lake Press, 2019), 363 et seq.

5. Alexander, *Korea*, 164–66.

6. Alexander, *Korea*, 164–66.

7. Borklund, *Men of the Pentagon*, 96.

8. Borklund, *Men of the Pentagon*, 103.

9. Borklund, *Men of the Pentagon*, 89–92.

10. Lynn Hudson, "The Confident Confidante: Anna Rosenberg Hoffman," *50 Plus*, August 1981.

11. Witt et al., *A Defense Weapon*, 67.

12. Hudson, "The Confident Confidante."

13. Anna Kasten Nelson, "Anna M. Rosenberg, an 'Honorary Man,'" *Journal of Military History* 68, no. 1 (January 2004): 139.

14. Stuart Svonkin, *Jews against Prejudice: American Jews and the Fight for Civil Liberties* (New York: Columbia University Press, 1997), 117.

15. Landon R. Y. Storrs, "Attacking the 'Femmocracy': Antifeminism in the Cold War Campaign against 'Communists in Government,'" *Feminist Studies*, 33, no. 1 (Spring 2007): 118–52.

16. Statement by Senator William Benton read into *Congressional Record*, December 21, 1950.

17. Booton Herndon, *Praised and Damned: The Story of Fulton Lewis, Jr.* (New York: Duell, Sloan and Pearce, 1954), 7.

18. "The Administration: Command Request," November 20, 1950.

19. Ed Lee Gossett Papers, Baylor University, Poage Library.

20. Eleanor Roosevelt and Lorena A. Hickok, *Ladies of Courage* (New York: G. P. Putnam's Sons, 1954), 199.

21. Arnold Forster and Benjamin Epstein, *The Trouble-Makers* (Garden City, NY: Doubleday, 1952), 26.

22. "Woman Is U.S. Assistant Secretary of Defense," *The Age* (Melbourne, Australia), March 3, 1951.

23. Borklund, *Men of the Pentagon*, 125.

19. ENEMIES WITHIN

1. "Rep. Rankin Loses Seat in Congress; Was Strongly Anti-Jewish," *Jewish Telegraphic Agency*, August 28, 1952; see also Ted Morgan, *Reds: McCarthyism in Twentieth Century America* (New York: Random House, 2003), 409 and 531.

2. Ed Lee Gossett Papers, Baylor University, Poage Library.

3. *Congressional Record*, December 12, 1950.

4. Charles R. Allen, Jr., and Arthur J. Dlugoff, "McCarthyism and Anti-Semitism: A Documented Exposé," *Jewish Life*, July 1953.

5. Arnold Forster and Benjamin Epstein, *The Trouble-Makers* (Garden City, NY: Doubleday, 1952), 27–28.

6. Forster and Epstein, *The Trouble-Makers*, 54.

7. Anna Rosenberg, oral history interview with Wall, 1958.

8. Anna Rosenberg, oral history interview with Joe Frantz, 1973.

9. Anna Rosenberg, oral history interview with Forrest C. Pogue, 1957.

10. Fred J. Cook, *The Nightmare Decade: The Life and Times of Senator Joe McCarthy* (New York: Random House, 1971), 336.

11. Eleanor Roosevelt and Lorena A. Hickok, *Ladies of Courage* (New York: G. P. Putnam's Sons, 1954), 202.

12. Rosenberg, oral history interview with Wall.

13. Rosenberg, oral history interview with Frantz.

14. Cook, *The Nightmare Decade*, 335–36.

15. Hearings before the Senate ASC, part 2, 97.

16. Hearings before the Senate ASC, part 2, 105.

17. Forster and Epstein, *The Trouble-Makers*, 49.

18. Roosevelt and Hickok, *Ladies of Courage*, 202.

19. "The Administration: Sea Gull's Nest," *Time*, December 25, 1950.

20. Cook, *The Nightmare Decade*, 336.

21. Morgan, *Reds*, 411–13.

22. David J. Krajicek, "Infamous Sen. Joseph McCarthy Brutally Attacked Reporter in 1950," *Daily News* (New York), June 4, 2017.

23. Morgan, *Reds*, 411–13.

24. Carl W. Borklund, *Men of the Pentagon: From Forrestal to McNamara* (New York: Frederick A. Praeger, 1966), 122.

25. Statement by Senator William Benton read into *Congressional Record*, December 21, 1950).

26. "Anna Rosenberg," *Charlotte News* (North Carolina) December 18, 1950.

27. Drew Pearson, "Figure in Anna Rosenberg Case Now GOP Radio-TV Director," syndicated column, *St. Joseph Gazette* (Missouri), October 16, 1956.

28. Matthew C. Ehrlich, *Radio Utopia: Postwar Audio Documentary in the Public Interest* (Champaign: University of Illinois Press, 2011), 149.

29. Robert Griffith,. *The Politics of Fear: Joseph R. McCarthy and the Senate* (Rochelle Park, NJ: Hayden, 1970), 163.

30. Marquis Childs, "McCarthyism's 'Grim' Meaning," *Wisconsin State Journal* (Madison), December 29, 1950.

31. Forster and Epstein, *The Trouble-Makers*, 60.

32. Maurine Neuberger, "Footnotes on Politics by a Lady Legislator," *New York Times*, May 17, 1951.

33. Roosevelt and Hickok, *Ladies of Courage*, 202–3.

20. A WOMAN IS RUNNING THE ARMY!

1. Frances Levison, "'Aunt Anna' Captures the Pentagon," *New York Times Sunday Magazine*, March 18, 1951.

2. Carl W. Borklund, *Men of the Pentagon: From Forrestal to McNamara* (New York: Frederick A. Praeger, 1966), 122.

3. Levison, "'Aunt Anna.'"

4. Levison, "'Aunt Anna.'"

5. Levison, "'Aunt Anna.'"

6. Lynn Hudson, "The Confident Confidante: Anna Rosenberg Hoffman," *50 Plus*, August 1981, and Leonard Mosley, *Marshall: Hero for Our Times* (New York: Hearst Books, 1982), 456.

7. Mosley, *Marshall*, 456f.

8. Lynn Hudson, "The Confident Confidante."

9. "Busiest Woman in the U.S.," *Life*, January 21, 1952.

10. Lynn Hudson, "The Confident Confidante."

11. ARH Papers, ASD File, Radcliffe Institute.

12. "Woman-Size Job," *Washington Post*, November 11, 1950.

13. Borklund, *Men of the Pentagon*, 121.

14. Lynn Hudson, "The Confident Confidante."

15. ARH Papers, ASD File, Radcliffe Institute.

16. Lynn Hudson, "The Confident Confidante."

17. *Person to Person* TV show, 1959.

18. Lynn Hudson, "The Confident Confidante."

19. "People: Women at Work," *Time*, January 29, 1951.

20. Levison, "'Aunt Anna.'"

21. Mitchell, Henry. "Homage to a 'Perfect American.'" *Washington Post*, November 20, 1980.

22. Levison, "'Aunt Anna.'"

23. Lynn Hudson, "The Confident Confidante."

24. Doris M. Condit, *History of the Office of the Secretary of Defense*, vol. 2, *The Test of War: 1950–1953* (Washington, DC: Historical Office, Office of the Secretary of Defense, 1988), 488–89.

25. Condit, *The Test of War*, 490.

26. Judith Bellafaire, "Called to Duty: Army Women during the Korean War Era," *Army History*, no. 52 (Spring 2001): 19–27, published by U.S. Army Center of Military History.

27. James F. Schnabel, *United States Army in the Korean War: Policy and Direction: The First Year* (Washington, D.C.: Center of Military History, U.S. Army, 1992), 43.

28. Anna Rosenberg, oral history interview with Joe Frantz, 1973.

29. "Man-Power—Her Task," *U.S. News & World Report*, November 24, 1951, AR on cover.

30. Levison, "'Aunt Anna.'"

31. "Design for Cooler Days," *Time*, August 6, 1951.

32. ARH Papers, DDE File, Radcliffe Institute.

33. Levison, "'Aunt Anna.'"

34. Levison, "'Aunt Anna,'" and "Armed Forces: Universal Service?" January 22, 1951.

35. Anna Rosenberg testimony to Congressional Committee on Reserve Policy, April 18, 1951.

36. "UMT–Not Now," *New Republic*, March 17, 1952, and Linda Witt, Judith Bellafaire, Britta Granrud, and Mary Jo Binker, *A Defense Weapon Known to Be of Value: Servicewomen of the Korean War Era* (Lebanon, NH: University Press of New England, 2005), 241.

37. Condit, *The Test of War*, 490.

38. Morris J. MacGregor, *Integration of the Armed Forces, 1940–1965* (Washington, D.C.: Center of Military History, United States Army, 2001), 394–96 and 618–19.

39. Bellafaire, "Called to Duty," 19–27.

40. Harry S. Truman, radio address, November 11, 1951, *Public Papers of Harry S. Truman* (Washington, D.C.: GPO, 1965), 627–28.

41. Microfilm reel M-142, 1 of 2, *Trade Winds*, May 26, 1951, ARH Papers, Radcliffe Institute. WAVES was established in WW II as the women's branch of the U.S. Navy.

42. Dwight D. Eisenhower, Pre-Presidential Papers, Anna M. Rosenberg File, Dwight D. Eisenhower Library.

43. "A Woman's New York," *Poughkeepsie New Yorker*, January 14, 1952.

44. Bettie J. Morden, *The Women's Army Corps, 1945–1978* (Washington, D.C.: Center of Military History, United States Army, 1990), 104.

45. Morden, *The Women's Army Corps*, 99.

46. Condit, *The Test of War*, 493.

47. Walter G. Hermes, *United States Army in the Korean War: Truce Tent and Fighting Front* (Washington, D.C.: Center of Military History, U.S. Army, 1992), 334, and David Coleman, "U.S. Military Personnel 1954–2014," History in Pieces, https://historyinpieces.com/research/us-military-personnel-1954-2014.

48. Levison, "'Aunt Anna.'"

49. Margaret L. Coit, *Mr. Baruch* (London: Victor Gollancz, 1958), 684.

50. Lynn Hudson, "The Confident Confidante."

51. "Woman-Size Job."

52. Patricia McCormack, "The Busiest Woman in U.S.," UPI, October 19, 1980.

53. *Person to Person* TV show, 1959.

54. Anna Kasten Nelson, "Anna Rosenberg, an 'Honorary Man,'" *Journal of Military History* 68, no. 1 (January 2004): 149.

55. "Busiest Woman in the U.S."

56. Michael D. Pearlman, *Truman and MacArthur: Policy, Politics, and the Hunger for Honor and Renown* (Bloomington: Indiana University Press, 2008), 170.

57. Pearlman, *Truman and MacArthur*, 170.

58. Walter Karp, "Truman vs. MacArthur," *American Heritage* 35, issue 3 (April/May 1984).

59. Bevin Alexander, *Korea: The First War We Lost* (New York: Hippocrene Books, 2004), 405–13.

60. Karp, "Truman vs. MacArthur."

61. Karp, "Truman vs. MacArthur."

62. Ed Lee Gossett Papers, Baylor University, Poage Library.

63. *American Jewish World* 40, no. 44, July 4, 1952.

64. *Jewish News* 3 no. 49, December 9, 1950.

65. MacGregor, *Integration of the Armed Forces*, 392.

66. MacGregor, *Integration of the Armed Forces*, 392.

67. MacGregor, *Integration of the Armed Forces*, 392.

68. Mosley, *Marshall*, 455–58.

69. "Side by Side," *Time*, August 6, 1951.

70. Michael Cullen Green, *Black Yanks in the Pacific* (Ithaca, NY: Cornell University Press, 2010), 17.

71. Correspondence between Earl McGrath and AR January 1953, HSTL.

72. Correspondence between Earl McGrath and AR January 1953.

73. Richard M. Dalfiume, *Desegregation of the U.S. Armed Forces: Fighting on Two Fronts, 1939–1953* (Columbia: University of Missouri Press, 1969), 220.

74. David W. Tarr, "The Desegregation of the Armed Forces," government report, January 7, 1960, Library of Congress, Legislative Reference Svc.

75. Tarr, "The Desegregation of the Armed Forces."

21. EVERY RIDGE A HEARTBREAK

1. Francis Levison, "'Aunt Anna' Captures the Pentagon," *New York Times Sunday Magazine*, March 18, 1951.

2. "Busiest Woman in the U.S." *Life*, January 21, 1952.

3. Doris M. Condit, *History of the Office of the Secretary of Defense*, vol. 2, *The Test of War: 1950–1953* (Washington, D.C.: Historical Office, Office of the Secretary of Defense, 1988), 490.

4. Levison, "'Aunt Anna.'"

5. Chester L. Cooper, *In the Shadows of History: Fifty Years behind the Scenes of Cold War Diplomacy* (Amherst, NY: Prometheus Books, 2005), 35–40.

6. Transcript of press conference with Assistant Secretary Rosenberg, 1952.

7. Anna Rosenberg and James C. Derieux, "This I Saw in Korea," *Collier's*, February 2, 1952.

8. Lynn Hudson, "The Confident Confidante: Anna Rosenberg Hoffman," *50 Plus*, August 1981.

9. Transcript of press conference with Assistant Secretary Rosenberg, 1952.

10. Condit, *The Test of War*, 497.

11. Rosenberg and Derieux, "This I Saw in Korea," *Collier's*, February 2, 1952.

12. Levison, "'Aunt Anna.'"

13. *York Dispatch* (Pennsylvania), "Pledge Reaffirmed," October 25, 1951.

14. Rosenberg and Derieux, "This I Saw in Korea."

15. "Armed Forces: Promise Kept," *Time*, February 4, 1952.

16. *Pacific Stars and Stripes*, August 15, 1952.

17. Rosenberg and Derieux, "This I Saw in Korea."

18. Ronit Yael Stahl, "God, War, and Politics: The American Military Chaplaincy and the Making of a Multireligious Nation (dissertation submitted in partial fulfillment of the requirements for the degree of Doctor of Philosophy [History], University of Michigan, 2014), 296.

19. *Person to Person* TV show, 1959.

20. Rosenberg and Derieux, "This I Saw in Korea."

21. Rosenberg and Derieux, "This I Saw in Korea."

22. Rosenberg and Derieux, "This I Saw in Korea."

23. SFC Doug Du Bois, "Angels of Mercy," *Stars and Stripes*, October 14, 1950.

24. Judith Bellafaire, "Called to Duty: Army Women during the Korean War Era," *Army History*, no. 52 (Spring 2001).

25. Tom A. Hamrick, "The Lucky 13: Army Nurses in Korea Bring Medical Aid and Morale to Frontlines," *Pacific Stars and Stripes*, clipping in Zane's notebook.

26. Linda Witt, Judith Bellafaire, Britta Granrud, and Mary Jo Binker, *A Defense Weapon Known to Be of Value: Servicewomen of the Korean War Era* (Lebanon, NH: University Press of New England, 2005).

27. Lisa Tendrich Frank, *An Encyclopedia of American Women at War: From the Home Front to the Battlefields* (Santa Barbara, CA: ABC-CLIO 2013), 344.

28. Witt et al., *A Defense Weapon*, 251.

29. Ann B. Zoss (later Roberts), teacher in the GED-Educational Center, as told to Kathleen Vander-Boom, March 26, 2000, Women in Military Service for America Memorial Foundation Archives.

30. *Pacific Stars and Stripes*, December 6, 1951.

31. *Pacific Stars and Stripes*, October 29, 1951.

32. Lynn Hudson, "The Confident Confidante."

33. *Pacific Stars and Stripes*, November 15, 1951.

34. James Daniel, "Pentagon Pin-Up," *Washington DC News*, May 30, 1952.

35. Rosenberg and Derieux, "This I Saw in Korea."

36. WNYC radio archives.

37. Rosenberg and Derieux, "This I Saw in Korea."

38. *Pacific Stars and Stripes*, February 19, 1954.

39. *Pacific Stars and Stripes*, November 12, 1952.

40. Lynn Hudson, "The Confident Confidante.

41. *Kansas City Times* (Missouri), "A Woman's Instinct Helping Run the Defense Department," June 22, 1951.

42. "Busiest Woman in the U.S."

43. Levinson, "'Aunt Anna.'"

44. ARH Papers, ASD File, Radcliffe Institute,.

45. David L. Roll, *George Marshall: Defender of the Republic* (New York: Caliber, 2019), 595 and 600.

46. CBS *Person to Person* transcript, June 12, 1959.

47. July 16, 1953, letter from Brigadier General Julius Klein to Walter Bedell Smith, in 1953, Personal Correspondence K, Dwight D. Eisenhower Library.

22. DRAFTING EISENHOWER

1. Telegram from DDE to Senator Styles Bridges in the midst of the hearings on Anna Rosenberg's nomination as Assistant Secretary of Defense, December 14, 1950, Dwight D. Eisenhower, Pre-Presidential Papers, Principal File, Dwight D. Eisenhower Library.

2. Cary Reich, *The Life of Nelson A. Rockefeller: Worlds to Conquer, 1908–1958* (New York: Doubleday, 1996), 141.

3. Alan R. Raucher, *Paul G. Hoffman: Architect of Foreign Aid* (Lexington: University Press of Kentucky, 1985), 156.

4. Raucher, *Hoffman*, 156.

5. Stephen Potter Amberg, "Liberal Democracy and Industrial Order: Autoworkers under the New Deal (dissertation submitted to M.I.T. February 1987), 199–200.

6. *Time*, September 6, 1943.

7. Raucher, *Hoffman*, 141–42.

8. Alden Whitman, "Paul G. Hoffman Is Dead at 83; Led Marshall Plan and U.N. Aid," *New York Times*, October 9, 1974.

9. Raucher, *Hoffman*, 109–10.

10. Raucher, *Hoffman*, 109.

11. Dwight D. Eisenhower Library, pre-presidential speeches.

12. ARH Papers, DDE File, Radcliffe Institute.

13. Dwight D. Eisenhower Library, pre-presidential speeches.

14. *NY Daily News*, "White House Boom in CIO for Gen. Ike," *Daily News* (New York), November 21, 1946.

15. George E. Sokolsky, "These Days," *York Dispatch* (Pennsylvania), March 18, 1958.

16. Blanche Wiesen Cook, *The Declassified Eisenhower: A Divided Legacy* (New York: Doubleday, 1981), chap. 3.

17. Dwight D. Eisenhower, Pre-Presidential Papers, Anna M. Rosenberg File (2), Dwight D. Eisenhower Library.

18. Eisenhower, Pre-Presidential Papers, Anna M. Rosenberg File (1), Dwight D. Eisenhower Library.

19. ARH Papers, DDE File, Radcliffe Institute.

20. Raucher, *Hoffman*, 92.

21. Raucher, *Hoffman*, 92.

22. Paul G. Hoffman, "How Ike Saved the Republican Party," *Collier's*, 1956. For glass remark, John Gunther, *Taken at the Flood: The Story of Albert D. Lasker* (New York: Harper & Row, 1961), 81.

23. ARH Papers, DDE File, Radcliffe Institute.

24. Doris Weatherford, *American Women during World War II: An Encyclopedia* (New York: Routledge, 2002), 399.

25. "Eleanor Roosevelt," *Time*, February 22, 2002 (reprint from earlier publication).

26. Eleanor Roosevelt, "My Day," June 1, 1954.

27. "4 Named to Board Authorized to Plan Memorial to FDR," *Boston Globe*, November 10, 1955.

28. A. H. Raskin, "The Outlook for Labor under Eisenhower: The Organized Need to Be Reorganized," *Commentary*, April 1953.

29. Steven Greenhouse, "When Republicans and Unions Got Along," *New York Times*, September 6, 2020.

30. Greenhouse, "When Republicans and Unions Got Along."

31. Stephen E. Ambrose, *Eisenhower: Soldier and President* (London: Simon & Schuster, 2014), 545.

32. Walter White, *New York Age*, April 11, 1953.

33. Stephen Ambrose, *Eisenhower*, vol. 2, *The President* (New York: Simon & Schuster, 1984), 625.

34. Paul Hoffman, *Peace Can Be Won* (Garden City, NY: Doubleday, 1951).

35. For Anna as a "virtual bachelor," see Frank Costigliola, "Broken Circle: The Isolation of Franklin D. Roosevelt in World War II," *Diplomatic History* 32, no. 5 (November 2008): 677–718.

36. Reich, *The Life of Nelson A. Rockefeller*, 246.

37. *Daily News* (New York), June 17, 1959.

38. "Centenary of George Catlett Marshall, *Congressional Record* (Senate), January 23, 1981.

39. *Person to Person* TV show, 1959.

40. Joseph Persico, *Edward R. Murrow: An American Original* (Lexington, MA: Plunkett Lake Press, 2020).

41. *Person to Person* TV show, 1959.

23. HAPPY BIRTHDAY, MR. PRESIDENT

1. Joseph P. Lash, *Eleanor: The Years Alone* (New York: W. W. Norton, 1972), 298–99.

2. Lash, *Eleanor: The Years Alone*, 298–299.

3. Patricia Zelman. *Women, Work, and National Policy: The Kennedy-Johnson Years* (Ann Arbor, MI: UMI Research Press, 1980), 37–38.

4. "Role of Women in U.S. Government Draws Speculation," *Indianapolis News*, October 23, 1964, and Cynthia Ellen Harrison, *On Account of Sex: The Politics of Women's Issues: 1945–1968* (Berkeley: University of California Press, 1988), 76.

5. Harrison, *On Account of Sex*, 74–75.

6. Harrison, *On Account of Sex*, 76.

7. "Le Beau Cat Man," *Time*, September 15, 1961.

8. Edna P. Gurewitsch, *Kindred Souls: The Devoted Friendship of Eleanor Roosevelt and Dr. David Gurewitsch* (2002; repr., New York: Open Road Media, 2014).

9. James Patterson, *The House of Kennedy* (New York: Little, Brown and Company, 2020). For LBJ's self-consciousness, Doris Kearns Goodwin, *Lyndon Johnson and the American Dream* (New York: Harper & Row, 1976), 166.

10. As set forth in an earlier note, the evidence strongly indicates Anna was born on July 19, 1899, which would make her sixty-three.

11. Alden Whitman, "Paul G. Hoffman Is Dead at 83; Led Marshall Plan and U.N. Aid," *New York Times*, October 9, 1974.

12. "Milestones," *Time*, July 27, 1962.

13. *Des Moines Register*, November 11, 1962.

14. *Louisville Courier-Journal*, October 12, 1963.

15. *Miami News*, October 31, 1963.

24. A TRUE FRIEND ACROSS ALL THESE YEARS

1. Anna Rosenberg, oral history interview with Joe Frantz, 1973.

2. Oral history of Lady Bird Johnson, LBJL.

3. Rosenberg, oral history interview with Joe Frantz, 1973.

4. Rosenberg, oral history interview with Joe Frantz, 1973.

5. Rosenberg, oral history interview with Joe Frantz, 1973.

6. Frances Levison, "'Aunt Anna' Captures the Pentagon," *New York Times Sunday Magazine*, March 18, 1951.

7. Oral history of Lady Bird Johnson, LBJL.

8. Patricia Zelman, *Women, Work, and National Policy: The Kennedy-Johnson Years* (Ann Arbor, MI: UMI Research Press, 1980), 39.

9. *Kansas City Times* (Missouri), January 17, 1964.

10. Zelman, *Women, Work, and National Policy*, 40.

11. Zelman, *Women, Work, and National Policy*, 45.

12. Zelman, *Women, Work, and National Policy*, 39.

13. Zelman, *Women, Work, and National Policy*, 46.

14. Credit quote is from Anna Rosenberg Hoffman, oral history interview with Michael L. Gillette, February 17, 1977, LBJL. For newspaper

articles, see, e.g., *Star Tribune* (Minneapolis, MN), May 3, 1964, and *The Gazette* (Montreal, QC), April 30, 1964.

15. Audio diary and annotated transcript, Lady Bird Johnson, 4/9/1964 (Thursday), Lady Bird Johnson's White House Diary Collection, LBJL.

16. Zelman, *Women, Work, and National Policy*, 50.

17. *Newsday* (Suffolk edition, Melville, NY), April 20, 1964.

18. Rosenberg, oral history interview with Joe Frantz, 1973.

19. Rosenberg, oral history interview with Joe Frantz, 1973. In the Frantz interview Anna says this lunch occurred when LBJ was Senate Majority Leader; in the Gillette interview she says it was in 1964.

20. Rosenberg, oral history interview with Joe Frantz, 1973.

21. Rosenberg, oral history interview with Joe Frantz, 1973.

22. Joshua Zeitz, *Building the Great Society: Inside Lyndon Johnson's White House* (New York: Viking, 2018), 72–74.

23. Rosenberg, oral history interview with Joe Frantz, 1973.

24. Zeitz, *Building the Great Society*, 72–74.

25. Lady Bird interview, LBJL.

26. *Newsday* (Suffolk edition, Melville, NY), April 20, 1964.

27. "Tribute to ARH," ARH Papers, Radcliffe Institute.

28. Rosenberg, oral history interview with Gillette, Feb. 17, 1977.

29. Rosenberg, oral history interview with Joe Frantz, 1973.

30. ARH Papers, Radcliffe Institute.

31. Rosenberg, oral history interview with Joe Frantz, 1973.

32. Zeitz, *Building the Great Society*, 315.

33. Rosenberg, oral history interview with Gillette, 1977.

34. Rosenberg, oral history interview with Gillette, 1977.

35. Rosenberg, oral history interview with Gillette, 1977.

36. Rosenberg, oral history interview with Joe Frantz, 1973.

37. "Anna Rosenberg, "High-Octane Femininity plus a Career," *Boston Globe*, July 16, 1966, and author interview with Thomas P. J. Rosenberg, April 2021.

38. Author interview with Thomas P. J. Rosenberg.

39. Rosenberg, oral history interview with Gillette, 1977.

40. Joseph A. Califano, *The Triumph and Tragedy of Lyndon Johnson: The White House Years* (New York: Simon & Schuster, 1991), 193.

41. Califano, *The Triumph and Tragedy of Lyndon Johnson*, 193–95.

42. ARH Papers, Radcliffe Institute.

EPILOGUE: THE LAST NEW DEALER

1. Lynn Hudson, "The Confident Confidante: Anna Rosenberg Hoffman," *50 Plus*, August 1981.

2. Author interview with Cleotha Gibbs, January 11, 2022.

3. Author interview with Owen Blicksilver.

4. "People," *Time*, April 2, 1951.

5. S. J. Woolf, "A Woman Sits in Judgment for NRA," *New York Times*, March 31, 1935.

6. Anna Rosenberg interview with Diane Sawyer of *CBS Morning News* on centenary of FDR's birth, January 1982.

7. Frances Levison, "'Aunt Anna' Captures the Pentagon," *New York Times*, March 18, 1951.

8. Anna Rosenberg, "Social Security and National Purpose," 1942.

9. Victor Riesel, "America's Busiest Woman," *HYC*, October 14, 1942.

10. Anna Kasten Nelson, "Anna M. Rosenberg, an 'Honorary Man,'" *Journal of Military History* 68, no. 1 (January 2004) and Doris Weatherford, *American Women during World War II: An Encyclopedia* (New York: Routledge, 2010), 398.

11. Ann P. Harris, "Hers" column, *New York Times*, June 14, 1984.

Selected Bibliography

NEWSPAPERS

Boston Globe

Brooklyn Daily Eagle

Brooklyn Times Union

Buffalo Evening News

Buffalo Times

California Eagle

Charlotte (NC) News

Chicago Defender

Chicago Tribune

Daily News (New York)

Democrat and Chronicle
    (Rochester, NY)

Des Moines (IA) Register

Glens Falls (NY) Times

Hackensack (NJ) Record

Honolulu Advertiser

Indianapolis News

Jewish Advocate

Jewish Daily Bulletin

Kansas City (MO) Times

Louisville Courier-Journal

Miami News

Montréal Gazette

Morning News (Wilmington, DE)

New York Age

New York Amsterdam News

New York Evening Tribune

New York Herald Tribune

New York Times

New York Tribune

New York World

New York World Telegram

P.M.

Poughkeepsie New Yorker

San Francisco Examiner

St. Joseph (MO) Gazette

St. Louis Post-Dispatch

Star Tribune (Minneapolis, MN)

Stars and Stripes

The Age (Melbourne, Australia)

Washington Post

Wisconsin State Journal

York (PA) Dispatch

MAGAZINES

The Atlantic	*Look*
Collier's	*New Republic*
Commentary	*New York Times Magazine*
Der Spiegel	*New Yorker*
Ebony	*Newsweek*
50 Plus	*Paris Match*
Fortune	*Reader's Digest*
Harper's Bazaar	*Saturday Evening Post*
Harvard Magazine	*Smithsonian Magazine*
Independent Woman	*Stars and Stripes*
Jewish Life	*Time*
Junior League Magazine	*U.S. News & World Report*
Life	*Vogue*

RADIO AND TELEVISION

CBS Morning News	*Person to Person*
Fresh Air	*Meet the Press*
Hear It Now	*WNYC archives*

ORAL HISTORIES, ARCHIVAL COLLECTIONS, AND AUTHOR INTERVIEWS

Eben A. Ayers, Harry S. Truman Presidential Library and Museum (HSTL)

Bernard Baruch, Princeton University Library

Owen Blicksilver

Cleotha Gibbs

Ed Lee Gossett, Baylor University, Poage Library

John Gunther, University of Chicago Library

Paul G. Hoffman, HSTL

Lady Bird Johnson, Lyndon Baines Johnson Library and Museum (LBJL)

Robert Kaprielian

Arthur Krim, LBJL

Mary Lasker, Columbia University Oral History Research Office

Erich Leinsdorf, LBJL

G. Rossi Lomanitz, Niels Bohr Library & Archives, American Institute of
Physics

Robert Patterson, Library of Congress

Frances Perkins, Columbia University Oral History Research Office

Asa Philip Randolph, Library of Congress

Eleanor Roosevelt, Franklin D. Roosevelt Presidential Library and Museum
(FDRL)

Anna Rosenberg, FDRL, LBJL, and Columbia University

Thomas P. Rosenberg

SELECTED WORKS

The following sources are the ones I found most useful in shaping this story.
For a full bibliography, visit www.christophercgorham.com.

Abzug, Robert H. *Inside the Vicious Heart: Americans and the Liberation of
Nazi Concentration Camps.* New York: Oxford University Press, 1985.

Altschuler, Glenn C., and Stuart M. Blumin. *The G.I. Bill: A New Deal for
Veterans.* New York: Oxford University Press, 2009.

"Anna Rosenberg—She Sells Intuitions." *Fortune* 50, no. 5 (1954).

Bennett, Jr., Lerone. "The Day They Didn't March." *Ebony*, February 1977.

Bennett, Michael J. *When Dreams Came True: The G.I. Bill and the Making of
Modern America.* Washington, D.C.: Brassey's, 1996.

Borklund, Carl W. *Men of the Pentagon: From Forrestal to McNamara.* New
York: Frederick A. Praeger, 1966.

Boyer, Richard O. "Middlewoman." *New Yorker*, April 23, 1938.

Coit, Margaret L. *Mr. Baruch.* London: Victor Gollancz, 1958.

Collins, Elizabeth A. "Red-baiting American Women: Gender, Loyalty,
and Red Scare Politics" (unpublished doctoral dissertation). History
Department, University of Illinois, Chicago, 2007.

Condit, Doris M. *History of the Office of the Secretary of Defense*, vol. 2, *The Test of War: 1950–1953*. Washington, D.C. Historical Office, Office of the Secretary of Defense, 1988.

Costigliola, Frank. "Broken Circle: The Isolation of Franklin D. Roosevelt in World War II." *Diplomatic History* 32, issue 5 (November 2008).

Dalfiume, Richard M. *Desegregation of the U.S. Armed Forces: Fighting on Two Fronts, 1939–1953*. Columbia: University of Missouri Press, 1969.

Davis, Kenneth S. *FDR: The New York Years 1928–1933*. New York: Random House, 1985.

Detzer, Karl. "Little Anna Goes to Washington." *Independent Woman*, January 1951.

"Dynamo in Bracelets; Anna Marie Rosenberg." *New York Times*, December 29 1959.

Forster, Arnold, and Benjamin R. Epstein. *The Trouble-Makers: The New Anti-Defamation League Report on Intolerance in the United States*. Garden City, NY: Doubleday, 1952.

Goodwin, Doris Kearns. *No Ordinary Time: Franklin & Eleanor Roosevelt: The Home Front in World War II*. New York: Simon & Schuster, 2013.

Gunther, John. *Roosevelt in Retrospect*. New York: Harper & Brothers, 1950.

———. *Taken at the Flood: The Story of Albert D. Lasker*. New York City, Harper & Row, 1961.

Harrison, Cynthia Ellen. *On Account of Sex: The Politics of Women's Issues, 1945–1968*. Berkeley: University of California Press, 1988.

Hassett, William D. *Off the Record with FDR, 1942–1945*. New Brunswick, NJ: Rutgers University Press, 1958.

Heidenheimer, Arnold J. "Case History of a Smear." *New Republic*, December 25, 1950.

Hudson, Lynn. "The Confident Confidante: Anna Rosenberg Hoffman." *50 Plus*, August 1981.

Israels, Josef, II. "Mrs. Fix It." *Saturday Evening Post*, October 16, 1943.

Lang, Daniel, and Geoffrey T. Hellman, "Outgoing Directrix." *New Yorker*, September 7, 1945.

Lash, Joseph P. *Eleanor and Franklin*. New York: W. W. Norton, 1971.

———. *Eleanor: The Years Alone*. New York: W. W. Norton, 1972.

MacGregor, Morris J. *Integration of the Armed Forces*. Washington, D.C.: Center of Military History, United States Army, 2001.

McCullough, David. *Truman*. New York: Simon & Schuster, 1992.

McGlade, Jacqueline. "Establishing Mediation as Enterprise: The Career of Anna Rosenberg." *Business and Economic History* 25, no. 1 (Fall 1996).

McGuire, John Thomas. "The Historical Presidency: In the Inner Circle: Anna Rosenberg and Franklin D. Roosevelt's Presidency, 1941–1945." *Presidential Studies Quarterly* 45, issue 2 (June 2015).

———."Between Two Eras: Anna Rosenberg and the Maintaining of the Alternative View of Public Administration, 1941–1945." *Administration and Society* 51, no. 2 (February 1, 2019).

Mosley, Leonard. *Marshall: Hero for Our Times*. New York: Hearst Books, 1982.

Nelson, Anna Kasten. "Anna M. Rosenberg, an 'Honorary Man.'" *Journal of Military History* 68, no. 1 (January 2004).

———."Caught in the Web of McCarthyism: Anna M. Rosenberg and the Senate Armed Services Committee." *Congress and the Presidency* 30, no. 2 (March 2010).

Nomination of Anna M. Rosenberg to be Assistant Secretary of Defense: Hearing before the Committee on Armed Services, United States Senate, Eighty-First Congress, Second Session. Washington, D.C.: U.S. Government Printing Office, 1950.

Perry, Elisabeth Israels. *After the Vote: Feminist Politics in La Guardia's New York*. New York: Oxford University Press, 2021.

Raucher, Alan R. *Paul G. Hoffman: Architect of Foreign Aid*. Lexington: University Press of Kentucky, 1985.

Reich, Cary. *The Life of Nelson A. Rockefeller: Worlds to Conquer, 1908–1958*. New York: Doubleday, 1996.

Roosevelt, Eleanor, and Lorena A. Hickok. *Ladies of Courage*. New York: G. P. Putnam's Sons, 1954.

Roosevelt, Elliott, and James Brough. *A Rendezvous with Destiny: The Roosevelts of the White House*. New York: G. P. Putnam's Sons, 1975.

Rosenberg, Anna M. "He Shared Our Lives." *New Republic* special edition, April 15, 1946.

———. "A New Look at Woman's Work." In *The Great Ideas Today 1966*. New York: Frederick A. Praeger, 1966.

———."Social Security and the National Purpose." In *The Family in a World at War*, edited by Sidonie Matsner Gruenberg. New York: Harper & Brothers, 1942.

———. "War and American Women." *Free World* 7 (June 1944).

———. "Women in National Defense." *Journal of Educational Sociology* 15, no. 5 (1942).

———."Women on the Job." *New Masses*, December 8, 1942.

Rosenberg, Anna M., and James C. Derieux. "This I Saw in Korea." *Collier's*, February 1952.

Rosenman, Samuel, ed. *The Public Papers and Addresses of Franklin D. Roosevelt, 1944–45*. New York: Random House, 1950.

Tarr, David W. "The Desegregation of the Armed Forces," government report, January 7, 1960. Library of Congress, Legislative Reference Svc.

Woolf, S. J. "Trouble-Shooter." *New York Times Magazine*, February 22, 1942.

———. "A Woman Sits in Judgment for NRA." *New York Times*, March 31, 1935.

Zelman, Patricia G. *Women, Work and National Policy: The Kennedy-Johnson Years*. Ann Arbor, MI: UMI Research Press, 1982.

Index

Adams, John, 68

African Americans. *See* Black Americans

Air Force One, 179, 291–92

Alaska Air Command, 257

All in One Lifetime (Byrnes), 172–73

Alsop, Joseph and Stewart, 217*n*, 235

Altschuler, Glenn C., 170

Amalgamated Clothing Workers of
America, 27

Ambrose, Stephen E., 277

America First movement, 75–76, 94

American Arbitration Association, 62

American Jewish Committee, 212

American Revolution, 44, 119, 120

Amsterdam Democratic Club, 18, 21, 25

Anti-Defamation League, 212, 235

anti-Semitism, 21, 39, 69–70, 75–76,
250–51
Anna's hearings, 212–13, 215–18,
224–26, 234

Arlington National Cemetery, 280, 281

Arliss, George, 54

Armed Forces Qualification Test, 245

Armstrong, George W., 251

Assistant Secretary of Defense, 215–68,
294
anti-Semitism during hearings,
215–18, 221, 224–26, 234
Black Americans and, 243–45,
251–55
chain of command, 241–42
confirmation, 233–35
confirmation hearing, 218–22, 224
loyalty hearing, 225, 226–33
Marshall's offer, 208–9, 215–17,
225–26

Marshall's paternal protectiveness,
238–40
recruitment of women, 245–47
resignation, 267–68
staffing, 237–38
streamlining personnel management,
242–45
wartime visits, 257–65, 265–66

atomic bomb
Manhattan Project, 142–48, 191
Soviet testing of, 206–7, 212

atomic bombing of Hiroshima and
Nagasaki, 191

attack on Pearl Harbor, 113–15, 119

Austro-Hungarian Empire, 1, 9, 12, 13,
14, 19, 51–52

Avery, Sewell, 125

Bacharach, Burt, 286

Bacskai, Marie, 12, 30, 124

Baer, Max, 54

Baerwald, Paul, 198

Bank of United States, 45

Baruch, Bernard, 3, 174, 269, 271, 280,
282
Anna as Assistant Secretary and,
214, 233, 238, 239, 248
during World War II, 79, 107,
150–55
Buffalo Plan, 133, 137, 138

Bataan Death March, 122

Battle of Bloody Ridge, 256

Battle of Châlons, 166–67

Battle of Dunkirk, 76, 88

Battle of El Alamein, 127

Battle of France, 76–77, 161–65, 166–68

Battle of Iwo Jima, 181

Battle of Leipzig, 183

Battle of Metz, 167–68, 168*n*

Battle of Midway, 127

Battle of Pork Chop Hill, 256

Battle of Pusan Perimeter, 209–10

Battle of Reims, 166

Battle of the Bulge, 175–76

Battle of the Falaise, 162–63

Battle of Trenton, 120

Battle of Triangle Ridge, 256

Battle of Yechon, 253

Battlle of Saint-Lô, 161–62

Beatty, Warren, 226*n*

Beaty, John, 251

Bellafaire, Judith, 245

Benevolence, USS, 262

Bennett, Lerone, Jr., 96, 104

Benny, Jack, 288

Benton, William, 82–83, 173–74, 215,
    271, 280, 289
        Anna as Assistant Secretary, 215,
            233, 234, 252, 268
        loans to Anna, 174, 191–92

Berlin Airlift, 204

Biltmore Hotel, 34–35, 36, 42, 61

Black Americans, 4, 21, 164, 257
        desegregation of the military,
            243–45, 251–55, 268, 277
        Truman's Executive Order
            9981, 203, 253–54
        Johnson and civil rights, 297–98,
            302–5
        labor issues during World War II,
            93–106, 125–26, 129–30
        FDR's Executive Order 8802,
            102–3, 125–26, 136,
            199–200
        women in the workforce,
            135–36
        returning soldiers, 191, 199–203

Blicksilver, Owen, 308–9

Bloch, Ernest, 54

Block, Adrian, 54

Bohr, Niels, 142

Borklund, Carl, 214

Boyer, Richard O., 61–62

Boynton, Amelia, 302

Bradley, Omar, 2, 160, 161–62, 184,
    210, 217

Bridges, Styles, 218, 220

Brienza, Angela, 259

British Board of Labour, 69

Brodsky, Frank, 110

Brooklyn Dodgers, 201

Brown v. Board of Education, 255

Brunauer, Esther, 214, 225

Buffalo Plan, 131–41

Burgoyne, Johnny, 44

Bush, Vannevar, 193

Byrd, Harry, 234

Byrnes, James F., 97, 113, 137–38, 139,
    172–73, 233, 311*n*

Cain, Harry, 218, 233–34

Camp Gerard, 47

Campobello Island, 37, 98

Cantril, Hadley, 89–90, 92

Carpenter, Charles, 260

Carpenter, Liz, 294–95

Carson, Johnny, 286

Caruso, Julius, 289

Catton, Bruce, 140

Chaplin, Ralph, 65

Childs, Marquis, 235

China, 76, 206, 208–9, 249–50

Churchill, Winston
        Anna and, 82, 151–54
        FDR and, 91, 148–54
        Québec Conference (1943), 148–50
        during World War II, 77, 82, 88, 91,
            113, 122, 130, 142, 148–54
        Yalta Conference (1945), 177–79

Civilian Components Policy Board, 242

Civilian Conservation Corps (CCC), 52,
    63–64

Civil Rights Act of 1957, 277

Civil Rights Act of 1964, 298

Clifford, Clark, 201–2

Cohn, Roy, 278–79

Coit, Margaret L., 248
Cold War, 181, 206–7, 212, 243, 249–50, 277–78
Collins, Elizabeth A., 27, 219, 228
Collins, James F., 211, 240–41, 242, 248, 259
Committee to Defend America, 76
Common Sense, 224, 251
Compton, Karl, 201
Compton Commission, 201
Conant, James, 170, 197
Condit, Doris, 258
Congress of Industrial Organizations, 146–47, 272–73
Congress of Racial Equality, 105, 201
Connichie, Elspeth, 110
Constellation, USAF, 266
Controlled Referral Plan, 137–38
Cook, Fred J., 228
Cook, Nancy, 39, 47, 71
Coolidge, Calvin, 21, 25–26
Corcoran, Thomas, 58–59, 77
Costigliola, Frank, 78
Coughlin, Charles, 215
Cox, James, 20–21
Creed, William, 70–71
Cronkite, Walter, 291
Curtiss-Wright P-40s, 131, 136, 139

Dalfiume, Richard M., 254–55
Dallek, Robert, 287*n*
Daniels, Jonathan, 182
Daniels, Roger, 105, 139
Davis, Henry, 10, 13, 14
Davis, John W., 26
Davis, Sammy, Jr., 281
Davis, William H., 66–67
Davis & Lederer, 10, 11, 13
Day-Lewis, Cecil, 68
Defense Advisory Committee on Women in the Services (DACOWITS), 242, 246–47, 268
Defense Weapon Known to Be of Value, A (film), 246*n*
Democratic Junior League, 47

Democratic National Conventions
    1924, 25–26
    1936, 61
    1948, 203
    1960, 285
desegregation of the military, 243–45, 251–55, 268, 277
    Truman's Executive Order 9981, 203, 253–54
De Sola, Ralph, 225, 226–32, 234
Detzer, Karl, 124
Dewey, Thomas E., 204, 205–6
DeWitt Clinton High School, 16
Dewson, Molly, 47, 84
Dicker, Herman, 188
Dickerman, Marion, 47, 58, 67–70
Dickerson, Earl B., 102
Dies, Martin, Jr. (Dies Committee), 73, 96, 118*n*, 204, 221, 225, 225*n*, 226
Dietrich, Marlene, 164–65
DiMaggio, Joe, 266
Dorchester Hotel, 67, 87, 159, 159*n*
Douglas, William O., 123
Douglas VC-54C *"Sacred Cow,"* 179
Dowd, Margaret "Peggy," 77
Dreyfus, Alfred, 212, 212*n*
Dubinsky, David, 27, 36
Dulles, John Foster, 278

Eagle's Nest, 1, 2–4, 188–89
Early, Steve, 182
Eckhoff, Phyllis, 217, 237, 247, 289
Efron, Edith, 197
Eichmann, Adolf, 163
Einstein, Albert, 142
Eisenhower, Dwight D., 272–75
    Anna and, 2, 180, 190, 244, 269, 272–76
    Black Americans and, 243–44, 277
    election of 1948, 205
    election of 1952, 265, 274–75
    election of 1956, 279

Eisenhower *(cont.)*
    presidency of, 276–77, 279, 281, 285
    during World War II, 2, 149, 163, 165, 168, 180, 184–85, 187
    Supreme Allied commander, 148, 149, 159–60
Eleanor Roosevelt Institute, 306
election of 1920, 20–21
election of 1924, 25–26
election of 1932, 49–50
election of 1936, 61, 89, 90
election of 1940, 89, 89n
election of 1944, 172–73
election of 1948, 203–4, 205–6
election of 1952, 264–65, 274–75
election of 1956, 279
election of 1960, 284–85
election of 1964, 297n, 298–99
Empire State Building, 45, 45n, 50, 192, 269
Employment Service, U.S., 129, 137–38
Encyclopedia Britannica, 192, 220, 270
Executive Order 8802, 102–3, 125–26, 136, 199–200
Executive Order 9835, 205
Executive Order 9981, 203, 253–54

Fair Employment Practices Committee (FEPC), 102–3, 105–6, 199–200, 202
Fair Labor Standards Act of 1938, 276
Falaise Gap, 162–63
Farley, Jim, 35, 39, 311n
Faubus, Orval, 277
Faure, Laura Hobson, 199
Fauset, Crystal Byrd, 110
Fay, Margaret, 18
Federal Bureau of Investigations (FBI), 145, 205, 225–26, 230, 234
Federal Writers' Project, 221
Fitzgerald, Ella, 288
Fitzgerald, F. Scott, 44
Fleeson, Doris, 284
Flint sit-down strike, 65–68, 73

Flynn, Edward J., 35–36, 42, 172, 311n
Fonda, Henry, 288
Ford, Henry, 21
Fort Bragg, 88, 254, 254n, 255
France, 76–77, 161–65, 166–68
Francis, Clarence, 220
Frankfurter, Felix, 38, 123, 251
Franklin Delano Roosevelt Memorial, 306–7n, 307
Frantz, Joe, 160n, 212, 300n
Franz Ferdinand, Archduke, 1, 12, 13
Franz Josef I, 9–10, 12
Freedman, Benjamin, 224, 225
Freedom Rides, 201
Fritchey, Clayton, 285

Gallup, George, 89, 90, 205, 274
Garner, John Nance, 61, 66, 73, 90
General Foods, 220
General Motors (GM), 65–68, 73
G.I. Bill of Rights, 4–5, 169–72, 180, 197, 268
Gibbs, Cleotha, 303, 307–8
Gibson, Truman K., 201
Ginsburg, Ruth Bader, 213
Goering, Hermann, 165
Goldman, Mark, 135, 139
Goldwater, Barry, 297n, 299
Golway, Terry, 40–41
Goodwin, Doris Kearns, 98n, 287
Gossett, Ed Lee, 216–17, 225, 251
Grant, Cary, 270
Great Depression, 44–50, 312–13
    New Deal and, 52–64
Great GM Sit-Down Strike, 65–68, 73
Great Society, 301, 303
Green, Theodore F., 138
Green, William, 36, 105, 121
Guderian, Heinz, 209
Gunther, John, 80–83, 97, 174–75, 195

Hagan, James Joseph, 18–19, 21–22, 30–31, 51, 84
Hagan, Walter, 21–22

Hallaren, Mary, 247
Halsted, Anna Roosevelt, 78
Hamburg American Line, 54
Hanford site, 144–45, 191
Harding, Warren, 20–21, 25, 25n
Harriman, Averell, 180–81, 306
Harris, Ann P., 313
Harris, Marcia, 225
Harrison, Earl G., 188
Harrison, Marcia, 214
Harrison Report, 188
Harrods, 69
Harvard Crimson, 88–89
Harvard Divinity School, 183
Harvard Law School, 38, 58
Harvard University, 47, 61, 98, 170, 197, 311
Hassett, William D., 86, 153, 178
Hayes, Rutherford B., 104
Head Start, 301
Hearst, William Randolph, 61
Hero Club, 15, 17
Hesley, Karl, 110
Hickok, Lorena A., 84, 276
Hillman, Sidney, 27, 62, 98, 100, 121, 126
Himmler, Heinrich, 163
Hinckley, Anne H., 312–13
Hitler, Adolf, 1, 3–4, 69, 75, 76, 122, 142, 155, 157, 162, 168, 168n, 175, 187, 188–89
Hobby, Oveta Culp, 233
Hobcaw Barony, 280
Hobson, Laura, 199
Hoffman, Anna Rosenberg. *See* Rosenberg, Anna Marie
Hoffman, Clare, 224–25
Hoffman, Paul Gray, 277–78, 287, 297, 303
    election of 1952 and Eisenhower, 274–75
    marriage to Anna, 289–90
    Marshall Plan, 203–4, 204n, 270, 280
    Peace Can Be Won, 277–78
    at Studebaker, 270–72, 280, 299

Homer, 177, 190
Hook, Charles, 67–70
Hoover, Herbert, 38, 42, 45, 47, 49, 76
Hoover, J. Edgar, 226, 234
Hoovervilles, 45
Hopkins, Harry, 4, 58–59, 76–82, 88, 97, 114, 125, 179, 251
Horace Mann School, 46
House Armed Services Committee, 242
House Un-American Activities Committee (HUAC), 73, 204–5, 212–14, 221, 226
Howard, Roy, 296
Howe, Louis McHenry, 60–61, 77, 88–89
    election of 1928, 34–35, 36–37, 36n, 38–40, 42, 43
    election of 1932, 49
Hughes, Everett, 164
Hughes, Langston, 93, 105n
Hughes, Sarah, 292
Hull, Cordell, 113, 311n
Humphrey, Hubert H., 252, 253
Hunt, Lester C., 231
Hyde Park, 70–72, 111, 153–54, 276, 285
Hyman, Irwin, 188

Ickes, Harold, 107, 311n
I. Miller, 29, 220
Independent Woman, 5, 22–23, 124–25, 240
International Ladies' Garment Workers' Union, 27, 297
Israels, Josef, II, 196

Japan, during World War II, 76, 94, 119, 121–22, 127, 181, 182, 191
    attack on Pearl Harbor, 113–15, 119
Japanese Americans, internment of, 115–16
Jewish refugees, 188, 198–99
Jews against Prejudice (Svonkin), 212
Jim Crow, 95, 199, 202, 253, 254, 298
job-hopping, 136–38
Jodl, Alfred, 187
John Reed Club, 221, 226, 226n, 231

Johnson, Charles, 129
Johnson, Claudia Alta "Lady Bird,"
    293–94, 295, 297, 299, 305
Johnson, Hugh, 53, 54
Johnson, Jack, 68
Johnson, Louis, 210, 251
Johnson, Lyndon B.
    Anna and, 59, 116, 243n, 244,
        293–304
        Assistant Secretary of Defense
            hearings, 222, 227, 230
    death of Eleanor, 290
    election of 1964, 297n, 298–99
    FDR compared with, 300–301
    JFK and, 287, 288–89
        assassination, 291–92
    Leinsdorf and, 59, 291
    presidency of, 293–305
        civil rights, 297–98, 302–3,
            304–5
        Vietnam War, 303–5
        women in the administration,
            293–96
        Robert Kennedy and, 287,
            287n
Joint Distribution Committee (JDC), 25,
    198–99

Kaiser, Edgar F., 129
Kaiser, Henry J., 129
Kaiserin Auguste Victoria, 10–11
Kaiser Shipbuilding, 129–30
Kaprielian, Bobby, 177–78, 183
Kardashian, Kim, 288n
Kaye, Danny, 68, 280, 288
Keenan, Joseph D., 240
Kelly, Grace, 270
Kelly, Joseph J., 131
Kennedy, David M., 96, 102–3, 140
Kennedy, Jacqueline "Jackie," 281, 284,
    287, 289, 292
Kennedy, John F., 190n, 284–90
    assassination of, 291–92
    birthday gala of 1962, 286–89
    election of 1960, 284–85

lack of women in administration,
    285–86, 294
Kennedy, Joseph P., 70n, 77
Kennedy, Robert F., 287, 287n
Kenyon, Dorothy, 213–14, 221, 225, 236
Kenyon College, 299
Kerr, Adelaide, 28–29, 132
Keyserling, Mary Dublin, 214, 221
Kidd, Gordon, 290
King, Martin Luther, Jr., 96, 105n, 302
Knowland, William, 226
Knox, Frank, 98
Knudsen, William S., 98, 100
Korean War, 208–11, 217, 235–36,
    242–43, 249–66
    Anna's wartime visits, 257–65,
        265–66
    desegregation of the military,
        243–45, 251–55
Krim, Arthur, 287, 288, 297
Kring, Walter Donald, 290
Kristallnacht, 70
Ku Klux Klan (KKK), 21, 25, 39, 225

labor strikes, 8, 26–27, 145–46
    Great GM Sit-Down Strike, 65–68, 73
labor unions, 26–29, 125–26, 146,
    276–77
Ladies of Courage (Roosevelt), 84, 276
La Guardia, Fiorello, 32, 51–52, 117, 233
    Anna and, 32, 51–52, 80, 107–9,
        115, 117, 130, 283
    Black Americans and, 97, 99, 100,
        103
    New Deal and, 51–52, 54, 58, 80
    Office of Civilian Defense, 107–9,
        115, 130
    World's Fair, 74
La Guardia Gluck, Gemma, 163
Land, Emory S., 128
Landon, Alf, 89
Lash, Joseph P., 83, 97, 105n
Lasker, Albert, 193–94, 220
Lasker, Mary, 192–95, 220, 280, 285,
    286, 294, 297, 301, 303

Lawford, Peter, 287–88
Lawrence textile strike of 1912, 8
Lazard Frères, 29, 220
League of Women Voters, 20
Leahy, William, 311*n*
LeConte, Phyllis, 262
Lederer, Albert, 1, 9–16, 30
Lederer, Charlotte "Mater," 9, 11, 13,
    29–30, 74, 269
Lee, John C. H., 164
LeHand, Missy, 35, 77–78, 80, 94,
    100–101, 112, 116
Lehman, Herbert, 38, 39, 40, 229, 234,
    235*n*, 252, 255, 279
Lehman Corporation, 142
Leinsdorf, Erich, 59, 291
Lend-Lease, 92, 94
Levison, Frances, 238
Levittown, 198
Lewis, Fulton, Jr., 215–18, 221, 230–31,
    234, 235
Liberty Bonds, 15
Liberty Ships, 130
Lichtenstein, Nelson, 151, 154*n*
Limbaugh, Rush, 215
Lincoln, Abraham, 92, 102, 298
Lindbergh, Charles A., 76
Lippmann, Walter, 178
Little Rock Central High School, 277
Livingston, John, 20*n*
Locke, Edward A., 123
Lodge, Henry Cabot, Jr., 274
Lomanitz, Giovanni Rossi, 146
Long, Huey, 61
Loomis, George, 197–98
Louis XIV of France, 164–65
Lucas, Jim G., 268
Luce, Henry, 239, 271
Lusitania, RMS, 11
lynching, 103, 172, 202

MacArthur, Douglas
    election of 1948, 205
    election of 1952, 264–65
        during Korean War, 209, 210,
            249–52
        Truman's firing of, 249–51, 253
        during World War II, 121
McCarthy, Joseph, 5, 205, 293
    Anna's confirmation, 212–14, 218,
        221, 223–27, 230–35
    Marshall and, 250–51, 265
    Murrow and, 278–79
McConnell, Viola, 262
McCullough, David, 172
McGlade, Jacqueline, 36
McGrath, Earl, 254, 277
MacGregor, Morris, 245, 255
McGuire, John Thomas, 36, 115
McIntyre, Marvin "Mac," 82, 182
McNutt, Paul V., 124, 125, 126, 137, 139
Macy's, 31, 45, 126, 134, 220, 271
Manchukuo, 76
Mandel, Ben, 221
Manhattan Project, 113, 142–48, 191
March on Washington (1963), 105
March on Washington Movement, 94,
    96–104, 106
Marshall, George C.
    Anna and, 160, 238–40, 271,
        280–81
        integration of troops, 251–53,
            253*n*
        job offer, 208–9, 215–17,
            225–26, 233
        resignation, 267–68
    death of, 280–81
    during Korean War, 210–11, 215,
        242–43, 250–51
    MacArthur and, 250, 251*n*
    McCarthy's accusations, 250–51,
        265
    Nobel Peace Prize, 204, 280
    during World War II, 113, 127, 148,
        149, 159–60, 184–85, 193,
        272
        Supreme Allied commander
            candidate, 148, 149, 159
Marshall Plan, 203–4, 204*n*, 270, 280
Märtha of Sweden, 77–78, 80

Martin, Dean, 281

MASH (Mobile Army Surgical Hospitals), 258–59, 262, 265–66

MASH (TV show), 258*n*

Matthews, J. B., 214

Maugham, Somerset, 68

Medal for Merit, 141, 202

Medal of Freedom, 5, 190–91, 190*n*, 202

medical care, 187, 195–97, 258, 258*n*, 262

Medicare, 301

mental health services, 195–97

Mercer, Lucy, 78

Meyer, André, 220

military draft age, 244

Miller, Emma Guffey, 286

minimum wage, 41, 48, 58, 61, 63, 104, 276

Missouri, USS, 191, 265

Miss Wolfhound 1952, 260

Mittelbau-Dora (Nordhausen) concentration camp, 2, 185–87

Monroe, Marilyn, 266, 286, 287*n*, 288–89, 288*n*

Montgomery Ward, 125

Moore, William, 196

Morgenthau, Henry, 38, 311*n*

Moses, Robert, 85

Moskowitz, Belle, 19–20, 24, 26, 33, 38, 45*n*, 47, 80, 84

Murphy, Frank, 66

Murray, Philip, 121, 146–48

Murrow, Edward R.
    Anna and, 68, 240, 248, 268, 281–83, 310
    MacArthur crisis, 250
    McCarthy, 234, 278–79
    during World War II, 75, 114
        Buchenwald tour, 186–87, 187*n*

Mussolini, Benito, 76

NAACP, 94–95, 99, 172

Nadich, Judah, 188

National Advertising Council, 245–46

National Advisory Commission on Selective Service, 304–5

National Biscuit, 137

National Cancer Act of 1971, 301

National Defense Advisory Commission, 88

National Guard, 66, 243

national healthcare, 193–96

National Institute of Health, 195

National Labor Relations Act of 1935, 145

National Mental Health Act of 1946, 195

National Recovery Administration (NRA), 52–60

National Science Foundation, 194–95

National War Labor Board, 121

National Youth Administration, 93, 95

Nazi Germany, 69–70, 76–78, 93–94, 119, 122, 148, 161, 163, 175–76, 181, 183, 187, 209

Nellor, Ed, 234

Nelson, Anna Kasten, 80, 105–6, 196, 220, 221, 312

Nelson, Don, 64, 122–23, 125, 137

Nesbitt, Henrietta, 311*n*

Neuberger, Maurine, 236

New Deal, 4, 52–64, 306–7, 308. *See also specific programs*

New Frontier, 285

Newhouse, S. I., 297

New Masses (magazine), 118*n*

New York Board of Education, 15

New York City, 4, 7–8, 10–11, 31–32, 50, 197–99

New York City strike of 1912, 8

New York City transit strike, 281

New York City Veterans Service Center, 195–96, 197–98

New Yorker, 32, 48, 61–62, 85, 116–18, 309

New York gubernatorial election of 1928, 33–43

New York Stock Exchange, 44

New York World's Fairs, 74, 297

Niles, David, 251

Nineteenth Amendment, 18

Nixon, Richard M., 232–33, 265, 284–85
Nordhausen concentration camp, 2, 185–87
Normandy landings, 157, 161
North Africa campaign, 113, 127, 130, 139, 196
Norway, 76, 77–78
nuclear weapons. *See* Atomic bomb
Nuremberg Laws, 69

Oak Ridge site, 144–46, 191
O'Day, Caroline, 39, 47, 48
Office of Civilian Defense (OCD), 107–9, 115
Office of Defense Health and Welfare, 111–12
Office of Inter-American Affairs, 116
Office of Production Management, 94
Office of Scientific Research and Development (OSRD), 193
Office of War Mobilization (OWM), 137–38, 150, 155, 211–12
Ohrdruf concentration camp, 184–85
Omaha Beach, 161
Operation Barbarossa, 100–101
Operation Overlord, 149–52, 157–58, 161–64
Operation S.O.S., 198–99
Oppenheimer, Robert, 143–44, 145
Ottinger, Albert, 38–39, 42

Paine, Thomas, 120, 224
Paley, William, 296
Paradise, Mildred, 266
Paris, 76–77, 163–64
Patrick, Stephen J., 261
Patterson, Robert P., 5, 125, 159, 190
Patton, George S., 2, 162, 165, 166–68, 184, 188
Peace Can Be Won (Hoffman), 277–78
Pearson, Drew, 84n, 232–33
Perkins, Frances, 84–88
    Anna and, 20, 67, 68, 82, 84–87, 87n, 128, 139–40, 173, 174, 310
    background of, 84–85

labor rights and, 36, 66–67, 68, 72
New Deal and, 58, 60
New York gubernatorial election of 1928, 36, 40, 41, 42–43
The Roosevelt I Knew, 86, 140, 311n
during World War II, 92, 139–40
Philippine campaign, 121–22, 127–28, 181
"Poem for a Man" (Hughes), 93, 105n
Pogue, Forrest C., 213, 225, 233
Poland, 19, 75, 76
poll taxes, 103, 202
Poole, Mildred B., 254, 254n
Poses, Lillian, 132
Postal Service, U.S., 246
Powell, Adam Clayton, 136
Pratt, Eliot, 110
Presidential Medal of Freedom, 5, 190–91, 202
President's Commission on Industrial Relations, 67–72
President's Committee on Civil Rights, 200, 202–3
Price, Margaret, 285–86
prisoners of war (POWs), 262–63
Proskauer, Joseph, 38
Protocols of the Learned Elders of Zion, 224
Pyle, Ernie, 157, 166, 169, 176

Québec Conference (1943), 148–50

Randolph, Asa Philip, 93, 95–106, 200
Rangel, Charles, 169, 304n
Rankin, John, 170, 224–25
Rauh, Joseph, 103
Ray, Bill, 288
Ray, Tom, 129–30
Rayner, William P., 213
Reagan, Ronald, 270, 307
Reds (movie), 226n
Reeb, James J., 302
Reed, John, 226n
Reilly, Mike, 311n
Renown, HMS, 148

Retraining and Reemployment
    Administration, 195
Rhee, Syngman, 265
Ridgway, Matthew, 253, 259
Robb, Jerry, 263
Robert E. Peary, USNS, 130
Roberts, Owen, 61
Robertson, Bill, 183–84
Robeson, Paul, 136
Robinson, Jackie, 201
Rockefeller, David, 112
Rockefeller, John D., 45–46
Rockefeller, Nelson, 29, 32, 45, 116, 174,
    191, 220, 239, 280, 290
Rockefeller Center, 45–47, 50
Rommel, Erwin, 127
Roosevelt, Eleanor
    Anna and, 33–34, 47, 81–82, 84,
        108–12, 115–16, 127, 165,
        177, 217, 236, 237, 275–76,
        280, 308, 310
    Black Americans and, 93, 97–98,
        101, 103–4, 105–6
    death of, 290
    death of FDR, 182
    election of 1928, 33–34, 35, 39
    election of 1960, 284–85
    during World War II, 78, 115–16, 123
Roosevelt, Elliott, 36*n*, 61, 77, 111, 311*n*
Roosevelt, Franklin Delano
    Anna and, 71–72, 78–84, 116–17,
        180–81, 219, 308, 310–12
        Buffalo Plan, 131–32
        congressional investigation,
            126–27
        G.I. Bill, 170–71
        gubernatorial election, 33–34
        New Deal programs, 59–60, 64
        offer of cabinet position,
            172–75
        wartime missions, 1–6, 157–59
    Black Americans and, 93, 94–106
    Churchill and, 91, 148–54
    election of 1932, 49–50
    election of 1936, 61, 89, 90

election of 1940, 89, 89*n*
election of 1944, 172–73
fireside chats of, 63, 90–91, 301–2,
    308
G.I. Bill of Rights, 169–72, 180
ill health and death of, 178–83
Johnson compared with, 300–301
New Deal and, 52–54, 56–57, 58–64
New York Governorship of, 44–45,
    47–49
New York gubernatorial election of
    1928, 33–43
during World War II, 75, 76–78,
    88–94, 152–55, 169–70
    attack on Pearl Harbor and
        declaration of war,
        113–15, 119
    Four Freedoms speech, 91–92,
        101
    Manhattan Project, 142–48
    Operation Overlord, 149–52
    Québec Conference (1943),
        148–50
    war production, 119–25,
        131–32, 140–41
    Yalta Conference (1945),
        177–79, 181
Roosevelt, James, I, 71
Roosevelt, James, II, 26, 77, 311
Roosevelt, John Aspinwall, 111
Roosevelt, Sara Delano, 35, 42–43, 111,
    112
Roosevelt, Theodore, 20, 34
Roosevelt I Knew, The (Perkins), 86, 140,
    311*n*
Rosenberg, Anna Marie
    Assistant Secretary of Defense.
        See Assistant Secretary of
        Defense
    birthdate of, 11, 11*n*
    Black Americans and, 97–98, 100,
        101, 103–6, 125–26, 129–30,
        135–36, 200–203, 243–45,
        251–55, 257, 277, 297–98
    business of, 26–29, 45–47, 126–27,
        173–74, 192–95, 219–20,
        220, 269–70, 299–300

children and family life of, 20,
    29–30. *See also* Rosenberg,
    Thomas John
congressional investigation of 1942,
    126–27, 173
death of, 308–9
death of FDR, 182
early life of, 9–16
early political career of, 18–32
FDR and. *See* Roosevelt, Franklin
    Delano, Anna and
Fifth Avenue apartment of, 191–92,
    207, 208, 223, 269–70, 280
G.I. Bill and, 4–5, 170–72, 180
during Korean War, 242–43
    wartime visits, 257–65, 265–66
labor rights and issues, 26–29,
    46–47, 48, 67–72, 103–6,
    125–26, 127–30, 144–49,
    297
La Guardia and, 32, 51–52, 80,
    107–9, 115, 117, 130, 283
legacy of, 308–13
loans given to, 174, 191–92, 214
marriage to Mike, 5n, 17–18
marriage to Paul, 289–90
media and press coverage of, 22–23,
    27–29, 48, 54, 55, 61–62,
    85, 116–18, 124–25, 126–
    27, 139–40, 192, 239, 240,
    247, 268, 281–83, 309–10
New Deal and, 53–60, 219, 221,
    276, 306–7
    Social Security, 60–64, 74
New York gubernatorial election of
    1928, 33–34, 40–43
postwar years of, 192–99
Social Security and, 312–13
wartime missions of, 1–4, 157–68,
    180, 183–84
    Eagle's Nest, 1, 2–4, 188–89
    Nordhausen, 2, 185–87
    during World War I, 15–16, 17
    during World War II, 88–92,
    114–15, 150
        Buffalo Plan, 131–41
        Manhattan Project, 144–48, 191

War Manpower Commission,
    123–24, 133, 137, 139,
    141, 150, 191, 219
war production, 120–21,
    123–41
Rosenberg, Ethel and Julius, 5, 5n,
    212–13, 275
Rosenberg, Jane Wade, 207, 269
Rosenberg, Julius "Mike," 46, 80, 156,
    196, 207, 269
    divorce from Anna, 279–80, 286
    marriage to Anna, 5n, 17–18
Rosenberg, Milton, 5
Rosenberg, Thomas John, 2, 20, 25, 46, 50,
    51, 75, 111, 156–57, 173–74,
    192, 207, 238, 269, 289
Rosenberg, Thomas P. J., 5, 240n, 303
Rosenman, Sam, 35, 39–42, 123, 153,
    171, 194, 202, 311n
rotation policy, 259–60
Ruml, Beardsley, 271
Russell, Richard, 219–20, 222, 225,
    227–28, 229

Sachs, Alexander, 142–43
Saltonstall, Leverett, 227, 229–30
Saratoga Battlefield, 44
Sarnoff, David, 105
Sawyer, Diane, 81, 83–84, 171
Schafer, Philip, 115–16
SC Hakoah Vienna, 29
Schechter Poultry Corp. v. United States,
    57–59
Schiff, Dorothy, 297
Schine, G. David, 278
Schlesinger, Arthur, Jr., 40, 289, 306
Schuetz, Alfred, 196
segregation, 199–203, 243–45, 251–55,
    268, 277, 298
Selective Service Act of 1948, 211
Selma March, 302, 305
Senate Armed Services Committee, 218–
    22, 224, 225, 226–36, 293
Servicemen's Readjustment Act of 1944,
    169
Shakespeare, William, 142, 156, 223

Shearon, Marjorie, 231–32

Shemya Air Force Base, 257

Sherwood, Robert, 311*n*

Shils, Edward, 142

Shoreham Hotel, 82, 87, 150, 180, 223, 269

Siegfried Line, 168

Sinatra, Frank, 281

Smith, Al, 19–20, 25–26, 39, 42, 80, 297

Smith, Genevieve, 262–63

Smith, Gerald L. K., 217, 224, 234

Smith, Harold, 123

Smith, Margaret Chase, 279

Smith, Walter Bedell "Beetle," 4, 79, 160, 165, 168, 187, 210, 233, 279–80

Social Security, 60–64, 74, 312–13

Social Security Act of 1935, 60, 62

Sokolsky, George E., 273

Solbert, Oscar, 165

Somers, Herman Miles, 139

Soviet Union

Cold War, 206–7, 212, 249–50, 277–78

during Korean War, 209

during World War II, 76, 94, 100–101, 113, 122, 127, 131, 180–81, 183–84, 187, 204

Spanish-American War, 7, 252–53

Sperling, Godfrey, 290

Sperry, Willard, 183

Stalin, Joseph, 94, 177, 178, 179, 181, 204, 277–78

Standard Oil, 29, 46

Standard Steel, 94

Star of Oregon, SS, 130

States' Rights Party, 203

Statue of Liberty, 11, 13, 70

Steinbeck, John, 63, 281

Steingut, Irwin, 25

Stevenson, Adlai, 265, 275, 279, 290

Stimson, Henry L., 113, 311*n*

employment of Black Americans, 97–98

Manhattan Project, 145, 146, 147

Operation Overlord, 148–49

war production, 122–23, 125

Storrs, Landon, 214, 220, 221

Stoughton, Cecil, 288

Straus, Jack, 134

Straus, Nathan, Jr., 30–31, 53–54

Studebaker, 270–72, 280, 299

Suckley, Daisy, 153, 311*n*

Sulgrave Club, 182, 232

Supreme Court

Brown v. Board of Education, 255

FDR's court-packing plan, 58–59

Schechter Poultry Corp. v. United States, 57–59

West Coast Hotel Co. v Parrish, 61

Supreme Headquarters Allied Expeditionary Force (SHAEF), 159, 164, 187

Svonkin, Stuart, 212

Swift, Wesley, 225, 230

Swope, Gerard, 67, 69–70, 71

Symington, W. Stuart, 220

Szilard, Leo, 142

Taft, Robert, 249, 251, 265, 274, 275, 276

Tammany Hall, 18–19, 23, 32, 40–41

Taylor, Elizabeth, 281, 286

Tennessee Valley Authority (TVA), 52

This I Remember (Roosevelt), 49

Timmerman, Karl, 181

Titanic, RMS, 10–11

Todhunter School, 33, 48, 67

Toland, John, 181

Toscanini, Arturo, 208

Townsend, Francis, 60

Townsend Plan Clubs, 60

Truman, Harry S.

Anna and, 141, 188, 189, 190–91, 195–98, 202, 212, 218, 231, 234, 239, 241, 243–45, 267–68

Black Americans and civil rights, 199–203, 243–45, 251–55

death of FDR, 182, 183

death of Marshall, 281

election of 1948, 203–4, 205–6, 273
election of 1952, 264–65, 274
during Korean War, 209–10, 212,
        243–45, 249–51, 264–65
MacArthur crisis, 249–51, 264
postwar presidency of, 141,
        190–207
        Jewish refugees, 198–99
        mental health services, 195–97
        national healthcare, 193–96
during World War II, 113, 188
Tully, Grace, 311n
Tulsa race massacre, 21
Twenty-Fourth Infantry Regiment,
        252–53
Tydings, Millard, 221–22
Tydings Committee, 213–14

unemployment, 3, 48, 49
United Auto Workers (UAW), 65–66
United Nations, 180, 209, 273, 278
United Nations Special Fund, 299
Universal Military Training (UMT),
        243–45
University of California, Berkeley,
        143–44, 145, 147
University of Chicago, 143–44, 145, 147,
        201
Utah Beach, 161

V-2 rockets, 160
Val-Kill Cottage, 48, 67, 71
Vanderbilt, Alfred, 220
Van Fleet, James A., 259
Versailles, 164–65
Vietnam War, 303–5
Villa Fiorentina, 280, 286
Von Arnold, Clare Lederer, 20n, 29–30,
        269, 289, 303
Von Arnold, John, 183
Von Kluge, Günther, 168n
Vultee Air, 94

Wadleigh High School for Girls, 13,
        15–18, 219, 283

Wagner, Robert F., 67, 287, 306
Walker, Walton H., 168, 184
Wallace, Henry, 90, 172
Wall Street Crash of 1929, 44–45
Warm Springs, 37, 43, 113, 178, 180, 181
War Production Board, 118, 122–23, 137
Warren, Earl, 277
Washington, George, 119, 120, 243n
Watson, Edwin "Pa," 79, 82, 96, 97, 143,
        179–80
Watt, Robert, 69
Webster, Milton, 102
Weinberger, Caspar, 240n
Welch, Joseph, 278–79
West Coast Hotel Co. v Parrish, 61
Wherry, Kenneth, 224
White, Walter, 94–95, 97–100, 172, 277
Whitney, Jock, 220
Whitney, John Hay, 29, 220
Wilhelm II, German Emperor, 8
Williams, Aubrey, 62, 93, 95, 96–98,
        100, 103
Williams, Clarence, 136
Williams, John, 244
Willkie, Wendell, 89, 89n, 90
Wilson, Woodrow, 7–8, 12–13, 20, 75,
        150, 158
Winchell, Walter, 235
Winner, Helen, 231
Witt, Linda, 262
Women in the Armed Forces Integration
        Act of 1948, 246–47
women in the military, 245–47, 262–63
        World War II and Buffalo Plan,
        131–41
Women's Army Corps (WAC), 2, 198,
        246–47, 262–63
Women's Memorial Corridor, 240n
women's suffrage, 8–9, 13, 14, 18–19
Woodard, Isaac, 200, 202
Woolf, S. J., 55, 104, 117, 118, 124–25
Workmen's Compensation Act, 41
"work-or-fight" law, 138, 151
Works Progress Administration (WPA),
        52, 61, 63–64, 221

World War I, 7–8, 12–18, 158
World War II, 4, 74–78, 88–92, 119–25,
   259
   atomic bombing of Hiroshima and
      Nagasaki, 191
   attack on Pearl Harbor, 113–15, 119
   Black Americans and, 93–106,
      125–26, 129–30, 135–36,
      164
   Buffalo Plan and, 131–41

   Manhattan Project, 142–48, 191
   Operation Overlord, 149–52,
      157–58, 161–64
   war production, 119–30
Wright, Bob, 282

Yalta Conference (1945), 177–79, 181